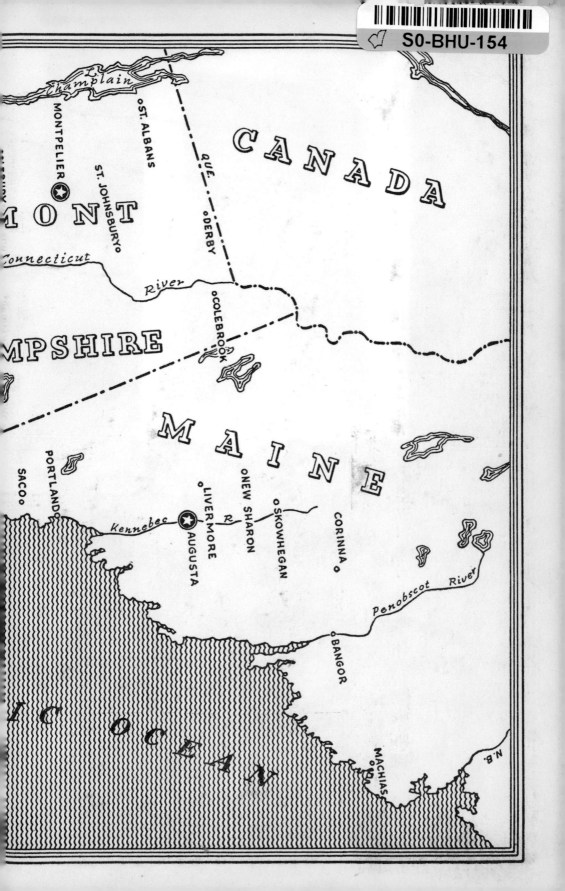

THE YANKEE EXODUS

THE
YANKEE EXODUS

AN ACCOUNT OF MIGRATION
FROM NEW ENGLAND

BY

STEWART H. HOLBROOK

1950

THE MACMILLAN COMPANY : NEW YORK

COPYRIGHT, 1950, BY STEWART H. HOLBROOK

All rights reserved—no part of this book may be reproduced in
any form without permission in writing from the publisher, except
by a reviewer who wishes to quote brief passages in connection
with a review written for inclusion in magazine or newspaper.

First Printing

PRINTED IN THE UNITED STATES OF AMERICA

FOR SIBYL

FOREWORD

My interest in migration from New England began some forty years ago, when I first became conscious of the many deserted hill farms in my native Vermont, and in New Hampshire where I also lived. The old cellar holes, the orchards being slowly throttled by encroaching forest, moved me deeply. I had a fairly good idea of what had gone into the making of those hill farms and homes; and the fact that they had been abandoned, after a century or more, seemed to me a great tragedy. It still does.

In good time I myself joined the exodus, and though I visit there almost annually, for thirty years and more I have lived outside New England. Everywhere I went, I met native Yankees or the descendants of Yankees; and came to the conclusion, in no way original, that Yankees must have had a good deal to do with civilizing the United States lying west of Lake Champlain and the Berkshires; and, of more importance, had perhaps exerted an influence in those foreign parts immensely greater than was commonly believed and also out of all proportion to their numbers. I sought to inform myself on the matter. But although I found several hundred works dealing with the migrations to America of all the many different peoples of Europe, and some from Asia, and although these books told exactly where the Irish, the Germans, the so-called Scotch-Irish, the Scandinavians, and on to include Poles and Russians and Italians and many another group had settled, and of their valuable contributions to America, I could discover in all that welter of books only one dealing with the movements of Yankees. This was a master's thesis by Lois Kimball Mathews, published as long ago as 1909, which, though able, brought the story down only to 1860 and only as far as the east bank of the Mississippi. It concerned itself, moreover, chiefly with the *numbers* of Yankees who migrated to this or that region. It did not tell who they were, what set them in motion, and, except for a few instances of politics, did not attempt to assess their effect in their new environments.

It seemed to me that the lack of a detailed work on the migration of Yankees and their influence constituted a sizable void in the American story. Yet, I then had no intention of attempting to fill that void. I merely read every article or essay I could find on the subject in the historical quarterlies of some thirty-odd states; and talked with every intelligent Yankee outlander I met. Little by little I accumulated information as to who among the Yankees migrated, and sometimes why; where they went, and what they did after they got there.

Then, three years ago I started in earnest to set down an account of what by then seemed to me the most influential migration in all our history. The strange race of Yankees not only permeated every last reach of the Republic; but almost always they made their impact felt. Their inventions, at home and elsewhere, changed the whole pattern of settlement in the West and South. Their fanatical respect for education led them to perform prodigies for learning in every state. Their shrewdness and great industry in business and commerce made them both welcome and feared. (I was charmed to discover that once upon a time the natives of New York City had organized a society for the avowed purpose of keeping the Yankees in Manhattan socially in their place.) Only too many of the emigrating Yankees also felt a powerful urge to make others like themselves, especially in the matter of so-called morals—including Temperance—and this was the cause of making them, properly enough, loathed or hated.

I had no desire to prove anything in particular about the Yankees. I simply wanted to know why they emigrated, and where to, and how effective they were in their new homes. I also came to wonder what if any influence the Yankees who stayed at home in New England exerted upon the rest of the country, and hence included them in my enquiry.

It may be objected that this book, dealing as it does with but one group of people, gives an exaggerated idea of their importance. The same, I suppose, might be said about any of the hundreds of books regarding the part played by the migrations to America of Europeans and others. All I will say is that the Yankees have been ignored, and that this book is a modest attempt to set them in their proper place in the great movements that civilized so much of the United States outside New England. The book is, of course, little more than a footnote to what is needed to tell the Yankee story in full. Yet it is, at least, a pioneer work. I hope that it may inspire some funded professor, or wealthy institution, to tell of the Yankee Exodus in, say, ten thumping-big volumes. They would be needed.

STEWART H. HOLBROOK

CONTENTS

ILLUSTRATIONS

THE YANKEE EXODUS

CHAPTER I

MELANCHOLY ON A HILL

THIS HILL, my great-great-grandfather had said, produces the best maple honey in Vermont and the biggest supply of material for stone fences you could imagine. He always had a plenty of the one, and far too much of the other.

When he went there, a little after the end of the Revolution, with the truly appalling idea of clearing a farm in the forest, the entire hill was enveloped with the immense hush of an illimitable wilderness.

Now, a century and a half later, the silence is returning, along with the wilderness that is marching from the edges of the old fields and pastures straight across and up and down, swallowing the miles of stone fences, tearing the pasture gate off its hinges, advancing to the barn to break its ribs, and arriving, at last, at the very slab of granite that served as doorstep, while the house itself, with a few decaying apple trees and a bush of lavender, is about to be crushed, then wholly obliterated, along with the rest of a typical hill farm of the Green Mountain State.

"Jonas Galusha is a pretty good governor," said my great-great-grandfather, who read the Montpelier *Argus* and kept up with affairs, "a pretty good governor, but he has no idea how many goddam rocks we have to pick in order to plant buckwheat, to pay taxes with." The old gentleman was seldom profane, except when discussing the War of 1812, or taxes of any sort. . . .

A sociologist may be alarmed at the return of the wilderness to so many hill farms in New England. A forester, on the other hand, might be pleased, and remark it is time and past for the wilderness to reclaim its own—that the hills of New England are suited only to the growing of trees. But to him who has lived on a Vermont hill, the matter of abandonment contains something other than alarm for coldly social reasons, or joy at the covering of the exhausted soil with handsome white birch and fragrant balsam. To him comes a sadness that has nothing to do with sociology or economics, but stems from some deep and imperfectly understood emotion about his own kind of people; namely, Yankees of the oldest stock. When the hill farms began reverting to forest—or, worse, to foreigners called city folks—New England's great day had passed. Her Yankees were on the move—either westward or into a Congregational Valhalla where God provided buckwheat cakes with maple honey at every meal, and angels who looked like a cross-fertilization of Henry Ward Beecher and Anne Hutchinson read snatches of the Good Book.

Even as late as my boyhood, early in this century, the farms on this hill all were occupied, and the district school filled at every term. The desks were the same our fathers and mothers had used, and so, too, were many of the textbooks. We learned that Ethan Allen and George Washington, working in splendid cooperation, had fought and won the Revolutionary War; and that the stomach of even a mild toper turned a hideous purple just before delirium tremens mercifully struck down and removed the besotted sinner.

I stood by the deserted schoolhouse on a fine September day recently, and looked in four directions. In every quarter, I saw abandoned farms. One small family now lived precariously on this entire hill, where once the soil had supported seven families—able to muster fifty-six persons for a picnic or a funeral.

Lilacs still grew in the schoolyard, and surrounded the tumble-down outhouse. The feeble grass grew high in the field, but it was thin and juiceless, not worth the mowing; and balsam and birch were stalking in from all sides. Was the field symbolic? I wondered. Was this woebegone grass, where timothy had once grown head-high and strong—was this grass a symbol of the Yankees? Were the birches and balsams taking over the tired land just as foreigners of all kinds had been taking over New England?

Fifty years ago this hill echoed to the axes of a hundred lumberjacks. One hundred years ago these pastures were rippling with the bell-music of many hundreds of sheep. One hundred and fifty years ago only two small clearings sparkled like stars in the immense night of a spruce forest. In that day, jays and crows furnished music.

The jays are back, and so the crows. The old clearings are fast closing. The Yankees have gone.

Why did they leave this New Canaan where they had tamed the savage forest and learned to live with the savage weather? They had piled enough stone to build a tower higher than Babel's in the land of Shinar. They had sent bale upon bale of wool, in oxcarts, two hundred miles overland to Portland; and although on this hill God did not temper the wind to the shorn lamb, their lambs survived winter in surprising numbers. Their women spun yarn in prodigious amounts.

They hauled their spruce to the banks of the Connecticut, then drove it like madmen chasing phantoms down the heaving stream to the mills at Mount Tom in Massachusetts, sixty days and nights to the south.

They tapped the great old maples by slashing the trunk and placing a birch-bark lunkin under the slash, then boiled the sap outdoors, a hunk of fat pork on a long stick in hand, ready to immerse the greasy meat, should the kettle start to boil over. They used the product on their tables, and what was left they sold, in prosperous times, for five cents a pound; or traded it for a little salt or even less of cream of tartar. And seemingly to hasten the day of reckoning, and when the big kettle was not boiling sap, they used it to make potash from the trees they felled and burned. The potash went to Portland, through the perilous Notch of Dixville, and a round trip meant a month gone.

Why did they leave this New Canaan they had worked so hard to fashion to their needs?

Where did they go, these Yankees who deserted the hills of Vermont and five other strongholds of a people who are said, at least by other Americans, to be flinty of character, chary of emotion, careful of money, and shrewd as can be?

What did they do when they got to where they were going, these strange Yankees who were as filled with yeasty ideas as they were with inventions of machines and gadgets? I am thinking of the kind of people who could and did form a *Vegetarian* Emigrating Society and head for Kansas; and who could and did conjure up Mormonism, Perfectionism, Christian Science, and in their lighter moments invent the friction match, the steam calliope, the normal school, the dollar watch, horsehair furniture, and barbed wire.

Not all of them went away, of course. A few remained, some to devise and build in New Hampshire the Concord coach that carried men and the mails across the Great American Desert and so up and over the Rockies. Mr. Colt went no farther than Hartford, where he manufactured his revolving firearm that was used to liquidate Indians and Mexicans and to hold up the steamcars in Iowa and Missouri. Mr. Estey stopped short in Vermont's Brattleboro, there to make the little sweet organs that went into the covered wagons, to be played in Congregational and Methodist bethels of Oregon and the tented saloons and whorehouses of the Mother Lode. Up in Maine, too, Joe Peavey, inspired by watching river-drivers break a log jam, went back to his little smithy in Stillwater and there and then forged the first Improved Cantdog or Peavey, the tool that was to roll untold billions of feet of logs into the Saginaw, the Chippewa, the St. Croix, and so on into Idaho. Even the Yankees who stayed at home thus had a vast influence on the American West.

No, not all of the Yankees went away. But by 1860, almost a half of them then alive had gone, nor was this greatest migration of native Americans done. It has continued into the middle of the twentieth century.

As recently as 1916 I had mowed with a hand scythe, here on Reed's Flat, where a field ranged both banks of the Mill Brook, and whetted my scythe on a stone quarried by the Pike family in New Hampshire. Thirty years later the only mowing done on Reed's Flat was done with ax and saw, for there the spruces were standing thick and tall, and the pulp-loggers were at them in force. The axes were now no longer ground on Pike family whetstones, for the Pikes had disappeared into the maw of a gigantic corporation. As for the spruce sticks, they would go either to Berlin or to Groveton to be made into cellophane, which only too many Americans seem to consider a wonderful symbol of Progress. . . .

Perhaps it is Progress, too, for there are so many ways of measuring imponderables as to bemuse a man who sees only that his own people went away and left their fields to grow into forests. I can wonder, too, if the slick, bright packages protected by cellophane contribute as much of importance to the Republic as a hill-farm family who in four generations fed and clothed themselves, schooled themselves, paid taxes, sent sons to serve in three wars and to help found a dozen states, sent daughters to six normal schools, and asked the government, in all that long period, for little more than a decent bounty on wolves and bears.

The old house has fared no better than the fields. Its faded red paint is mellow in a September sun. Wasps wind in and out of their paper home under the ridgepole. The dustily opaque panes of the windows would shock any New England housewife; yet they serve to obscure sight of rooms that are more shocking than dusty panes. Here was the parlor, its hand-carved molding still hugging tightly the walls; but one wall is now reeling outward, revealing both lath and plaster. The fireplace is half filled with crumbling bricks and the remains of a fire that was kindled when James Madison was President and went out during Wilson's last administration.

Here by tallow dip, by candle, then by lamp, but never by Mazda, four generations read the *Watchman,* or the Springfield *Republican,* or the Boston *Globe,* and studied textbooks and the *Old Farmer's Almanac* that warned of winds and snows and assorted storms but was fatuous in admonishing a Vermont hill farmer to see that *his* woodshed was filled to the rafters.

Here were weddings which often took the pair of them to Buffalo, or Beloit, or Topeka, or even to Oregon, a land well beyond the moon. And funeral services for bodies that still lay along Antietam Creek, at San Juan, and in the woods of the Argonne. On occasion this parlor must have shook to the awful doom promised by itinerant Adventist preachers, or shivered to the seductive calls of the earnest young men from the State of Deseret, which had been founded by a fellow Vermonter born in Whitingham. . . .

They all came to call on their fellow Vermonters—the Dorrellites, the Perfectionists, the Christians (from near-by Lyndon); and so, too, the Antimasons, the antinicotine forces, the Temperance shouters, the hydrotherapists, the anticalomel men, the hosts of assorted Sabbatarians, the sellers of lightning rods. So, also, the Abolitionists, the Friends of Liberia, the vegetarians, the Grahamites, the Thomsonians, the homeopaths.

And when times became dreadfully hard, and Yankees in their desperation started to make gadgets and such for sale to other Yankees—because they had no other market—this house resounded to the heralds of tin calf weaners and Seth Thomas's clocks, of mouth-organs and patent water-witches, of soapstone stoves and Thayer's Slippery Elm Lozenges. Once, at least, came a persuasive man who sold mulberry bushes, complete with worms, on which, he vowed, any hill farmer could make a fortune from silk.

At other times, to this same house, came aggressive men in spanking democrat wagons, who sold, or tried to sell, impressive-looking certificates representing stock in the Vermont Turnpike Company, the Passumpsic & Lake Memphremagog Canal Association, and the Upper Coös Railway Company.

Meanwhile, too, in this savage clime where man worked hard and long to earn his keep, Temperance and only Temperance, of all the new ideas, seemed to take hold on the farms and retain its grip. I wonder seriously how many bottles of varied elixirs gurgled away in this kitchen—bottles of Dr. Herrick's Liver & Blood Invigorator, of Perry Davis's Painkiller, of Green's August Flower, and Boschee's German Syrup. No matter the amount of "preservative" alcohol they contained, it was never mentioned on the labels, and thus generations of Temperance males and females were able to look upon both the times and the weather with more equanimity than they otherwise could have mustered and at the same time keep the faith. All praise be, then, to good Dr. Herrick and the rest—that is, all save Dr. Joseph Walker, a perverse person who came out with Walker's Vinegar Bitters, Free From All Alcoholic Stimulants. . . . What little balm had been left in Gilead was dissolved and ran away in the wry and non-soothing bitters of the antisocial Dr. Walker.

There were, of course, births in this or that bedroom, and the Bible was thumbed to name the results who, bearded or otherwise when grown, sounded like all the prophets and heroes of the Old Testament, together with their wives and concubines and sons and daughters; and when biblical names gave out, or wore thin from use, the heroes of the American republic came in: Jethro lies in Ohio soil, near Oberlin; Solomon drove his stakes in Northfield, Minnesota. Sally Ann got only as far as Cattaraugus in western New York. It was Rufus they covered up on Antietam Creek. Amos simply went away and was never heard of again. Abijah went to Colorado to work for Mr. Tabor, who came from near-by Orleans County, Vermont. Ethan took no forts but took, instead, the fever, and died somewhere in a surveying crew of the Santa Fe railroad, which was being extended by Mr. Strong of Brownington, Vermont.

Jerusha went to work tending spindles in Mr. Lawrence's brand-new heaven in Massachusetts called Lowell, where her morals and the morals of uncounted other Yankee maidens were tended as carefully as the spindles; and they got, and probably earned, two dollars a week for preserving their virginity and at the same time making the finest cloth in all New Canaan. "Dear Mamma," Jerusha wrote home, in 1840, "The Mill owners here are the kindest men imaginable. All of us employes are encouraged to read the Bible and the North American Review, which has some very fine Thoughts expressed in elegant language; and those few girls who are derelict in their attendance at Sabbath School are called upon gently and chided seriously by our Mill overseers, all good Christian men who are also our Teachers on the Sabbath." But not a great deal was done about protecting the maidens from the machines, and many a Yankee girl who had pretty fingers lost one or more in Lowell.

Sharon was the real traveler. She worked her way through the new normal school at Lexington, near Boston, then in one great leap landed in Beloit, to teach the youngsters of that rising town a much broader A than was commonly heard in Wisconsin. From Beloit she went on to Burlington, Iowa; and still again, when the steamcars crossed the plains, into California, where she closed her life drilling multiplication tables—and Temperance—into the heads of children of Southern Pacific employees, a railroad project that had been carried out by three Yankees and one foreigner from Troy, New York. Lucy and Deborah also taught school, in Kansas, where they married two other transplanted Vermonters and demonstrated that Yankee women were far from sterile.

Some of these far-ranging Yankee girls doubtless carried a sprig or two of this same old lavender bush, now struggling amid encroaching forest, in their linen, as they moved westward. And perhaps a flower from this climbing rose, that will soon be done. I know that Yankees in far places often yearned for a taste of the wry fruit of these so-called native apple trees. The fruit was never else than hard and tart, but it contained a mystic flavor for which, apparently, there was no substitute. So, small boxes of these bullets of apples went in the wake of the migrating Yankees, to be eaten in the lush paradise of California and to the great scandal of most Californians.

If you wanted to know exactly where the Yankees had gone, you could walk into the office of the Cross Company, bakers of Montpelier and St. Johnsbury, Vermont, and see on the books which western stores in Minnesota, Iowa, California, and Oregon had been clubbed, by transplanted New Englanders, into ordering Montpelier or St. Johnsbury crackers. None but a Yankee wanted them. It was much the same with Mr. Gorton's dried codfish from Massachusetts, and the Portland Star Matches from Maine, which came in flat cards and were said to be the seven-day kind because it required several seconds before the blue flame of their sulphur ignited the wood and ceased to smell of the Pit that hath no bottom.

With them, along with their crackers, their codfish, and their theology, they carried their peculiar ideas of government and managed, in spite of Kentucky statutes in Illinois, to impose their township system throughout the state. With modifications they did the same to or for Michigan, and also installed the whipping post, in words taken from Vermont's original laws. When Wisconsin was carved out of Michigan, Yankees poured in so fast as to dominate politics, supplying eight of the state's first eighteen governors, and seven of its early United States senators. In California, Yankees worked even greater wonders, when an immigrant from Maine planted the first seedless orange tree and his wife founded the first cult in the southern portion of the state.

It did not seem to matter much, once they had got away from home, where they landed. John Pierpont Morgan, an emigrant from Hartford, Connecticut, made something of an impression on the metropolis of New York, as well as on much of the West. The Doles from Maine founded an empire in the Sandwich Islands and then made the Islands into Hawaii. The original American settlement in Texas was projected by an emigrant from Durham, Connecticut, named Moses Austin and was carried out by his son, for whom the city is named.

Oh, it was pitiful to contemplate the way they left New England in such vast numbers, but it was true that they often prospered in the sight of their Lord, for were they not his chosen people? If in their trunks as they moved westward went bottles of their favorite patent medicines, they also carried their idea of salvation by works, which settlers from other and less fortunate parts sometimes said was intolerance. In Anoka, Minnesota, founded largely by men from Maine—the first Prohibition state—the new Empire Saloon was soon raided by a vigilante group one evening and all the excellent liquor spilled. It was at this period that James Madison Goodhue, late of Hebron, New Hampshire, and Amherst College, 1833, who was putting out Minnesota's first newspaper, wrote with grim satisfaction that Minnesota was "destined to become the New England of the West." The James-Younger gang discovered what *that* meant when, in what turned out to be their supreme moment of disaster, they attempted to rob the Yankee bank in Yankee Northfield. . . .

It seemed, too, that wherever they went, they took with them their native inventiveness. Eli Whitney of Westborough, Massachusetts, was teaching school in the South when he thought up the cotton gin. Samuel Morse, a native of Charlestown, Massachusetts, had set up as a portrait painter in New York City when he invented the telegraph. The Great Plains of western United States could not be fenced, and thus settled, until Joseph F. Glidden, an Illinois farmer from New Hampshire, patented what he called barbed wire.

No, there was little use in fighting back the brush on this hill—not when Yankees were shooting robbers in Minnesota, building railroads across Texas, founding colleges in Iowa and Oregon, cutting a swath of timber from the Penobscot to Puget Sound. Only a few of them came back. In this attic is still a brass-studded trunk that once upon a time went as far as Omaha. Francis Holbrook took it there and thought he was going to homestead a quarter-section. He soon returned home. "I never," he said, "see such a damnable country in all my life." He complained that the farmers in Nebraska lived in sod huts and, even when they had windows, couldn't see anything.

But Francis did not stay on this hill. He moved to a river farm, and thus became a part of the inner-migration that went on for a hundred years. "The gods of the valleys are not the gods of the hills," Ethan Allen remarked on a famous occasion, yet thousands of hill Yankees were glad to exchange their gods for a valley farm.

Behind the kitchen door, here, there once sat upon the floor, as a doorstop, a great pink and white conch shell which was used daily to announce that the sun, or at least the Seth Thomas clock, had reached meridian and it was time for dinner. My great-grandmother and my great-aunts, so I am told, would pick up this same shell, step to the granite slab at the door, and wind a trump that was heard in the far corner of the field, that was heard in the Back Forty, that was heard on a quiet day across five farms, two brook valleys, and halfway up Monadnock Mountain—a great, long gusty, booming, and mellow note, deep and vibrant as the lowest note of an organ. It was a note to stop an ax in mid-air, to arrest the stroke of a scythe in the wheat.

In that tremendous low-pitched blast was also the quality of assurance. Here was no squeal, no irritating treble, no pleading, but the hoarse authentic note of certainty, bidding all who heard it to know that God had been pleased to pass His sun across the meridian once more and to tell the menfolk, and anyone else who heard it, that they had best be spry and prompt, in the orderly manner of Yankees. No bell, no whistle, no siren ever carried such assurance, such urgency or, I repeat, such authority.

There is no telling when the note of the conch shell was last heard on this hill. Were it blown today, its solemn tone would be heard, at most, by four persons, five cows, a horse, a dog, and perhaps, in season, by a hunter or two following the old beech ridge, looking for bear.

Is there such a thing as an accumulated memory, a sort of inheritance, by which a people, removed for generations from their source, can recognize instinctively, and by no other process, a sight or a sound that was important to their forebears? If there is, I should be tempted to ask some radio network man to come, on a hot day in August, to this hill farm and set up his paraphernalia on the granite doorstep. Then, I should persuade a middle-aged relative of mine, who is said to look like great-grandmother, to pick up the great pink and white conch and wind a long note fair into the microphone.

How would that note echo in Greybull, Wyoming; in Beloit, Wisconsin; in Bemidji, Walla Walla, Modesto, and Denver? Would listeners here and there, men and women who had never been on this hill and perhaps never in New England, would they instantly conjure up the breathless heat of August on a Yankee hill farm—so near the sun—and hear the cicadas at their last farewell to summer, with an obbligato of tinkling bells of sheep in pasture? Could they hear the slow, steady swish of scythes, one following the other to the end of the swath, and the creak of the hayrick moving from tumble to tumble? Would something deep in their blood remember something they had never seen, or perhaps never heard of, and bring before their Western eyes a small calicoed woman, ringleted, sharp-eyed, sharp-featured, her bosom rising, then falling slowly as the conch shell in her hand gave out its melancholy warning that a Yankee God had brought noontime again? Would the lingering echo of the note exert in far places a pull, an uneasy tug, that could be explained in no rational manner?

It might. It would matter little, anyway, except perhaps as an experiment toward assessing the influence of heredity. It would matter little because this hill—like many another hill in the six Yankee commonwealths—has long since passed meridian. The conch shell sounded, for many of these hills, as long ago as 1830, and as recently as 1940 for others. But it has sounded for them all, and they are no longer of importance, unless as summer homes for city folks, or for the purpose for which Nature intended them, the growing of forests. Blow, Jerusha. . . . Blow, Sharon. . . . Blow, Sally Ann. They may hear an echo of your shell in far places. . . .

CHAPTER II

THE OTHER SIDE OF THE MOUNTAIN

THE PATRON SAINTS of emigration from New England are or ought to be the Reverend Roger Williams and the Reverend Thomas Hooker, founders respectively of Rhode Island and Connecticut, and the far from reverend Colonel Ethan Allen, whose real estate operations had a great deal to do with the establishment of Vermont. None of these men left the New England region, yet they contained the very essences of purposeful movement. Williams and Hooker were *Come-Outers* who migrated because of religious controversies. Allen was a *Go-Awayer* who most certainly had the idea of bettering his worldly condition. Doubtless all three men also had in great measure a desire to see what was on the other side of the mountain.

Direct in the line of apostolic succession and right on the heels of Ethan Allen came the first of the influential Yankee emigrants, who was General Rufus Putnam, head of the Ohio Company of Associates. It was this group more than any other that set the Yankees on the move into foreign parts, chiefly the West, which has endured for more than one hundred and fifty years.

The Yankee exodus to all parts of the American West, and occasionally into the South, is the most influential movement our country has known. The Yankees began to leave New England even before the Revolution, at a time when Maine, Vermont, and to a lesser degree New Hampshire still contained unknown thousands of acres of howling wilderness. But at that time the movement away was neither large nor continuous; the great migrations had to wait until the fighting was over.

Their leaving has been explained in generalizations about poor land, differing religious opinions, heavy taxes—or any taxes—and dislike of the climate. Easier than such generalizations, and probably nearer the truth, would be another sweeping statement—that Yankees were born with an uncommon urge to see, with their own eyes, if the grass on the other side of the mountain really was greener. Certainly, it was some such curiosity and little

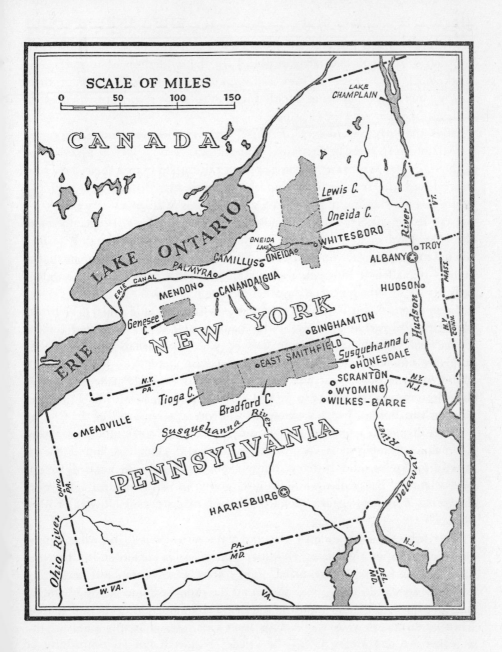

SCALE OF MILES

0   50   100   150

CANADA

LAKE CHAMPLAIN

LAKE ONTARIO

Lewis C.

Oneida C.

ONEIDA LAKE

WHITESBORO

CAMILLUS ONEIDA

PALMYRA

ERIE CANAL

MENDON CANANDAIGUA

Genesee C.

ERIE

NEW YORK

BINGHAMTON

Susquehanna C.

EAST SMITHFIELD

HONESDALE

SCRANTON

Tioga C.

Bradford C.

WYOMING

WILKES-BARRE

MEADVILLE

Susquehanna River

PENNSYLVANIA

HARRISBURG

Ohio River

ALBANY TROY

HUDSON

Hudson River

VT.

MASS.

N.Y. CONN.

N.Y. N.J.

N.Y. PA.

Delaware River

N.J.

OHIO PA.

PA. MD.

DEL. MD.

W. VA.

VA.

[11

else that prompted many a well fixed New Englander to leave a prosperous vocation or a productive farm and head for the wilderness of western New York and Pennsylvania, of Ohio, and even of what is now Mississippi, there to hang out his shingle amid smoldering stumps, or to grow corn where mean Indians lurked around the clearings.

With the early come-outers, of course, the urge to leave stemmed from the varied interpretations of Scripture. Thus it was with Roger Williams, and if New Englanders were in the habit of raising statues to their men who pushed back the frontier, they could hardly do better than to erect a bronze figure to him, the first migrant. The greener grass Williams was seeking was not tall hay in a field, but a field, any field, free from the rail fences of State theology. He had to go over the mountain, over several mountains, to find his unfenced field; but find it he did, and in the moment of his great thankfulness he called it Providence Plantations, a much happier name, incidentally, than the name it bears today, that of Rhode Island.

Except for his birth, which took place in old England, Roger Williams would be the perfect symbol for the Yankee emigrant. He studied for the Established Church, then became imbued with the Puritan heresy and left for New England, where a man, so he believed, needed no patent to commune with the Lord. That was a mistake. He discovered that he had merely moved from one strictly conforming land to another just as bad. He refused to preach in Boston. He was welcomed to Plymouth, but soon, as the leading man of Plymouth remarked, he "begane to fall into some strang oppiions. . . . which caused some controversie between yᵉ church & him." So, he moved to Salem, and bettered himself but little. The General Court of Massachusetts Bay Colony found him guilty of disseminating "newe & dangerous opinions, against ye aucthoritie of magistrates." He was ordered banished.

This time the other side of the mountain turned out to be what is now Providence, where Williams and his heretical followers founded the first settlement and presently organized a new colony. His geographical pioneering was now done, but he still had not found the promised land of the mind. He turned Baptist, for a few months, but found this faith, too, to be rail-fenced. Then he turned away from all creeds and called himself simply a Seeker, and a Seeker he remained. "God," he cried, "requireth not an uniformity of religion." He meant it, too, and said it at length in his most famous work, *The Bloudy Tenent of Persecution*. He meant it, and welcomed to his colony the untouchables of that day, who included Jews, Quakers, and Catholics. No other New England pioneer, perhaps, did so nobly, nor so much, with what he found on the other side of the mountain.

Thomas Hooker was no such heretic as Williams, but he was a come-outer all the same. He found the rail-fences of Newtowne in the Bay Colony, where he preached, too confining. After a noted controversy with John Cotton, Pope of the Puritans, he led his band of faithful over the mountain to found a new church and settlement he called Hartford, in which was the genesis of Connecticut.

Neither Hooker nor Williams was a missionary in the way that term is now understood. They were come-outers, not go-ye-outers, who are agents of the Lord sent into the wilderness to convert heathens of any and all kinds. New England was to become a never-failing source of go-ye-outers. Their line was begun by the Dorchester Colony Company, organized in the town of that name in Massachusetts. In 1695, the Reverend Joseph Lord and his parishioners left their established home on a long and arduous journey. Their stated intention was to "promote the extention of Religion in the Southern plantations." Within the next year they had founded Dorchester in South Carolina, where a hamlet and a county still bear the name. Although this first group of migrating Yankee missionaries may have had no great or lasting influence in "the Southern plantations," they nevertheless founded a long line of Yankee activity by toting their own particular brand of salvation to the other side of the mountain. There would be many more of their kind later.

Ethan Allen had no desire whatever to promote the Gospel in foreign parts. He was a lost soul, a freethinker, who had become something of a police-court character in his native Connecticut by disorderly conduct, including the crime of blasphemy. Possibly his many jousts with the law made him restless, but he was highly mobile by nature; and when the lands of the New Hampshire Grants came into the market, just before the Revolution, Ethan took off on snowshoes to look them over. He found them fair indeed. Then, with brothers Zimri, Heman, and Ira, and cousin Remember Baker, he organized the quaint Onion River Land Company. The company promptly, and by devious means, acquired 60,827 acres of land, the title to which was rather more than dubious, in what is now Vermont.

Both New York and New Hampshire claimed the land involved, and for the next several years the Onion River Land Company, whose military genius and public relations counsel was Ethan Allen, fought a guerrilla war to hold their empire. They did hold it, too, and advertised it so enthusiastically that Connecticut settlers flowed in continuously. In the *Connecticut Courant* the company declared that its lands contained broad treeless intervales along the Onion River, which, it appeared, was fairly alive "with a diversity of sorts of excellent Fish particularly the Salmon." In fact, "there is no tract of land of so great quantity Between New York and the Government of Canada, that in a state of Nature can justly be denominated equally Good. A number of men are already gone to cut a Road to the premises from the Otter Creek which is about twenty miles, and a Settlement will forthwith be carried into execution."

Then, in the advertisement, came a line that warned prospective settlers against purchasing the same land from New York claimants. "Said purchase and settlement," it stated coldly, "is Insured on a title derived from under the Great Seal of the Province of New Hampshire." The "settlement" referred to was in reality a rugged log fort containing thirty-two purposeful loopholes, a roof so made that it could be thrown off if set afire, and within the inclosure was a fine spring of water. "In this situation," wrote Ira Allen, "we were a terror to New York claimants."

It took a deal of doing, but the Allens did protect their settlers, and most of them stayed. Soon what had been called New Connecticut became Vermont, an independent republic, and a bit later the fourteenth state. It was the first state to become such without benefit of clergy.*

Ethan Allen was unquestionably more typical of the Yankee migrants of subsequent years than Roger Williams or Thomas Hooker; he left home with the idea of bettering himself materially, nor was he too particular as to how it came about. No matter his motive, his Onion River Land Company was surely a great stimulus to Yankee migration, both within and from New England; many of the first generation born in Vermont were the first to pick up and leave for western New York, Pennsylvania, and Ohio.

Before the Onion River boys had fairly consolidated their position, another group of Connecticut people was on the move, led by General Phineas Lyman of Suffield, a relic of the French and Indian War. General Lyman had first attempted to get a grant of land along Lake Champlain for settlement by veteran soldiers. Nothing came of it, so he made a trip to England and applied for lands along the Yazoo River, in what is now Mississippi, a country about as remote as could then be imagined.

The king's men apparently made promises which General Lyman considered equivalent to a grant. He returned to America, and in 1773–1774 headed a band of some four hundred Yankee families, called Military Adventurers, into the South. Some went by sea to the Gulf of Mexico, then up the Mississippi, others cruised down the Ohio on flatboats, still others plodded overland across Tennessee. They settled near the old French town of Natchez, and had little more than put up their cabins when they were informed there was no land grant. They were merely squatters. So, they

---

* The status of Ethan Allen among the godly is made clear by a passage in the diary of the Reverend Nathan Perkins, a Connecticut missionary who traveled through Vermont shortly after Allen's death. "All ye men of learning deists in this state," he wrote, and "Arrived at Onion-river falls, & passed by Ethan Allyn's grave. An awful Infidel, one of ye wickedest men yt ever walked this guilty globe. I stopped & looked at his grave with a pious horror."

squatted—the Comstocks, the Sheldons, the Wolcotts, Weeds, Cranes, Bowens, Knapps, Phelpses, Bradleys, Cases, and members of the Hotchkiss and Ellsworth families—in what well-meaning but deluded General Lyman said was "Georgiana Colony." Before the first year was out, the general had died. But the Yankee settlers remained, for the most part, and many of their descendants live in and about Natchez today. Although the Lyman colony created much interest in New England at the time, it does not seem to have inspired other Yankees to invade the South in mass movements.

Just before and during and after the Revolution, the migration of Tories was continuous. They fled out of New England into Quebec and the Maritime Provinces, and to a lesser extent into Ontario. Nova Scotia alone received, in all, some 30,000 of these refugees, many of whom were substantial people and were to contribute much to the history of the Dominion.* They went by ship from Boston and Portsmouth and Providence by the hundreds; and in small groups or even as individuals fled across the vague border at night. The ancestor of a friend of the author's made his entry into British territory inside a packing box which allegedly contained a spinet. These people were not emigrants in the real sense of the term, but they did leave New England. They were not seeking the greener grass beyond the mountain, but felt sure that whatever they found there would be preferable to living amidst king-haters and such rabble.

With the coming of peace the restlessness of New Englanders increased notably. More and more of them moved from Connecticut into Vermont and New Hampshire, to settle new Derbys, Fairfields, Litchfields, and Water-burys. A Rhode Island group headed by Jonathan Arnold settled St. Johnsbury, Vermont. People of Massachusetts went into the wild district of Maine, then governed by the Bay State, to settle a new Andover, a New Vineyard. Other Maine towns, such as Hermon, Freedom, Dexter, Hartland, and Exeter, were founded by New Hampshire people who had hardly cleared their own farms before taking off into new country.

In the meantime, too, other dreamers, or discontented or discouraged Yankees, were turning westward. Often they were prompted to move by men who had already seen the land beyond the mountain and reported it to be wonderful. There was Kirkland, New York. Seven pairs of brothers, from seven families of Plymouth, Connecticut, had served in the American army during the Revolution. In the process they had marched over a goodly portion of York State. Upon their discharge from the service, they went West and founded Kirkland in Oneida County. No few of their townsmen

---

* In his excellent *Colony to Nation*, A. R. M. Lower cites such well known New England family names as Tupper, Borden, and Fielding, which became prominent in Canada.

and neighbors were quick to follow, among them Judge Hugh White of Middletown, who in 1784 moved with his four grown sons into charming Oneida County and became an influence in Yankee migration. Having founded Whitesboro, and naturally wanting it to flourish, the judge continuously sent back to Connecticut the biggest stalks of Whitesboro corn he could muster, and samples of the finest oats, wheat, and potatoes. This early-day boosterism was most effective. The samples "so far excelled anything they had seen," the good judge observed, "that soon many came to see the country, and in general were so well pleased that they located in the vicinity."

Among the many Connecticut people attracted to Oneida County were Nathaniel and Betsey Babbitt, whose son Benjamin Talbot turned out to be something of an inventive genius. While working as a wheelwright in Utica, young Babbitt persuaded a few of his fellow workmen to rise an hour earlier, so that they might quit an hour sooner two days a week and attend lectures in chemistry given by a professor from Hamilton College whom he had induced to come from Clinton for the purpose. Babbitt invented and patented a fire engine, a brush-trimming machine, and other gadgets; but his great success stemmed from his early interest in chemistry. By 1843 he had established a factory and was successfully manufacturing saleratus, baking powder, soap powder, and soap. He took into partnership a cousin, Isaac Babbitt, late of Taunton, Massachusetts, who had already devised the alloy that still bears his name as a common noun, babbitt; and their factory soon led all soap producers in the country. They spent money to advertise, not only in newspapers and by posters, but also on theater curtains. By mid-century, at latest, "B. T. Babbitt" was considered a mark of honest quality on soap, and the Babbitt brands still flourish a century later.

Many Yankee veterans of the Revolution received grants of land in Oneida County and other parts of New York. These were in lieu of what today would be called a cash bonus. Though many of the old soldiers never saw their lands, but sold them for whatever they could get, a considerable number migrated. New Hampshire veterans who settled in York State included David Adams, Northumberland; Stephen Adams, Palmyra; Solomon Aldrich, Owego; Phineas Allen, Chautauqua; Joel Baker, Smithfield; Nathan Barrus, Boonville; Nathaniel Bean, Batavia; Allen Breed, Hope; and William Bell settled down to clear his well wooded acres in Yankee-dominated Oneida County.

The York Fever was long in the air. A group of thirty Quakers, all fishermen of Nantucket and Marthas Vineyard, pooled their resources to buy New York land and found the town of Hudson. A company organized at Dighton

in the Bay State bought 46,000 acres of New York land and planted Richmond. Two Massachusetts speculators, Oliver Phelps and Nathaniel Gorham,
went into the York land business in a large way. For $100,000 they bought
preemptive rights to a vast tract in the western part of the state, divided it
into conventional townships six miles square, then set up a land office in
Canandaigua. This began the "Genesee Fever," so called from a handsome
river valley on the claim, which threatened for a while to depopulate many
towns of southern New England.

The Genesee Fever could be seen running its course through Albany. One
winter's day in 1795 an observer there counted 500 sleighs passing westward
through that town between sunrise and sunset. During the following summer
an average of twenty boats daily went up the Mohawk River. A majority of
the first emigrants to the Genesee paradise were from Massachusetts and
Connecticut; later came others from hilly Vermont and New Hampshire,
attracted no doubt by advertisements which offered ten thousand acres to
"the industrious yeomanry of Vermont and New Hampshire who wish for
farms not lying edgeways."

Into this flood of movement to western New York went two young boys
who were to have an immense influence on New England, and on the United
States. In 1804, John and Abigail Young, together with their children including Brigham, moved from Whitingham, Vermont, to roam the Genesee
country. A dozen years later Joseph and Lucy Smith, together with their
children including Joseph, Jr., moved from Sharon, Vermont, to settle in
Palmyra. It was at Palmyra that Joseph, Jr., talked to the glorious angel
Moroni and was shown the glistening golden plates that became the Book
of Mormon. Two years later Brigham Young, by then a farmer of near-by
Mendon, became a convert. In another ten years Smith and Young—and
Moroni—were to set off an emigration from their native New England
that shook and scandalized Yankeeland as nothing before had done.

When the flood tide of Yankees moving into York State showed any
sign of abating, the land speculators began to talk up their wares in New
England newspapers. In 1821 subscribers to the *New-Hampshire Patriot*
of Concord could read that 20,000 acres "in the county of Herkimer, township of Norway, 90 miles from Albany," were being offered at prices ranging
from $1.50 to $2.50 an acre. Joseph Andrus, New Hampshire agent for
speculator Brabazan Noble, reported enthusiastically if none too gram-
matically that "there is now about 15 settlers on this tract; with a new Saw
Mill—and a Grist Mill will be put thereon this summer."

Although York land speculators were advertising in Vermont newspapers
as early as 1801, Vermonter Matthew Lyon struck out in that year for distant

Kentucky, taking better than a score of relatives and friends with him, to increase the population of Eddyville. Lyon was easily one of the most able men who had a hand in founding the fourteenth State of Vermont. A close associate of Ethan Allen, he had settled the town of Fair Haven, Vermont, in 1783. He started an ironworks, made good paper out of basswood, and founded a rabid political sheet called the *Scourge of Aristocracy*. Vermont sent him to Congress, and there he fell afoul of the notorious Alien and Sedition Acts. Sent to jail, he at once became something of a national hero. Funds were collected in Virginia and other states to pay his fine, but fellow Vermonters already had raised four times the needed amount by a lottery. Vermont returned him to Congress, where he cast the decisive vote for the election of Thomas Jefferson. Then, Lyon picked up and moved, bag and baggage, to Kentucky, which promptly sent him to Congress, again and again. But he was still the pioneer. When he died in 1822, he had just been elected congressional delegate from the Territory of Arkansas; and one can wonder if the old man, then aged seventy-two, had found the grass greener in Arkansas than in Kentucky, or in Vermont.

Although New York got a majority of the early migrants from New England, Pennsylvania was not wholly overlooked. A colony of Yankees had settled Pennsylvania's beautiful Wyoming Valley, then undergone a horrible massacre by Indians in 1778. When peace was restored, those who had escaped the scalping returned to carry on, and other Yankees joined them, to such an effect that the state of Pennsylvania became alarmed. Not without reason. In 1796 the Susquehanna Company, strictly a Connecticut group of high-powered real estate operators, met in Hartford to set up a provisional government for the several states they hoped to form by the simple process of dismembering a good part of Pennsylvania. The company went so far as to draw up a constitution and elect officers.

Thoroughly alarmed at last, Pennsylvania quickly erected Luzerne County, established Pennsylvania courts there, and introduced Pennsylvania laws. No matter if Connecticut people owned the land, Pennsylvania was to govern it. The Yankees kept coming, too. In Poultney, Vermont, which for some reason or other was to appear prominently in the later migrations to other states, a group first organized a Congregational church, then with their pastor leading set out across country to settle East Smithfield, in northern Pennsylvania. Other Yankees laid out Honesdale, in Wayne County, complete with town hall, a common with shade trees, and houses set gable end to the street after the fashion of so many New England villages.

Yankee veterans of the Revolution were moving into Pennsylvania, too. From New Hampshire came James Blair, to settle at Erie; John Blaisdell, at Rush; Isaac Brown, at Brooklyn; Daniel Chamberlain at Silver Lake, and Moses Chamberlain at Gibson.

Then, shortly after the death of William Bingham, late of Philadelphia, the heirs of that incomparable speculator were trying to induce Yankees to buy land. Bingham deserves notice in any study of landowning in the United States. He made a fortune from privateering in Revolutionary times; and a part of it he used to buy wild lands. At the time of his death in 1804, he owned three million acres of timber in Maine. He also owned much land in New York, where he founded the town of Binghamton. And now his heirs were offering for sale, through New England newspapers, no less than "250,000 acres in the counties of Bradford and Tioga, Pennsylvania, at from $2.50 to $3 an acre . . . and 500,000 acres in the counties of Potter, Mc-Kean, Venango, Armstrong, Jefferson, and Lycoming" at a mere $2 an acre. Robert H. Rose, stationed at Silver Lake, Pennsylvania, was the man to see about these lands, and he swore that "the land is generally of good quality, well watered, intersected by important roads, and in a healthy situation."

It is impossible to know how many Yankees came to purchase and to settle on the 750,000 Bingham acres in Pennsylvania. But among them was not George Whitfield Scranton, born in Madison, Connecticut, who migrated first to New Jersey and went into the iron business. In about 1839 he and partners bought extensively of land in Lackawanna County, Pennsylvania, and a year later established the town of Scranton, as the center of their coal-mining and iron-making activities. The new venture was highly successful, and rightly so, for George Scranton was a man of "inexhaustible energy and great moral integrity."

In the far northwestern corner of the state Yankees, with a few Yorkers and Germans, settled Meadville. To Meadville soon came, from Portsmouth, New Hampshire, the Reverend Timothy Alden, a vision in mind—that of a Yankee college set down fair in this wilderness. This was Allegheny, founded with $461 in cash, some dubious land, a good collection of books, and $6,000 in promises from the Meadville settlers; and it turned out to be one of the brightest stars in western Pennsylvania.

With Meadville and Crawford County thus safe for Yankees, other New Englanders poured in to settle Tioga and Bradford counties. New England settlement was spotty in the Keystone State, but it was nudging the Ohio line, where began the Northwest Territory and where God, in combination with the Ohio Company of Associates and the Connecticut Land Company, had reserved large portions for the sole use of Yankees.

Conditions were now ripe for the founding of a new New England. And now to the Bunch of Grapes Tavern in Boston came General Rufus

Putnam—a man, said General Washington, "of strong mind but with nothing conspicuous in his character." But if he had failed to win in the textbooks the heroic place accorded his cousin Israel, he was now to achieve importance by starting the greatest emigration of Yankees up to then.

In 1786, when he went to the Bunch of Grapes with a large idea in mind, General Rufus Putnam was forty-eight years old. He had served in the Continental army with bravery, displaying also a ready resourcefulness in action at Stony Point and other engagements. He had done, in peacetime, a good deal of surveying in New England and the so-called West, and he early became imbued with the idea of settlement of veterans of the war in the Ohio country. In 1783 he had framed a petition to Congress asking that Ohio lands be considered in bounties which several states had promised to their soldiers. Two years later, when Congress appointed him a surveyor of western lands, he sent as substitute an old comrade, General Benjamin Tupper.

General Tupper, like his friend, had served in the war. On his return from the western survey he, with Putnam and one other man, determined to organize a group of ex-officers and soldiers to settle in the Ohio River country of the new Northwest Territory. To this end, the meeting was called in the Bunch of Grapes—incidentally, one of the several taverns in which Samuel Adams and other propagandists had planned the agitation which hastened the coming of the war.

The third man was Manasseh Cutler of Ipswich Hamlet, one of the most remarkable men of his time. Dr. Cutler, Congregational clergyman, had served in the war as a chaplain and thus become acquainted with Putnam and Tupper. Now, on the first day of March, 1786, Dr. Cutler joined with Tupper, Putnam, and a few other ex-officers in organizing the Ohio Company of Associates. The purpose of the company was to acquire land in the Ohio country for settlement, for settlement, in short, by what the company's petition to Congress described as "the most robust and industrious people in America," meaning, naturally, Yankees of sound New England stock.

Dr. Cutler himself patently fitted the Ohio Company's description of a Yankee, so far as it went; but it in no manner did him full justice. Tall and portly, he liked to wear a suit of black velvet, together with black silk stockings, silver knee and shoe buckles, his long hair in a single braid. His manners, one may judge from contemporaries, were more courtly than was common in New England.

After graduation from Yale in 1765, he married, studied for the ministry and in 1771 was ordained pastor of Ipswich Hamlet, now Hamilton, Massachusetts. On that great April day in '75 when New England exploded, Dr. Cutler addressed the Minute Men of his town, then rode with them to the camp at Cambridge. He later served as chaplain with several regiments. He studied medicine under Dr. Elisha Whitney and later practiced successfully. He had immense curiosity about a diversity of subjects. He used a sextant and telescope to measure distances to certain stars, observed hairs through a microscope, inoculated people for smallpox, and experimented with an electrical machine.

One wonders if the so-called flowering of New England did not begin with Dr. Cutler. In 1784 he made an expedition to Mount Washington in New Hampshire solely to measure the peak. He was the first to prepare a systematic account of the flora in his region, examining some three hundred and fifty species and classifying them according to the method of Linnaeus. He read for the law. For more than twenty-five years he conducted a private boarding school for boys, which he taught himself.

The Ohio Company of Associates could hardly have had a better associate than Dr. Cutler, for he was as persuasive with men as he was brilliant in his other fields.

The company's first petition to Congress failed to find favor. So, in the summer of 1787, Dr. Cutler got into his sulky and drove to New York, where the Continental Congress was sitting. He found that body enmeshed in and bemused by the problem of what to do with its Western lands, known as the Northwest Territory. This was the country bounded by the Ohio and Mississippi rivers and the Great Lakes. Squatters already were there, and more were pouring in. The region must have government. Dr. Cutler was asked by the committee which was formulating an ordinance to make suggestion. Never bare of ideas, the genial doctor submitted a number of suggestions, several of which were incorporated into what history knows as the Ordinance of 1787.

This document provided that the new Territory should be ruled by a governor and judges appointed by Congress until such time as 5,000 male inhabitants were of voting age, when they could elect a legislature of their own and send a delegate, without vote, to Congress. Slavery was forever forbidden.

The famous Ordinance was adopted on July 13. Cutler now went to work on influential members of Congress. By gracious but astute and persistent lobbying, and considerable maneuvering to defeat Southern congressmen, he beat down a strong opposition minority, and on October 27 the Treasury Board of the United States granted to the Ohio Company the right to take up one and one-half million acres of Territorial land at approximately eight cents an acre.

General Benjamin Tupper knew exactly which acres were best suited to a robust and industrious people. They were to be found near the confluence of the Ohio and Muskingum rivers. He had seen them with his own eyes. The Ohio Company of Associates prepared for the great trek.

They lost no time about it. At early dawn on December 1, 1787, Rufus Putnam and a contingent of twenty-one men, including General Tupper, paraded before the parsonage of Dr. Cutler in Ipswich Hamlet, and the good doctor gave his Godspeed to the first contingent of the Ohio Company. The doctor himself was to follow later.

The pilgrims moved on. They paused a moment in near-by Danvers to fire a salute, then continued westward toward what cautious neighbors with fine Yankee sarcasm were calling "Putnam's Paradise." Some eight weeks later they arrived at the upper reaches of the Ohio in Pennsylvania, where they were joined by a second contingent of Associates from Hartford, Connecticut. They were now on the other side of the mountain, though not yet in New Canaan.

The combined Yankee groups went to work with a will to construct a sort of floating shed, which they called a galley and which, being their flagship, they sought to name. Some called it the *Adventure* but, true to the excessive individualism in the group, others called it the *Union Galley,* while still others insisted it was the *Mayflower.* Nor was the latter name wholly out of place. One of the scow's builders was Major Robert Bradford of Plymouth, lineal descendant of William, one-time governor of Plymouth Plantation.

At this period the migrating Associates numbered forty-eight. Notable among them were the Reverend Daniel Story of Boston, James Varnum of Dracut, Colonel Ebenezer Sproat of Middleboro, Captain William Dana of the Cambridge Danas, and Captain Robert Oliver of Boston. Not all were from Massachusetts. There was a true hero of the Revolution, Abraham Whipple of Rhode Island, who had taken part in the burning of the British *Gaspée,* and Jonathan Devol of Tiverton in the same state. From New Hampshire came two Gilmans of Exeter, and Dr. Jabez True of Hampstead, the first leech to practice in the Ohio country. The surveyor of the group was Return J. Meigs of Middleton, Connecticut. Colonel Meigs had probably seen more of battle than any other veteran in the group, and his brilliant raid on the British at Sag Harbor, in '77, had brought him the thanks of Congress and a handsome sword.

The flotilla was ready in early April. It consisted of a flagship, no matter its name, and a vessel described merely as a flatboat, plus several canoes. The forty-eight men climbed in and moved with the current. Five days later, on April 7, they tied up on the Ohio bank of the stream near the log walls of Fort Harmar, just beyond the mouth of the Muskingum.

The oxen bellowed, the horses whinnied, men shouted, and all hands went ashore to start building what was first called Adelphia, and later Marietta for a French queen who was overly fond of cake, but who gave aid to Americans against the English.* It was the first permanent settlement in the Northwest Territory.

Marietta was to be no typical frontier hamlet, jerry-built to save time and work. A row of stout log cabins went up, and around them a rugged stockade of pointed poplar logs, under the practiced eye of General Putnam, who had erected fortifications at Boston and West Point. On higher ground the careful general laid out a fort that would have given pause to any raiding party, Indian or white. It was of heavy logs, blockhouses at the four corners, dwellings making up the walls between. Around the whole went a most formidable log palisade. A bit later this stronghold, which the settlers liked to call Campus Martius, was to shelter hundreds of refugees from the smoldering settlements up the Muskingum. For the present, the Campus Martius was used as an office in which to draw the detailed plot of Marietta.

The town was laid out in the Yankee manner. Each settler was given an in-lot for his house and barn, and an out-lot of eight acres for his farm. A town common was naturally provided.

All had been timed well. The cabins and fort were hardly finished when the first families began to arrive. The women and children were in season to pick wild fruits and harvest the first vegetables the men had planted. And presently Dr. Cutler himself was on the way. On July 21, 1788, the doctor left Ipswich Hamlet in his faithful sulky. God must have been with him, too, for he "covered 750 miles in 29 days." He remained almost a year in Marietta, advising, treating the ill, investigating the curious mounds in the neighborhood which he concluded were the work of ancient tribes. Dr. Cutler, or anyone else, could see, too, that Marietta was the work of "robust and industrious" people, Yankees. Within a few months a school was being held, taught by Miss Bathsheba Rouse. There had been preaching from the very day the pioneers landed when Founding Father David Story had, on the part of the Associates, thanked God for their safe passage and prompt arrival.

The school was presently Muskingum Academy, later to grow into Marietta College. General Putnam and several Associates were influential in starting a state university. In 1795 they went up the Hocking River in canoes and laid out two townships for the support of a state seat of learning. The Marietta settlers also gathered what became locally famous as the "Coonskin Library." This was a community enterprise. Lacking cash, they trapped raccoons and exchanged the peltry for books, volumes like Locke's Essays,

---

* Some accounts of the name derive it from the two daughters of General Putnam, Mary and Etta. However come by, it was an improvement over Adelphia.

Gibbon's *Decline and Fall of the Roman Empire,* Schlegel's *Philosophy of History,* and Smollett's *History of England.*

Orderly government was set up in Marietta almost upon arrival of the first party. And when General Arthur St. Clair, first governor of the Northwest Territory, came to Marietta in 1788 to take over his duties, the Pilgrims there persuaded him to name December 25 not as Christmas, but as Thanksgiving Day, a true Yankee occasion.

The pattern was now complete. Yankees had made the first settlement in the Territory. They had brought their culture as well as their industry. They had managed to prescribe the first official holiday in all Northwest Territory. One doubts not that they ate pumpkin pie on that glorious occasion. Others might settle in the Ohio country, but the Ohio country was also safe for Yankees. By the time the first Maretta harvest was in, other Yankees were heading for the New England of the West.

CHAPTER III

SETTLING THE WESTERN RESERVE

BRIGADIER GENERAL MOSES CLEAVELAND began living up to the implications of his Old Testament name in 1795, when he turned prophet and helped to organize the Connecticut Land Company; and a year later led fifty-two other Yankees out of New England and into New Zion of the Western Reserve along the shore of Lake Erie. He had been interested in the West ever since his good friend and comrade-at-arms, General Rufus Putnam, had induced him to take two shares in the Ohio Company of Associates, the already successful founders of Marietta.

The Western Reserve was a result of the prehensile qualities inherent in the people of Connecticut. The British charters to Massachusetts, Connecticut, New York, and four Southern colonies gave to those provinces an indefinite claim to Western lands, extending in certain cases across the continent to the Pacific Ocean. After the Revolution, when Congress was setting up the Northwest Territory, it had to settle the claims of the several states. Maryland, which had no claim, urged the other states to yield theirs for the federal good, and all but Connecticut and Virginia did so. The latter reserved for itself the so-called Virginia Military District, while Connecticut kept its hand firmly on a strip along Lake Erie. This became known as the Western Reserve, sometimes called New Connecticut.

The Connecticut Land Company, formed of thirty-six men including General Cleaveland, purchased approximately three million acres, and the directors prevailed on Cleaveland to inspect and survey their new property, and to lay out a few likely townsites. The directors could hardly have done better; General Cleaveland, though Connecticut-born, was perfectly at home in the West. He had ranged a good deal. He was as swarthy as an Indian. He got along well with the red men and was probably just as good a woodsman as they. He did his surveying job with dispatch and returned to his home in Canterbury before the harvest of 1796, to report that two towns, with a few

[25

settlers in each, had been laid out at Conneaut and Cleaveland.* All that remained to be done, by a speculating concern such as the Connecticut Land Company, was to promote sales and instigate migration.

The Marietta colony's success had brought the name of Ohio into the talk and the press of New England. The New Haven *Gazette,* among others, said the Marietta corn grew fourteen feet high. When Colonel John May of Boston returned from a Western trip he related that a seven-acre farm in Ohio had produced 700 bushels of corn. When Thaddeus Harris got back to his native Dorchester, Massachusetts, he continued to marvel at the fine farms and neat fences of the Marietta settlers.

Because this talk also concerned the Ohio country, it was excellent promotion for the Western Reserve; and presently an unnamed writer came out in the Providence *Gazette* with an article entitled "Advice to American Farmers," which helped fan the ready flame of Yankees to migrate. The writer warned against taking land in either the Niagara or the Kentucky region. Neither was so salubrious a climate as Ohio; and so far as Kentucky was concerned, he said, all decent emigrants would naturally avoid all regions that had not prohibited Negro slavery. He also had some practical advice for emigrants. They should take with them apple, peach, and garden seeds, a kettle in which to boil maple sap, and of course a gun and ammunition. A Bible should be included in the settler's effects—naturally—and the writer thought that it was best if those of the same faith settled together, "in order the sooner to secure a minister and schoolmaster." All in all, it was his considered opinion that the emigrants to the Ohio country were "creating new forces for independence and affluence."

Similar notices were appearing in papers in all parts of New England. The news sounded attractive, for instance, to Elder Morris Witham, Hard-Shell Baptist of Standish, Maine. In 1796 he made a lone journey to Ohio and bought a tract of land, not in the Western Reserve, but in what is now Clermont County, bordering the Ohio River. Then he returned to Maine to astound his fellow townsmen along the Saco with what he had seen. He told of soil black as gunpowder, of fountains of water inexhaustible and sweet as nectar; of natural grasses on which cattle grew hog-fat in a few weeks; of tall chestnut trees from which fence rails could be split with one stroke of the ax—as straight as a line, said Elder Witham. And he vowed that in Ohio the potatoes grew as large as "Caleb Kimball's foot."

---

* Accounts of the founding of Conneaut are conflicting. "With their *tin cups,*" says a pious version, "dipping from the broad lake the crystal waters with which to pledge the national honor," the Ohio pilgrims raised the first log cabin there. General Cleaveland himself said that he caused rum to be poured for all the party, and that after salutes had been fired and the toasts drunk, the affair closed "with three cheers. Drank several pails of grog, supped and retired in remarkably good order."

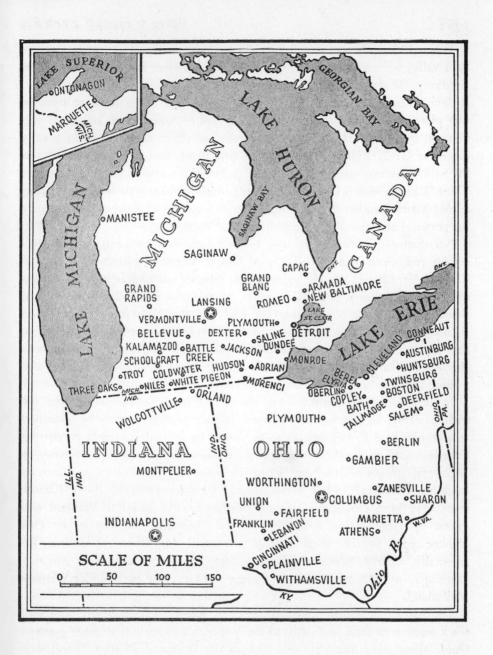

SCALE OF MILES

0   50   100   150

When Elder Witham took off again for paradise, several families of the Saco valley went too. On a second trip went still more families, among them Bradbury, Warren, Lane, Townsend, Bennett, Rounds, Wentworth, and Ridlon. When they got there, all their houses and barns were grouped in one place, making the village of Withamsville. And though the town survives in mid-twentieth century, there must have been sore times in the early days, for G. T. Ridlon, who knew at first hand, said the whole affair was "a wild, reckless venture, and nothing but the unsanctified selfishness of Elder Witham would have caused him to induce these well-housed and contented Maine families to sacrifice all they had gained in generations to gratify his personal ambition for selling land in the West."

No matter the complaints, the Ohio Fever was spreading to the most remote reaches of Yankeeland. Up in Derby, Vermont, plumb on the Canadian border, Charles Wright, aged twenty-one, set out on foot to see what was out there in the new land of wonders. In the next four months he walked through New York State, a part of Pennsylvania, then into Virginia, and so north again to Putnam, Ohio, having covered more than 900 miles, on foot and alone. He attended "the Ohio university at Athens," taking both English and surveying. Soon he was teaching school at Reading. He was also writing home to his brother, Erastus, in Derby.

In those times letters cost a lot of money, but newspapers went through the mails cheaply. So, the brothers carried on their correspondence by a method so common, and so heinous, as to be forbid by federal law. In a newspaper Charlie would mark whole words that he wished to include in a sentence by horizontal strokes of the pen. Words he wanted to spell out were made by marking individual letters with dots. However he marked them, Charlie must have been eloquent, for soon brother Erastus had left Vermont and "gone up Illinois river teaching school." Such was the way of it: One Yankee gone to the West usually accounted for others following. Incidentally, Charlie Wright never got home again, but died near Monroe, Louisiana, in 1827, while with a government surveying party under William McFarland.

The hamlet of Hollis, New Hampshire, heard the call clearly, and sent forth many a migrant, not only to the Western Reserve but to other parts of Ohio. Many were men of God, such as the Reverend Phillips Wood who went to Piqua, the Reverend William P. Eastman to preach at Union, and the Reverend Luther Smith at Zanesville. The Reverend Eli Sawtell, after serving in foreign parts as agent for the American Seamen's Friend Society, settled down in Cleveland, which by then had dropped one letter from its name, to found a female academy and to teach. Sam Worcester of Hollis went into Ohio politics and so to Congress.

The small New Hampshire village of Peterborough sent the Reverend Solomon Laws to aid in civilizing the Western Reserve; David Scott and Gustavus Swan to become prominent citizens of Columbus; and Professor George Moore to teach in Cincinnati. From Peterborough Dr. Reuben D. Mussey went forth to teach and at last to die at the Ohio Medical College in Cincinnati.

Out of New Hampshire's Cornish and Dartmouth College went Philander Chase, to be the first Episcopal Bishop of Ohio and, of greater import, to found at Gambier a notable place of learning which he named Kenyon College. The good bishop called his own farm the Valley of Peace, yet he himself was often in controversy and after much bickering resigned his office and moved on to Gilead, Michigan, there to start another school. Another Chase, Salmon P., also from Cornish, followed his Uncle Philander to Ohio but refused to study for holy orders. Instead, he studied for the law and was soon a devout and aggressive antislavery man, on the way to the United States Senate and Lincoln's cabinet; and still on to act as chief justice of the nation's supreme court.

Although Vermonters did not go to Ohio in any great number, about half of them who did migrate to that country settled in the Western Reserve. Among them were early pioneers at Hiram, and Wadsworth. Several more families went to wild Geauga County, where people from Cheshire, Connecticut, had preceded them. Sugar maple grew in abundance in this region and, more than a century later, the town of Chardon has a maple sugar festival. Rutherford Hayes and wife, both of Brattleboro, Vermont, migrated to Delaware, Ohio, where a son was born, later to be a President. Ohio's reputation as a birthplace of chief executives was further assured when Abram Garfield of Massachusetts married Eliza Ballou of Rhode Island and migrated to Cuyahoga County, where son James Abram was born—the last President to be born in a log cabin.

He who surely was Ohio's most remarkable senator of all time was born Benjamin Franklin Wade, near Springfield, Massachusetts, in 1800, and later migrated with his parents to Andover, Ohio. Wade worked as farmer, drover, teacher, and studied law. In 1851 he was elected to the United States Senate, to serve there a total of eighteen years. He was an honest, rough, and bold man who did something toward the taming of Southern fire-eaters in the Senate. When one of them challenged him to a duel, Wade responded quickly and called for rifles. The duel did not take place. Wade's most spectacular feat was at the First Battle of Bull Run. In a buggy he had driven out to see how the North was doing. It wasn't doing very well. The lads in blue were in wholly disorganized rout. Wade placed his buggy across one of the roads of retreat, took his position with rifle in hand and threatened to shoot the first soldier who attempted to pass. He succeeded in stemming a portion of the Union rout. Half a dozen Wades might have stopped all of it.

Aging relics of the Revolution went along with younger men to the New Zion of Ohio. The New Hampshire veterans included Elijah Averill, who settled at Lafayette; Alvan Bingham at Athens; Ebenezer Buck at Salem; Jonathan Cass at Dresden; Jonathan Cilley at Hamilton; and John Clark at Northfield.

Although all six Yankee states felt the Ohio Fever in varying degrees, it was Connecticut that often must have seemed to be moving en masse to the new country. Among the early settlers of Portage County were several Bierces from Cornwall, including Lucius, later to play a prominent part in the so-called Ohio-Michigan, or Toledo, War, over the proper boundary. Another branch of the same Bierces did not tarry on the Reserve but moved direct to Meigs County, well down the river, where a son was born and named Ambrose, in 1842. The proprietors of Bath were Ezekiel Williams and Thomas Bull of Hartford, and the first legal settlers in that town were Jason Hammon of Bolton and Jonathan Hale of Glastonbury; and the Bronsons— Harmon, Levi, and Azor—of Waterbury were moving spirits in founding the Ohio Boston, aided by Alfred Wolcott of Hartford. The first town clerk, justice of the peace, and schoolmaster in Copley was Jonathan Starr from Norwich, and with him were William Green of Canaan and Thomas Beckwith of Hartford.

Copley had the first formal temperance society in Ohio, and its members gave no quarter to the Demon: one of them, Harvey Baldwin, went so far as to refuse spirits to the men who helped him to raise a gigantic cider press on his farm. To refuse passing out rum at a raising of any sort was to be about as fanatical as a man could be.

The town of Canfield had a full-bodied Yankee flavor from the first, due in part to Elijah Wadsworth, from Connecticut, who erected a fine house there in 1800, and to Elisha Whittlesey, also from Connecticut, who settled here with his partner, Eben Newton, to practice law. Whittlesey's business took him to all parts of the Ohio country, and in 1815 he helped to found another new village, this time on the Firelands.

The Firelands, also known as the Sufferers' Lands, was a twenty-five-mile-wide strip on the western portion of the Reserve. This half a million acres was set aside by the Connecticut legislature, in 1792, for the citizens of the Connecticut shore towns who had suffered great property losses during the Revolution in the destruction by British troops, one expedition of which was led by Benedict Arnold, a native of the region. The towns burned included the several Havens, Norwalk, Danbury, Greenwich, Ridgefield, New London, and Groton. Setting aside the Firelands was a generous thing, but it was thirty years before they were properly surveyed and open to settlement; and the Firelands then settled slowly indeed. Forty-year-old men who had lost their homes in the war, were now in their seventies, rather old to migrate; but their descendants at last moved into the new country.

Lawyer Whittlesey, ranging out from Canfield, discovered a fine site for a town on the Firelands, a high and pleasant place; and with two other Connecticut men, Platt Benedict and Fred Fallig, founded Norwalk, named for the martyred village back home. Whittlesey had sufficient influence to have Norwalk made a county seat. He fetched maple saplings and planted them along its main street; and under his leadership villagers erected a three-storied building and established Norwalk Academy. Young Rutherford B. Hayes was schooled here.

Almon Ruggles, from Danbury, Connecticut, was chief surveyor of the Firelands, and selected the town of Berlin for a settlement. John Beatty from New London drove his stakes near Sandusky Bay. He became mayor twenty years later of the thriving town of Sandusky.

Cleveland, which was to outstrip everything on the Reserve, had a most discouraging early period. In 1800, when Samuel Huntington of Coventry, Connecticut, put up a log cabin there, it was something less than a hamlet. Ten years later it had a population of but fifty-seven. Huntington had moved in the meantime to Painesville, where he was elected the second governor of Ohio. But Cleveland gradually forged ahead. Samuel L. Mather, grandson of a heavy stockholder in the Connecticut Land Company, settled there in order to look after his family's interests, and saw vast possibilities in the newly discovered iron ore of Michigan's Upper Peninsula. He organized a company which brought the first load of ore down the lakes to Cleveland, and thus founded a noted iron and shipping dynasty. Meanwhile had arrived Captain Alva Bradley, born in Connecticut, whose first job in the West was the stamping of charcoal in wooden-soled shoes. Bradley built a boat and got into lake shipping. He invested heavily in Cleveland real estate. He died wealthy and honored, called Admiral of the Lakes.

The Leonard Hannas, who had first settled in New Lisbon, moved to Cleveland, bringing young Marcus Alonzo, whose mother had been Samantha Converse, a Vermont schoolmarm. Marcus was to have a considerable influence, in Cleveland, in Ohio, and on the United States.

A great and contrasting influence was that of Clarence Darrow, who was born in Kinsman of pure Connecticut stock. This village, founded by John Kinsman from Connecticut, never grew into a city, but it had a fine academy; and there young Darrow, son of the village infidel and furniture maker, got his first schooling. His first law practice was in neighboring Andover.

The most talked-about settlement on the Reserve for many years was Kirtland, one of several villages founded by Turhand Kirtland, a stockholder and general agent of the Connecticut Land Company. One day in January of 1831 a sleigh drove into Kirtland and stopped in front of Gilbert & Whitney's store. Out of the sleigh leaped a tall handsome stranger, who ran into the store and stunned one of the proprietors with the greeting: "Newel K. Whitney, thou art the man!" The stranger was Joseph Smith, native of Vermont, who proceeded to tell Mr. Whitney: "I am the Prophet Joseph. You've prayed me here, now what do you want of me?" The Prophet remained in Kirtland, where gathering Mormons erected a massive Temple, the most impressive in Ohio, and it was headquarters of the sect for a decade. The New Zion, however, turned out to be farther west. Yankee Gentiles were too numerous in Ohio for Mormon comfort.

Among the swarming Gentiles was the superbly named surveyor Birdseye Booth, who ran the lines of Stow township, owned by Joshua Stow and William Wetmore of Middletown, Connecticut; and the lines of Tallmage, settled by Roger Newberry from Windsor. Middlebury was founded by Captain Joseph Hart, born in Wallingford. Twinsburgh got its name, rightly enough, from identical brothers Aaron and Moses Wilcox, who came from North Killingsworth in 1823 to settle and to donate eight acres for a public square and the sum of $20 "to improve the Common." All Yankees liked to see a good common in the center of town. The twins married sisters and died within a few hours of each other, aged fifty-seven. Early Twinsburgh settlers included Ethan Alling, Major Elisha Loomis, and E. W. Mather, all from New Haven. Coventry, Ohio, was founded by men from Groton, Connecticut—Jesse Allen, Nathaniel Allen, and Amos Spicer.

David Hudson of Goshen, Connecticut, named his Ohio town for himself. Here in 1802 he built a Congregational church and a schoolhouse. Among the early settlers was Owen Brown of Torrington, Connecticut, who opened a tannery where, for a dozen years, worked his son John—after 1859, the only Brown in the United States that needed no further identification than his first name. At Hudson, in 1826, was founded the institution of learning that became Western Reserve University.*

Now and again some lone Yankee set out upon a journey merely to satisfy his curiosity to see exactly how the emigrants at the West were getting along. Such a one was young Elisha Niles, of Chatham, Connecticut, who on June 3, 1811, left home for a tour of Ohio, which he called New Connecticut. At Lima he visited with the Benjamin Roots, formerly of Lyme. At Clarence he saw Charles Knight, once of Colchester; and at Morgan ran into a whole

* See Chapter XX.

slew of old Chatham friends—the Philip Goffs, the Cornelius Phelpses, the Stephen Knowltons. Young Niles thought that all the ex-Nutmeggers were doing extremely well; and he must have said something to that effect when he returned to Connecticut, for on September 14, 1815, he watched while "on this day some forty souls left Chatham, to Remove to New Connecticut in Ohio." Included in this mass migration were the families of Isaac Hinckley, Stephen Brainard, Asa Brainard, and Elijah Young; and three bachelors named Ira Clark, Elijah Abel, Jr., and Ephphas Bolles.

The Connecticut migration contained, early and late, many an Atwater. One or more Atwaters were in the group of Plymouth who founded Plymouth, near Ashtabula, Ohio. "Nearly all of this company," wrote Francis Atwater, "were Episcopalians," and they numbered the families of Zadoc Mann, Warner Mann, John Blakeslee, Asher Blakeslee, Lynus Hall, Titus Seymour, Elias Cook Upson, and Dr. David Warner. Captain Moses Hall was notable among the Plymouth settlers. Incidentally, Historian Atwater remarked that the Western Reserve "comprising some 3,250,000 acres, was sold by the State of Connecticut to a syndicate of her sons for a sum about equal to the present [1895] cost of building a viaduct across the Cuyahoga river at Cleveland."

The records of the time fail to show that any appreciable number of Yankees, once they had got settled in Ohio, ever returned to New England for more than a visit. They stayed where they were and, by letters to their old homes, were doubtless of the greatest influence in persuading more to follow them. The seductive calls of the professional realtors, no matter their eloquence, could not touch the homely letters that told of stoneless soil; could not match the naked truth, when a brother in Berea, Ohio, told a brother in hilly Bath, New Hampshire, of land as level as a barn floor.

Back home, of course, a few sour and sobering notes were mingling with the songs of praise for the New Connecticut. One Yankee, writing in the Hartford *Courant* under the name of "Robinson Crusoe," laid about him with fine sarcasm, making sport of the pretentious names given to public improvements in Marietta—such as Campus Martius—and by Munchausian exaggerations casting doubt on the stories of gigantic pumpkins and tall corn in Ohio. Other Yankee correspondents and writers of letters-to-the-editor displayed ribald derision for the claims of the Ohio settlers. By 1819 one irritable and determined Yankee named Henry Trumbull could remain quiet no longer. He published, in Boston, a strange little pamphlet embellished with fanciful woodcuts, entitled *Western Emigration: Journal of Doctor Jeremiah Simpleton's Tour of Ohio.* In his preface the author said flatly that New England was all that any man could desire, yet because man was

by nature restless, many a one had been ruined by leaving his Yankee home
for Ohio.

"Yes," says the mythical Dr. Simpleton, "I have been to Ohio, and if the
crows do not deprive me of all that is left of my poor old Dobbin, I will at
last get home . . . where I will sit myself down contented to remain all
the days of my life an inhabitant of old Massachusetts—and be thankful
even for a scanty meal of codfish and potatoes." The emaciated Doctor then
goes on to relate, in boring detail, his ghastly trip to Ohio—and return.
When he got there, the town he sought was virtually non-existent. All the
several offices he held—colonel, justice of the peace, doctor, schoolmaster—
meant nothing at all; they were mere titles, empty of all but sound. "The
place was inhabited by musquetoes and swamp flies, wolves and wildcats."
The story closes with the Doctor extolling—somewhat surprisingly for a
Massachusetts man—the state of Maine and its way of life. Maine, says he,
is not a country where the inhabitants walk on all fours.

If the Doctor's prose was not sufficient to give pause, the woodcuts showing the dreadful region of Ohio, and the morons who had settled there,
certainly would have stopped short any person who put faith in pictures.

The exodus to Ohio, more than any later migration, was attacked all over
New England. One judges that fear prompted a portion of it, fear both of
social and of economic changes that might follow the loss of population. If
so, the fear was not unfounded; long before the Ohio Fever had run its
course, the effects were felt at home. And the attacks continued. Favorites of
the Yankee press were cuts representing the travelers going to Ohio in good
wagons drawn by sleek and fat horses, robust men surrounded by healthy
and smiling families; then, returning to New England, wrecks of wagons
with the tattered legend "I Have Been to Ohio," attached to skeletons of
horses, and containing haggard, ragged, almost depraved-looking families.

Probably these fantastic cuts, and the often fantastic prose, had some effect
on tempering the tone of advertisements of speculators in lands. But the
Ohio Fever had sent Yankee temperatures to a high mark, and nothing,
except time alone, could quite lay the epidemic. The moment Moses Cleaveland returned from his expedition, and the realtors got busy, the newspapers
of Connecticut and Massachusetts broke out with a rash of advertisements
and another rash of unquestionably inspired "news" stories. Both were to
continue for years.

An active agent in the exodus was the firm of Uriel Holmes and Ephraim
Root, of Hartford, who paid for space to "call to the attention of all industrious and enterprising persons" the wonders of the acres Holmes and Root
had bought from the Connecticut Land Company and were now prepared to
exchange for Connecticut farms. Thus did many an ancient farm pay, at least

in part, for land in the New Connecticut. Root alone disposed of some 100,-000 acres of Western lands. Lemuel Storrs of Middletown disposed of even more, and finally sent agents into the Western Reserve, to care for settlers on the spot.

When in the early days of migration to Ohio the Indians, desperate at the influx, started to butcher Yankee settlers, here and there a Yankee editor at home sought to slow the exodus by featuring accounts of battles and the massacre of isolated Yankee settlers. The Boston *Gazette's* editor was good at this. He started an Indian Department and was no man to be queasy in reports of scalpings and burnings. When General Arthur St. Clair's campaign against the redskins turned into a bad defeat for the soldiers, the *Gazette* called its story "A Melancholy Affair," which surely it was; and also gave sanguinary details of the disaster.

Even the geographer, Jedidiah Morse, turned propagandist in an effort to stay the Yankees. "Actual calculation has evinced," he wrote, "that any quantity of the best mowing land in Connecticut produces about twice as much clear profit as the same quantity of the best wheat land in New York or Ohio."

For all his great authority in the field of learning, the Reverend Dr. Morse might just as well have remained silent about opportunities in the West. Neither propaganda about wheat nor news about scalpings could offset the fact of fourteen-foot-tall corn and fields that were stoneless. The Yankees continued to migrate. The first settler in Butler County, Ohio, was Jeremiah Butterfield of Chelmsford, Massachusetts, whose forefathers had helped to settle not only the Bay State but New Hampshire and Maine as well. General Edward Paine, born in Bolton, Connecticut, went forth at the age of fifty-four, to lead a group of sixty-four people to found Painesville. John Walworth, a native of New London, bought 2,000 acres in Painesville, and moved in on sleds in 1800 to begin clearing land. Lewis Day, with son Horatio and two other men, all from Granby, Connecticut, arrived overland in wagons to establish the village of Deerfield, which he named for his mother's native town in Massachusetts.

Although Yankees were doubtless known better for individualism than for cooperation, the frontier forced them into certain group efforts. In 1818 the settlers in Medina County were so bedeviled by bears and wolves that they organized a mighty hunt. On Christmas Eve more than six hundred armed men, most of them Yankees, assembled at Judge Hinckley's place. They spread out in military formation, and began driving all wild animals before them to a center. The gunfire must have sounded like full-dress battle, for when the chase was over, the huntsmen counted seventeen dead wolves, twenty-one bears, three hundred deer, and turkeys, foxes, raccoons, and other small animals beyond knowing. The country around Medina was wonderfully forested; but the Yankees quickly cleared it, and the region became notable for its stupendous crops of wheat and corn. Ohio wheat and corn were among the many things that contributed much toward the decay of rural New England.

James Kilbourne of New Britain, Connecticut, was no man to accept either the fabulous tales about Ohio lands or the stories of the scalping of Ohio settlers. He was one who liked his information at first hand. So in 1802 he went out to the Northwest Territory and, it seems, looked over pretty much all of it, including a part of Michigan, before he returned home to organize a company of pioneers. They went to Ohio, though not to the Western Reserve, and in 1803 put up a log church, a schoolhouse, and cabins not far from present Columbus. They called it Worthington. The only untypical part of the new town was its church, which was not of the true, Congregational brand, but Episcopal, the first one in the whole region. Kilbourne, however, was otherwise typical of his race. He founded the first newspaper in central Ohio, the *Western Intelligencer,* was elected president of Worthington Academy, and in 1812 was sent to Congress. He also organized one of the earliest Abolitionist societies.

Something of a one-man migration was Stephen Pomeroy of Northampton, Massachusetts. Lugging a Bible, and "Watts' Hymns and the Shorter Catechism," and leading his wife and six children, he traveled west for six weeks, then drove his stakes in what became Huntsburg.

How important to these migrants was their church is seen in the founding of Granville, Ohio. Before the pilgrims took off from the town of the same name in Massachusetts, they formally organized a congregation, and then pastor and deacon went with them into the wilderness. The Granville exodus numbered one hundred and seventy-six persons. The first thing they did on arrival at the site of their new home was to release their oxen and listen to a sermon by their pastor: "O Lord, Thou hast delivered us safe through the valleys and shadows . . . "

If one of these new Yankee towns did not have a suitable pastor when the first cabins went up, it soon had one. In Austinburg, on the Reserve, Betsy, wife of Eliphalet Austin, the first settler, packed her saddle bags one day in 1811, and rode a thirty-day journey overland to Bristol, Connecticut, and there prevailed on the good and Reverend Giles H. Cowles, D.D., to move with his wife and eight children to tiny Austinburg, where he remained nineteen years.

If the early settlers liked neither Congregational, nor Baptist nor Episcopalian preaching, they might on occasion get a good sound dose of Emanuel Swedenborg, when the eccentric John Chapman passed by. This man was the Johnny Appleseed of legend, born around 1775, either in Springfield or in Boston, Massachusetts, who took to the Ohio roads and trails as a sort of educated tramp, planting apple trees as he went, and roaring passages from the great Scandinavian mystic to all who would listen, or couldn't help themselves. Johnny liked the primitive region and died there, being buried near Fort Wayne and going simultaneously into consecrated legend.

An eminently named son of Darien, Connecticut, Ethan Allen Brown, migrated to the New Connecticut in 1804, and by 1818 was governor of Ohio. Vermont sent a small but continuous wave of migrants, many of whom were to make their mark: Joel H. Linsley became president of Marietta College; to Congress from Ohio went Vermonters Aaron F. Ferry, Heman Allen Moore, John Fassett Follett, Columbus Delano, and Edson B. Olds. Another Follett, Martin D. of Enosburg, became an associate justice of Ohio's supreme court. Curtis Sawyer Barrett, born in the green hills in 1839, became a notable Ohio operator in coal and steel. Vermont also exported journalists: Charles B. Murray established the Cincinnati *Commercial Review*, Joseph H. Barrett edited the *Gazette* in that city, and for twenty-five years Joseph W. Gray, born in tiny Bridport, published the Cleveland *Plain Dealer*.

By the turn of the century, a continuous migration into Ohio was under way from New Jersey, New York, Pennsylvania, and Virginia, and the pioneer Yankee influence was being modified—or watered, as any true Yankee would have put it. But the Western Reserve itself retained both the appearance and the character of Connecticut, as well it should. Many of its towns even duplicated, to the future harassment of the United States Post Office, the names of Connecticut places. As early as 1800 the roll went: Berlin, Bloomfield, Bristol, Brookfield, Chatham, Chester, Colebrook, Danbury, Fairfield, Farmington, Franklin, Greenwich, Guilford, Hartford, Hartland, Huntington, Litchfield, Lyme, Middlebury, Monroe, Montville, New Haven, New London, Norwalk, Saybrook, Sharon, Southington, Thompson, Trumbull, Vernon, Warren, Windham, and Windsor.

One Gershom Flagg traveled pretty much all over the state of Ohio, and he did not think too much of the settlers in other than the Western Reserve. Those of the central and southern portions, said Vermonter Flagg, had come from Kentucky, Virginia, Pennsylvania, and other foreign places. And, said he, "They are the most ignorant people I ever saw. . . . I am persuaded the people who come from Connecticut who are settled in the north part of this state are more enlightened." What seemed to trouble smug Mr. Flagg more than anything else was that these non-Yankees called townships and towns what Flagg and all other New Englanders called towns and villages.

Mr. Flagg did not exert any particular influence on the new state, but a fellow Vermonter did. He was the Reverend Isaac Jennings, late of Bennington, who urged and badgered the people of Ohio, then gave most of his time to establishing primary and grammar schools in Akron under a system that was widely adopted over the state.

Working hand in hand with Jennings, and often leading him, was Caleb Atwater, who left North Adams, Massachusetts, to settle in Circleville, far south of the Reserve, in 1815. Atwater was one of the giants. He pushed through bills to aid roads and schools, and wrote an essay on education that was of the greatest influence in Ohio. Many a writer has termed him the founder of the state's school system. He wrote valuable studies on the Ohio mound country. He was a mover for the railroad, in the face of ridicule by powerful canal interests of that means of transportation. He was, indeed, interested in almost everything except the making of money. He lived and died a poor man; and before his death, in 1865, he had written the first history of Ohio and put forth an able statement as to why the forests of the state should not be butchered without some provision for new growth. Caleb Atwater was, wrote a historian of Williams College, one of the finest flowers ever to have been graduated from that institution.

Atwater's influence unquestionably was great in his adopted state. The influence of Ohio on all other Western states, however, stemmed largely from the Yankee college in Yankee Oberlin.

CHAPTER IV

A BEACON IN THE WILDERNESS

COMPARATIVELY FEW Yankee emigrants went forth with any conscious plan to influence the regions where they were to settle. All of them, of course, casually took their Yankee notions along—such as their baked beans of a Saturday night, their religion, which was usually headed by a Congregational God of Old Testament size and temperament, their love of schooling, and their political leanings which, except in the matter of antislavery where they were adamant, were as changeable as New England weather. Yet their primary reason for leaving their old homes was not to implant their customs and beliefs in whatever new state was in the making. Most of them went away for the sole purpose of bettering themselves.

There were, of course, exceptions. A few individuals moved upon the West hot-eyed, with the avowed purpose of influencing that new and savage country, especially in education and religion, which in that day were considered by a majority of people to be one and the same thing. That was the way Oberlin in the Western Reserve came into being, to rise and shine like a bright beacon in the immense night of the great forest of the Northwest Territory; and Oberlin Collegiate Institute was to influence the culture of Ohio and the newer states to the west as perhaps nothing else before or since.

Oberlin was the dream of two obscure Congregational preachers and fanatics, Philo Penfield Stewart and John Jay Shipherd, who had been schoolmates in the Academy at Pawlet, Vermont, and had been inspired by the good works in the American West of David Bacon, Joseph Badger, Thomas Robbins, and other agents of the Connecticut Missionary Society. So, Stewart and Shipherd went into the wilderness along the shore of Lake Erie to carry the torch for the true religion. In 1832 they were stationed at small Elyria, Ohio, and they were discovering that the backwoods was truly a benighted region, in no manner anxious to serve the Lord of the Pilgrims and Puritans. They were grievously dismayed, but not disheartened; and presently they be-

[39

came obsessed with the idea they should found a school, right here in the Devil's own region, that should train missionaries to spread out and Christianize—for Congregationalism—the whole vast valley of the Mississippi.

By training young men on the spot, and not in far-away and civilized Connecticut and Massachusetts, they would better fit the acolytes for the work in hand; and young women, too, would be trained, because the school they were planning was to be quite revolutionary—it would accept females. It was also to be a manual labor school where students would learn to work with their hands and thus be equal to the frontier conditions they were certain to meet. Would it not be a happy thing, Shipherd and Stewart asked each other, if a young preacher could direct with professional assurance the construction and the raising of a church building, and advise about planting and harvest or about the making of clothes, or administer to the sick such simples and medicinals as could readily be found in the clearings? The idea was perfectly sound. Moreover, by their labor at the college, students could help to pay the cost of their education in higher matters.

Philo Stewart and John Shipherd were true and uncompromising fanatics, the sort who often accomplish the impossible things they set out to do. Before they left Elyria to locate their school they prayed for days on end, for guidance; and when they were cruising the deep woods of the Western Reserve they stopped often and asked further divine aid. Finally, in the township of Russia, Lorain County, the Lord responded: here was to be the Place. That the spot was one of the most unprepossessing in all the Reserve, that it was little more than a swamp, gave the seekers no pause whatever. A Congregational God was a God who knew what He wanted. . . .

Before anything else was done the two dreamers, there in the dark swamp, declared that it should be and was named Oberlin, honoring a pastor who, in Alsace, had given sixty years of "almost incredible devotion to redeeming an ignorant and degraded population." The very reason for chosing Oberlin's name was thus conclusive evidence of what Shipherd and Stewart thought of the work ahead of them.

So, while the ignorant and degraded settlers of the Western Reserve continued to live happily in that condition, John Shipherd started on horseback for Connecticut and New Haven, there to see the Messrs. Street and Hughes, speculators, who owned the consecrated land in Russia township.

Now, the Devil was patently as real to John Shipherd as to Martin Luther; and he had not gone far when a sinister form assailed him which he instantly identified as the Adversary—assailed him with doubt, with terror, ridicule, apathy. Shipherd faltered, he later admitted, but not for long. There in the dark wilderness haunted by an even darker figure, the young missionary sent forth prayers, then started his horse again and triumphantly rode down the Evil One who with satanic prescience dreaded what an Oberlin Collegiate Institute would do to his domain in the Western Reserve and elsewhere in the Mississippi valley. And the Lord remained with his pilgrim, and Shipherd prevailed on Street and Hughes to sell the tract wanted, "at a reasonable figure."

Philo Stewart meanwhile was not idle. With characteristic foresight and ingenuity he was working to perfect a cooking stove of new design, the profits from the sale of which he planned to use in support of the new school in the great swamp of Lorain County. No more typical partnership of Yankees could be found. Here was one of them riding down a horned Devil; the other sweating to make a homely domestic contrivance that every pioneer family would buy, thus giving support to the school that was going to drive the same horned Devil and all his minions straight back into Hell, where they belonged.

Then and later, the school at Oberlin was seldom to lack either idealism or practicality.

But Philo Stewart was having as difficult a time with his stove as John Shipherd with the Devil. By mid-May of 1833 he had cast only "the greater part of four stoves," which he felt was woefully little. Certain things, he said, had to be worked out most carefully if the stove were to be as good as he intended. He continued to labor hard. A little later his labor was to be of wonderful aid to Oberlin.

Clearing ground for the Oberlin colony, or village, and the school, went ahead swiftly throughout 1833, and in December a building was ready for the first class, which was composed, as the founders had planned, of both young men and young women. This first coeducational place of higher learning in the United States was presently chartered by the State of Ohio. The Reverend Seth H. Waldo, graduate of Amherst College, was secured as the first principal. James Dascomb, M.D., Dartmouth, came to teach botany, chemistry, and physiology. All the other pedagogues, then and for years to come, were "the products of New England culture and ideas."

The Oberlin Yankees were also busy with the new village, for Shipherd and Stewart had recruited several families who wanted to establish a thoroughly New England settlement on the Reserve. A flour mill was soon running, turned by a genuine steam engine, in which the colonists took the greatest pride; and also a sawmill. At the first town meeting, when the conventional three selectmen were elected, it was voted, quite in character, that the village houses and school buildings should be painted red, for red paint was "the most durable and least expensive." This was merely an old Yankee notion in extreme degree; in New England most of the farm and village houses were painted white, so far as the front and sides were concerned; but the back, away from the street or road, was the most durable and least expensive red. Oberlin was merely radical and went whole-hog; there could be no half-measures.

The first year of the Institute must have been most successful, for the second season began with slightly more than one hundred men and women enrolled. Cofounder Shipherd now sought to depart even further from conventional college practices of the time. *"Resolved,"* he wrote, in what one hopes were italics, *"that Students shall be received into this institution regardless of color."*

Here was a radical departure. Even the antislavery Yankees of the Western Reserve thought it was going too far, and many of them made protest. Oberlin did not waver. It even encouraged Negro families to live in the village and to send their children to the Institute. Oberlin also stood without compromise for Abolition. Not so the Lane Theological Seminary at Cincinnati. This school, headed by the eminent Dr. Lyman Beecher, a Connecticut Yankee who had moved to Ohio with his brood of talented children, was presently split asunder on the snag of slavery.

The splitting was done by young Theodore Dwight Weld, born in Connecticut, who had already converted the faculty of Western Reserve College at Hudson to Abolition. He then entered Lane and quickly organized most of the student body in favor of Abolition. Lane's trustees expelled him. So great was this young man's leadership that he took virtually all the student body with him, direct to Oberlin; and there gave a series of lectures on slavery so popular that Oberlin could not begin to accept all the applications of men and women who wanted to enter the Institute. The "ignorant and degraded" inhabitants of Ohio had turned out to be far from fearful of the light from Oberlin's beacon.

From one of Weld's lectures at Oberlin, "American Slavery as It Is," Dr. Beecher's daughter Harriet crystallized *Uncle Tom's Cabin.* One of Weld's converts, Gamaliel Bailey, edited the *National Era,* which ran her story as a serial before it went between covers to help shake the Republic apart. With Theodore Weld's lectures and the consequent excitement, Oberlin began a long period of explosive ferment that put Ohio safely in the antislavery ranks and also expanded into great influence in other Western states and territories. Soon to the now much-discussed school came the Reverend Charles G. Finney, Presbyterian revivalist, Abolitionist, bringing what was called, with capital letters, the Big Tent, in which to hold mass meetings of students and townsmen. To speak in the Big Tent came Stephen Foster, the songster, and wife; and Frederick Douglass, and Garrison of the *Liberator.*

Negroes continued to move steadily into Oberlin village. Between 1850 and 1860 they numbered 5 per cent of the student body.*

The Reverend Dr. Finney remained at Oberlin to head its theological department; and from Lane Seminary came Dr. Asa Mahan, Abolitionist, to head Oberlin itself. New endowments came to the school from Arthur and Lewis Tappan. Cofounder Shipherd became restless, and soon wandered off into the deeper wilderness of Michigan seeking a site for another Oberlin. He found it in Eaton County and there, with his wife and children and six other families, he established Olivet College, destined to survive and, in turn, to send out its young men and women to start still newer schools along the lines of Oberlin and Olivet. The process continued until late in the century.

As early as 1837 the first missionaries went out from Oberlin. A graduate of 1838, John S. Griffin, did not stop until he had reached the Oregon country. Scores, then hundreds, of graduates ranged the country in between, starting churches, founding schools, always taking with them Oberlin's idealism and Oberlin's intolerances. Oberlin itself had become so famous that it could not begin to accommodate all who wanted to enter, and subsidiary Oberlins were opened temporarily at Sheffield and Abbeyville in Ohio.

Reforms of all sorts stewed and steamed in Oberlin; and then went out into the West. One of the least popular of its crusades was that of dietary reform. For several years the ideas on food of Sylvester Graham were as dogma. Graham bread and burnt-toast coffee graced, if that is the word, Oberlin tables. Condiments were taboo. Students grumbled. One professor thought the fare so hideous that he provided from his own meager funds a box of pepper for each table. He was disciplined. Yet, after 1842 both coffee and tea reappeared, and also meat. Even Dr. Finney, an honest if a strange man, admitted that Grahamism had been a delusion.

The colony and the college, however, remained dynamic. Little by little its graduates founded new Oberlins at Berea, Kentucky, Hillsdale College in Michigan, Ripon College in Wisconsin, Northfield (now Carleton) College in Minnesota, and Grinnell and Tabor colleges in Iowa. Students, faculty members, and townspeople of Oberlin made the place an important station of the Underground Railroad. When slave catchers dared to come there, Oberlin turned against them as a man, nor did it turn the other cheek. Violence broke out on occasion, and one incident of taking a slave from the clutches of his captors resulted in several students' going to jail, to become

---

* The Negro grandparents of my friend Edwin C. Berry of the Urban League moved to Oberlin in 1849. Their sons and daughters and grandsons and granddaughters have been graduates of the college.

martyrs to Abolitionist sympathizers all over the country, including the fairly remote reaches of Iowa where the Congregational Association took up "a collection of $46, which was forwarded to the Oberlin Rescuers." The record indicates that an escaped slave was never taken away from the village of Oberlin.

The name of the village spread up and down and across the filling West and into the Deep South. Free Negroes heard of it and went there to live. Wild stories circulated about the town and the college. Miscegenation was said to be rife. This did not happen to be true, but it served to fan Oberlin's fame, or notoriety, and kept it well in the news. Something was always happening there. The town's aversion to liquor and tobacco was well known, and when a few bold saloonkeepers attempted to do business there, they found the going rough indeed. Rocks crashed through their windows; fires broke out on their premises. Tobacco, after many a battle, was at last stocked by several storekeepers, though no college youth or professor dared to patronize such places. Oberlin's tolerance did not include living with the works of that sinister Adversary whom good Dr. Shipherd had ridden down ahorseback. . . .

The Sabbath was also to be kept holy. When Dr. Finney was on his way hither, to begin his long service with the college, he discovered to his sudden horror that his last day of travel would come on the Sabbath. He forthwith had himself set on shore and spent Sunday in meditation, then resumed his journey on the next boat that came along. For three decades and more, Oberlin was solidly against any normal enjoyment of what most Christians—the Adventists excepted—call, with a handsome disregard for the calendar they use, the Seventh day of the week.

A steady flow of cash into Oberlin College coffers continued through the years, a goodly amount of it from New England. Josiah Chapin of Providence, William Chapin of Lawrence, Willard Sears of Boston, J. P. Williston of Northampton, and Miss Mary Holbrook of Holbrook, Massachusetts, were continuous contributors. So, too, were Mrs. Valeria Stone of Malden, and untold Sunday schools and Congregational societies of the six Yankee states.

Oberlin's bright name acted as a lodestone to emigrating Yankees, hundreds of whom went there, many to remain, others to fan out through the Western Reserve, and so on into Michigan, Wisconsin, Minnesota, Illinois, and Iowa. Among the early Oberlin families were the Hamiltons, Saffords, Penfields, Peases, Turners, Steels, Gastons, Ryders, Taylors, Littles, Platts, Captons, Ingersolls, Parishes, Hoveys, Weeds, Duttons, Copelands. One might call the roll of townsmen of Oberlin at any time during its first century and be answered in accents that ranged all the way from Danbury in

Connecticut to Bangor in Maine; from North Hero, Vermont, to Tiverton, Rhode Island.

Meanwhile, the name of Oberlin was being stamped proudly in the metal of more than one hundred thousand copies of Philo Stewart's Improved Cooking Stove, commonly admitted to be the best stove in all the Northwest Territory. ("Let them fry on an Oberlin stove," said an impious Oberlin student, "or let them fry in Hell.") A portion of the profit on every stove went to the college. Stewart himself reflected perfectly the reform spirit of the school he had helped to found and support. In Troy, New York, he opened a water-cure establishment, a feature of which was "an original system of gymnastics." The place quickly failed. Incidentally, it was Stewart that had first imposed the dreadful dietary system on Oberlin college.

The caldron of Oberlin boiled over again and again. When the Civil War started, Deacon Beecher of that town protested the fighting and went forth to induce the North to enlist hundreds of thousands of unarmed citizens who were to mass along the Mason and Dixon line and there to pray, to send up a mighty chorus of supplication to God "until the rebels are vanquished and brought to terms." But the North stuck to gunpowder. Another typically Oberlin worthy was Hiram Pease, who was so filled with missionary zeal that he spent sermon time counting the "supernumerary buttons on the garments of the brethren present," then reckoned up how much they had cost in money and, hence, how many Bibles were thus withheld from the ignorant and degraded population of the Mississippi valley. Mr. Pease did not do this lightly, but put forth his findings and criticism in open meeting. Doubtless it called for just such fanatics to make Oberlin's impact felt so strongly in the West.

Fanatics? There was Lucy of the dark brown hair, born of the Stone family back in Massachusetts—Lucy Stone she was born and so she died, though married to a Blackwell. She weighed one hundred and five pounds, with all her many clothes on; and out of this small body, for five decades, there came a cry, a demand that Woman be accorded a status other than that of a chattel. Endless work on a Yankee farm had made her discontented. Nor did it help when she discovered that before the law a woman was forever a minor, incompetent to give or to receive, though she might pay taxes. So, Lucy Stone looked at Woman and was desolate. "Is there nothing," she asked despondently, "that will put an end to me?" There wasn't, and she packed her extension suitcase and went away to far-off Oberlin, the only college in the United States that would accept a chattel as a student. Here she supported herself by manual labor.

She emerged from the school a seething radical, her gray eyes burning, to free not only the blacks but women, too. Hers was a voice of great and singular beauty, low vibrant, as haunting as an echo in a mountain valley; and she used it effectively to hasten Abolition and to arouse the silly dolts who called themselves females, urging them to become people. Woman's Rights? Hardly a female of the time knew that she had any Rights; but they all felt differently, once they had heard the strangely moving voice of Lucy Stone. Some of them snickered when Miss Stone married Henry Blackwell but retained her family name, while their husbands spoke gravely of the anarchistic tendencies of the time.

Lucy Stone spoke in every city and in most of the hamlets of the East and Middle West. She was mobbed many times. Once she was felled by a missile thrown. Hoodlums made charivari of her meetings. Still she talked on. She stood under the withering sun of Kansas and cried aloud that the state's new constitution should give woman a say in government. Kansas turned her down. So did New Jersey, where she had gone to live awhile; and in Jersey she refused to pay taxes, and so the sheriff came and sold her household goods. . . . Aye, Lucy was fanatic. When she was threescore and fifteen she stood on a platform at the World's Fair in Chicago and there, her liquid voice still like a harp of many strings, she attempted to speak of Woman's Rights to females who had come to see the sights and their consorts who had come hoping to see a female called Little Egypt, who weighed many pounds more than Lucy Stone and could dance, it was said, merely by use of her hips and stomach muscles. And *what*, pray, were Woman's Rights compared to a ride in a gondola poled by a romantic Venetian, or a sight of the hootchy-kootchy?

There was no denying that Oberlin turned out people who had ideas and determination. Perhaps they were fanatics, too; yet they had a great pity in their hearts, pity like that which moved Lorenzo Coffin, who had come to Oberlin from New Hampshire, to go forth and become in his grizzled age the Air Brake Fanatic, to club the railroads into protecting the lives and limbs of their employees by installing safeguards. A pity like that in Mary Ann Ball, who married a Bickerdyke and became a "large heavy woman, strong as a man, with muscles of iron, and nerves of steel," who set out alone for the Civil War as a free-lance nurse. When a suspicious Union officer demanded to know under whose authority she was picking up the wounded and lugging them in her own arms to an ambulance station, she replied— for she could be tart—that her authority was God Almighty, "and have you, sir, any authority to rank *that?*" She never forgot her Oberlin training, for she was a terror to officers she found in liquor, many of whom she managed to have discharged. Later, she devoted her energies to relieving the sufferers from the great locust plagues in the West, and kept house at the Chicago

Home for the Friendless. Mary Ann earned the handsome monument to her memory that is set up in Illinois at Galesburg. . . .

And there was pity in the heart of brilliant Erastus Milo Cravath, class of '57, who might well have headed any great university in the land, but chose instead to found the school for Negroes called Fisk, and to be its first president.

To do any of those things in those times called for courage, a courage founded in conscience; and often for determination of a quality little less than fanaticism. Oberlin's beacon may have sometimes burned a little too brightly, but it was never clouded.

The college sent out its propaganda, after 1838, in the *Oberlin Evangelist*, an aggressive and influential periodical in all matters pertaining to Abolition, temperance, antinicotine, and Sabbatarianism. Coupled with the hundreds of devout and often able young missionary-teachers, who for decades circulated throughout the expanding West, the total effect was probably much greater than can be measured. At least two historians of the Northwest Territory have cited Oberlin as having incomparable influence on the culture of Ohio and the newer states. One can scarcely pick up a book dealing with the early Middle West that is not liberally salted with references to the college or the town.* Even if the Adversary was not quite routed from the region, he was given pause, was driven underground, and to this day has never enjoyed the immunity he had before good Dr. Shipherd rode roughshod over him in the forest. As for good Dr. Stewart, it might please him to know that Ohio still stands high in the manufacture of cooking stoves. And both of the founding fathers would be happy that Oberlin College, even if no longer denominational, is in a flourishing condition, with more than one thousand "female students," along with twelve hundred men; that Negro students are as welcome now as they were when Oberlin erased the color line; that there are no sororities or fraternities; and that better than one-half of all its students earn all or a part of their way while absorbing some of the learning, as well as the idealism which not even the somewhat materialistic twentieth century has been able to remove entirely from the Collegiate Institute in the swamp of Russia Township, Ohio.

* In the twenty volumes of the *Dictionary of American Biography,* published 1928–1936, are listed 5 eminent Americans who attended Hiram College; 22 who went to Western Reserve University; 23, to Ohio State University; 27, to Kenyon College; and no fewer than 59 who were students at Oberlin.

CHAPTER V

THE HERALDS OF MORONI

AT THE TIME Philo Stewart and John Shipherd were addressing their Lord in the wilderness of Ohio, and preparing to establish a Western font from which Congregationalism should flow to inundate the whole Mississippi valley, another Yankee had moved into Ohio. This was Joseph Smith, whose astonishing arrival at Kirtland has been mentioned. Prophet Smith had much larger plans than those of Shipherd and Stewart; he had in mind a religion that would embrace all the known world, including even the Congregationalists. He had left Vermont with his parents to move west in 1816.

That had been a year of great exodus from New England, especially from Vermont—the Year of Two Winters, the infamous Eighteen Hundred and Froze to Death, when snow fell a foot deep in June and was of aid in helping thousands of Yankees to make up their minds. They sold out, if they had anything to sell, and they got out—New York, Ohio, anywhere to flee the wrath of a savage God displeased with the War of 1812 and the general breakdown of the True Faith.

No Yankees had been more sorely tried by their life and times in the Green Mountains than Joseph, Sr., and Lucy Mack Smith, parents of the future prophet. They had tried farming at Tunbridge, at Norwich, at Royalton, at Sharon, where Joseph, Jr., was born; they had lived awhile in Lebanon, New Hampshire. Nothing had gone well, not even the ginseng root they had speculated in. There had been much illness. Then came the snow in June, the bitter frosts in August. A year later found the Smith family in York State, settled near Palmyra.

Joseph, Jr., grew into a tall, fair-haired, blue-eyed man of rather distinguished appearance, usually jovial but given, as early as his fifteenth year, to spells of melancholy. He was commonly believed, around Palmyra, to be no great shakes in the matter of hard labor. Visions came to him, during which he had conversation with an angel later identified as Moroni who, on subsequent visitations, commanded him, in the name of the Lord, to restore

48]

the true church of Christ to the earth. All existing sects, it appeared, were in complete and hideous error. Then, on September 22, 1827, Joseph Smith, Jr., was led by Moroni to the hill Cumorah, near Manchester, Ontario County, New York, and there permitted to see and eventually to take away with him certain plates of gold upon which was recorded the history of "the true church on the American continent, following its migrations from Jerusalem." The Yankee Prophet was now in the making. He was twenty-one years old.

The history inscribed on the golden plates—thin as sheets of tin, bound together with rings—was in some ancient and forgotten characters; but the Angel Moroni directed Joseph to translate them by using the pair of miraculous spectacles discovered with the plates, which would automatically, and without any effort of learning, permit the rendering into English of the hieroglyphics.

Now appears the second New Englander to play a part in establishing a new and a wholly American religion. He was Oliver Cowdery, a schoolmaster from Middletown, Vermont. He acted as amanuensis for Joseph, putting down on paper and in English the words that Joseph, sitting behind an opaque screen with the golden plates and the spectacles, called out. The work of translation required three years. The result was the Book of Mormon.*

The Book of Mormon, called the Mormon Bible, was published at Palmyra, New York, in July of 1830. Joseph had already, on the preceding April 6, formally founded, at near-by Fayette, what is now known as the Church of Jesus Christ of Latter-Day Saints. The communicants at the founding were Joseph's relatives and a few neighbors. A year later the Prophet Joseph led his little band on the first of many moves, stopping at Kirtland, Ohio, to make it the first headquarters of the faith. From Kirtland he sent out the original Mormon missionaries. *"God's work,"* promised the Book of Mormon, *"shall hiss forth."* These incredibly courageous and determined men scattered for the most part over Ohio, New York, Pennsylvania, and Maryland, though a few of the ablest were sent to New England.

Neither the Mormon nor non-Mormon writers on the early history of the church indicate that any formidable number of Yankees accepted the message brought by the young heralds of Moroni and the Prophet. The continuous exodus from New England during the thirties and forties was not mainly, or even largely, an exodus of new Mormons. But the record is

* It has always appeared ironic to me that conventional Christians attack the Book of Mormon for its miraculous discovery and translation. The miracle of the Book of Mormon pales beside that of the birth of the founder of Christianity. The antiquity of a miracle, apparently, is of the greatest importance.

clear beyond doubt, that a majority of the leaders among the Mormons during the formative period, and even later, were natives of New England. The Prophet himself, the first and early presidents of the church, the counselors of the presidency, two of the patriarchs, a majority of the twelve apostles, many of the seventies, many of the First Company of Pioneers into Deseret, were born in one or another of the six Yankee commonwealths. If New England as a whole did not embrace Mormonism, then those Yankees who did accept it did so to some purpose. No emigrants from New England ever had a greater influence on the American West.

The first converts made on New England soil appear to have been the twenty-seven men and women of Benson, a hillside village in Rutland County, Vermont, who heard the fullness of the gospel preached there in 1831, when the Book of Mormon was scarce a year in print, by Elder Jared Carter, a man not to be trifled with. In 1831 the people of Benson could not have heard of Prophet Joseph Smith, nor of the Angel Moroni and the golden plates, when Elder Carter entered their village. But then they did hear the miraculous tidings, and they could not have heard them from a more impressive messenger. Elder Carter not only preached but commanded the ill and the halt to stand up and walk, and they did. The meetings in Benson, says an old account, "witnessed many manifestations of the Spirit in regard to healing."

It was not yet time for the going out, the Exodus; that would come later, when Zion was ready to receive them. For the present, Elder Carter organized a branch of the church in Benson, blessed the new Mormons, then passed on. Mighty feats elsewhere in New England awaited him, and in the West, too, for Elder Carter was to become captain-general of the Danites, the secret and militant group formed to defend the Mormons against their almost continuous persecution at the hands of Gentiles.

In the next year, 1832, Elder Carter returned to the native state of the Prophet, bringing his brother Simeon; and they were joined by another pair, Elders Orson Pratt and Lyman E. Johnson. Working in pairs, as was the Mormon custom, these four men walked over much of Vermont, holding meetings where permitted, earning their way by work on the farms, meanwhile searching out the spots where the Restored Gospel might find a welcome. In the old time there were prophets and apostles, there were visions and miracles: was there any reason it should not be so in these latter days? . . . Was Moroni less an angel because he did not appear in the Old and New Testaments of the Gentiles?

The Restored Gospel apparently was not welcome in Sharon, the native town of the Prophet, nor in Whitingham, birthplace of Brigham Young, soon to be a power in Zion. At least, no converts were reported in those villages.

But in remote Charleston, far up the state and near the border of Canada, Missionaries Pratt and Johnson found a ripe harvest. At Charleston they promptly baptized fourteen converts in the chilly Clyde River. They healed the sick. There was the wife of Winslow Farr, "unable to leave her bed in three years" who, on command of Elder Pratt, arose and walked, and she, too, was baptized. Mr. Farr himself was convinced, and so many another townsman who had been skeptical of these agents for a new religion in which unfamiliar prophets and kings and angels stalked—strange names, Nephi, Laman, Lehi, yet with the right flavor of ancient times: Zenos, Neum, Zenock, and Mormon himself, who had foreseen that false Christs and prophets would arise. . . .

There were other notable healings in Charleston, and the Elders organized a branch of the church there, which included the families of William Snow and Zerubbabel Snow, and several converts from the neighboring town of Brighton. Elders Pratt and Johnson moved on, asking nothing of the Gentiles for their keep but to mow a field, to pick rocks and build fence, to cut a cord of wood. They earned their way, these Mormons, and never begged in the manner of only too many Gentile missionaries.

Three years later, three of the most eminent men of the church *walked* from Ohio to St. Johnsbury, Vermont, to hold a conference. These men, all members of the quorum of twelve Apostles, were Heber C. Kimball, born in near-by Sheldon, Vermont, Orson Hyde, native of Connecticut, and William E. McLellin. More than a thousand of the curious came to hear their first Mormon preaching. Few of them fell under its spell, only nine being baptized, but one of these was to be a lion of the Lord and an Apostle of the first mark, young Erastus Snow.

The conference took occasion to survey Mormon progress in the Green Mountains. Converts numbered but 107, with a mere 29 converts across the Connecticut River in New Hampshire. This small harvest did not discourage the missionaries in the least, for the total did not include those families who already had left for the new Zion in Ohio, and hence were not counted in the present summing up. The soft spots—the towns where the heralds of Moroni had made their harvest among the Yankees—were topped by St. Johnsbury, which mustered 41 converts. Next came Danville, 23; Charleston, 21; Andover, 15; and Benson, 7. The figure for Benson indicates either that there had been backsliding after 1831, when Elder Jared Carter had baptized no fewer than 27, or that some 20 converts had already gone west. The latter is the more probable.

The spearhead of the Saints in New Hampshire was formed by Elders Orson Pratt and Lyman Johnson. In twenty-six days of 1832 they baptized fifteen new Mormons including Amasa Lyman, later one of the Apostles. The pioneering missionaries were followed by Elders Orson Hyde and Samuel H. Smith, a brother of the Prophet. And a year later came a second pair, Elder Stephen Burnett and the same Lyman Johnson. Among them they converted, then ordained to the priesthood one Hazen Aldrich, who "preached with great fidelity" in the northern villages of the White Mountain region. He surely required all the fidelity he could muster, for these people possessed some of the qualities of the granite boulders of their hilly pastures. Mormons came sore hard in this region, but the towns of Lyman and Littleton softened in spots. From the former, Zadoc Parker and wife at last were thoroughly converted and moved to the West where, says a local historian, "Zadoc Parker became an Elder and a leading member of the society." A hill above Young's Pond in Lyman retains the name of Mormon Hill because of meetings held there in the 1830's. The converts in Littleton who migrated West included James Parker, and Phineas Parker and wife; and a decade later Jane, daughter of Levi Cobleigh, went out to Deseret.

Indicative of Mormon perseverance is the fact that again and again, during the next three-quarters of a century, Mormon missionaries returned to this same neighborhood in the White Mountains. Converts, however, were pitifully few. Yankee folklore against Mormons had long since become case-hardened and could not be dissipated by the most eloquent of missionaries. Although adultery was probably practiced in the White Mountains with as great an industry as anywhere else, it was not condoned. And what, pray, was polygamy? Mormon missionaries were classed in one respect with gypsies; they were said to be on the watch for pretty little girls to steal; and these pretty little girls, it was told, were destined for the seraglios of the Mormon elders. And that, naturally, was a fate worse than death. Fear of polygamy could in no manner be offset by the fact that Mormon missionaries never asked for charity, but earned their way wherever they went by labor. The early missionaries did not have to defend polygamy, for it was not yet a revelation of the Mormon God. But, whatever the reason, early and later, New Hampshire, along with Maine, seems to have been poor soil for the Restored Gospel.

In September of 1832 Orson Hyde and Samuel Smith left New Hampshire in a canoe and paddled across the pleasant Piscataqua River into virgin Maine. They were presently laboring in the town of York, near the coast, where they held meetings in the house of a Mr. Langley. Next, they walked eight miles to Wells, where the Freewill Baptists, eager to hear of the new revelations, were glad to let the Saints speak in meeting. The missionaries reported later that "the people offered no objection to what the Mormons said, but on the other hand, showed no anxiety to hear them preach again." On th next day Hyde and Smith walked to Kennebunkport, where they "attended a meeting of the deluded sect whose members were known as Cochranites." The missionaries appear to have left no other written comment on the Cochranites, of whom they were to hear more later.

The two Saints moved on to Saco village, where a kindly old gentleman named Branner treated them with great good will. They had no difficulty getting permission to use Central Hall, and here they preached. At a second meeting the crowd was much greater. "I spoke with great power and authority," Elder Hyde related, "and made a profound impression on the people who were about to raise a contribution for us, but as we had money enough for our present purposes we thanked them for their kindness and told them we were not in want." This fact, too, must have made a tremendous impression on the people of Maine—strange missionaries for a strange gospel who refused money. One can believe it was nigh incredible.

Hyde and Smith continued their labors in Saco and in neighboring Bidde-ford. They did not overlook the outlying farms, where they not only gave news of the Restored Gospel but turned to and worked like beavers in the harvest fields. On the last day of September they baptized their first convert in Maine, who was Timothy Smith; and in the next few weeks they baptized Simon Waymouth and wife Esther; Sally Taylor and Lovey Dennet. Mrs. Dennet's husband presently gave in, and he too was baptized. Convert Simon Waymouth proved so quick and able that the two missionaries ordained him Elder and "instructed him in the duties of that high and holy office."

Elders Hyde and Smith now proceeded to Waterboro, where they preached with no noticeable results; and after one more meeting in York they again crossed the Piscataqua into New Hampshire. The Maine people had been most friendly, but they were "more ignorant," said Elder Hyde, than other people in New England. But Maine, or a small portion of it, had now heard the Restored Gospel preached in its fullness, and a little later the results of this pioneer work were to become apparent. For the present, Elders Hyde and Smith had to move on, to spearhead other parts of New England. Elder Hyde considered his and Smith's mission into Maine as "one of the most arduous and toilsome ever performed in the Church." The two men had walked on foot from Ohio, "teaching from house to house, and from city to city, without purse or scrip, often sleeping in schoolhouses after preach-ing in barns, in sheds, by the wayside." It was a task calling for sinews in the mind and in the body; but in good season all of Maine would hear of the miracle at the hill Cumorah. . . .

The heralds of Moroni needed something of the power of that miracle to keep them steadfast in the face of the hostile Gentile world. "When one of us would be teaching in private families," recalled Elder Hyde, "the other would be frequently nodding in his chair, weary with toil, and want of sleep. We were often rejected in the afterpart of the day, compelling us to travel in the evening, and sometimes till people had gone to bed, leaving us to lodge where we could. We would sometimes travel until nearly daylight before we could find a barn or shed in which we dared to lie down; must be away before discovered, lest suspicion rest upon us. Often we would lie down under trees and sleep in the daytime to make up loss."

In that same pioneering year of 1832 Elders Orson Hyde and Samuel H. Smith were the shock troops of the Saints in every New England state. Rhode Island proved particularly difficult. The two missionaries labored there but one week, during which they barely escaped, on three occasions, from mob violence. They baptized but one convert, who must have been a lonely man even in small Rhode Island, and left the state which Roger Williams had planned should be a haven for any and all religions.

Conditions were only a little more favorable in Massachusetts. Hyde and Smith preached in Boston in August of 1832 with some success, then in Lynn, where "hundreds of people came to hear us." They held a meeting in Salem without molestation; but Beverly turned out to be scandalous. A crowd of ruffians disturbed the meeting by setting off firecrackers; and after the services "the rabble went through town, making the night hideous with their hues and cries. They finally surrounded the house where the brethren were and howled like a pack of wolves." This was the worst experience Hyde and Smith had experienced to date. They got out of dreadful Beverly without being mobbed and walked sixteen miles to Byfield, where "they found friends and believers."

Hyde and Smith and their comrades of these pioneering days were setting a style and a discipline for other missionary Saints to follow. No sect was ever more devoted, more self-sacrificing. Even the Catholic friars in their exploring and proselytizing efforts in the new America were no more indifferent to life, to scorn and insult, to health and comfort, than were the Saints, early and later. The Mormons were also both moderate and circumspect, though no missionaries ever showed greater courage. They were often arrested and jailed. They were beaten and mobbed. Almost always, in sound Christian communities, they were ridiculed. On their long journeys on foot, as often as not, their only sustenance was the water trickling from the rocks along the road and wild berries from the bushes in which they slept at night.

In spite of these characteristics, the Saints were not to bring about any wholesale conversion of Yankees. Work as they would and did, the best they could accomplish for their Mormon God was a family here, a few families there, hardly a trickle compared to the goings-out for Mammon. The material success in Minnesota of a Pillsbury from New Hampshire, as we shall see, or the election of a Washburn from Maine as governor of Wisconsin— these and other like happenings probably inspired more emigrants from Maine and New Hampshire than did the promise of a New Zion in Kirtland, in Nauvoo, or in Deseret.

Yet, it should be stressed, the quality of the Mormon converts in New England was exactly right for the work in hand, that of establishing firmly a brand-new and wholly American religion, as well as founding a new and unique state in the Republic. The Mormon success in New England was not in numbers. When the energetic Hyde and Smith penetrated Connecticut in 1832, they seem not to have made any converts. But Connecticut could well wait. In that same year a Connecticut native, Wilford Woodruff, born in Avon, had just migrated to western New York where, within the year, he joined the Saints. Woodruff was shortly to become one of the most notable Yankees in the church, and at last to be its president.

One of the great characteristics of the Mormon church from its very founding was its perseverance. It did not leave the seed planted in New England by pioneers Hyde and Samuel Smith to shrivel or rot for lack of cultivation. In 1833 missionaries of the Saints were back again to call on the Yankees. Massachusetts was still resistant, even aggressive. When Elder Evan Green and comrade tried to speak in Westminster, near Fitchburg, "the people railed against us, calling us impostors, counterfeiters, pickpockets. . . . We bore testimony of the gospel and then left the place." Poor Elder Green and his partner were scarce two miles out of the village when they were overtaken by three chaises loaded with hostile fellows, who searched them, then cursed them roundly.

The elders went wearily on to Wendell, in Franklin County, and here, though meeting with much opposition "led by the Presbyterian priest," the Saints held out for four weeks, their meetings constantly growing. Six converts were the harvest. Massachusetts remained stoutly recalcitrant until 1838, when Brigham Young himself came all the way from Missouri, Brother Joseph Young his comrade, to preach and to establish several branches of the Church. They were followed in 1843 by a gifted elder, George J. Adams, who drew immense audiences, among them "men of renowned learning and high social standing."*

* The Mormons were basically not a revivalist sect. The Prophet discouraged holy rolling, the jerks, speaking in tongues, and all such mass hysteria. The Saints thus drew to their ranks many able men who had been revolted by the excesses of the evangelistic sects. See Mrs. Fawn Brodie's magnificent study of Joseph Smith, *No Man Knows My History*, New York, 1945.

The Mormons always returned. In 1833 the seed sown in Maine the year before was ready to be tended, and into the Pine Tree State went Elders John F. Boynton, Henry Harriman, and the same Evan Green who had been treated so infamously in Massachusetts. This time the Saints brought in a harvest, especially in those towns—said a local observer—where Cochranism had preceded Mormon preaching.

Jacob Cochran, long since forgotten, was one of the many minor Yankee prophets. He was born in Enfield, New Hampshire, in 1782, and preached with some success in his native region. Then he moved into the Saco River valley in Maine and stirred that ordinarily quiet neighborhood into great turbulence. Among other things, he favored the exchanging of wives among his converts. A popular feature of his meetings was "a demonstration of the Garden of Eden, with real people dressed exactly as Adam and Eve had dressed." Cochran labored chiefly in the Saco valley towns, including Kennebunkport where Elders Hyde and Smith of the Saints had attended a meeting of Cochranites, in 1832. Now came the Mormons a second time. "The Mormon excitement," relates the local historian, G. T. Ridlon,* "spread into every town where Cochran had made converts and the inhabitants had been washed from their moral and rational moorings by Jacob."

Yet, unfriendly though he is, Historian Ridlon cannot help admiring the missionaries of the Saints. "The Mormon preachers," says he, "had great covered wagons, drawn by large spirited horses, in which those who would emigrate were carried away to their settlements. Their temple was a barn on the Millikan farm in the town of Buxton. Here was headquarters of the crusade in Maine.

"Like flaming heralds," Ridlon continues, "the Saints traveled from town to town, and their evident sincerity and unbounded enthusiasm drew thousands to hear them." Ridlon remarks, too, that wherever the Saints were persecuted, there they "immediately rose in the favor of the community." Not all the Yankees were intolerant; a generation or two of pioneering in the Maine pines and spruces had softened the Puritan influence.

Either in the barn temple at Buxton or in the general neighborhood, the Saints of 1833 made a large but unnumbered group of converts, among them Nathaniel Millikan, who owned the barn. Others who came forward and were baptized carried typical old Yankee names, like Sylvester Stoddard and Josiah Butterfield; like Hannah Lord, Susan Lowell, Sally Mason, Martha Bradbury, Susan Boynton, Polly Butterfield, Rebecca Andrews, and Eliza Bradbury. Brother Butterfield was ordained Mormon priest and left in charge of the Church in Maine.

Aye, the Saints always returned. Korihor the Anti-Christ must be driven

* *Saco Valley Settlements and Families,* Portland, Me., 1895.

out. God's word should hiss forth in darkest Maine. So, they came again to the Pine Tree State four years later, this time in the persons of Elders Wilford Woodruff and Johnathan Hale. Woodruff had just married a Maine girl, Phoebe Carter, whose parents lived in Scarboro, and now she heard her inspired husband preach to her relatives and their neighbors. He preached with great power, too, for converts were made; and Woodruff and Hale went on to labor with great success in the Fox Islands, off the Maine coast. Fruit was being laid up against the season. . . .

A little more than a year later a company of fifty-three Maine converts took off in a group, heading for the Promised Land, which was now designated as Jackson County, Missouri, where headquarters of the Saints had been moved from Kirtland, Ohio. The long caravan moved slowly yet steadily west in great wagons, passing through Andover and Ashburnham, Massachusetts, through Fitzwilliam, New Hampshire, on through Vermont, pausing to camp overnight at Brattleboro and at Bennington; camping at Utica and Rome and Manchester, in New York; moving on, a marvel of order and discipline, attracting citizens all along the route, running into bad weather near Erie, Pennsylvania, where they were glad to make five miles in a day's journey; then into Ohio, touching at Conneaut, Concord, and Xenia, at Terre Haute, Indiana, and so on into Edgar County, Illinois. Here the plodding caravan received terrible news, of the "severe persecutions and drivings of the Saints in Missouri." The caravan halted while the leading men took counsel. It was thought best to remain in Illinois until conditions settled. The Saints made one more move, the few miles into Rochester, Sangamon County. Here they set up a semipermanent camp. Not for long. The Prophet was preparing a haven for them, and all other Saints, at Commerce, which he renamed Nauvoo. It was ready for the band from Maine within a year of their arrival in Illinois.

The Saints always returned. Before he left New England, in 1837, Elder Wilford Woodruff succeeded in planting the Church in Connecticut by founding branches at Canaan and at Hartford. Then he started out on foot for Rowley, in eastern Massachusetts, where Elder Hale was forming a branch. He was to witness a miracle on this journey. "I walked 52 miles the first day," Woodruff recalled, "48 miles the second day." On the second day he grew most weary when within a mile or two of his stopping place. "Every step was made with painful effort. Just then a gentleman came dashing along in his carriage. As he came up I prayed to the Lord that he should invite me to ride. Instead of doing so, he went by with great speed." But he did not go far: the Lord heard his poor disciple, and acted swiftly. "When the carriage had got about ten rods ahead of me, the horse, without being spoken to, or reined up, and for some cause unknown to the driver, came to a sudden stop." But Elder Woodruff knew the reason; he knew what had happened. "It appeared as if a barrier, unseen by others, stood in the horse's way. Instantly the gentleman turned and asked me to ride . . . and we sped on our way." There was no sense in contending against a man like Elder Woodruff. . . .

It was little wonder the Church made Woodruff an Apostle in 1839, or that he was for the ensuing half-century one of the stalwarts, or that he became president of the Church of Jesus Christ of Latter-Day Saints in 1889. In the ripeness of his years in Salt Lake City, which he had helped to found with his own hands and head, Fourth President Woodruff, the third Yankee to head the Church, recalled that between 1834 and 1895 he had "traveled 172,369 miles; held 7,655 meetings; preached 3,526 discourses; organized 50 branches of the Church and 77 preaching places." How many New Englanders and others the eloquence and determined effort of Wilford Woodruff brought to Kirtland, then to Nauvoo, then to Deseret, is not known; but the number must have been formidable.

The Saints came back, always, even to hostile and dangerous Rhode Island, which Elders Orson Hyde and Samuel Smith had left in 1832 after undergoing much persecution and making but one lone convert. In 1840 young Erastus Snow, the convert of St. Johnsbury, Vermont, who was to go far in the Church, went into the darkness of Providence and Newport and labored for more than a year. He left a branch with twenty-one members in Newport. Elder Miner G. Atwood came later and established a branch in Providence. The total was not great, but the point was, the Saints had not been defeated. And in 1876 Providence was the scene of a "Grand Sunday School Jubilee of the Saints in Rhode Island." If Korihor the Anti-Christ had not been wholly destroyed, he was nevertheless kept in reasonable bounds. . . .

One of the most forceful of all the heralds of Moroni was Heber Chase Kimball, born in Sheldon, Vermont. He was a huge man of tremendous vigor, who was ordained as one of the Apostles as early as 1835, then sent out to spread the Restored Gospel. This he did with such notable success in New York, and in Vermont, that in 1837 he was named head of the first mission to England, a vastly successful enterprise with which, however, this book is not concerned. But Apostle Kimball fired many a less experienced Saint with the fanaticism needed to uphold a man in the face of discouragement, persecution, and the poverty which went with being a Mormon missionary. Whether in the great city of London, England, or in the village of St. Johnsbury, Vermont, Apostle Kimball did not hesitate to stand in the streets and, Jonah-like, cry repentance unto the inhabitants. "Ye are ripening in iniquity," he shouted at them. "Ye are preparing for the wrath of God, and like an ox going to the slaughter, know not the day of your visitation."

Heber Kimball was in the famous First Company of Pioneers which in 1847, and in the great wastes of Utah, heard Brigham Young say *This is the Place;* and the place became Salt Lake City. Kimball was later chief justice of the state of Deseret, which an idiotic Congress insisted be called Utah. He and Woodruff and Orson Hyde were surely three as influential emigrants as ever came out of New England, except, of course, Joseph Smith and Brigham Young. But there were other Yankees in the hierarchy, too. Few Mormons today, and even fewer Gentiles, are aware of the large number of New England men among the early leaders of the Saints.

The powerful Council of the First Presidency, next to Brigham Young in authority, numbered Heber Kimball, Yankee Hyrum Smith, born in Vermont, Frederick G. Williams, born in Connecticut, and Willard Richards, born in Massachusetts. A Yankee too, through his parents, was the Fifth President of the Mormon church, Lorenzo Snow, though he happened to be born in Ohio. He was converted to the Saints by his own sister, Eliza, a native of Berkshire County, Massachusetts, who became a noted Mormon poet and also composed the favorite Mormon hymn "O My Father, Thou That Dwellest."

Among the Twelve Apostles, Yankees were much in evidence: Thomas B. Marsh, Ezra T. Benson, and Franklin D. Richards, all of Massachusetts; Orson Hyde of Connecticut; Amasa M. Lyman of New Hampshire; and Vermonters Luke S. Johnson, William B. Smith, Erastus Snow, and Albert Carrington—a Dartmouth graduate.

Presiding bishops of the Saints have included Edward Partridge and Newell K. Whitney, both of Vermont. Then there were, as there are today, the seventies of the Church, a special order of Latter-Day Saints whose chief duty is missionary work. Notable in the early group of seventies were such Yankees as Joseph Young, Levi Hancock, Henry Harriman, and Albert P. Rockwood, of Massachusetts; Josiah Butterfield of Maine, Salmon Gee of Connecticut, and Zera Pulsipher of Vermont.

Thus, and though New Englanders were a minority among the Saints at Nauvoo, and an even smaller minority at Salt Lake City, their quality must have been better than average. The present (1949) assistant historian of the Church does not know* and says he has no way of estimating the number of Yankees who have been taken into the Saints. But he supplies a list of the New Englanders in the celebrated First Company of Pioneers. This was the group led by Brigham Young across the plains in 1847, out of the United

* A. William Lund, Salt Lake City, Feb. 8, 1948, in a letter to the author.

States and into the then Mexican region which Young designated as Deseret
and in which the Saints performed a miracle in state building that was never
to be matched in North America. This company was made up of volunteers,
and it numbered 140 men and three women. Forty-one of the men and
one woman—wife of Brigham Young—were natives of New England.
Thirteen were from Vermont, thirteen from Massachusetts, ten from Connecticut, three each from Maine and New Hampshire. Rhode Island, the
difficult, was not represented.*

Two bold converts from Rhode Island, however, were in a later company that came to the Salt Lake in 1847, along with 218 other Saints from
New England. This group contained 100 from Massachusetts, 44 from Vermont, 40 from Connecticut, and 17 each from Maine and New Hampshire.
Doubtless those figures are in reasonable proportion in respect to the manner
in which New England responded to the missionaries of the Saints.

It was to be expected that Massachusetts, the most populous of the New
England states, should supply the greatest number of converts to the Saints.
But it is another matter to explain why Vermont, the least populous of the
six states, should have furnished the second greatest number. The history of
the Saints intertwines from the first with the history of Vermont. The Prophet
was born there. So was the incomparable leader of the Mormons, Brigham
Young. Vermont was the first Yankee state into which Mormon missionaries
were sent. It was the one state to which, in 1843, the Prophet sent a last
desperate appeal, addressed to the "Green Mountain Boys," to redress the
wrongs done to the Saints in Missouri.

The Prophet seems also to have been partial to the women of the Green
Mountains. Six of his wives were Vermont natives, three were born in Maine,
and two each in New Hampshire and Massachusetts.†

It will be recalled that a Vermont youth, Oliver Cowdery, acted as
amanuensis to the Prophet while the Book was being translated.

Nor was the Vermont influence done. It was quite likely hatred of the
Saints that prompted Luke Poland, Congressman from Vermont, to introduce
the bill in 1874 that curbed the jurisdiction of the Mormon courts in Utah.
And it was the long-time senior senator from Vermont, George Franklin

* Good Yankee family names of long standing were coupled with good biblical given
names of even more ancient origin among these pioneers into Deseret—among them Hosea
Cushing, Benjamin Franklin Dewey, Datus Ensign, Joseph Hancock, Andrew Shumway,
Seth Taft, Phineas Howe Young, Solomon Chamberlain, Philo Johnson, Rodney Badger,
Ozro Eastman, Aaron Farr, Levi Jackman, Shadrach Roundy, Amasa Lyman, John Tibbets.
    † See Brodie, *No Man Knows My History,* Appendix C. Mrs. Brodie lists among the
plural wives of the Prophet the Vermont natives Nancy Johnson Hyde, Delcena Johnson
Sherman, Almera Woodward Johnson, Lucy Walker, Fanny Young Murray, Mary Ann Frost;
Maine natives Olive Andrews, Olive Grey Frost, Jane Tibbets; New Hampshire natives
Clarissa Reed Hancock, Sophia Woodman; Massachusetts natives Ruth Vose Sayers, Vienna
Jacques.

Edmunds, that in 1882 introduced the bill to disenfranchise polygamists, by which, of course, was meant nothing more or less than members of the Mormon church. The bill passed. It was strengthened in 1887, and it is generally credited with breaking the Mormon political power and causing the Saints to do away with their plural marriages.

From the first revelation on Hill Cumorah to the entry into the Union of the State of Utah, in 1896, Yankees have played leading parts in the Church of Jesus Christ of Latter-Day Saints. Their influence is most characteristically displayed on the great seal of the State of Utah, by a thumping great beehive surmounted by a favorite Yankee word, *Industry*.

CHAPTER VI

IN EDEN WAS A GARDEN

THE CHARMING COUNTRY of Indiana was never the goal of any great number of Yankees. Long before that state contained much of a population, the New Englanders were passing it by for Illinois, for Michigan, and, above all, for Wisconsin. Although the reasons for this are far from clear or convincing, it has been explained in the fact that Indiana's southern counties were early settled chiefly from Kentucky, Tennessee, and Virginia. Men of the Old Dominion held virtually all the territorial offices. Then, hard on the heels of the cold year of 1816, long remembered as "Eighteen hundred and Froze to Death," people of western New York and of Pennsylvania began to move in and were followed, during the next decade and more, by others of the same regions.

Here and there, of course, a few venturesome Yankees mingled with that stream of settlers. Montpelier, Indiana, was of almost unadulterated Vermont stock, Wolcottville was the result of efforts of George Wolcott of Torrington, Connecticut, who drove his stakes in Hoosier soil in 1837. Orland, in Steuben County, later to become a notorious Free Soil town, was settled in 1834 by John Stocker and his neighbors in Windham County, Vermont. Stocker chose the site because he liked the look of the large groves of oak.

Another Vermonter who came early had considerable influence in Hoosierland. He was James Whitcomb, born in Windham County, who moved west with his family as a boy, worked his way through Transylvania University in Kentucky, then set up as a lawyer in Bloomington, Indiana. He was elected governor in 1843 and undertook successfully to adjust the state's staggering debt after its disastrous experiment in the building of canals and railroads. He began to promote education, until then a subject that had not interested Hoosiers. He created the office of superintendent of public schools, and also promoted schools for the deaf and the blind, and a state hospital for the mentally ill. More than any other man, perhaps, Whitcomb was the founder of Indiana's school system. He is also remembered for

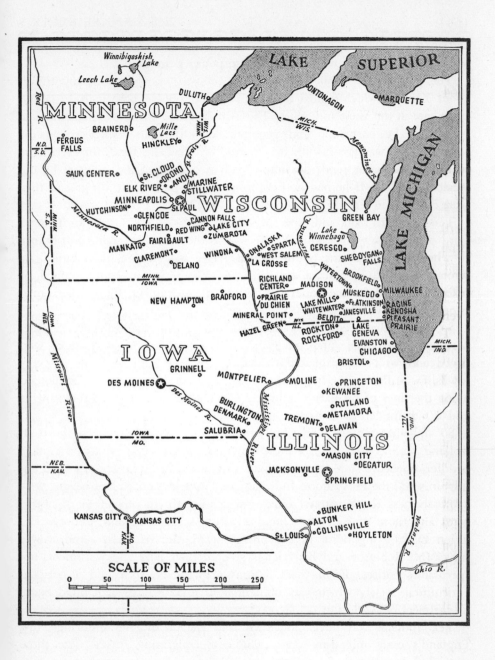

certain Yankee traits, among which his "personal charm and social grace were strangely crossed with habits of penuriousness in small matters."

The pinchpenny habit in small matters was one of the many things about Yankees which tended to make them unpopular, both in Indiana and elsewhere in the West and South. The man from the South was likely, almost certain, to be hospitable and generous to individuals, either friends or strangers. He was lavish with his liquors, his food, his time; for even if he had little liquor or food, he simply had to live up to the code set by the wealthy planters. If he had nothing more than a mess of turnip greens, they were cooked and served with a flourish.

The Northern man, and especially the Yankee—so said Governor Thomas Ford of Illinois, who was no Yankee—was the most liberal in contributing to whatever was for the public benefit. "Is a schoolhouse to be built," he wrote, "a road to be built, a school teacher or a minister to be maintained, or taxes to be paid for the honor or support of government, the northern man is never found wanting."

So, few as they were, the Yankees in Indiana did have influence. Supplementing Whitcomb's work came Caleb Mills, late of Dartmouth College, who urged and wrote and agitated constantly for free public schools in every township. Mills was the first president of Wabash College, which he molded along the lines of his native Andover and Dartmouth. Between them, Mills and Whitcomb left their mark.

So did that strange and ebullient character Solon Robinson, born in Tolland, Connecticut, an orphan at ten, who made his way west as a Yankee peddler, opened a store in the Indiana woods and had a large trade with immigrants and the Potawatomi Indians. In 1836 he organized and headed with aggressiveness the Squatters' Union, which sought to protect his doubtful acres and those of some five hundred other settlers in Lake County. The union made a big noise in the press, locally and nationally, and it was successful; Robinson and his friends secured their land at government, not speculators' prices. From there, Robinson went on to found a national agricultural society which was influential in establishing the United States Department of Agriculture.

Yet, Indiana was never much in the talk or the news during New England's early migrating days. The new emigrating fevers were those generated by Illinois, Michigan, and Wisconsin. For every Yankee who stopped in Indiana, approximately four Yankees passed into Michigan, eight into Illinois, six into Wisconsin, half a dozen more into Minnesota.

Illinois and Michigan first felt the migration at about the same period, which is to say the 1830's. Although southern Illinois was being peopled chiefly from Kentucky, among the earliest settlers there were four brothers named Collins straight from Litchfield, Connecticut, and direct, too, from the teachings of Dr. Lyman Beecher of that pretty village. In 1817 the Collins boys laid out Collinsville, near St. Louis, and set up a sawmill, a gristmill, and several shops, all turned by water power, and opened a distillery. They started a general store and a tanyard. No such energy and enterprise had been seen in the region. Nor, as it turned out, had such idealism for when some of Dr. Beecher's temperance tracts reached Collinsville the brothers read them at once, and scrapped their distillery immediately. The serpent's lure to death and sin should not be of their making. Nor would they encourage its manufacture: they forthwith stipulated that neither wine, the mocker, nor strong drink, in which lay babbling and raging, might be sold on land purchased from them.

Nor is one to think the Collins boys contributed only in a negative way to the cause of Temperance. Had not Cotton Mather said that Yankees were children of God who had settled in what once were the Devil's own territories? The Collins boys of Collinsville presently built a steamboat for traffic on the Mississippi and named it *Cold Water*. You may be certain the boat carried no bar; and on its first trip to St. Louis its revolting name so offended the residents that they attempted to prevent its landing. It is not too difficult to understand how a vessel named *Cold Water* would be as inflaming to the easy going people of St. Louis as a speech on Abolition. . . .

A few years later the father of the remarkable Collins boys came west to see his sons and remained to help, with work and no little cash, in the founding of Illinois College at Jacksonville. This budding institution stemmed direct from New England by way of the Yale Band, a group of young missionaries who believed that "evangelical religion and education must go hand in hand," and had set out in 1829 to found Congregational churches and a college in Illinois. To head the new school came Edward, third child of Dr. Lyman Beecher, direct from his pulpit in the Park Street, or Brimstone Corner, Church in Boston.

The school at Jacksonville was from the first a mighty influence in central and southern Illinois, where proslavery settlers were in the majority. President Edward Beecher began at once to snipe at the South's peculiar institution, and in a little while was discharging full salvos. Mr. Herndon, father of young William, was so dismayed and frightened at Dr. Beecher's teaching that he snatched his son from the college, though not soon enough. The Abolition poison had taken root. William Herndon was to become a law partner with Abraham Lincoln.

One of the new college's first graduates, Richard Yates, became an antislavery governor of the state. President Beecher himself was one of the volunteers helping to guard Elijah Lovejoy's printing press on the night mobsters of Alton shot and killed the fiery Abolitionist from Albion, Maine; and thereafter Beecher gave every support to Owen Lovejoy of Princeton, Illinois, the dead editor's brother, in his antislavery meetings throughout the state.

This town of Princeton was a thoroughly Yankee village, founded in 1831 by a formally missionary group from Northampton, Massachusetts, led by a namesake of the great Cotton Mather. Perhaps Princeton's most influential settler was John Howard Bryant, of Cummington, Massachusetts, who came in 1833 and was soon joined by his brothers Austin, Arthur, and Cyrus, though another brother, named William Cullen, remained in the East to edit a newspaper and to write poetry. John Bryant married a Yankee girl, Harriet Wiswall, who had come west with her parents from Norton, Massachusetts. For the next seventy years John Bryant split rails, built roads and bridges, edited a newspaper, made brick, was recorder of deeds, lectured on Abolition, and in his spare time wrote verse.

Farmer John Bryant was a fine example of the Yankee settler at his best. He was instrumental in organizing Bureau County, and in erecting at Princeton the first township high school in Illinois. He also played a part in forming the Illinois State Agricultural Society. "He was," said a biographer, "probably the most useful citizen in his community." But some may have doubted his usefulness, for his home often lodged as many as fifteen fugitive Negroes who were heading for Canada.

That Illinois remained safe for Yankee ideas of culture, in the face of an "alien" population, was due in large part to the New England idealists, and fanatics, who went there early and stuck. Not all Yankee notions were to stick, however, for in spite of the Herculean efforts of Temperance lecturers like Yankee John M. Peck, the rum evil was never downed.

But Yankee education dominated. Professor J. B. Turner, who came from Templeton, Massachusetts, to teach at Illinois College, was influential in founding the University of Illinois at Champaign. The Monticello Female Seminary at Godfrey was the idea of Benjamin Godfrey, from Chatham on Cape Cod. Anna Peck Sill, of Connecticut stock, was the first principal of Rockford Female Seminary, one of the founders of which was Stephen Peet of Sandgate, Vermont. Anna Sill was typical of the migrating Yankees; she commonly talked with the Lord, and on the day she opened the seminary (later, Rockford College) she spoke again. "O Lord," she wrote in her journal, "fit me for my work and glorify Thyself thereby." Benjamin Shurtleff of Boston was so generous with cash to endow a struggling college at Alton that it was named for him. The seminary called Almira at Greenville came largely from the efforts of two Yankees, one from New Hampshire, the other from Brown University.

In 1837 there came to open a blacksmith shop at Grand Detour a Yankee who never had any influence in educational matters but was of the greatest importance in making this raw country into what its boosters liked to call it; namely, the Garden State. John Deere was a Vermonter who had made plows in his native Rutland, and now he started to make them in Illinois. He quickly discovered the conventional type of wooden moldboard was not suitable for turning the heavy, compact prairie sod. He tried sheet steel, which he cut from an old sawmill saw. It worked finely in the soil of this new Eden, and Deere continued to experiment, making plows that grew steadily better. He could not fill the new orders coming in.

Deere sold his blacksmith shop and moved to the new Yankee village that had been founded by Joel, Levi, and Huntington Mills, and Michael Bartlett. This was first called Rock Island Mills, then Moline, from the French word for "mill." Deere's move there was to make Moline the Plow Capital of the World, for his product grew better and more popular every year. If the Beechers, Bryants, and their kind did much for the intellectual atmosphere of the new Eden, John Deere's plows did much to civilize the soil and to make the Garden bloom as never before.

The gardeners were coming. Throughout the thirties small groups of New Englanders were moving into Illinois in bands like that from Gilmanton, New Hampshire, led by John Page, which settled Metamora; and the Maine colony at Rockton, headed by Ira Hersey who had scouted the site in 1837, then returned to the Pine Tree State to fire his neighbors with enthusiasm for the Rock River valley. Hersey's band went from Portland to Boston by ship; to Providence by rail; by water to Philadelphia; by rail to Pittsburgh, where they took passage down the Ohio to Cincinnati. Here they bought wagons, oxen, and provisions, then floated up the Mississippi and up the Illinois River as far as Ottawa, from which they rolled on wheels overland to their new home. Almost the first thing they did was to start building a church of the Congregational persuasion, as the phrase had it.

Mount Hope was settled from Rhode Island by the Providence Farmers' & Mechanics' Emigrating Society. Another group from Rhode Island staked out Delavan, in Tazewell County. Tremont, in the same county, was settled by people who could not well have come from anywhere else than Massachusetts. Both the Bay State and Connecticut were responsible for Kewanee, the streets of which were named Dwight, Edwards, Hollis, and Payson. But Kewanee's first citizen was a New Hampshire man, Rufus P. Parrish of Gilmanton, who in himself was a complete cargo of Yankee notions brought to Illinois. In Boston he had been one of the sixteen men to organize the first Y.M.C.A. in the United States. He held Abolition a religion and voted for James G. Birney, the antislavery candidate for President. Within thirty days of his arrival in Kewanee, that village had its first Sunday school, and a bit later its first Lyceum, both of them organized by Parrish, who went on to bring to the town such diverse figures as John B. Gough, Abraham Lincoln, Mary Livermore, and Stephen Douglas. With these matters attended to, Parrish labored for and at last founded Kewanee's Free Public Library, which was his pride. Meanwhile he had constantly hounded his fellow citizens for more and better schools, himself serving many years as director of education. He lived to a great old age, nor was he at a loss to explain why. "By regular temperate living," said he, "I have by God's help reached considerably more than four score years." Note well the certainty of it— "temperate living" and "God's help." Here is no man lost from moorings. The frontier did not change *him,* but the frontier felt *his* impact, for he was the kind of New England emigrant whose settler's effects included not only some graceful old Yankee furniture, but a generous parcel of old Yankee culture, as impervious to wild prairie winds as the very granite of New Hampshire.

At the foot of Lake Michigan, meanwhile, old Fort Dearborn, named for a New Hampshire general, was becoming Chicago, named for a wild and pungent onion. The change of name was possibly symbolic, for, although fantastically energetic Yankees were a majority among the city's earliest builders and boosters, the influence of the frontier, where grew the stout wild onion or garlic, which the redmen called "chickagou," was to prevail. Chicago was never, then or later, to remind any New Englander even faintly of home.

Nevertheless, three early comers, all Yankees of purest stock, were to have enormous effect in making Chicago. The first was Long John Wentworth, born in 1815 in Sandwich, New Hampshire, who grew six feet six inches high and weighed a little more than three hundred pounds. Shortly after his graduation from Dartmouth College in 1836, he went to Detroit and there advertised, in the *Free Press,* the fact that he wanted and needed a job. No job was forthcoming, and so he took off for Chicago, doing the last stretch of thirty miles on foot. He arrived on the night of the 25th of October and —as he always liked to relate—took dinner and lodgings at the boarding house of Mrs. Harriet Austin Murphy at Lake and Wells streets, an event he recalled yearly for the next half-century by having dinner with the same Mrs. Murphy on each 25th of October.

Within a month of his arrival Wentworth took charge of a newspaper, the Chicago *Democrat.* He was also in charge of the activities that resulted in a charter for the city, being aided, among others, by young Walter L. Newberry of Windsor, Connecticut, who was to make a fortune from Chicago land which he bought by the acre and sold by the front foot, and leave much of it to found a magnificent library. The third Yankee was John Stephen Wright, and his influence was perhaps greatest of all. This native of Sheffield, Massachusetts arrived in the wild onion swamp in 1832 and together with his father whacked up a log cabin and opened shop in what he called the Prairie Store. A year later young Wright took the first census of the city and published a handsome lithographed map of the bog and its shacks, which he termed "edifices" and "buildings." He also went into the real-estate business. No matter what he was doing, John Wright was forever lauding the new city by the lake, and at least two historians of the town have called him the great-grandfather of all boosters and boomers.*

By Barnumlike promotion Long John Wentworth and John S. Wright made Chicago into the Convention City, climaxing on July 5, 1847, in a spectacular River and Harbor Convention that attracted 3,000 delegates from eighteen of the twenty-nine states of the Union and sent most of them home marveling—many marveling in the press—at the vitality of this new metropolis. "In ten years," cried Thurlow Weed, one of the great men of the period, in his Albany *Journal,* "in ten years Chicago will be as big as Albany." This was a gross understatement, though it seemed otherwise at the time. The gigantic meeting turned Eastern eyes toward Illinois as nothing before had done. Eastern bankers began to inquire about investments there. Eastern businessmen had seen, with their own eyes, a raucous town whose flimsy hotels were packed to the eaves, where the streets were crowded day and night, where money was changing hands at a dizzying rate, where local citizens spoke of Chicago's FUTURE in capital letters.

If one point, date, or single event started Chicago on its amazing growth, it probably was the River and Harbor Convention, which did nothing at all about any river or any harbor but did a plenty for old Fort Dearborn in its new guise.

John Stephen Wright did not cease writing his interminable letters of enthusiasm to friends and strangers in the East, nor cease his buying and selling of lots in Chicago. At twenty-one he had made $200,000 in his activities. A year later he lost it all in the panic of 1837. Next, he founded the *Prairie Farmer* and traveled about much in a buggy over the flat lands, taking subscriptions, getting news, telling the people how wonderful were Illinois and Chicago. His paper prospered. He went east to interest financiers in seeing Chicago at first hand. He wrote articles on Illinois for Boston and New York papers. With Jearum Atkins he began manufacture of the Atkins Automaton, a gadget that was the sensation of rural America for five years.

Atkins was another Yankee, born in Vermont, who migrated to Chicago

* See *Chicago: The History of Its Reputation,* by Lloyd Lewis and Henry Justin Smith, New York, 1929.

as a millwright. A fall from a wagon put him into bed for twenty-four years, and here he devised his Automaton, a mechanical gadget to rake the severed grain from the platforms of reapers. The device imitated the motion of human arms and was so wondrous in action as to awe the crowds that came to see it on trial. Wright took hold of the invention. Forty machines were made and sold in 1853; three hundred, a year later. By 1856 Atkins and Wright were making five thousand of the Automatons. Agricultural societies showered medals and handsome resolutions on the invention, and praise on the Yankee who had brought somewhat of ease to the workers in Eden.

But tragedy came soon. Just as it appeared that the Automaton was to conquer every wheatfield in America, a new batch of the machines began coming back to the manufacturers in a flood. They had been made of green, unseasoned wood, and they broke down everywhere. Back they came in such numbers that Atkins and Wright were put into bankruptcy.

Wright bounded back into real estate, forming a land company and bringing in much Eastern capital. After the Great Fire, he talked louder and better of the Gem of the Prairies, predicting a million population. But he lacked balance. His mind gave way entirely, and he had to be committed to an institution in Philadelphia, where he died. Attendants said Wright still rambled on about his great love, and one does not doubt that his last words may well have been the phrase he made famous. "Low land? Low land?" he had shouted back at Chicago's detractors. "We do not have to grade hills in Chicago, or to fill valleys!"

The third of Chicago's early Yankees, Walter Newberry, continued to prosper from the land he had bought at low prices. But he had public spirit a plenty. One of his pets was the Chicago Public Library, to which he gave much time and money, and he held many a position of trust. Poor John Wright is forgotten, and so is Long John Wentworth; but Newberry's name survives in the library that bears his name.

The specific industry for which the city on the lake was to be most celebrated, that of killing and packing, got its start as early as 1835 when Gurdon Saltonstall Hubbard, a native of Windsor, Vermont, built an immense warehouse at La Salle and South Water streets and started to kill pigs and salt and smoke pork greatly in excess of the day-by-day needs of the rising town. A few years later came Philip D. Armour, young man of Stockbridge, New York, born of Yankee Stock, to start packing meat in Chicago; and after him came Gustavus Swift, born in 1839 at West Sandwich on Cape Cod, to kill and pack too, and to experiment successfully with a refrigerator car, invented by William Wallace Chandler of Randolph, Vermont.*

Growing up with the turbulent city were merchants, among them the grave

* So Vermont authorities claim. See *Vermonters,* by Dorman B. E. Kent, Montpelier, 1937.

and attentive Marshall Field, born in Conway, Massachusetts, whose first job in Chicago was to clerk in a store at $400 a year. He slept on a cot in the store, thus to be never far from his work. He rose naturally enough to partnership, then started his own firm, which became and remains Chicago's incomparable institution of its kind. Field's fortune was the largest in the city, and much of it went into the Field Museum, for though the merchant had few if any intellectual interests he honestly wanted to do something handsome for a public that had treated him so well.

Looming large in the city's early days was J. Young Scammon, born in Whitefield, Maine, who came to Chicago in 1835 to hang out his shingle as a lawyer but became identified with banking and with the daily *Inter Ocean,* which he founded. Mr. Scammon did very well for himself, and thanked Chicago for it, bequeathing $30,000 to the struggling Dearborn Observatory.

The Yankee migration to Chicago was filled with "firsts." The first lawyer (1827) was Russell E. Heacock from Litchfield, Connecticut. Philo Carpenter, born on the southern slope of the Hoosac Mountains in Massachusetts, arrived in 1832 to open the first drugstore. He was quite in character, for he organized the first Sunday school in the brawling, carousing village of false-front shacks and gave the first local talk on Temperance. He was also an Abolitionist in his spare time and was reputed to have aided two hundred black men and women on their way to Canada. The first M.D. was Elijah Dewey Harmon of Bennington, Vermont, who came in 1832, closely followed by Dr. Philip Maxwell of Guilford in the same state.

One of the founders of Northwestern University arrived in a buggy, being fifteen days on what passed as a road from Detroit. He was Jabez K. Botsford, late of Newton, Connecticut, soon to be king of the local stove business. Silas Cobb, from Montpelier, Vermont, set up as a leather merchant and made the first stout buckets used by the volunteer fire companies, but soon branched out into the horsecar business and became one of the traction moguls.

Yankees surely were many and influential in the town's early days, but they were soon outnumbered and swamped by the hordes of other Americans and Europeans who took over the city and, by the end of the Civil War, were running it.* By that time, such Yankee influence as remained, in its purest form, had picked up and moved to the new suburb of Evanston.

Thus, such visiting Yankees as came to see the big city at the foot of the big lake were prone to be critical. One of them was John H. W. Hawkins, a star performer in the Temperance field. Said he: "I have never seen a city which was so much like the universal grog-shop as Chicago." The town, he

* By 1870, when the city had a population of 298,977, the Yankee bloc numbered only 13,752, "including 45 blacks born in New England." Massachusetts led with 5,991; then, surprisingly enough, came Vermont with 2,226; Connecticut, 2,063; Maine, 1,656; New Hampshire, 1,335; and Rhode Island, 436.

thought, was wholly lost; and he seems to have been content to leave it to
stew in its own fermented and distilled juices. Nor did it improve. Long
after Hawkins came another Yankee, Dwight Moody of Northfield, Massachusetts, to enter the shoe business. But Moody was so shocked at the sin and
poverty on every hand that he gave up his job and started to "sell" religion.
He was a valiant soul, able and determined; but, though he could fill the
city's biggest auditorium with weeping sinners, the Devil never relaxed his
hold very much, and Chicago's corruption and vice grew with its population,
coming at last into full bloom, as gigantic and evil as some deadly weed of
the tropic jungle. "What would Christ say if He came to Chicago?" asked
a visiting Briton, W. T. Stead, and was aghast to contemplate the answer. . . . *

Thousands of migrating Yankees were carefully avoiding the Sodom of
Chicago. They were taking up land in the open spaces which men of vision
and many acres to sell were hailing as the Garden State of the West. The
new Illinois Central Railroad Company was largely responsible for the
sudden influx. No railroad before or since, in Eden or out, has been so effective in populating a region, or acting so intelligently.

The Illinois Central was chartered in 1851, two of its most active directors
and heaviest stockholders being David A. Neal, who had made his first pile
from Salem ships in Massachusetts, and Robert Rantoul, Bay State senator.
Among its promoters was Stephen A. Douglas, from Vermont. The company's chief attorney was James F. Joy, late of Durham, New Hampshire.
Its construction chief was a Yankee named Roswell B. Mason. The Reverend
Wendell Philips, Abolitionist of Boston, was a prominent stockholder. So
was Mrs. Harriet Beecher Stowe, a Yankee novelist. One of the railroad's
busiest publicists was Parke Godwin, son-in-law of William Cullen Bryant,
a Yankee poet.

By its charter, the railroad agreed to build 700 miles of line in six years
and to pay the State 7 per cent of its gross, not its net, income, forever more.
If the terms were met, the road should have a grant of 2,295,000 acres of
Illinois land.

* The city may well have been as hideous as Dr. Moody, Mr. Stead, and other visitors
said it was, yet many a Yankee continued to live there and to like it. In 1878 the Sons of
Vermont Resident in Chicago numbered almost 300 members. Gurdon S. Hubbard, Windsor,
was president. Other officers came from all parts of the Green Mountain State: Judge John
Jameson, Irasburg; Judge Mark Skinner, Manchester; the Honorable D. K. Pearsons, Bradford; John N. Hills, Arlington; Norman Williams, Woodstock; Judge C. V. Lawrence,
Vergennes; L. G. Fisher, Derby; Professor Albert D. Hager, Chester; L. L. Coburn, Mont-
pelier; and Frank B. Williams, Chelsea. In the same year the Sons of Maine in Chicago
had more than 100 members, and met for a sumptuous banquet and much oratory about the
Pine Tree State, presided over by Judge Thomas Drummond, Bristol; Leonard Swett, Turner;
J. Young Scammon, Whitefield; John N. Jewett, Palmyra; John J. P. Odell, Eastport, and
John S. Brewer, Calais. The migrated sons of other New England commonwealths do not
seem to have formed similar groups.

The planned colonization of a railroad's territory was a brand-new undertaking, and the Illinois Central went ahead to devise, by trial and error, a successful method. A handsome poster was prepared in which the railroad lands were described in prose of great power. Prices and terms of sale, neither of which favored the company at the expense of the buyer, were listed. One hundred thousand copies were sent to selected lists of farmers in Eastern and Southern states. Post offices were glad to post them prominently too. A newspaper advertising campaign was begun. The Boston *Traveler* was among the mediums used. So were three papers each in Vermont, New Hampshire, and Connecticut, one each in Maine and Rhode Island, and four more in Massachusetts, then or a bit later.

The company's sweet singers also prepared the first of many ecstatic pamphlets which went into some detail regarding the wonders of Illinois, chiefly the wonders of Illinois lands close to the Illinois Central Railroad. These lands, it appeared, were easy to plow, non-rocky, and were of incredible and inexhaustible fertility. Not since the ancient Egyptian farmers had such soil been known.

The Illinois Central did not trust its case to words alone. It employed graphic artists, who created pictures to prove the words of Illinois Central poets were right. Here is a snug farmhouse, a trace of sheer beauty in the gingerbread decorations around the eaves. Gorgeous trees shade it—astounding, when you come to think of it and recall that elsewhere in the pamphlet these fine prairie lands were said to be treeless. Everything is neatly fenced, in the best New England manner, and genteel horned cattle chew their cuds in the foreground. A stanch plow rests beside a superb field of corn of truly Gargantuan size. The honest and happy husbandman himself is seen moving from house to barn, a splendid structure; and just at the far side of the cornfield is a train of cars, trailing a plume of smoke across the otherwise rustic and wholly charming scene.

Look, ye sons and daughters of New England, look at what a farm can be in Eden. Come down out of your granite hills, where only sheep can live. Come up out of your terminal moraines, which you foolishly call farms. Here in Illinois the life of the husbandman is fed by the bounty of the earth and sweetened by the air of heaven.

It all fetched the Yankees, too. They were stirring restlessly, on their rocky or hilly farms, and when they gazed at the magnificent picture of life in Illinois unfolded by the philanthropists of the Illinois Central Railroad Company, the urge became too strong to subdue. Out of Vermont promptly came two hundred families of the Vermont Emigration Association to settle New Rutland in Illinois. Fourteen Massachusetts families left home to found

Rosemond. In 1855 the Working Men's Settlement Association was formed in New London, Connecticut, and within the year its vanguard was platting Lyman in the new Garden State.

The movement of Yankees continued. One could tell where they settled by the Congregational churches that were built as soon as possible at Monee, at Kankakee, Clifton, Bulkley, Loda, Paxton, El Paso, La Salle, Tonica, Nora, Galena, Dunleith, Amboy, Mendota, Bloomington, Sandoval. A Yankee village was set down even at Hoyleton in the section called Egypt, where Yankees were heartily loathed by the earlier settlers from the South and often threatened with violence. But under leadership of the Reverend J. A. Bent, who had himself purchased 2,640 acres, the Yankees stood fast and thrived, founding the necessities of life; namely, a Congregational church, a seminary, and a Temperance society.

By the middle of 1857 it looked to many a Yankee editor as if rural New England were going swiftly into tragic decay. "More than 300,000 people of New England will leave before the end of 1857," wrote one. In Maine, a scribe saw the young men and women leaving almost daily and said the movement was "taking from us the most vital elements of progress and our future good condition."

It was true, too. Many a New England village, in Maine and elsewhere, reached its population peak in or about 1850. Illinois figured in the decline that set in shortly after the century's halfway mark.

In 1854 a Connecticut firm was advertising throughout New England for agents to peddle a new book, *The Great West*. Western pastors of Congregational faith were writing home urging good Christians, presumably Congregationalists, to come and help to save the West for God. As for the pastors at home, Lewis Stillwell has pointed out, "all they could do was to accept the exodus and to urge emigrants to be faithful in the new homes in the West."

The Exodus was on the way, seemingly from every corner of New England. In Skowhegan, Maine, which had felt not a tremor of the earlier Ohio Fever, the Garden State of the West was calling loud. Increase Sumner Weston landed in Bunker Hill, Illinois. Then, a sizable group of Skowhegians sold their Maine places and migrated to Buda, among them Joseph and Martha Webb, Joe Weston and wife Hannah, Alex Jewett and "2 or 3 sisters," Eben Weston, William H. Bigelow, and the hardly forgettable Aholiab Bigelow.

The Reverend Edward Everett Hale added to the excitement when, on May 9, 1852, he preached a sermon in the Old South, Boston, on "The Christian Duty of Emigrants." By "emigrants" he meant both those arriving from Europe and those Yankees who were packing up and leaving. Their duty, it appeared, was to go as soon as possible to the boundless and bountiful West.

"There," cried one of New England's great figures, "God has provided for them the Western Prairie, white with the harvest, waiting for them to reap it. He has reared the forest, which will build them cheerful cabins; it waits for them to fell it."

The harvest was truly plenteous, good Dr. Hale indicated, but the laborers were all too few. Let the Yankees gird their loins and be up and about. Let their lights be burning in those cheerful cabins in the West.

One of Dr. Hale's friends did not agree: "It makes little difference," said Henry Thoreau, "whether you are committed to a farm or a county jail." But another Yankee lifted his voice. "When tillage begins," shouted Dan'l Webster, "other arts follow. The farmers, therefore, are the founders of civilization." And still another voluble Yankee, Horace Greeley, late of New Hampshire, had long been telling of the glories of the West. "Fly," he had cried in print, again and again, "fly, scatter through the country, to the great west. It is your destination!" He continued his admonition in his *Tribune* days. "Greeley does the thinking for the whole West at $2 a year for his paper," observed Ralph Waldo Emerson in 1856.

Meanwhile, the Illinois Central kept up its drumming. New posters and new pamphlets appeared, each surpassing those that had gone before. Agents circulated in person, talking with influential Yankees in towns and cities. And the exodus flowed on.

Out of small Hollis, New Hampshire, went Dr. Calvin Wheeler, to practice medicine in small Bristol, Illinois; and to the same new town, to save the souls of those whose bodies Dr. Wheeler failed to cure, went the Reverend William P. Kendrick, also of Hollis. From Hollis to Rockport went the Reverend Ralph Emerson. From Canaan, New Hampshire, went Nat C. Pierce and wife, who had been Dolly Pattee, to take up land near Princeton where, it is good to know, "they lived, labored, prospered, and died." From Pembroke, New Hampshire, went Edward Southworth Fitz, both M.D. and D.D., to practice both professions in new Mason City.

Dinsmore's *American Railroad and Steam Navigation Guide* for 1856, an exciting affair with many advertisements of land in Illinois and other Western states, helped the movement. It said of Alton, for instance, that "in its vicinity, besides fine farming land, are deposits of limestone, stone-coal, and abundance of timber." For Chicago, Mr. Dinsmore could hardly say enough. "Nothing," he wrote, "can exceed the animation of its business and railroad districts."

Chicago was indeed more animated than godly. Although, as noted, the most effective of its pioneer businessmen and boosters had been Yankees, they had hardly made it an orderly New England city. Neither religion nor education stood high in the town. Yet, all was not lost, for Orrington Lunt retained the integrity he had been born to in Bowdoinham, Maine. Having made a small fortune in Chicago wheat and the Chicago & North Western Railway, he was active in founding Northwestern University. It was Lunt who alone waded through the dismal swamp along the lake shore, to find the ridges and hardwood groves which he selected for the university site and campus. His fellow trustees of the college wanted to name the new town Luntville, or Orrington, but he would have none of it and it was named for another trustee, John Evans.

But Lunt moved promptly to Evanston, happy to be away from the loud and unseemly noises of Chicago, and became its foremost citizen, rejoicing in the fine new university, and taking considerable comfort in the life and works of a Yankee girl, Frances Elizabeth Caroline Willard, the daughter of Vermont parents and Oberlin graduates, who became president of the Evanston College for Ladies and the incomparable bellwether of the National Woman's Christian Temperance Union.

The university and college at Evanston, as well as the W.C.T.U., had a large influence, in Illinois and elsewhere; but just what it has been cannot be assessed by a layman. It must be left to professors and divines.

CHAPTER VII

THE LAND OF MICHIGANDIA

No MATTER where they went, nor how many, there were almost as many reasons for leaving as there were emigrants. The rich fields of the river lands at last played out. Spruce, or pine, or the devil's own paintbrush (*Hieracium aurantiacum*) crept into the mowing. Sheep chewed the hill farms down to the granite. There were gimlet-eyed bankers who took mortgages at 10 per cent, and were seldom sentimental when it came to foreclosure. There was weather, and once, in 1816, came a whole dose of weather that is still remembered, when a foot of snow piled on top of June's daisies, and forced many a farmer's family to eat boiled nettles and hedgehog. There were plagues like the spotted fever that swept the Yankee commonwealths and frightened the survivors into the tents of the revivalists; and a galloping consumption that seemed at last to be endemic. In 1811 a vast cloudburst beat down on Vermont, stripping whole farms of their soil, piling debris upon others, washing away nearly all the sawmills and gristmills. In 1821 in New Hampshire, on the 9th of September, there was no sun before noon, or after. All was gloomy, and the stout old maples and beeches shivered their mantles in quick, sharp breezes that died as soon as they came. The people became alarmed. At about six o'clock the heavens opened and discharged, says an old account, their watery contents in torrents, and there came simultaneously such a gale as the oldest citizen could not remember. Warner Village was wiped out entire. Many homes around Sunapee Lake were blown away like chaff. Salisbury Village suffered dreadful damage.

Were these sinister happenings mere warnings of the Last Days? Many a rustic prophet said they were, and pounded home the warning with hair-curling sermons that brought cold sweat to congregations in sweltering meetinghouses in July. Aggressive Baptists and Methodists were on the march, men who knew Signs when they saw them and spoke plainly and directly of Jehovah's intentions and plans. Farmer William Miller had been spending the long winter evenings calculating the days of Man, and now he stirred to some purpose, preaching the Advent, the Second Coming, and the saving of exactly 144,000 Faithful, the destruction of all others.

The young men of Nauvoo, still only halfway to Deseret, were back in their New England homes, not to stay but to depopulate, taking whole villages west with them to live under the Prophet named Joseph Smith, a former Vermonter.

Was the Ark of Noah not only a fact but a symbol? Somewhere in the American West was there perhaps an Ararat? Certainly the balm was flowing no more here in Gilead. Strange signs and portents were to be seen in the heavens, and, moreover, water was now flowing in the Erie Canal, the eighth wonder of the world, leading west toward a new and incredible land the name of which, after about 1825, was said to be Michigan.

Still and all, there were almost as many reasons for leaving New England as there were emigrants. If it wasn't the weather, or the plague, or a mortgage, or the restlessness conjured up by revivals, it could be a pregnant maid on a hilltop farm. It could be an unfounded charge of murder. It could be the rumor that wages in the West were a dollar a day, twice the Yankee wage. It could be, in all truth, almost anything, or nothing. Many a Yankee must have been hard put to explain, even to himself, why he had left familiar places for some region still largely unknown except to trappers.

One fine morning, in Montpelier, capital of Vermont, there started from his home to his office a citizen of substance and standing, who had, so far as anyone was aware, not a care in the world beyond his excellent law practice. On this morning he did not stop at his office, but walked on, over the Green Mountains, to arrive, in good time, in Louisiana. Here he made a good living, begat several children out of wedlock, and then, one day twenty-two years later, just as casually walked into his home in Montpelier, put his hat on the rack, and inquired if supper were ready.*

No one ever knew why the Montpelier lawyer went away, or why he returned. It was much the same with Daniel Pratt, of Prattsville in the town of Chelsea, Massachusetts. One day Dan'l disappeared and was seen no more in his home district for twelve years. In the meantime he had wandered from New Brunswick to the remote Dakotas. In time he referred to himself as the Great American Traveler and insisted he be called general. For another fifty years General Pratt walked the turnpikes and the trails of the United States, lecturing on "The Four Kingdoms" and "The Solar System," unable until his seventy-ninth year to overcome the restlessness of his soul and body. Only death could take him from the road.

There were many Yankees, however, who knew why they were leaving

* This account came direct to the author from one of the eccentric's descendants.

home. They knew where they were going, and how. The whole affair was planned to the last detail, even set down with ink on paper, in a form more than incidentally remindful of the Mayflower Compact of the original Yankees called Pilgrims. An outstanding group of this sort was the Union Colony, organized in East Poultney, Vermont.

It is probable that the Reverend Sylvester Cochrane, Congregational minister of the village, was the originator as well as the moving spirit of the Union Colony emigrants. It was he who, in the autumn of 1835, set out alone on a prospecting trip by way of the wonderful new Erie Canal to Buffalo, thence by steamer, stage, and horseback to Detroit and beyond. When he returned to East Poultney he was a confirmed emigrant to Michigan —by all odds, said he, the heart and soul of the continent. He talked up the idea of an emigrating company to townsmen and to others in neighboring villages. Throughout the winter the subject was discussed; then he called a formal meeting in March of 1836, at Castleton. Some fifty-odd men of Poultney, Castleton, Sudbury, Bennington, New Haven, West Haven, West Rutland, Orwell, Benson, and Dorset attended.

First, they drew up their "Considerations for locating a colony" by quoting the Bible: "And Moses sent them to spy out the land of Canaan." Then came the Constitution and By-Laws of Union Colony. Right away, in the first paragraph, the budding emigrants stated their belief that "a pious and devoted emigration is one of the most efficient means, in the hands of God, in removing the moral darkness which hangs over a great portion of the valley of the Mississippi." Thus they showed they were acquainted with the sermons of Dr. Lyman Beecher of Boston, who had permeated all New England with the words, "Population is rushing into the West like the waters of the flood, demanding for its moral preservation the immediate and universal action of those institutions which discipline the mind, and arm the conscience and the heart." By which Dr. Beecher meant nothing other than the Protestant church, and the New England kind of education.

Hence, the Union Colony emigration was for the purpose of removing some of that moral darkness in the Mississippi valley. But the members of the Union Colony were also inclined to be intellectually honest, and in the next paragraph of their Constitution they vowed: "We believe that a removal to the west may be a means of promoting our temporal interest." Then they quickly returned to their first thought by trusting that their temporal interest would "be made subservient to the advancement of Christ's kingdom." In formal language they pledged themselves to carry with them into the great void of pagan darkness their institutions of the Gospel, and also "the same literary privileges that we are permitted here to enjoy." They swore that the Sabbath should remain holy with them, that it should be observed "rigidly"—meaning that neither they nor their children, nor their workmen, nor their beasts should desecrate the day of rest by either labor *or* recreation.

The matter of Rum was not forgotten; and, because "ardent spirits have invariably proved the bane of every community into which they have been introduced," the Union Colony men prohibited manufacture, sale, and use of alcohol in the proposed settlement.

With the matter of morals thus out of the way, the colonists got down to business. Each member must advance $212.50, for which he should have a farm of 160 acres.

Trustees were elected, and the biblical spies for the New Canaan chosen' to go forth and locate. The spies were Simon S. Church of Sudbury, Wait S. Squier of New Haven, and William G. Henry. No time was lost, for early in April the spies, based on the rising new town of Kalamazoo, were exploring Ionia County, Michigan. Next, they went into Eaton County, which looked fine, and of which they purchased a tract of some 5,000 acres, much of it with fine groves of rock maples.*

The spies sent notice back to Vermont, then went to felling maple, beech, ash, oak, cherry, and basswood, planting potatoes, putting up log cabins. The "savage solitude of centuries" had passed. God and his Yankees had come, and they knew how to tame the backwoods, to make it safe for Congregationalism and Temperance.

Back in Vermont, the main body of emigrants was ready. They took off at once, and arrived in what they called Vermontville in time to erect several more cabins before snow-fly. There were twenty-two families in all, mostly farmers, though with a diversity of skills that augured well for Union Colony. Hiram J. Mears was an accomplished wheelwright. Jacob Fuller was a cooper. Simeon McCotter was a cabinetmaker, Walter Fairfield a printer, Martin Norton a blacksmith, and Dewey H. Robinson had a degree in medicine. Wells Martin and Charles Imus were experienced surveyors—an art of immense importance to the settlers. Bazaleel Taft listed himself as machinist. Daniel Barber was a merchant.

The parcels of land appear to have been drawn by lot, but only after a suitable prayer was offered by the Rev. Mr. Cochrane. A church with sixteen members was organized. A school was opened in one of the cabins, and continued thus until 1843, when Vermontville Academy was dedicated with the Reverend W. U. Benedict as teacher. The tuition was $2.50 a quarter. Board and lodging could be had at from $1.00 to $1.25 a week.

The first year was naturally marked by hardships, but the settlers were hardy too. They were proficient with ax and saw, and soon developed in

* This land is now a part of Barry County.

William F. Hawkins a true terror to trees, both broadleaf and conifer, known all over the county. Hawkins and the other Vermontville axmen favored the superb axes made at Hoosick Falls, New York, by Isaiah Blood.

The first white child born in Vermontville was Henry Sanford. He was followed by many another, and several became prominent, even distinguished within the state. Nor was Vermontville the only Yankee village in Eaton County. The town of Eaton Rapids mustered 330 citizens when Michigan's first census was taken, and Bellevue had a population of 413. These two towns were settled by Yankees, mostly Vermonters, among the Bellevue colony being Willard Davis, George Browning, and Oliver Stiles. Henry A. Shaw of Benson, Vermont, whence came the Barbers and Griswolds to Vermontville, settled at Eaton Rapids in 1839, finding a few Green Mountain boys already there. And Nathan Barlow cut his way into the forest of what became Barry County to help found Yankee Springs.

Yet, early as these Vermonters were, other Yankees were ahead of them. In 1805, when Congress organized the Territory of Michigan, General William Hull of Massachusetts was appointed governor, and the quite remarkable William Griswold of Torrington, Connecticut, secretary. Griswold, a former preacher and editor, was "a correct, honest man, paid his bills and sang David's Psalms"; but he held many opinions very strongly, and after a quarrel with Hull was forced to resign. It was Hull, of course, who surrendered Detroit without a shot to the British in 1812. When Americans reoccupied the town a year later, the man who was to become the good genius of Michigan was put in charge of the territory. He was General Lewis Cass, born in Exeter, New Hampshire, a man fit to make an empire out of the long abused and benighted region.

Cass had already distinguished himself above most American army officers in the War of 1812, and now he turned his abilities to making peace with the local Indian tribes and forming an administration to bring order to the most chaotic part of the United States. He also had a direct and large influence in attracting settlers. Having discovered that early government surveyors had reported most of Michigan to be a vast and dismal swamp, he ranged the region in person, on horseback and in canoe. He found the country good. He put on his cocked hat and went to Washington, to tell Congress and the press that Michigan was God's own country. For eighteen years, between 1813 and 1831, Cass gave Michigan good and strong government, and never ceased lauding the land and the climate. Later, for twelve years he served as senator. Little wonder settlers named their babies for him, as well as a county, a river, and a town.

When General Cass first came to Detroit, in wartime, he found a few Yankees already there. Among them was Solomon Sibley, formerly of Sutton,

Massachusetts, and Marietta, Ohio, who became Michigan's territorial delegate to Congress and a judge of the territorial supreme court. A son, Henry Hastings Sibley, born in Detroit, was to become the first governor of Minnesota.

Stephen Mack of Lyme, Connecticut, was keeping store in Detroit as early as 1810. His wife was Temperance Bond, and the couple were two of the first four settlers of Pontiac. Another Connecticut Mack, Andrew of New London, drove a band of Merino sheep over the Cumberland Mountains in 1804 and started a woolen factory in Cincinnati. Then he joined the army and served at Detroit, staying on through the troublous times to become mayor in 1834.

One of the most widely known Yankees in the early days was Rix Robinson of Richmond, Massachusetts. He was a trader and trapper who ranged the whole territory and established several trading posts, among them Ada, where he made his home as the first permanent settler in Kent County. He married an Indian, held various state offices, and refused a nomination for governor "at the request of Mrs. Robinson."

Although the Erie Canal (1825) was to be the great highway to Michigan, a number of hardy souls did not wait for it. Reuben Atwater was one. The Atwaters of Connecticut surely developed a notable urge to emigrate. One finds the name among early settlers in all the Midwestern states. Reuben, a native of Wallingford, came to Michigan in 1808, to act as secretary of the Territory. Ezra P. Baldwin of Claremont, New Hampshire, arrived, aged seventeen, in Detroit. Zephaniah Bunce, later to hold various public offices, also came in 1817. Henry C. Chipman, of the famous Vermont family, arrived in 1823, and a bit later sat on the territorial supreme court. Another Chipman, John S., tarried a while in Centerville, then went on to California.

Nor did Samuel Dexter of Boston wait for canal boats. In 1824 he made a clearing and called it the town of Dexter, which indeed it was; and he also founded the *Emigrant,* first paper in Washtenaw County. Dexter was a good Unitarian, who "preached at country stations without pay" and was a man of strong convictions and reputedly a powerful reasoner. His home, with its twenty-five rooms and nine fireplaces, survives in mid-twentieth century.

William Poppleton could not be bothered with canal boats. In the very year that water was let through the ditch, he put his family into a covered wagon and went overland to Troy, Michigan, being thirty-two days on the way, and settled on land he had purchased two years before. It is interesting to know that Poppleton's old home was in Poultney, Vermont, and one wonders if it were from him that the Reverend Mr. Cochrane of East Poultney and the Union Colony group first heard of the wonders of Michigan.

Cochrane may have had contact with Orange Risdon, surveyor of Rupert,

Vermont, who helped to lay out the New York cities of Lockport, Brockport, and Buffalo, then went on to survey seventy-five townships in Michigan. He settled down in Saline, named for the salty mineral springs there. Or perhaps it was still another Poultney man that told Cochrane about Michigan, for Poultney appears to have sent out many adventurous men ahead of the Vermontville colonists. This was Warren Tuttle, who in 1824 planted pioneer potatoes among the stumps of Livonia, Michigan, where he stayed and made the wilderness, said a local historian, "bud and blossom as the rose."

With the opening of the canal the trickle of migrants went into flood, reaching its crest, so far as Michigan was concerned, in the middle and late thirties. The manifest of a canal boat at this period often read: "Flour, wool and hides eastbound; farmers westbound." In one month (July) of 1830, four thousand farmer families passed through the canal. The very peak came later. The trek into Ohio had never been anything like this.

It was a time of sadness for those who would not or could not leave the old farm or the old village where they had been born and reared, for grass grew high in dooryards for the first time in a century or more. Hedgehogs gnawed at wooden sinks in kitchens where bricks were beginning to tumble into fireplaces. Well sweeps creaked in the wind. In the ancient town of Candia, New Hampshire, a reflective citizen looked around him. "On High street," said he, "there are now not over eight persons who live upon lands which were owned and occupied by their ancestors previous to the year 1800." Between 1800 and 1825, he recalled, Candia's natives had migrated either to Maine or to New York State; from the later date up to about 1840, "our young men and women have settled in various Western states."

At least one of the young New Hampshire men from Chesterfield was going to make his mark on Michigan. He was John D. Pierce. In boyhood the Word had been instilled in him by his tutor, the noble Enoch Pond, who inspired many young men to carry the beacon. John Pierce went on, to work his way through Brown University in Rhode Island, then through Princeton Theological Seminary, and so to a church in Oneida County, New York. Pierce was a Mason and in 1830, during the height of the Antimasonic movement, was forced to resign his pulpit. This he did cheerfully enough. Taking his family in an open oxcart, he drove to Marshall, Michigan, then a hamlet of a few huts, and preached a fine sermon on the evening of his arrival.

John Pierce believed devoutly and fiercely in education. In 1836 he was made superintendent of public instruction for Michigan. With the help of a neighbor, General Isaac E. Crary, from Colchester, Connecticut, Pierce managed to secure for the state a trusteeship over important lands. A million acres were set aside for educational purposes. He went on to draft plans for a primary school system and a state university. These were put into effect with virtually no change, and proved most successful. During his administration, Pierce also founded the *Journal of Education,* the first such periodical in the old Northwest Territory.

It is often difficult, if not impossible, to learn why Yankees settled in specific districts. The logical assumption is that the first settler, or settlers, wrote home to friends and relatives, or even letters to Yankee newspapers, relating the joys of the new region. Michigan was a subject much in the news of the thirties. Newspaper editors of the period were great hands to exchange subscriptions with one another, and to reprint, usually with credit, items they thought would be of interest locally. Possibly that is the manner by which the Coldwater district of Michigan attracted Yankees at an early date. William P. Arnold of Clarendon, Vermont, put up one of the first homes in Coldwater. That was in 1833. Within a year several other New Englanders were clearing land in the neighborhood, among them Hiram Alden from Ashfield, Massachusetts, the Upsons of Southington, Connecticut, and the Gilberts from Vermont. Near Coldwater grew up a settlement with the name Quincy, indicative of New England parentage. Incidentally, Hiram Alden of Coldwater became an outstanding person in his adopted state. He served it as commissioner of internal improvements and was so highly thought of that his body "was followed to the grave by 600 officials and laborers," who came from all parts of Michigan, "willingly paying their expenses as their tribute to a friend and an honest man."

White Pigeon was another goal of the first New Englanders. Edwin Kellog of Sheffield, Massachusetts, went there in 1830 to set up as a miller of flour, and John Stewart Barry of Amherst, New Hampshire, was right on his heels. So was Columbia Lancaster, who came from New Milford, Connecticut. Lancaster, however, yearned for still remoter places; and eight years later he loaded up a wagon and did not stop until he had reached the Oregon country. Barry remained and was three times elected governor of Michigan. Isaac Willard, born near Worcester, Masachusetts, was an early settler in White Pigeon. One of the first stores in the enterprising village was the business of Washington Pitcher, from Norwich, Connecticut.

Small successive waves from three Yankee states went into the establish-ment of Romeo. In the first wave was Minot T. Lane of Marlboro, New Hampshire, who was followed in 1837 by Adonijah Strong Welch and family from East Hampton, Connecticut. Mr. Welch taught school in a log cabin, and later became principal of the state normal college. Then in 1843 Isaac Abbott and family came from New Hampshire, followed in a few years by

Daniel B. Briggs, of Adams, Massachusetts, who was made superintendent of public instruction.

The John Hancock Carletons of Massachusetts settled at Hudson in log-cabin days, and there became the parents of Will, who grew into something of a poet. Will Carleton's verse often celebrated pioneer virtues and was widely read. Harper's published some of his poetry as *Farm Ballads,* which was sensationally popular. His best known poem was "Over the Hill to the Poor-House," which vibrated chords in multitudes of Americans, many of whom were shamed by it into taking their indigent parents from poor farms. As a recitation it became a close second to "The Wreck of the Hesperus." No school exercises were quite complete without a calicoed girl or homespun youth declaiming, "Over the hill to the poor-house I'm trudgin' my weary way."

For reasons long since lost in the mists, Kalamazoo County turned out to be the goal of many Vermonters. Cyrus Lovell left Grafton in 1829 to build the first frame house in Kalamazoo City; other Lovells named Enos, George W., and Lafayette W. were among the first settlers in near-by Climax. The first white child born in the county was William Rufus Shafter, the son of Hugh and Eliza, who had migrated from Windsor, Vermont. Shafter achieved a notable record for courage and ability during the Civil War and became one of the great Indian fighters of all time; in 1898 he commanded American land forces in the taking of Santiago. A leading spirit in the founding of Kalamazoo College was Nathaniel Balch from Athens, Vermont. Early Yankees in neighboring Schoolcraft village were Edwin H. and George Van Ness Lothrop from Easton, Massachusetts.

One of the greatest stands of white pine on earth was what brought Yankee loggers and lumbermen to Michigan. As early as 1838 lumbermen who had migrated from Maine to Michigan were advertising in the Bangor *Whig & Courier,* offering fine jobs at good wages to Maine natives who would come to the West. They went, too, and their migration was one of the phenomena of the Yankee exodus; for their sons went on to cut pine in Wisconsin and Minnesota, their grandsons to cut pine in Idaho and fir in Oregon and Washington, and redwood in California. Michigan's Saginaw River was the first to feel the impact as the Maine operators moved in, among them families of Murphys, Dorrs, Gubtils, Leadbetters, Merrills; and Charles K. Eddy, with son Walter, from Corinth.* In this migration was Horace Butters of Maine, who in Michigan invented a skidding machine for loggers

* A distant relative was Ezra Butler Eddy, born in Bristol, Vermont, who moved into Ontario to start logging and in time to become the Match King of all Canada.

which in time brought a revolution in the industry, and is much used today in the Far West.

One of the greatest Saginaw lumbermen was a Vermonter, Ammi W. Wright. He later moved into Minnesota, where his Swan River Logging Company operated for many years. Another Vermonter, Charles T. Hills, moved to Muskegon and, with the Rynersons as partners, helped to make it second only to Saginaw as a sawdust city. Frank W. Gilchrist, from Concord, New Hampshire, built a sawmill at Alpena and did his logging around Thunder Bay. John Canfield, from Sandisfield, Massachusetts, was a noted pioneer logger at Manistee, where his mills smoked day and night for decades. But the greatest timber owner of all the Yankees was probably David Whitney, born in Westford, Massachusetts, who first operated along the Saginaw and later, from his home in Detroit, bought timber and did an immense amount of logging in Wisconsin, Oregon, Washington, and northern California.

How many common lumberjacks these lumbermen were responsible for bringing west is not to be known, though the number was probably well into the thousands. People living along the Erie Canal heard their howls as they migrated, and came in time to call them Bangor Tigers, no matter they came from the Penobscot, or from the Kennebec or even the Connecticut. In Michigan they established their breed as most able with ax and saw, and they were catty of foot, in their calked boots, driving billions of feet of the great pumpkin pines down the Saginaw, the Muskegon, the Au Sable, and turning the towns into roaring bedlams when the drive was in and the urge came strongly upon them to make love and drink alcohol.

Michigan was in the very air of New England. Some writer of dreadful doggerel, quite possibly a land promoter, wrote a batch of it and set it to music. Its lyrics sneered at the stay-at-homes, challenged the young to break away, and became immensely popular:

> Come, all ye Yankee farmers who wish to change your lot,
> Who've spunk enough to travel beyond your native spot.
> And leave behind the village where Pa and Ma do stay,
> Come, follow me, and settle in, Michigandia—
> Yea, yea, yea—in Michigan-d-i-ay.

They sang the Michigan song in Addison County, Vermont, and away went ten whole families to settle Sylvan in Washtenaw County, Michigan. This was a favorite region for Vermonters, possibly because Orange Risdon, the celebrated surveyor from the Green Mountains, had settled here at

Saline in 1824, and was joined two years later by the Orin Parsons family of Yankees.

What was called Monroe colony was first settled by two brothers from Royalston, Massachusetts, and by 1834 was known as a stanch, or sometimes as a pigheaded, Yankee community. David A. Noble of Williamstown, Massachusetts, came to make his home here in 1831, and to be sent to Congress. To found the first newspaper in these parts came Edward G. Morton of St. Albans, Vermont. Other settlers arrived from Scituate, Rhode Island, and from New Hampshire, in such volume and with "such intelligence and strength of character" that Monroe was often called the independent state of Monroe. It was the center of excitement during the bloodless "Toledo War," a boundary dispute with Ohio, when Monroe posses raided Toledo and the entire region was filled with threats and alarums.

Not only the border counties but the interior of the state was filling. Charles Dickey and family of Londonderry, New Hampshire, moved into Calhoun County at Marshall, where Charles T. Gorham of Danbury, Connecticut, had already settled, along with James Wright Gordon, of Plainfield, Connecticut, who was to become a lieutenant governor of Michigan. They were soon joined by Samuel S. Lacey of Bennington, Vermont, a man difficult to please. Lacey had ranged pretty much over New York State and most of Arkansas before coming to rest in Marshall, where he was soon elected state land commissioner. To practice law in the new village was Henry Taylor, who had pulled up his stakes in pretty Deerfield, Massachusetts.

Up in Detroit, John Farmer was happy to see the flood coming in. He had had much to do with it. While surveying in the party of Orange Risdon, young Farmer had made and taken out copyrights on several maps of Michigan. One of these was published in 1826, just after the Erie Canal was opened; and four years later came another edition, with an informative gazetteer, describing the marvels of this new country. It proved to be as popular as the Michigandia song, and doubtless ten times as influential. Yankees by the thousand pored over it. They read the sparkling words in the gazetteer, looked at the great map dotted with odd and somehow attractive names, and then a great many of them made up their minds. They sold their farms or village property; often they sold or gave away the good will of their profession, be it medicine or law; and away they went—a majority of them—in the 1830's to Michigan, a map of John Farmer's in pocket.

Darius Comstock of Cumberland, Rhode Island, was well in the vanguard. After fulfilling contracting jobs on the Erie Canal, he floated on its waters westward, and finally planted himself in Raisin Center, Lenawee County, in 1826. The John Barbers of Perham, Massachusetts, found Adrian in the same county to their liking. One of Adrian's most useful citizens turned out to be the scholarly Daniel K. Underwood, born in Enfield, Massachusetts, who got his M.D. at Dartmouth. He opened a drugstore in the new town, practiced medicine, and donated land for the site of Adrian College. Underwood was a fanatic on fruits, to which he gave much study, and wrote valuable monographs on fruit growing in Michigan. The Comstocks, Darius and Addison, promoted the Erie & Kalamazoo Railroad, which became a part of the Michigan Central.

Other primeval settlers of Lenawee County included George Crane of Norton, Massachusetts, who in 1833 bought 2,500 acres at Palmyra, and was soon engaged in railroad building. But wooden roads preceded the iron rails, and it was George Mathews, born in Watertown, Connecticut, who helped to promote, then took charge of Lansing and Detroit Plank Road. He also laid out, founded, and named the town of Meridian, which unfortunately no longer exists as such. To the Lenawee region's Hudson also came a second minor poet, John W. Turner, from Putney, home of the Perfectionists, to practice law in Michigan. Elias J. Baldwin from Massachusetts was one of the first settlers in Morenci.

At the far southwestern corner, Berrien County was taking on many of the aspects of New England. Moses Chamberlain of Pembroke, New Hampshire, had discovered its charms after ranging over parts of Ohio and Michigan in 1835. He purchased a large tract of this New Canaan, and returned to New Hampshire. Then with his family, including able sons Henry and William, he went by the Erie Canal and the lakes to Chicago, and overland eastward into Berrien County at New Buffalo. Son Henry promptly founded the town of Three Oaks and took part in politics, once being nominated for governor. The Three Oaks Congregational Church had for its pastor the Reverend Waters Warren from Ludlow, Vermont, a son of whom founded the Warren Featherbone Company, which flourishes in mid-twentieth century.

The little town of Pembroke in New Hampshire sent other sons elsewhere in Michigan. Byron McCutcheon practiced law in Manistee and Grand Rapids, and went to Congress. His brother, Sullivan McCutcheon, also became prominent in politics.

During a dozen years after 1831, Berrien County drew heavily from Norwich, Stamford, and New Milford, Connecticut; from Leominster, Chicopee, and Harwich, Massachusetts; from Weybridge, Shoreham, Westminster, Addison, and—naturally—East Poultney, Vermont; and from Nelson, New Hampshire. The state of Maine is not represented in that migration; but its sons, more often than not, struck into the tallest green timber they could find, no matter the state; and thus, from Skowhegan, Maine, Maximilian Webb went to Saginaw, Michigan's greatest lumber town; and Francis

Drew to Grand Rapids, which thrived on lumber. From Skowhegan, too, Solomon and Willard Lambert went to Livonia, Lorenzo Pooler to Plymouth, John Linnell to Blanchard, and Isaac Stewart to Allis.

John Perrin's family of Woodstock, Connecticut, was something of a migration in itself. Taking wife, five sons, and four daughters, he boarded ship for Albany, canalboat to Buffalo, and steamer to Detroit. Leaving the rest behind, Perrin and two sons hit out into the back reaches to find a farm. On a pretty slope in Jefferson, Hillsdale County, they found it—with a fine spring bubbling up out of solid rock. It all looked, said John Perrin, like familiar country, only the soil was much better. He and the two boys built a cabin, then went to Detroit and fetched the remainder of the family. The population of Jefferson township had thus increased exactly elevenfold in 1835.

It is little wonder that the stay-at-homes brooded. Was New England destined to be a mere reservoir on which the West was to draw for its "best educated and most energetic people"? Were the tinklings of sheep bells, which were becoming more numerous on deserted hill farms, actually a knell? Schoolhouses were boarded up. The list from which to select the grand jury was slimming. The trade fell off at crossroads stores. Was it true that farm produce from the new West, coming east over the Erie Canal, was making mock of Yankee farming? Many a discouraged Yankee farmer, who simply would not move away, began tinkering with inventions.

Northern Michigan, the so-called Upper Peninsula, attracted but few of the earliest settlers. Its sovereignty was in doubt, anyway, until after the Toledo War, when the strip was presented to Michigan; and even then it was too remote. A Yankee named William Burt dramatically brought the Upper Peninsula to the attention of all adventurous men, especially the go-getters of 1844, who had no Reverend Dr. Russell Conwell to bid them look in their own back yards for diamonds.

William Austin Burt, a native of Petersham, Massachusetts, had educated himself in various fields, including surveying, and had invented both a typewriting machine and Burt's solar compass. In 1824 he had bought a piece of land in Michigan's Macomb County and settled his large family there. With the help of his five sons he surveyed the Upper Peninsula and, upon the death of Douglass Houghton, took charge of the geological survey also. Late on the afternoon of September 19, 1844, the needle of the magnetic compass he held in his hand began to dip and flutter furiously. It pointed north, then west, then south, describing wild arcs, pointing nowhere for long.

Burt shouted to his sons. "Look around, boys," said he. "Look around and see what you can find."

The boys looked around and discovered several large outcroppings of ore that appeared like almost pure iron. Iron it was. From that moment the Upper Peninsula ceased to be a howling wilderness. The Great Cold Lake, which Americans called Superior, lying there so vast and quiet, was rimmed with a collar of iron—iron, it turned out, more than a mile deep. It was not long before there were traffic jams at the "Soo," as men of Boston and other places worked their boats up through the boiling white water or carried them around in a costly portage.

Settlements grew quickly up around the mines—Ishpeming, Negaunee, Republic, Escanaba—as the Marquette, and then the Menominee, Range came into being. The piles of ore grew, but they remained where they were. There was no way to get the stuff to market—not until Charles T. Harvey, a young Yankee salesman for Mr. Fairbanks's weighing scales, made in St. Johnsbury, Vermont, had first the vision, then the ability, and finally the great determination needed to build the Soo Canal and locks—one mile of clear, open water that was largely responsible for making the Upper Peninsula the first great iron-mining region in the United States.

There was copper up there, too, and when the canal was opened both copper and iron went through. Worcester (now Marquette) grew suddenly and was first named for the home town of Amos R. Harlow, influential pioneer. Samuel Livingston Mather, born in Middletown, Connecticut, who had come west to dispose of his family's lands in Ohio, promptly organized the Cleveland Iron Mining Company to explore and buy ore lands; and the company was soon one of the giants of ore, as it remains today under the style of Cleveland-Cliffs Iron Company.

The Upper Peninsula's copper country was of interest, too, to David Henshaw, the Massachusetts-born Secretary of the Navy under President Tyler. He resigned to organize a company to exploit his holdings on the Keweenaw Peninsula, a part of the Upper Peninsula's rugged shore line. Meanwhile, a group of Bostonians including Clarkes, Bigelows, and Eliots, and headed with great astuteness by Quincy Adams Shaw, was forming the Calumet & Hecla Mining Company, which became and remained the great producer of Michigan copper. But Sam Knapp of Vermont, who went to Michigan in 1844 for what he said was his health, did very well too. After four years of prospecting in the Keweenaw region, he uncovered a six-ton nugget of pure copper. The site became the Minnesota mine, which made Sam and his backers wealthy. Sam retired in 1868, to settle in Jackson, where he died, leaving all to the Methodist church.

But neither the copper nor the iron mines attracted Yankee laborers in any great number. This work was left to immigrants from England, Ire-

land, and Europe, with many French from Canada. The mining development, however, "opened up the country," and Yankee lumbermen moved in
to exploit the vast reaches of timber that covered much of the Upper
Peninsula. One young man, Orrin W. Robinson of Cornish, New Hampshire,
with a fourteen-year-old sister and an aunt, landed at Ontonagon in 1854.
He went to work for an uncle who had charge of the Derby mine—Samuel
Stillman Robinson from Windsor, Vermont. But he saw the great trees all
around, and he left the ore to tackle them. Twenty years later Orrin was
operating one of the largest logging and sawmill outfits in the region, an
industrial concern that carried on until 1928.

Of fully as much value to Michigan as the wealth of iron and copper
was the exciting publicity attendant on the discoveries and development.
Michigan continued to be much in the news in New England, especially in
the Boston papers, and unquestionably many a restless Yankee, wanting to
go somewhere but not knowing where, was influenced by the reports of
continuous discoveries of iron and copper. It was romantic—and let no man
think for a moment there was nothing romantic in the Yankee nature. Then,
there were the annual reports of Calumet & Hecla, of the Pittsburgh &
Boston, of the Minnesota, and of other concerns in which Yankee money was
invested. For half a century these reports indicated there was wealth as
well as adventure in northern Michigan.

The flood continued, though mostly it poured into the part of the state
below the Straits of Mackinac. John Almy of Rhode Island, a trained
engineer, laid out the village of Kent, which became a part of Grand
Rapids, second city in the state. John Ball of Grafton County, New Hampshire, who was graduated from Dartmouth in 1820 and was teaching school
at Fort Vancouver on the Columbia River in 1832, started east again in 1837
but got no farther than Grand Rapids. He liked it and settled down. The
Simeon Baldwins of Canterbury, Connecticut, came to stay; and another
Connecticut man, George W. Allen of Enfield, after trying Painesville, Ohio,
went on to Grand Rapids. Charles C. Comstock of Sullivan, New Hampshire,
started in 1853 to build a fortune on Grand Rapids lumber. As early as 1836
sixteen-year-old Solomon L. Withey arrived with his parents from St.
Albans, Vermont. He became a noted judge, and his courts "were always
models of propriety and decorum."

Cass County, properly honoring the name of Michigan's greatest citizen
of pioneer times, was being populated in part from General Cass's native
New Hampshire. Two of Cassopolis's first citizens were Abiel Silver of
Hopkinton—who with two brothers opened a pioneer store and himself

served on the state land commission—and James Sullivan of Exeter, grandson of the noted General John Sullivan of Revolutionary times. James practiced law in Niles, later at Cassopolis.

One of the first (1832) settlers in Niles was Rufus Landon of Falls Village, Connecticut. Rodney C. Paine from New Milford in the same state was an early mayor of Niles. He arrived the same year as one of the many traveling Chipmans—John S. of Shoreham, Vermont. George Redfield, later a secretary of state for Michigan, settled in Cass County from Connecticut in 1835.

Incidentally, the New Englanders appear to have taken a most active part in politics in the early years. The second governor was William Woodbridge, born in Norwich, Connecticut. The fourth governor was born in Amherst, New Hampshire, the fifth in Limerick, Maine, and the seventh, who was Epaphroditus Ransom, came from Shelburne Falls, Massachusetts. But no more Yankees sat in the governor's chair until the fourteenth, a native of Dartmouth, Massachusetts.

The long-time political boss of the state was born in Bedford, New Hampshire, in 1813, as Zachariah Chandler. He emigrated to Detroit at twenty, made a fortune in trade, banking, and land speculation, and sat in the United States Senate for almost two decades. A number of early-comers from New England were sent to the House or Senate. Henry P. Baldwin, from Coventry, Rhode Island, was both governor of Michigan and Senator. To the national House went the former Vermonters Fernando C. Beaman of Chester, Alexander Buel of Poultney, Jacob Howard of Shaftsbury, and William A. Howard of Hinesburg; David A. Noble from Williamstown, Massachusetts, Oliver L. Spaulding from Jaffrey, New Hampshire, and Alpheus Williams from Saybrook, Connecticut. For two years James Witherell of Mansfield, Massachusetts, was acting governor of the territory. The brothers May, Charles S. and Dwight, who came from Sandisfield, Massachusetts, both served terms as lieutenant governor. George Martin, from Middlebury, Vermont, was a noted chief justice of the supreme court.*

* Other Yankees who became prominent in Michigan communities, both large and small, often in the matter of education, included the following men, most of whom arrived in the 1830's. From *Massachusetts:* Isaac Adams, Andover; Francis Baker, Sheffield; Edward Bancroft, Westfield; Hale E. Crosby, Ashburnham; Charles Larned, Pittsfield. From *Maine:* Nathaniel W. Brooks, Castine; Francis Stockbridge, Bath; Royal T. Twombly, Portland; John Welch, Augusta. From *New Hampshire:* Joseph Estabrook, Bath; Henry B. Lathrop, Hanover; Cummings Sanborn, North Haverhill; Oliver P. Strowbridge, Claremont. From *Vermont:* Lovatus C. Allen, Huntington; Samuel F. Anderson, Ira; Edward W. Harris, Bradford; Oramel Hosford, Thetford; Horace Mower, Woodstock; Joseph B. Pierce, St. Johnsbury; Oel Rix, Royalton; John L. Standish, Benson; Campbell Waldo, Middletown Springs. From *Connecticut:* John Q. Adams, Cornwall; Levi Bacon, Jr., Ellington; Horace B. Lathrop, Norwich; Henry Pennoyer, Norwalk; Elias M. Skinner, Woodstock; Ralph Wadhams, Goshen. From *Rhode Island:* Oliver C. Comstock, Warwick; John W. Hopkins, Providence.

Among the Yankee migrants were Baptists, Methodists, Episcopalians, Universalists, and Unitarians, to say nothing of the later Seventh Day Adventists. But Congregationalism largely prevailed among the Protestants. In 1835 it had six churches in Michigan. Twenty years later there were 106, with 5,000 members. By 1880 the number of such churches had doubled, the membership more than tripled.

Yankee churchmen and Yankee politicians worked together to implant in Michigan what they considered the great boon of local government, which was to say the town meeting. Michigan was the first Western state to adopt this form, and her example was followed—with certain modifications—by others, including Wisconsin, Minnesota, and Illinois.

During the years after Michigan became a state there were several distinct eras of wildcat towns—synthetic places built mostly on paper for the purpose of selling lots. A fair sample was White Rock, in Huron County, no longer to be found on a map. Elaborate maps displayed in Detroit and Grand Rapids barrooms—and sent to New England by the bale—depicted White Rock as already a gigantic city, with courthouse, banks, and other great buildings, with a teeming industrial section shooting smoke in all directions. Lots were sold wholesale and retail. The hamlet once achieved a population of 600, never more.

Few Yankees settled, even if they bought, in White Rock. But many did settle in well advertised towns that are no longer to be found on maps or in the Postal Guide. There was Commerce, where in 1833 Hiram Barritt of Alford, Massachusetts, erected the first frame house. There was Boston, in Ionia County, where in 1837 came the Stannard family of Newport, New Hampshire, and three years later the Trains of Tunbridge, Vermont. There was Rawsonville which, in 1837, looked good to Eurotas Morton from Hatfield, Massachusetts, and Hampton Rich of Sharon, Vermont. And there was Gratton, where in 1844 Milton C. Watkins of Rutland, Vermont, came to teach school. These and many other towns were mentioned with varying degrees of pride in early times but are no longer in existence.

Other Yankees must have had visions of a metropolis in many a crossroads hamlet that was outstripped by neighboring towns. Joshua K. Abbott of Concord, New Hampshire, chose Grand Blanc. Joseph G. Ames from the same state settled at Armada. The Babcocks of Orwell, Vermont, were among the first to clear ground in Southfield. Sherwood fetched Isaac Beall from Clarendon, Vermont. Noah Beach of Whiting, Vermont, came to Springfield. Charles T. Cady from Putney, Vermont, was the first sheriff in Dundee and was also and otherwise a good citizen, "expending money liberally for churches, schools, and Temperance." Gilbert Hathaway of Plymouth County, Massachusetts, did as much for New Baltimore by "donating $15,000 to found Hathaway Institute."

In his later years Elisha J. House, born in Chesterfield, New Hampshire, in 1813, liked to recall that he pioneered the town of Paw Paw. Zimri D. Thomas of Rowe, Massachusetts, did the same thing for Allen, Michigan. Osmond Tower of Cummington, Massachusetts, was proud that he had built the first school house in Michigan's Grand River valley. DeWitt C. Walker of Vermont laid out the village of Capac which, one hundred and twelve years later, had a population of 835.

A majority of the great Yankee inventors remained in New England; the New York Fever, the Ohio Fever, the surge into Illinois, and now the trek to Michigandia—none of the continuous excitement seemed to move them. Now and then one of the breed broke away; for instance, Hiram Moore, who came to Kalamazoo from his native New Hampshire in 1845, and proceeded to devise Moore's Harvester, which cut a fourteen-foot swath and found high favor with growers of grain. But Moore and his machine went down in front of the onslaught of the aggressive McCormicks of Chicago.

The original excitement over Michigan, which began almost simultaneously with the opening of the Erie Canal in 1825 and the publication of John Farmer's map in 1826 (plus the official and genuine enthusiasm of General Cass), was at its height in the middle and late thirties. But it never quite died in New England. Nearly all Yankee emigrants were literate, and they were a letter-writing people who told the stay-at-homes of both the bad and the good things they had discovered about Michigan. The advantages of the new homes must have far outweighed the faults; the Michigan movement continued, even after Wisconsin and Iowa and Minnesota were much in the public eye.

Then, in the 1870's, the Jackson, Lansing & Saginaw Railroad Company, which had a grant of 600,000 acres, started to romanticize about the lands on both sides of its rails—and the lands where its rails ran only on paper. In 1875 this company came out with a booklet and a most gorgeously colored map—a map in which vermilion counties vied with magenta counties, in which the dullest shade was of a yellow to startle the astigmatic. Nor was the accompanying text difficult to read. The railroad said it had for sale "the best PINE and FARMING lands in a belt 30 miles wide" which, moreover, was in a section of the state not surpassed for salubrity of climate, fertility of soil, abundance of valuable timber, and convenience to markets. The prices, so the J., L. & S. people swore, were LOW; the land could be paid for, too, "one fourth down and the balance on ample time."

Was it wheat? These lands could not be topped IN THE NATION. The same went for sheep raising. Apples? God save you, stranger, good Mother Eve never knew more seductive fruit—nor finer peaches, plums, pears, cherries, quince—aye, and if these were not enough, then consider the COAL and the SALT with which the J., L. & S. lands were infested. As for scenery, why, it appealed alike to the pleasure-seeking tourist and the contemplation of the PHILOSOPHER, while "the fanciful imagination of the poet may rest on the varied landscape with a pleasure that may never be realized in distant lands that are more celebrated in poetry and song."

The landscape was varied enough, for the railroad's lands were in such widely separated counties as Gratiot and Antrim, Saginaw and Cheboygan. No matter how wild large portions of this region were—and they were wild in 1875—the railroad company bragged vaguely of "the schools," which all good Yankees believed were as necessary as meetinghouses.

But for all its rich prose and bombast, the Jackson, Lansing & Saginaw Railroad was discriminating. In a good stiff warning, the company said to be sure "you have the necessary means." It was difficult, even in such a Utopia as Michigan, to make progress without some capital. Mr. O. B. Barnes, the company's land commissioner, would be happy to advise prospective settlers in this regard.

Exactly how the railroad's booklet was received in New England is not to be known; but assuredly it still found many Yankees who had been trying to make up their minds about Michigan, and helped them to do so. It was that kind of literature. In any case, the wild and remote counties of the J., L. & S. lands were soon resounding to the axes—and often the saw-mills—of thousands of Yankees, or of Yankees once removed. In this respect, it is interesting to note, though not easy to explain, why so many residents of Michigan of the time were "born in Camillus, New York, of New England parentage." One finds this remark in dozens of biographical sketches. Camillus must have been a notable Yankee settlement to send so many men and women of New England parentage on to Michigan.

Another statement often repeated in the sketches of old-timers who were born in Michigan's early days is "Born of American parents," or sometimes "Of wholly American descent." These statements were doubtless prompted by the fact of the heavy immigration from Ontario and other Canadian provinces.

By the middle of the eighties the early migrants to Michigan were dying. These had come in the 1820's, the 1830's. The dates most often cited are 1836 and 1837. The Yankee women who came to Michigan were seldom mentioned in the early annals, but the Michigan Pioneer and Historical Society *Collections,* which were published from 1879 onward, happily took cognizance of them. One of the earliest to come must have been Harriet

Row, born in Sharon, Connecticut, in 1810, who migrated in 1832. The date of Hannah Waterbury's arrival is not given, but she was born in 1789, in Stamford, Connecticut. Coraline Hubbell came to Oakland County from Fairfield, Connecticut, in 1839. Among other early settlers were Electra Allen of Vermont, Margaret Stiles of Massachusetts, and Sarah Bingham and Mrs. Benjamin Colborn, both of New Hampshire.

Perhaps the most influential on Michigan of all Yankee women was the seeress, Ellen Gould Harmon White, born in 1827 in small Gorham, Maine. Mrs. White, sometimes called the Prophetess of Doom, was the leader of the Seventh Day Adventists, founded in New Hampshire on the remnants of William Miller's millennial group. Although this remarkable woman was patently obsessed with the Last Days, she believed that people ought to enjoy good health until Gabriel should come to blow. In 1866, in response to a vision, Mrs. White founded at tiny Battle Creek the Western Health Reform Institute. Next came Battle Creek College, the sect's first training school for adult youth.

In time, under the extremely competent Dr. John Harvey Kellogg, son of an Adventist pioneer, the health institute, its name changed to Battle Creek Sanitarium, became known all over the world; and the Kellogg breakfast "health foods" grew, under Dr. John's brother, Will K. Kellogg, into an immense business. The influence of Battle Creek Sanitarium on migration to Michigan has never been estimated, but the institution has perhaps attracted more visitors and possibly permanent settlers—both Yankees and others—than did the Jackson, Lansing & Saginaw Railroad Company.

CHAPTER VIII

TROUBLE AT PUTNEY

ONLY ONCE in the long history of the exodus, after the Revolution, did actual exile play a part, and the thing responsible for banishing the Perfectionists from New England was one of the tenets laid down by their founder and prophet. "In a holy community," said he, who was John Humphrey Noyes, "there is no more reason why sexual intercourse should be restrained by law, than why eating or drinking should be—and there is as little occasion for shame in the one case as in the other."

This was strong meat, in nineteenth century America. It would be no light fare today, a century and more later, and although the unorthodox sect led by Prophet Noyes was to make a huge success of its steel traps, and an even greater success of its plated silverware, yet its odd idea and actual practice of Complex Marriage, which most Americans designated as Free Love, caused the non-Perfectionist Yankees bid them begone. It was a case of expulsion, even of flight.

The cult was a product of the great intellectual and emotional ferment of the 1830's and 1840's: a time when angels came to earth, one of them to deliver the golden plates of the book called Mormon to Joseph Smith, a Vermonter; a time when William Miller, also a Vermonter, saw visions of foreboding in the skies above the Green Mountains and confidently set the exact date for the Second Coming and the end of things. It was a period, too, when other prophets said that heaven could be reached on earth by communal living, as in the colonies at New Harmony, Indiana, and Brook Farm, Massachusetts.

John Humphrey Noyes rejected the idea of a Second Coming. It had, he said, already taken place. He rejected an end of the world, a day of reckoning. He rejected, too, the notion of angels, just as he scoffed at the theology of both the Catholic and the Protestant churches—including Congregationalism. Yet Noyes was as devoutly religious as any priest or parson. Man, he held, may have been born sinful, as the Bible seemed to indicate, but man could also achieve absolute perfection, not in heaven but here on earth, even in Vermont.

Noyes was born at Brattleboro in the Green Mountain State in 1811, the son of a well-to-do family. His father served on occasion as a member of Congress. His mother, who was Polly Hayes, was an aunt of Rutherford B. Hayes, later President of the United States. The Noyes-Hayes families were among the most distinguished in New England.

Young Noyes entered Dartmouth College at fifteen, was graduated with the highest honors, and began the study of law. He was soon carried away with the religious excitements that prevailed in New England and were particularly virulent in Vermont. He gave up his law studies for the Yale Divinity School. But the dogmas of conventional theology were not for him. He founded in New Haven what he called a free church. In 1834 he said from the pulpit that he himself had attained a state of perfection, of sinlessness. This was shocking, and he was dismissed from Yale.

The young man was neither discouraged nor in the least subdued. He set out on a tour that took him over much of Massachusetts and into York State, visiting small groups of forward thinkers—perhaps fanatics—who had formed themselves into communities. These he attempted to weld into a single group; but he discovered each was too sure of its own rightness to merge with others. At Brimfield, Massachusetts, where he and a comrade named Simon Lovett preached, the group of forward thinkers included a coterie of handsome and emotionally exuberant young women, two of whom, late at night, made their way to the bed of Brother Lovett. The news got around the village and was presently known as the Brimfield Scandal. It seems also to have become known pretty much over all New England.

The incident made Noyes "acutely aware of the dangers of an unguarded freedom among the sexes." In good time he was to formulate certain restrictions in this regard that made his own Perfectionist colony both successful and notorious. But now he gave up his attempt to make anything whole and good from the scattered and only too often wild groups of people who called themselves Perfectionists. He returned to Vermont, this time to small Putney where his father, mother, and brothers and sisters were living.

Noyes was a fine figure, tall and shining, with a disordered halo of russet hair. His speech, in contrast to the florid and bombastic style of the period, was simple and direct. While preaching in small near-by Westminster, he became acquainted with Miss Harriet Holton, granddaughter of the Honorable Mark Richards, a former lieutenant governor of Vermont and a wealthy man, who doted on her. Miss Holton was a maid who knew what she wanted— but for the time she seems to have made no impression on Noyes.

Noyes felt he had a tremendous message to impart to the world. He took off alone to lecture; and he wrote a letter that was published in a cultist periodical named *The Battle-Axe* and caused a sensation. In it he made a bitter attack on the sacred institution of marriage. Men and women, said he, had better change partners twenty times over than live together in any kind of strife and disagreement. And he said more, all to the same purpose.

The letter in the *Battle-Axe* brought John Noyes, until then merely another of the radical young men of New England, into prominence as scandalous as it was sudden. Letters poured in upon him, and the cultist paper he was just starting, the *Witness,* was sold out at once. Among the many letters was one containing $80 in cash, from Miss Harriet Holton of Westminster, Vermont, who intimated that the views of Noyes, as set forth in the *Battle-Axe,* were also her own.

Noyes presently proposed marriage—that is, a kind of marriage—to Miss Holton. He said he desired his partner in matrimony to "love all who love God, whether man or woman, and as freely as if she stood in no particular connection with me." This privilege, he specified, was to be reciprocal. He was not to monopolize his wife, nor she him. Harriet thought the proposal perfect, and on June 28, 1838, they were married in a legal, though un-churched, manner. The Honorable Mark Richards provided a handsome dowry, sufficient money "to support the young couple for six years."

The first thing the young couple purchased was a printing press, and they, together with Noyes's two sisters, started publication of a periodical, the *Perfectionist.* This paper was to promote the views which he called Bible Communism, and was sometimes known as Heavenly Association, though generally called Perfectionism. To prove the practicality of communal living, Noyes now organized the Putney Corporation of Perfectionists, parent of the later Oneida Community.

The group began to grow at once, although slowly. John Miller, a Quaker teacher from New Hampshire, showed up and asked to join. One day soon he married Harriet Noyes, the tall, red-haired and impulsive sister of the prophet. The more beautiful Charlotte, at the behest of brother John, married John L. Skinner, another convert. Now came a tramp printer, Harry Bowles, to be made welcome. The hand of fellowship in Perfection was offered to William Sherwood and wife. Within a few months four more male con-verts and one woman joined, but the young lady and one of the men were soon expelled because, apparently, they were more interested in the sexual freedom than in the other ideals of the colony. By March of 1843 the group numbered twenty-eight adults and nine children.

Meanwhile, Prophet Noyes had imparted what he always considered as his "greatest discovery" to his disciples. He called it male continence. (Physicians were to term it *coitus reservatus.*) He also inaugurated the practice he called complex marriage. Members might cohabit with whom they pleased, within the group, but the conceiving of children was expressly forbidden. Procreation was to be carried on by selected unions within the group.

In those days, as now, Putney was a small community. Unorthodoxy in any field could not long remain a secret. The Perfectionists were talked about, in plenty, and on June 10, 1847, Noyes was charged in a grand-jury indictment with adultery. Arrested, then released under heavy bond, Noyes, on advice of a brother-in-law who feared violence in Putney, fled the state.

Prophet Noyes was no man to bemoan the fate of his exile. Out in the wilds of the old Oneida Reservation, in Madison County, New York, one of his friends and admirers, Jonathan Burt, had attempted to found a Perfectionist colony along the lines of Putney. He had put up a sawmill and, gathering a few like-minded families around him in the clearing, was moving steadily toward financial bankruptcy at the time Noyes fled Vermont. Burt invited the Prophet to visit them. This Noyes did. In a short time, with his remarkable personality and abilities, he was able to put new heart into the colony, to fire the tired and discouraged members with new enthusiasm. He also gave Burt five hundred dollars in gold with which to meet an overdue payment on the colony land.

Burt suggested to him the possibility of bringing the Putney group to join the sawmill settlement in the wilderness. Noyes liked the idea and sent out the call. In February of 1848, the Prophet's wife and the Cragins, Mary and George, arrived. These pilgrims received a warm welcome from Noyes and Burt; but Mrs. Burt was as cool as the weather. She had not yet been converted to the idea of complex marriage. The arrivals, however, turned to with a will, and during the next few weeks wonders, as the prophet had promised, were indeed accomplished. Logging was started, the sawmill dam repaired. The making of furniture was begun. Mary Cragin opened a school in one corner of a cabin, having twelve youngsters for pupils.

Now came on the next contingent from Putney—the prophet's two sisters and their husbands, the prophet's brother George; the Hinds family, including young William who had driven the sleigh that took the prophet out of Putney and out of Vermont on his way to exile; and others.

On their heels came those who had scattered from Putney when the prophet had fled. They were still faithful. Louisa Tuttle came from her Connecticut home, and the Gould family from New York. Then, from Vermont, arrived Lemuel and Sarah Bradley, James L. and Catherine Baker, with daughter Mary; Henry Burnham and family; and the numerous Barrons and Joslyns. One should not get the idea that these were merely poor and disgruntled people, the sort who often joined any new church that seemed

to promise the security on this earth they had never known, or a respectable
and certain place in heaven, or both. These people were anything but ignorant
rustics or hillbillies hot for the millennium. For the most part they came
from substantial families, intelligent and progressive. A fair sample, perhaps,
was Albert Kinsley of Fletcher, Vermont.

Albert Kinsley was a deacon of the local Congregational church, a justice
of the peace, and sheriff of the town. He was an innovator, too, and had
introduced the first cooking stove into his region, and the first matches, at a
time when a majority of his neighbors considered stoves and matches to be
works of the Devil. In person he was of striking appearance, and had
steady, somber eyes filled "with a courageous certainty of vision." He was
also the perfect disciple. When he heard the call of Prophet Noyes from
Oneida Reservation he did not hesitate. He sold his farm and home, disposed
of all family possessions except certain cherished items, which he packed into
a covered wagon, and then set out with his wife and children. These were
four: the sons, Martin, fourteen, Myron, twelve, and pretty daughters Sarah,
nineteen, and Jane, seventeen.

The Kinsleys were ferried in their wagon across Lake Champlain. From
here they rolled to the east end of the Erie Canal and were boated along the
ditch to Durhamville, the port nearest Oneida and Perfection. From Durhamville they plodded through deep mud to the settlement in the clearing.

In this first year of what was called the Oneida Community of Perfectionists, the colony numbered fifty-one. The members were prodigious
workers, and the group rich with artisans—a stonemason, a part-time
architect, several carpenters, a maker of pails, a maker of lead pipe, a blacksmith, shoemaker, printer, several millwrights, and one who, almost incredibly in that day, called himself a landscape gardener. As for the women,
nearly all of them had been brought up on Vermont farms or in Vermont
villages, places where girls were trained in all of the common domestic
pursuits, and were also competent at the retting of flax, the carding of wool,
and both spinning and weaving. Most of them could make hats and baskets.
The industry of the entire group was such as to amaze even the hard-working
farm people of Madison County, New York.

The story of Oneida Community from its founding down to the present
day, when the heirs of the founders are operating at Niagara Falls one of the
most successful industrial enterprises in the United States, is one of the most
astonishing, as well as interesting, in our history. It has been told and retold
in many excellent books, and it is not within the province of the present
work. But something more must be said of the additional Yankees who
played parts in Oneida's successful industrial life.

Probably the most important of all, after Noyes, was a fellow Vermonter born, as was the prophet, in Brattleboro. He was Sewell Newhouse, a trapper who made his own traps, a man who had ranged the backlands of the Green Mountains and the Adirondacks and was much given to abstract contemplation. Newhouse, said one who knew him well, was as dignified as an Iroquois chief and had the measured tread of a stag. His lined face and smoldering eyes reminded some of a sullen eagle. He and his wife had been among the early converts at Oneida; and, as his contribution to the general welfare, it was his custom to pound out a dozen or so of his remarkably fine traps to be sold by the community.

In 1854, Oneida Community had financial troubles, due chiefly to the cost of its periodicals, which, whether paid for or not, were sent out to the non-believing world to bid it reform and come to Perfection. It was a time of great need to the community, and now Noyes went to Newhouse to suggest that he teach some of the younger men of the colony his secrets of tempering steel; that the colony go into the manufacture of fine traps in a large way. At first, Newhouse, who kept his methods as secret as any necromancer, demurred. For many years he had worked behind locked doors. Noyes, however, was a match for the iron will of the convert, and after a large amount "of communizing and the democratic power of inspiration" he prevailed on Newhouse to initiate a few young Perfectionists into his methods.

From that point on, Oneida Community was never again in need of cash. A brick factory was put up. Power was added. A virtual assembly line was inaugurated. The product was already known to trappers from coast to coast, in both Canada and the United States; and now orders began to flood the community office. One day there came an agent from the great Hudson's Bay Company who wanted to purchase the entire output of the new factory. The trap business grew so rapidly that outsiders had to be employed—first a dozen, then fifty men, then two hundred and fifty. For many years the community produced and sold almost 300,000 traps annually.

After the traps came manufacture of plated ware. It was started in the so-called branch community at Wallingford, Connecticut, where Farmer Henry Allen, a convert, had gathered several like-minded families on his place and was conducting a smaller Oneida Community, complete with complex marriage. The power-manufacture of tinned iron spoons grew slowly though steadily. Later, the community took over a large manufacturing property at Niagara Falls, installed modern machinery, and moved the Wallingford business there. This resulted in another migration out of New England, for many if not most of the Perfectionist families of Wallingford moved to the new factory. Pierrepont Noyes, one of the prophet's sons, grew up in the Oneida tableware business, and he is generally credited with making it into the big business it has been almost since the turn of the century. Community Plate, or Community Silver, is known the country over.

The two migrations of Perfectionists—one from Vermont, the other from Connecticut—and the scattered converts who also moved to Oneida from New England, probably did not involve more than four hundred persons. Yet, for quality, the exodus stood very high. A majority of the emigrants was unquestionably of well above average intelligence, and also people of some means in their neighborhoods. They were certainly as industrious and determined a folk as ever left the region. The children born of their complex marriage system, products of what today would be called eugenic marriages, appear to have stood, and to stand to this day, high in intelligence and health. The industry started by the Wallingford branch is a notable success in mid-twentieth century, and many of its stockholders and employees are sons and daughters, or grandchildren, of original Perfectionists. When one considers the material success of Oneida Community, as well as the useful and socially responsible lives of an overwhelming majority of its sons and daughters, one is forced to the conclusion that New England never lost better stock than it did through Perfectionist migrations.*

Unquestionably the most unsuccessful group of Yankee emigrants to the West was none other than the all but incredible Vegetarian Settlement Company. This forgotten and fantastic organization was thought up—"planned" is hardly the word—by Henry Stephen Clubb, a devout and fanatical disciple of a Yankee named Sylvester Graham. Graham, of course, was the reformer for whom graham flour, and bread, and crackers are named. He was a man never short of new ideas. He advocated bread made from unbolted wheat, never to be eaten until twelve hours after baking. He recommended fresh fruits, vegetables, open windows, good hard mattresses, loose clothing, cold shower baths, pure drinking water—or, for "medicine," the saline product from Saratoga Springs that was bottled as Congress Water—and cheerfulness at meals.

But the Vegetarian Settlement Company cannot be wholly laid at Graham's door, for he was four years in his grave when Disciple Clubb organized the group which was to establish in the very center of the United States a permanent home for vegetarians. Here the faithful would gather and set to growing their "favorite articles of food, such as different kinds of fruits and farinaceous productions."

The faithful would also and naturally, said Mr. Clubb, disseminate practical vegetarian information from their center and never cease to call

* See Robert Allerton Parker's fine book, *A Yankee Saint,* for a detailed account of Oneida Community and its men and women.

the public's attention to the subject of universal vegetarianism. He vowed it was a diet best adapted to the highest and noblest principles of human nature because "the use of the flesh of animals as food tends to the physical, moral and intellectual injury of mankind."

Members of the Settlement Company were obliged to sign a pledge in which they voluntarily "agreed to abstain from all intoxicating liquors as beverages, from tobacco in every form, and from the flesh of animals."

Clubb already had found the site for his dream city. It was, he said, "on the Neosho River between Latitude 38° and the boundary of the Osage Indian lands, and between 18° and 19° Longitude West from Washington." The spot so described was in southeastern Kansas.

Although vegetarianism was his great love, Mr. Clubb's was no one-track mind. His settlement was to be on what he called the Octagon Plan, a thing of eight equal sides and sheer beauty, which the originator said was the only sensible way to "commence a city."

The townships, sections, and quarter-sections of Kansas had been laid out, like lands elsewhere in the West, in quadrangles; and one may wonder at the remarks possibly made by Mr. Clubb's surveyors as they ran lines for four Octagon Villages each composed of "16 farms of 102 acres each; 16 triangular divisions of the Central Octagon, to be held in common, 13 acres to each; 4 corners, to be held in common, 36½ acres to each farm; 8 roads, 85 chains long, 10 square chains to the acre."

The Plan contemplated four such divisions and subdivisions which, in turn, would form Octagon City—16 square miles with a square in the very center of 584 acres on which was to be built, said Mr. Clubb with all the assurance in the world, an agricultural college and a model farm. One of the reasons for this elaborate and complicated arrangement, he explained, was that every settler would thus "live in a village, and at the same time be in the best possible situation on his farm—between pasture land in front and arable land in the rear of his dwelling."

If prospective settlers did not immediately grasp the significance of the Plan, then Mr. Clubb was ready to enlighten them. "The social habits of improvement occasioned by such proximity," he said, "must be evident, for in isolation, men become indifferent to the refinements of civilized society, and sometimes sink into barbarism. But living in proximity in this manner will cause emulation to excel in the arts of domestic & social life, and in the elevating influences of mental and moral cultivation." Moreover, said the original Mr. Clubb, with an eye to the possibility of the speculating nature being present in vegetarians, "the pecuniary advantages of this Plan arise from the fact that the foundation of the village always increases the value of the land all around."

The land in Octagon City was to sell at $1.25 an acre. Members of the Vegetarian Settlement Company were charged an entrance fee of $1, and 10 cents installment on each $5 share—and "a member is entitled to as many city lots as he takes shares in the Company."

It all sounds somewhat complicated now, and perhaps it sounded complicated in 1856, when Mr. and Mrs. William H. Colt, natives of Lyme, New Hampshire, and Mr. and Mrs. William Sommerville, of Lonsdale, Rhode Island, and assorted other vegetarians of New England and elsewhere, decided to join up. But they appear to have had implicit faith in Mr. Clubb, as well as in John McLaurin, noted water-cure physician, who was treasurer of the company. A recent bulletin from the Company had reported stock subscriptions to have passed $33,000, and the private capital of members, many of whom, it appeared, were already on the ground, amounted to well over $100,000. It seemed too, from reading the bulletin, that the immense and gorgeous Central Octagon Building was ready to welcome new members. Sawmills and gristmills were at work. . . . *Hurry, you Vegetarians. Hurry, lest you be too late.* . . . In March of 1856, according to the Bulletin, a party of eighteen settlers had just arrived. Mr. Clubb himself was in St. Louis, to return to the octagon paradise soon with a second party. . . . *Hasten, you eaters of carrots, you lovers of unbolted grain. The rich land awaits the seed. In autumn ye shall have the full-headed wheat.* . . . And on April 20 Vegetarian Waston Stewart was to take off from Lafayette, Indiana, with a third party of settlers.

So, in mid-April, from scattered New England points, vegetarian Yankees began the hegira from the meat-eating hell to the happy land of the Neosho River and Octagon City in far-off Kansas. Only one of them seems to have left a record. The aforementioned Mrs. William H. Colt, though obviously and understandingly distracted and numbed by her dreadful experience, managed coherence enough to set down a narrative. If her story was widely read in New England, surely it had the effect of keeping Yankees, if not at home, then at least out of the Neosho country.*

Mr. and Mrs. Colt arrived on the desolate scene on May 13, 1856. They strained their eyes to catch sight of the vast Central Octagon House. It turned out to be a modest log cabin, hardly a lean-to for the big old houses in Lyme, New Hampshire. No other structure of any sort was in view. There was no rollicking sawmill, cheerfully whining away at boards and timbers. There was no gristmill, thumping out unbolted grain. As far as the eye could reach, the prairie stretched on, bare, illimitable, and in some way sinister to people

---

* Even Mrs. Colt's title is discouraging: *Went to Kansas, Being a Thrilling Account of an Ill-Fated Expedition to that Fairy Land, and Its Sad Results.* It was published at Watertown, N.Y., in 1862.

used to hills and mountains. "The Company directors," wrote Mrs. Colt on her first day in Octagon City, "after receiving our money to build mills, have not fulfilled the trust reposed in them. In consequence, some families have left already."

Mrs. Colt does not report how many persons were in her own party, but one thing is clear: Four days after their arrival "the greater number of the company that arrived with us, and others that were here, left this morning for Kansas City. . . . It is saddening to think about." The Colts were of sterner stuff. They would remain. So they did—for a while. They worked like demons, plowing the sod, planting corn—that is, during lulls between the terrible storms and the hellish heat, which alternated with prairie fires, with clouds of flies and mosquitoes, with searing winds, with winds that froze the blood. And in spite of the healthful vegetarian diet, which did not include potatoes because they cost four dollars a bushel, there was much illness.

Mr. Clubb seems to have been bustling about. He would arrive at the settlement, read a sermon on the Sabbath, then away again, God only knew where. There was no direction, no management, and no new settlers. Weeds grew high in the corn. Reassured gophers, seeing no sign of an Octagon City, or even an Octagon village, began to return to their old holes. By September even the hardy Colts gave up, for there was great weariness in their hearts. The Capital, the Hub of proper eating and living—the dream that had fetched them across these grasshopper barrens—had been blown away somewhere beyond the muddy Neosho.

On the second day of September—it was still 1856, though to Mrs. Colt it seemed that years had passed—she, her husband, and children started the dreary trek to the non-vegetarian region of New England. One son died along the way. Mr. Colt himself died a few days later. For the Colts it had been indeed an ill fated expedition.

The Vegetarian Settlement Company, of course, had no perceptible influence in taking Yankees away from their native homes. I am prepared to believe it had the opposite effect, after Mrs. Colt's realistic first-hand account of the affair got into circulation. But the whole business was indicative of the idealism of the time, an idealism which, more often than not, could be termed nothing less than fanatical.

I do not believe that the Octagon City plan was merely a land-selling scheme of Mr. Clubb and his associates. The affair has all the stigmata of the mad, earnest, humorless idealism that flowered at Brook Farm, at New Harmony, at Ceresco, Wisconsin, and was to flower even again at Greeley, Colorado. One fanatical idea was not enough, but must be combined with something else. Vegetarianism must be practiced on farms having not four but eight equal sides. One feels certain, too, that the great dream of Mr. Clubb and his associates would have had the blessing of their inspiration and master, Sylvester Graham, a true fanatic to the last, who when on his death-bed refused medical attention and died, doubtless on a good hard mattress, with the windows of his room full wide, after "submitting to a tepid bath and a dose of Congress water," aged almost fifty-seven years.

As for Kansas, it was to be settled and settled quickly, settled in no small numbers by Yankees who ate pork with their beans, codfish with their pota-toes, and preferred—no matter what they said in church—fruit in the form of rugged apple cider. The Octagon City disaster was the last attempt of vegetarians to civilize Kansas.

CHAPTER IX

THE "FORESTERS" MOVE OUT

THE ELDER Timothy Dwight, president of Yale College, believed devoutly that New England could well do with a great deal of emigration. He was a keen observer, so far as surface matters went, in addition to being a hidebound man; and his travels up through the wilder parts of Connecticut and Massachusetts, and especially into frontier New Hampshire and Vermont, convinced him of the need of getting rid of a large number of Yankees. These were of that sort he termed the "forester class," meaning the pioneering type, and he bade them begone to the West.

Indeed, Dr. Dwight saw the very hand of Providence supporting his view, for God had just opened, "in the vast raw wilderness" of the old Northwest Territory, a "retreat sufficiently alluring to draw them from the land of their nativity." This, said he, was surely a mercy to the sober, industrious, and well disposed inhabitants of New England; for, if the forester class remained at home, then New England was certain to have many grievous troubles. These pioneers, said the pope of Yale College, were too talkative, too passionate, too prodigal, and too shiftless to acquire either property or character. He was speaking of the region out of which soon came James Fisk, who acquired more property than Dwight ever dreamed of, and Brigham Young, who had character in plenty. He was speaking of the class of Yankees out of which came H. A. W. Tabor, called Silver Dollar Tabor because of his immense fortune; and lonely, tragic Jehudi Ashmun, who gave his life to founding a home for freed slaves in Liberia.

Dr. Dwight was unquestionably a great teacher, but few men have been so mistaken in their judgment as he. He looked at his forester-class Yankees and pronounced them "unfit to live in a regular society." He said they were too impatient of the restraints of law and religion. He was right in this matter; for among the forebears of this same forester class were the Reverend Thomas Hooker, founder of Connecticut, and the Reverend Roger Williams,

108]

founder of Rhode Island, two men fit to talk with Dr. Dwight's own grand-father, the great and Reverend Jonathan Edwards.

Dwight also complained of the dram taking of the forester class.* Yet, these were the very people who attempted to saddle Ohio and Illinois with Prohibition, which they insisted on calling Temperance, and in Wisconsin gravely interfered with the happy customs of the hordes of German im-migrants in regard to beer. But one senses, on reading Dr. Dwight, that what really troubled him was that these pioneers were come-outers in everything, open to every new idea, whether religious, dietary, medical, or mechanical. Dr. Dwight was not so hospitable to new ideas and new things.

Perhaps the biggest piece of misjudgment by Dr. Dwight was to term these pioneers "shiftless and ignorant." They were neither; Dwight didn't know what he was talking about. Much closer to the frontier farmers of New England than Dwight were the makers of almanacs. These men knew the rural Yankees as no president of Yale could know them; and, being in the business of publishing almanacs that would sell, they made certain the pamphlets contained just the right ingredients. Hark to the Old Farmer while he instructs his clients on how to begin the month of November, in 1804: "Now let the noise of your flail awake your drowsy neighbors. Bank up your cellars. Now hire a good schoolmaster and send your children to school as much as possible." In the same month six years later the Old Farmer reverted to the same duties: "Send your children to school. Every boy should have a chance to prepare himself to do common town business." What Yankee parents did not want a son to be fit for office of first select-man of the town—whether the town was in New Hampshire or Wisconsin? Twenty-five years later the Old Farmer was still harping. "Secure your cellars from frost," said he, "Fasten loose clapboards and shingles. Secure a good schoolmaster."

Dwight did not reflect that once the Puritan, even a forester-class Puritan, had convinced himself one of Satan's purposes was to keep men from reading the Scriptures, then education was sure to follow. Nor did Dwight grant the foresters intelligence enough to figure that a man who could read and write would be less likely than an illiterate to be hornswoggled by some slick man of the city, even a city so godly as New Haven.

As for being shiftless, poor Dr. Dwight could hardly conceive of the work that went into the clearing of a single acre of Vermont or New Hamp-

---

* In an unnamed town in Vermont, said Dwight, "we lodged at an inn, where we found, what I never before saw in New England, a considerable number of men assembled on Satur-day evening, for the ordinary purposes of tavern-haunting. They continued their orgies until near two o'clock in the morning, scarcely permitting us to sleep at all. Early the next morning, these wretches assembled again for their Sunday morning dram, when we left the inn and went to a neighboring house as early as possible, disgusted."

shire land of its timber. By the time he was in his grave, his forester class were clearing western New York of its woods and working on into Ohio. A few had reached Illinois and Michigan. Moreover, in the very year of Dwight's death, which was 1817, a veritable graduate of Yale College was roaming the region beyond Michigan with the idea of founding a new state which should be named Petersylvania.

This man who first put Yale graduates into the forester class was the Reverend, though not Congregational, Samuel Peters, an Anglican, born in Hebron, Connecticut, and now, in 1817, a venerable relic of better than fourscore years. Peters had fled New England just before the outbreak of the Revolutionary War. In London he met another displaced Yankee, Captain Jonathan Carver, author of a remarkable volume of *Travels Through the Interior Parts of America* that was soon, in 1778, to be a fantastically popular book throughout the New United States.

Captain Carver had been around a good deal. During the period of the French and Indian War, he had ranged all over the regions later known as Michigan, Wisconsin, and Minnesota. He had made this exploration under orders of another Yankee, Major Robert Rogers of Methuen, Massachusetts, who hoped it would result in discovery of the Northwest Passage. Carver found no Passage, but he did receive a grant—so he said—of an immense area of land from his excellent friends, the Sioux Indians. The grant had been made, according to Carver, in a cave near the present site of St. Paul.

Captain Carver never formally claimed his grant, but died in poverty in England. Somewhat later, at the request of his American heirs, the Reverend Samuel Peters returned to his native land and set about claiming the vast empire. The business looked so good that he actually bought off the heirs and in 1806 appeared before a United States Senate committee to present his claim. While the Senate was ruminating—a good twenty-one years—the energetic Mr. Peters was far from idle. He bustled about despite his years and succeeded in organizing a group of speculators in a scheme to colonize Petersylvania. Now, in 1817, while waiting for Congress to make good the Carver claim, the kinetic Reverend Dr. Peters girded his loins for his first trip into Petersylvania. He was almost eighty-four years old.

At almost the same time, young Willard Keyes of Newfane, Vermont, decided to see what was on the other side of the Green Mountains. On June 2, 1817, he set forth on foot, doing a good thirty miles the first day. His only plan, he wrote in his daily journal, was to "travel into the Western parts of the United States." Although this was quite an order, young Keyes was just the man to handle it.

It is doubtful that Willard Keyes ever had heard of the Carver Grant when, a little west of Albany, he fell in with a "Gent. traveller Constant A.

Andrews by name" who was one of the party of Dr. Samuel Peters, heading, naturally, for Petersylvania. Andrews, who must have been somewhat of the forester class himself, looked young Keyes over and recognized a good man. He talked him into joining the party, partly by "executing a deed of 100 acres of land in Carver's Tract." Keyes found old Dr. Peters quite infirm, but quite as determined to devote the rest of his life, if need be, to securing the Carver Grant. So, westward they went.*

But Petersylvania was not to be. When the party arrived at Prairie du Chien, in what is now Wisconsin, the Army commander of the fort, Colonel Talbot Chambers, forbade it to go farther west. After waiting six months, old Peters, disappointed but not despairing, turned about and went back to New York. Eight years later the ruminating Congress got around to the matter of Petersylvania; it disallowed the Carver claim, and Dr. Peters promptly died, aged ninety-one.

But Willard Keyes, late of Vermont, stayed on in Prairie du Chien, teaching school, helping erect a sawmill, doing some logging. In the spring of 1819 he piloted a raft of lumber down the Black River and the Mississippi and never returned. He was the second Yankee schoolmaster to practice in what became Wisconsin, and perhaps the first Yankee logger there. In Willard Keyes were thus two of the outstanding Yankee qualities, or abilities, which made the New England forester class able to cope with the frontier and competent not only to tame it by clearing and plowing, but to civilize it with schools.†

Harriet Martineau, an English visitor to America, got deeper into New England life than did Dr. Dwight. "All young people in these villages," she wrote in 1836, "are more or less instructed. Schooling is considered a necessary of life." Miss Martineau saw New England at the time when Wisconsin was just beginning to rival Michigan and Illinois as the New Yankee heaven in the West.

Until the finish of the brief but singularly cruel Black Hawk War in 1832, Wisconsin received little attention except from trappers, fur traders, a number of missionaries, and a few speculators in doubtful land. The war brought the region into the news, and the 4,000 or more soldiers who had chased the wily Black Hawk dispersed to their homes in all parts of the nation to talk, as old soldiers will, of the scenes of their valor. Many of them were of

---

* Even at that early date, young Keyes noted that other Vermonters were ahead of him. In Rome, N.Y., where he attended a sitting of the superior court, "a large number of criminals indicted, among whom I recognized one familiar face, viz., Benjamin Flint a native of Newfane, Vt., for counterfeiting."

† Willard Keyes turned up a bit later as one of the founders of Quincy, Ill., where he died, full of honors, and left no small property.

the opinion that the new land in Wisconsin was superior to Michigan and Ohio. This was sufficient for the forester class of the Yankees: the advance guard moved in and squatted.

Southerners already were mining lead in the southwestern part of the territory. The federal government went ahead with its surveys. Land offices were opened at Green Bay and Mineral Point in 1834, at Milwaukee two years later. And, although the 1840's were to be the great decade of early settlement here, many a New England pioneer was ahead of the boom. One of the true breed was Caleb Blodgett, born in 1785 on a farm in Randolph, Vermont, a man who could well be, and was, characterized, with no exaggeration, as possessing restless energy and an indomitable will that nothing could daunt. Blodgett and his family helped to settle Alexander, New York, then moved on to Conneaut, Ohio, where they prospered by reason of a store, a hotel, and a mail contract. Fire destroyed everything, and so the Blodgetts moved on again, this time to what is now Wheaton, Illinois, where soldiers returning from the Black Hawk campaign told marvelous stories of the rich land to the north. So, in 1836, Caleb and Phoebe Blodgett, together with sons and various in-laws, moved into Wisconsin Territory, making claim to some 20,000 acres in and around what was soon to be Beloit.

The land was not yet officially open to settlement, which did not trouble Caleb Blodgett too much: any man who had "settled" in western New York, in Ohio, and in Illinois knew what to do. He hitched his oxen and plowed a furrow around a hundred acres. This was his "improvement," necessary to make his whole claim substantial and legal in the eyes of the government.

While Blodgett was plowing his long furrow, restless natives of Colebrook, New Hampshire, were yeasting. A number of Colebrookers already had gone "to live at the West," as almost any place the other side of Lake Champlain was known in New Hampshire, and now Colebrook's young physician, Horace White, called a meeting that resulted in formation of the New England Emigrating Company. The title was too-inclusive and misleading, in that the company's membership consisted of the heads of exactly sixteen families, all of Colebrook.

There seems to have been no reference in the company articles to God or Moses, as in many another Yankee colonizing society; and so, with only lay benediction, Robert Crane and Otis P. Bicknell, scouts, took off in a two-horse wagon. They were followed by Dr. White himself, who drove alone in a sleigh across New York, into Canada at Niagara, then around the north shore of Lake Erie to Detroit. The three men met at Ann Arbor, where Crane had an uncle from Colebrook already settled, and planned their scouting campaign. They appear to have had no specific region in mind, but were open to suggestions along the way and their own preferences as they should become manifest. They moved next to Calumet, Illinois, where another Colebrook man, Charles Messer, was working in a store. For one reason or another this part of the West did not appeal to the scouts. They moved still west, on foot and with packs on shoulders, to Rockford where, doubtless with no astonishment, they found still another Colebrook native, Harvey Bundy, clerking in a trading post operated by George Goodhue—a Yankee, sure enough, though unfortunately not a native of Colebrook.

Dr. White was no man to purchase land on hearsay. He began to range. His travels took him south as far as Quincy, west into Iowa as far as Dubuque, then north into Wisconsin and to the Turtle River where Caleb Blodgett had plowed his long primeval furrow. Dr. White liked the place. So did his two fellow scouts. In March of 1837 they paid Blodgett $2,500 for approximately one-third of his claim, amounting to between 6,000 and 7,000 acres. Crane and Bicknell fell to work putting up a big boarding house to welcome the main body of immigrants. Dr. White took off for Colebrook. There was no hitch; White found the company both solvent and in haste to settle "at the West."

Throughout the summer and autumn of 1837 members of the New England Emigrating Company continued to arrive at the Turtle River settlement, nor on arrival did they have to camp out. The boarding house was ready, and into it they moved until other shelter could be provided. They laid out the village streets, naming one "College" as an indication of things to come. Almost at once they opened a school called The Academy, in which was the root of Beloit College. And, of course, they soon erected a building for the Congregational Church society. Within a year the new village's population had reached two hundred, not all from Colebrook but one and all Yankees.*

For the next twenty years the thriving Yankee village was known variously as Blodgett's Settlement, New Albany, or simply as The Turtle. In 1857, so local tradition goes, one of the Yankees proposed an original name, and his attempt to pronounce the French words which he said meant "handsome ground" (was it *belle endroit?*) came out something like Beloit; and Beloit it was and is. A full decade before the village got its name, the Yankees had

---

* The Colebrook group and other Yankee settlers of 1837 included the Bicknells (Capt. John, Dr. George, and Otis P.), Horace Hobart, David J. Bundy, Heman Beach, Asahel Howe, Alfred Field, Cyrus Eames, Peter Field, Samuel G. Colley, Eleazer Crane, Leonard Hatch, five members of Capt. George Crosby's family, Lucius and George Fisher, J. Bradford Colley, Tyler Moore, Royal Wadsworth, Hiram Hill, Silas Tasker, John Reed, John P. Houston, James Carter, Horace Clark, Paul Field, Chauncy Tuttle, William Grimes, Charles Messer, William Jack, Harvey and William Bundy, and John Doolittle. In this same period the new settlement had a notable addition to its population when the redoubtable Ira Hersey, Illinois pioneer from Maine, was engaged by the emigrating company to help get the village settled.

their college going, one of the most influential founders being the Reverend Stephen Peet, a Vermont native of the forester class who had somehow been graduated, in 1823, from nowhere but Yale College.

The new city now had a name, a Congregational church, and a college; the pattern was complete except for one thing, and that was Industry. Beloit had from the first, of course, the varied shop and home industries which Yankees took with them wherever they went; and Charles Parker had taken hold of the Appleby twine binder, improved it, and with partner Stone manufactured the device by the thousand. But the pure strain of Yankee industry arrived direct from St. Johnsbury, Vermont, in the person of Charles Hosmer Morse, who became a partner of the Fairbanks scale family and founded, with them, Fairbanks, Morse & Company, long Beloit's greatest manufacturing house.

The original migration from Colebrook doubtless touched off an interest in this New Hampshire settlement in Wisconsin's Rock County. Yankees began moving into the county on the heels of the Colebrookers, settling both sides of the Rock River. Josiah Flint Willard and wife Mary hewed out a farm near the new village of Janesville. Both were Vermonters, both graduates of Oberlin College, and they presently produced a daughter, Frances, who was to have an influence not only in Wisconsin, but in pretty much all the United States. Samuel John Todd of Peterborough, New Hampshire, moved to the Beloit settlement; and the news of it also penetrated Connecticut, from which Abel Lewis and family of Groton set forth, to settle for a time, in Rock County and operate a sawmill. The Lewis family was the sort that inspired a visiting Frenchman to marvel at the casualness of the New England pioneer. Said M. Michel Chevalier: "Loading a wagon with a plow, a bed, a barrel of salt meat, the indispensable supply of tea and molasses, a Bible and a wife, and with his ax on his shoulder, the Yankee sets out for the West, without a servant, without an assistant, often without a companion, to build himself a log hut, six hundred miles from his father's roof, and clear a spot for a farm in the midst of the boundless forest. . . . He is incomparable as a pioneer, unequalled as a settler of the wilderness."

That statement hardly did justice to Abel Lewis and family. After a few years near Beloit, they heard about the gold strike in California. Without more ado they sold out, packed a double wagon, and set forth for the Pacific coast. They were only as far as the portage between the Fox and Wisconsin rivers when the wagon broke down. The oxen were unhitched and the family camped for the night. They liked the looks of the place; so, they upended the wagon body and lived beneath it until they could build a cabin, which

MANASSEH CUTLER
OF THE OHIO COMPANY OF ASSOCIATES

THE FIRST COVERED WAGON FOR THE WEST
LEAVING IPSWICH HAMLET, MASS., IN 1787

GOOD CHANCE FOR "RICH AND ENTERPRISING FARMERS"

Land for Sale,
TO ACTUAL SETTLERS.

On the first of September next, will be opened for Sale to Actual Settlers, that remarkably fine Tract of LAND, commonly called the CAZENOVIA TRACT, lying six miles on each side of the great Turnpike Road to Olean Point, on the Allegany River, within four miles of the Court-House of the County of Allegany, *State of New-York*, and within ten miles of the Susquehanna waters, whence Grain may be transported to Baltimore, at Two Shillings per Bushel.

The excellence of the soil, the purity and abundance of the water, and general healthfulness of the country;—the small expense of sending Produce to market, particularly of Butter and Cheese, to the South-Western States, by means of the Allegany River;—the facility of the communication afforded by the Turnpike, as the Mail Stage will shortly run from Angelica to New-York, through this Tract, in five days,—added to the ease with which Religious Institutions and Schools may be established—render this one of the most eligible and desirable Tracts of Land ever offered to rich and enterprising Farmers, as a Settlement either for themselves or their Children; especially on the following very liberal terms and low price at which the Subscriber will open the Land for sale:—

Per Acre, $ 4.50——for Lots fronting on the Turnpike, ⎱ 1-20th at the time of Sale, the residue in Ten
$ 3.50——for Lots in the Rear, ⎰ Yearly Payments, with Interest.

A Reduction of 25 Cents per Acre will be made if 1-10th of the Purchase Money is paid down, and the remainder in five equal annual Instalments; or, if 1-5th is paid down, and the residue in three equal annual Payments, an abatement of 50 Cents per Acre will be made.

Also, about 60,000 Acres,

In a state of rapid Settlement, for Sale upon nearly similar Terms. Apply to the Subscriber, BELVIDERE, near the Village of Angelica, Allegany County, New-York.

JUNE, 1819. *Philip Church.*

J. Bogert, Printer, Geneva, N. Y.

FIRST MORMON TEMPLE, KIRTLAND, OHIO

A VIEW OF EARLY SALT LAKE CITY

A BUSY CORNER IN OLD CHICAGO BEFORE THE GREAT FIRE OF 1871

"My Father's House"

THE MANSION HOUSE AT ONEIDA COMMUNITY, FOUNDED BY YANKEE NOYES

JOSIAH B. GRINNELL

THIS WAS SALUBRIA, IOWA, FREETHINKERS' COLONY

LUTHER C. TIBBETTS OF MAINE
GAVE CALIFORNIA ITS SEEDLESS ORANGE
MRS. LUTHER C. TIBBETTS
FOUNDED CALIFORNIA'S FIRST CULT

YANKEE ISAAC KALLOCH SHOT BY A WOULD-BE ASSASSIN

was made into a hotel. The place became Lewiston, and there the Lewises remained.

Kenosha (originally Southport) like Beloit was founded by a company, this one from New York, although Yankees were in its vanguard—among them George Kimball from New Hampshire, whose son Julius helped to found the first literary magazine in the territory, the *Garland of the West*, and Salmon Stebbins, another Granite Stater, from Plainfield, who preached the Wesleyan doctrine over much of the territory—"finding the Lord always present to help"—before settling in Kenosha. From Turner, Maine, came William Rolvin Bradford, to help found the Kenosha Fanning Mill Company, makers of a device of the greatest importance in pioneer agricultural country.

One early settler at Kenosha contained virtually all the many vagaries which migrating Yankees brought to Wisconsin. He was Warren Chase from New Hampshire, who was "absolutely honest and looked like the gorged gourmand of gloom." He was a teetotaler, a vegetarian, sometimes a Spiritualist, and always ready to try anything else. In Kenosha, he was a moving spirit in founding the Lyceum. In 1844 he was a leader in founding Ceresco (now Ripon), which he named for Ceres, and led there a company of Fourierist converts, to build the Long House, a splendid structure 32 by 208 feet, and also huge barns. Twenty families took up quarters there and for five years operated the community with great success, running sawmills, gristmills, and a fine school, and at last numbering almost two hundred. Then they gave it up, sold out, and found they each had made a small profit on the venture. Many of the members remained on the ground, to live in Ripon and to help found Ripon College. Both Ceresco and Ripon had a strong religious flavor, and alcohol was frowned upon.

It was different at Green Bay, a town that was lost to the Devil before Yankees in number could save it. A stray missionary arrived there in 1836, good Moses Ordway, a graduate of Middlebury College in Vermont, and he was staggered at what he found—a busy city of 4,000 inhabitants who "seemed to be agreed in only one thing and that was to blaspheme God and indulge in all kinds of wickedness." Almost every other night, said he, "they would have a bonfire and by the help of a whiskey band would have a dance so wicked and so wild that many of both sexes would lie drunken on the ground the next morning." The shocked Moses Ordway made an attempt which he must have felt was doomed beforehand. "My first discourse," he said, "was on the subject of the carnal mind being at emnity against God." But he gave it up, and went on to clear a farm at Waukesha, where he settled his family and for many years continued to preach the Presbyterian message.

Another Yankee, however, went to live in Green Bay and stayed there for much of his life—and Green Bay had reason to know it. He was Samuel Dexter Hastings, born in Leicester, Massachusetts, who arrived in 1845, to carry on as farmer, merchant, banker, and real estate operator. He hated but one thing—Rum. As head of the influential Order of Good Templars, he exerted a sinister power on the German brewers, harassing them at every turn, running for governor of Wisconsin on the Prohibition ticket, and at last going to all parts of the United States to speak for teetotalism.

Yet, of the two early settlements of Green Bay and Kenosha, the latter was much the more favored by Yankees. One of the earliest was Joseph V. Quarles of Ossipee, New Hampshire, who was thirty-seven years old on arrival at Kenosha in 1837. His letters to the old home are indicative of the efforts of enthusiastic settlers in the West to fetch more Yankees. Soon after coming to Kenosha, he wrote home to Isaac Thurston, postmaster at Ossipee and thus a good man to spread the news: "B. Canney talked of coming to Wisconsin. He with his boys would do well." Quarles offered to let Canney have land on which to plant and sow "as much as he can attend to." The low "prararas" were flat and wet and produced grass abundantly. They would grow grain and corn vastly better than New Hampshire lands. Quarles knew his New Hampshire rustics, and he put into his letters everything possible to seduce them to the West. "The game here is in plenty," he wrote, and spelled the name of one game bird exactly as it was and is commonly pronounced in New Hampshire, namely, "pattridge."

Quarles was proud of Kenosha village, too, which he reported to be a considerable place, with "4 stores and other buildings and one Lawyer not very smart—I think you would do well here." What he called the state of society in the village could hardly have been better: "a large portion of the inhabitants are N. Englanders—intelligent and polite— I believe it is a healthy climate." He still liked the place two years later, and was writing jubilantly to Ossipee to say that settlers were coming in from New York, Massachusetts, and Vermont, and also from the western part of New Hampshire. But none from the eastern portion of that state, even though, as Quarles declared, it was the last place God had made, when he got tired. Quarles thought that Samuel Sugget ought to migrate to Wisconsin, and said it was no great journey, anyway. Better run out and see the country. Why, the government was going to dredge a fine harbor at Kenosha, and when that was done "we should shortly be a right smart place."

A little later Quarles displayed a deep disgust for New Hampshire Yankees who would not migrate to Wisconsin. He thought he knew why they remained at home. "I can think of but one solution," said he, "the land in New Hampshire is so poor & hard that if a man should cease laboring long enough for an idea in relation to emigration to shoot across his brain, then his whole family would perish with hunger." Apparently, the home folks had asked Quarles if he were not going to return to Ossipee long enough to get a Yankee girl for wife. But he did no such thing; in 1843 he wrote that he had "fortunately succeeded in catching a prairie girl." She was Miss Caroline Bullen, daughter of a leading citizen of Kenosha.* Let the Yankee girls remain maids, if they would not emigrate. . . .

But if Ossipee citizens were slow to move to Kenosha this did not hold true elsewhere in New England. A census taken in 1843 showed Kenosha to contain 1,434 persons of American birth. Of these 141 were Vermonters, 77 came from Connecticut, 76 from Massachusetts, and 52 from Ohio. There were also 746 from upstate New York. Many and probably a majority of the Ohio and New York group were either native New Englanders or children of such.

Louis Harvey of East Haddam, Connecticut, got his start in Kenosha. He taught school there, then opened his own academy. He edited a Kenosha newspaper. In 1847 he moved to Waterloo and was horribly upset when a distillery was opened in the town. He bought it, tore it completely down, then used the material to erect a gristmill. In 1862 he was elected governor of the state, only to die from drowning a month after he took office, in the Tennessee River while on an errand of mercy, delivering supplies of food and comforts to Wisconsin soldiers in the Union army.

A Connecticut Yankee became famous in Wisconsin because of a distillery. He was Charles M. Goodsell, a man of strongly held opinions who supplemented them with action. He settled at Lake Geneva, Walworth County, and built a gristmill. A distillery near by sent him a grist of corn to be ground. He refused to touch it. The distillery demanded that its grist be "ground in turn," as the law plainly stated it should be. Goodsell was adamant. The distillers brought suit, and won. Goodsell appealed, and meanwhile went to Madison where, such was his influence among Yankee lawmakers, the legislature adopted an amendment to the statute reading, in effect: Nothing in this section shall be construed to compel owners or occupiers of mills to grind for distilling, or for sale, or merchant work.

In Walworth County, Goodsell had other Yankees all around him. Whitewater alone contained twenty families from New England—twelve from Vermont, three each from Massachusetts and Connecticut, one each from Rhode Island and New Hampshire. Whitewater's social origins, says its historian, were "largely New England." The county's first lawyer was Charles Minton Baker from Vermont. Walworth was the new home of Christopher

---

* A son of this marriage, named for his father, became a United States senator from Wisconsin and a federal judge.

Douglass, Connecticut-born, who settled at Big Foot Lake—now Lake Geneva—where his son built and operated the Big Foot Mills, both saw and grist. Walworth attracted Elbridge Gerry Ayer, late of Haverhill, Massachusetts, father of Edward Everett Ayer, who became both prominent and distinguished in Chicago. Charles L. Baker of Addison County, Vermont, heard the call: "On the 10th of September, 1838, with my family, consisting of wife, a daughter and two sons, with only such articles as were necessary for traveling, bid adieu to friends and the Green Mountains and started for the prairies of the West." In December the Bakers were settled at Lake Geneva, in a log house.

But Yankee pioneers did not long live in a log home. It seems to have been a matter of pride with them to get out of a cabin as quickly as possible and to live in a frame house. In Wisconsin, at least, most Yankee settlers simply put up a big board box and called it a house. Few appear to have troubled to erect a typical New England colonial-type house. Another Yankee characteristic was to build close to a road. Joseph Schafer, the Wisconsin historian, noted this. He thought it was because it "enabled them to keep in touch with the world." As for farming, he thought the German better than the Yankee, though he declared it was Yankee leadership that brought about the cooperative dairying in which Wisconsin was the leader.

It was a Yankee of Walworth County that Wisconsin sent to Congress in 1857, there to perform a great and lasting service for the nation at large. He was John Fox Potter, born in Augusta, Maine, in 1817, arrived in Wisconsin in 1838. A stanch Abolitionist, Potter was in no manner impressed by the fiery Southerners who infested and dominated Congress. At the close of a stormy debate, in which he had paid his respects to the South, he was challenged to a duel by Congressman Roger A. Pryor of Virginia. He accepted with promptitude and, as was the right of the challenged, chose the weapons. "Bowie knives," said he. Pryor was horrified, and declined. The incident was played up in the national press and had the effect of making dueling appear ridiculous, as it probably was. The affair is credited with killing the sophomoric custom, which from that point fell into obsolescence, and made Congressman Potter a celebrated national character.

Although a majority of the Yankee pioneers were of Timothy Dwight's unadulterated forester class, and preferred farm or small village to city, New Englanders were among the early notables in founding Wisconsin's largest cities. Byron Kilbourn of Connecticut stock owned one-third of the site of Milwaukee, which he called Kilbourntown, and was a promoter of high-pressure methods. He established a newspaper, the Milwaukee *Advertiser,* to boost his lots, operated a boat on the river, and was continuously active in canal and railroad operation and thus, naturally enough, in politics. Harrison Reed claimed to have opened the first general store in Milwaukee, having come from Littleton, Massachusetts, to do so. Later he edited the *Sentinel*. Among the early merchants were Levi Kellog and L. A. Wheeler, both from Vermont, H. H. West from Connecticut, Abner Kirby from Maine, and Franklin J. Blair from Massachusetts. George Greenleaf Houghton, from Guilford, Vermont, did very well in Milwaukee; and Daniel Wells of Waterville, Maine, operated from his Milwaukee office a vast business in lumber.

In 1836 Timothy Johnson and family from Middletown, Connecticut, staked out a claim of one thousand acres which became Watertown, Wisconsin. The Garlands from Maine helped found La Crosse. Prominent in early Racine was James R. Doolittle, son of Vermont natives, who became a governor of Wisconsin and a national figure in the Republican party. Peyton Randolph Morgan, from Maine, became a law partner of Judge Doolittle. Lucius Blake from Vermont and Rufus Kellog from Massachusetts were among Racine's early settlers. The Merricks of Exeter, New Hampshire, and the David Atwoods of Bedford, New Hampshire, were early on the scene at Madison, where William Francis Allen of Northboro, Massachusetts, came to teach at the University.

The Kellogs of Canaan, Connecticut, must have been one of the most notable family migrations to Wisconsin. Austin settled in Kenosha in 1835. A year later Thaddeus and family came, traveling with a two-horse team across Michigan. Young Amherst Willoughby Kellog never forgot the trip: "At Ypsilanti we had our first taste of venison. At Niles we stopped overnight in a big log tavern where the crowd was so great we could get for our family of five only one bed, in a room with others. . . . After passing Pike River, it grew dark and it seemed a long cold drive before we caught sight of the light in Uncle Austin's window and then the glad welcome and the comforting cheer of the blazing logs in his chimney place." Another Yankee family had at last come to Eden, or at least something like it. The new arrivals, however, went on to settle in Milwaukee; and within the year came more Kellogs from Connecticut—Uncle Chauncy, Uncle Seth, and their families, together with four grandparents of the Kellog and Howe lines. This group settled near Sylvania, Racine County, and was so numerous the place was known as Kellog's Corners. It was a custom of the Kellogs, all of them, after the supper dishes were done, to "gather for prayers." Each had his or her own Bible or Testament. They belonged, said a local historian, "to the large class of deeply religious and Puritanical New Englanders whose influence on Wisconsin history for many years was dominant and is still felt."

The influence was not felt at first, for the heaviest populated region in early days was the lead-mining section, around Mineral Point, and the miners were largely from the South. These people preferred a county form of government. The Yankees and Yorkers were used to a town government, and in 1841 their influence was sufficient to pass a law permitting popular vote in the matter. All except three counties voted for the modified town government, and seven years later the legislature established this form throughout the state.

From the first, the New England immigrants were active in politics. Of Wisconsin's governors the 1st, 3rd, 7th, 11th, 12th and 18th were born in New England.* Four more had Yankee parents. The president of the first constitutional convention was Don Alonzo Joshua Upham, born in Weathersfield, Vermont, a lawyer who had served as mayor of Milwaukee where, as early as 1850 and though greatly outnumbered by the Germans, there were sufficient Yankees to support a flourishing Sons of Pilgrims Society. Both the first and second constitutional conventions contained many New Englanders, Vermont leading with eighteen. Congressmen and senators were often transplanted Yankees; most of them were Republicans, after that party came into being, though one of the most notable was a thorough Democrat, William Freeman Vilas, a native of Chelsea, Vermont, who had gone west with his parents in 1851. Vilas was postmaster general and secretary of the interior under Cleveland, later a senator, and always an orator of great puissance. Among the Republicans was Timothy O. Howe, from Livermore, Maine, who came to practice law at Green Bay, be elected to the senate, and refuse appointment as minister to Great Britain. Long the state boss of the Republican party was the rough, irascible, kind-hearted, and often profane Elisha Keyes, born in Northfield, Vermont, who migrated with his parents to Wisconsin, where his father founded the village of Lake Mills and sent him to Beloit College. Fifteen years later Elisha was called the Bismarck of Wisconsin politics.

The first white woman to settle at Madison was Roseline Peck. She came to town in 1837, riding an Indian pony, at the instigation of her good friend, Governor Doty, and opened there an inn for the refreshment of politicians, surveyors, and catchpolls of all sorts. She was a native of Middletown, Vermont, and had married Eben Peck of Shoreham. Roseline gained a reputation for a "fiery, caustic wit," which seems likely, for Eben left home one day, without a word, and disappeared into the mists. When heard of next, many years later, he had acquired a farm, a wife, and five bouncing children in Texas, a safe distance from Baraboo, where Mrs. Peck had retired to live to

* Respectively Nelson Dewey, William A. Barstow, Louis P. Harvey, all of Connecticut; C. C. Washburn, Maine; William R. Taylor, Connecticut; and William H. Upham of Westminster, Massachusetts.

a great old age while her portrait hung in the Historical Society at Madison.*

Wisconsin may have attracted few Yankees from the Ossipee region of New Hampshire, and thus disappointed Ossipee's migrating Joseph Quarles, but the call was clear and strong in Vermont. Consider but one county (Orleans) of the Green Mountain state, and but one profession, that of the law: Lawyer Daniel F. Kimball married, and moved to Janesville, Wisconsin, in 1839, and was followed shortly by Attorney and Mrs. Charles H. Parker. Hoel H. Camp of Derby went in 1850 to Milwaukee, and five years later—such is the Law as a preparation for life—was president of the First National Bank. From Derby, too, went Henry Francis Prentiss and wife, who was Ruth Colby, in 1855, also to Milwaukee. Levi B. Vilas and family migrated to Madison, where he soon was mayor and a regent of the University. George Baldwin went to Chilton, in Calumet County, to practice. George P. Keeler settled in Waterloo, Jefferson County. Indeed, so many lawyers left Orleans County, Vermont, in the years right after 1840, one wonders if the Green Mountain bar was overstocked. Almost one-fourth of all the counsel named in the official list of Orleans County migrated to the West.

Were these attorneys good men in a "line case," dealing with the boundary lines of two or more farms? Were they competent to deal with claim jumpers? Or, did their talents run to the formal organizing of corporations? Not many of them had had a large criminal practice in Orleans County, for the rate of criminal offenses there was low. But a majority of them must have had experience in contests about land, for rural Vermonters were terrors in the matter of lines, as quick to fight for a dubious foot of rocky soil as though it had been frontage on Broadway, New York City.†

Perhaps the most influential member of the migrating Vermont bar was from Rutland County. He was Moses M. Strong, a stocky, strong-featured graduate of Dartmouth, who opened an office at Mineral Point in 1836, and a year later was appointed United States surveyor, a job which gave him a splendid opportunity to observe the lay of the land. He quickly acquired an immense fortune in timber, mineral, and other lands, and was active in the promotion of railroads. A relative, Marshall M. Strong, moved out of the Green Mountains in the same year, to become the first attorney in Racine County, and one of the founders of Racine College.

A notable influence on education in Wisconsin left Bradford, Vermont, in the family of J. W. D. Parker. He was young Warren Downes Parker,

* An amusing piece about Mrs. Peck by Collamer M. Abbott appears in the *Vermont Quarterly* for July, 1948.
† The New England stone fence was often the "line" between two farms; moving a stone fence was a task in itself. Doubtless this fact had a bearing on many line-fence lawsuits. The stone fence looms large in New England history and song and is the subject of many fine lines in *Yankee Boundaries,* the collected verse of Harry Elmore Hurd, of Plaistow, New Hampshire.

who taught school in his adopted state, then became head of the new state normal school at River Falls, and still later superintendent of education. Parker was held in the highest regard, and when he retired his many admirers presented him "with a handsome marble clock and a gold-headed cane." The great Henry Barnard, a Rhode Island Yankee, visited Wisconsin early in the interest of better education. At Madison and Milwaukee he spoke eloquently for free public schools, which the constitution of 1846 provided, much to the satisfaction of New England migrants. One of them, Joel Allen Barber, from Georgia, Vermont, founded Lancaster Academy; and others, like Josiah Pickard, Edward Searing, Lyman Draper, William Whitford, Jesse B. Thayer, and John Q. Emery, served in turn as state superintendent of schools.

Varied talents were coming west with the mobile Yankees. Marius and Sarah Wheeler left Thetford, Vermont, to set up a home in pioneer Johnstown Center, Wisconsin, where in 1850 a daughter named Ella was born. Ella loved to read Mrs. Holmes, Mrs. Southworth, and Ouida, and presently she was writing herself, first a book of poems dealing—characteristically for a Yankee girl—with Temperance. She continued to write, achieving a national reputation, or notoriety, with *Poems of Passion,* which did not deal with Temperance. She married a Mr. Wilcox but never stopped writing, and for forty years her verses and prose were "of great comfort to millions of weary or unhappy Americans."

Of a different talent was Frank Lloyd Wright, born in Richland Center of Yankee stock, his father being a Unitarian minister who also taught music; and Hamlin Garland, born in West Salem, the son of Richard and Isabelle Garland, immigrants from Maine.

Medicine was moving with the rest. Perhaps the first Yankee physician in Wisconsin was William Beaumont, born in Lebanon, Connecticut, in 1785, who studied under two Vermont physicians, then went with the Army to Green Bay and other Wisconsin outposts. Dr. Beaumont achieved permanent fame by his study of the digestive processes of the stomach, through a gastric fistula in the person of one Alexis St. Martin—a rewarding but most difficult subject. More typical of migrating physicians, probably, was James Heath of Vermont, who set up in Rock County and was the first permanent doctor in that part of the territory. Another was A. P. Cummings, who left his native Colebrook, New Hampshire, in 1850 to hang his shingle in Prairie du Sac. Cummings, said Dr. J. V. Stevens, who knew him well, "was typical of the locality from which he came . . . calm of demeanor and speech, seldom showing surprise or excitement under any circumstances." Until the very last, good Dr. Cummings continued to act as dentist too, if required, and he always used an ancient extractor called a turnkey. Just before setting this horrible instrument, he invariably spoke to his patient the words: "Now you hold still, and I won't hurt you a bit." Dr. Cummings considered hurt to be a comparative thing.

There were many early railroad builders in the New England contingent, far too many even to mention. S. S. Merrill from New Hampshire was general manager of the Milwaukee Road in primeval days; and John Catlin of Vermont, its president. William R. Sill and H. I. Bliss, both from Connecticut, were its chief engineer and assistant. One of their men, Charles I. Linsley, surveying in 1852 on the Whitewater-Madison line, liked the region and wrote many letters about it to the home folks in Middlebury, Vermont. The country around Whitewater was especially good, "quite hilly around here and more resembles N. England than the everlasting Prairie." He found many Vermonters scattered through the region and these, naturally, were "universally liked & considered the best population." He said they were the most hospitable of all, which seems a bit surprising, and said, "They have never taken a cent from us in pay for their hospitality." Madison was indeed a pretty town: "I. T. Marston and Mr. Vilas of Vermont have fine places here." But the region had one notable curse, in the eyes of young Linsley: Apples were very scarce, and cost fifty cents a dozen in Janesville. As for cheese, "they appear to be too lazy to make it." His immediate boss, also one of the founders of the Milwaukee Road, was Benjamin Hyde Edgerton, a native of Saybrook, where the Connecticut River empties into Long Island Sound.

Leading men of the Omaha System included D. A. Baldwin and H. H. Porter, both from Maine; John C. Spooner, Indiana-born of Yankee parents, and Edwin W. Woodman from Massachusetts. The Wisconsin Central was largely built under the direction of Gardiner Colby, his son Charles, and the Abbott family, all from New England. One Yankee railroad builder, E. H. Brodhead, a large-framed and self-willed man, was active in Wisconsin railroads for a long period, and a town was named for him. Daniel M. Kelley of Massachusetts is generally credited with building the Green Bay Line. A distant relative was Oliver Hudson Kelley, from Boston, who founded the order commonly called the Grange, which harassed the Green Bay Line and all other railroads, in Wisconsin and elsewhere, and tamed them in measure. Oliver Kelley himself organized many of the local granges in Wisconsin, though his farm in Minnesota was his home.

Then there were, as always, the Yankee logging operators and lumbermen. Several of them had stopped in Michigan before moving into Wisconsin; and many of the Wisconsin operators logged also across the St. Croix or the Mississippi in Minnesota. Here came the family of Dorrs who had migrated first to Michigan, and other Maine families, including the Washburns—among whom Cadwallader was sent to Congress and later elected governor of Wisconsin; and the Morrisons, DeLaittres, Lovejoys, Robinsons, Days, Prays, and Boveys; and the Farnhams and Robinsons and Ard Godfrey. Sawyer County in Wisconsin was named for the state's greatest lumberman of Yankee stock. This was Philetus Sawyer, a native of Whiting, Vermont, who in 1847 settled near Oshkosh, made a fortune, and went to Congress. Oshkosh became one of the typical sawdust cities of the migration. Here settled Daniel Libbey, from Whitefield, New Hampshire, who owned several mills and sent back to his native region for lumberjacks. Ferdinand Armstrong came from Bangor to erect mills at Beaver and Peshtigo, and went through the great forest fire of 1871, which took the lives of 1,152 settlers and lumberjacks but was never noticed because Chicago burned at the same time and occupied the newspapers.

Eau Claire was another bustling, brawling lumber city. One of its leading lumbermen was Orrin H. Ingram, from Southwick, Massachusetts, who also invented a piece of machinery, the gang edger, and later teamed with Frederick Weyerhaeuser and his syndicate of sawmills and timber holdings. Another Eau Claire Yankee who joined the same group was James T. Barber, native of Ashfield, Massachusetts; his timber stands included yellow pine in Idaho, where the town of Barber is named for him. In the early 1900's, there were natives of Maine working in the Barber mill in Idaho who had also handled lumber in Maine, Michigan, Wisconsin, Minnesota, and Louisiana.

Prominent in the press of Wisconsin was a Massachusetts man, Albert G. Ellis. Newspaper editors Daniel W. Ballou and Sterling P. Rounds came from Vermont; Charles S. Benton, from Maine; and Davis Atwood, from New Hampshire. Of a slightly later period was Ellis B. Usher, born in Buxton, Maine, who migrated with his parents in 1855. For many years he was editor of a most successful paper in La Crosse.

There were builders of towns like Nathan Myrick, born in Old Newbury, Massachusetts, who laid out the first townsite and erected the first sawmill in Crawford County. The towns of Onalaska, Farmington, and Hamilton, says an early record, had many pioneer families from New England, among them the Giles, Pettengills, Bradburys, Emerys, Chases, Couches, Baileys, Lewises and, of course, several named Adams. Aurin Z. Littlefield, who left Skowhegan, Maine, about 1832 to set up as a storekeeper in Sheboygan Falls, may not have been the founder of that handsome village, but he was one of the first to publicize it in New England. In letters to the *Clarion* in his old home town, Littlefield said that farming in Wisconsin could be made profitable with less than half the labor necessary in Maine; that Wisconsin had the healthier climate; and that, so far as the journey was concerned, a man could make it "in a comfortable conveyance for about $20." That seems very cheap, even for the period. Perhaps Littlefield was optimistic.

The influence on migration of these letter-writing Yankees can hardly be gauged, but they must have had an effect. At a later period than Littlefield were Warner Davis and family, who came from insignificant Brownington, Vermont, to settle in West Salem, Wisconsin. Both Davis and his wife Persis liked to write home, with the news that counted. Davis reported the church in West Salem to number sixty members. There was an "interesting Sabbath school." He did miss Vermont apples, but he had no idea of returning. "This is my *home,*" he wrote. "I should hate to go back to old Brownington and go to farming." He could raise more on his seventy-five Wisconsin acres under cultivation than "on any two farms in Brownington."

George Gale of Burlington, Vermont, left his mark on Wisconsin in the town of Galesville, which he founded after editing the *Western Star* at Elkhorn for a time. One of the first settlers in Dane County was Ebenezer Brigham, from Massachusetts—a man careful of his substance, said a caller to whom he served "a nice, frugal Yankee dinner." To be frugal was part of their tradition. To be cautious was another. The New Englanders who came to Wisconsin, said a local observer, were generally shrewd judges of land. He cited the plat entries of the town of Whitewater, which "show with what determination the Yankee pioneers shunned the swails, the thin land, and the rough land of that town." They did much the same in Sparta, where half of the first settlers were from New England, among them Emerys from Maine and families named Mather, Newton, Blake, and Thayer from Vermont and Massachusetts. Oddly enough, Yankees were a small minority in the town named Plymouth; but in Brookfield they were the second largest group, mustering large families named Parker, Story, Spears, Hatch, and Adams. In the town of Mount Pleasant, the settlement of Mygatt's Corners was almost solid New England. Almost at once "a library, and temperance and literary societies were organized." The first decade of Primrose was dominated by several Chandler families from Maine, but by 1860 they all had been "swallowed up in the Norwegian influx." Yankee population was heavy in early Pulaski, there being ten Vermont families, seven from Rhode Island, five from Massachusetts including many Snows, and three from Connecticut. They had their own parson, too, the Reverend Alfred A. Overton of Connecticut.

Here and there was an immigrant who was identified with no specific town but belonged, rather, to the entire region. One such was Martin Rich of Vermont, a builder of homemade dams. He was imported to erect a dam at Winnebago marsh, which then became Lake Horicon. Another was John

Starkweather, born in Putney, Vermont, in 1816, who went to Wisconsin before he could vote and there spent the next forty-two years building bridges, in more towns and across more creeks and rivers than he could recall. For a time, too, he carried the mails, and once made a notable trip in bad weather, by taking the mail on foot from Milwaukee to Aztalan in four and a half days.* John Starkweather the bridge builder may well have been one of the most useful migrants in Wisconsin.

A Vermont surveyor who turned into something else and had an immense influence on future Wisconsin was Milo Jones, a native of Richmond, who went west in 1835, set up as a dairyman at Fort Atkinson, and became the first cheese maker in the state that now leads the nation in that business. The first labor agitator in the state was a Yankee, Newell Daniels from Massachusetts, who organized a lodge of the Knights of St. Crispin (shoemakers) in Milwaukee.

If Timothy Dwight of Yale could have observed Wisconsin late in the nineteenth century he would have been appalled at his errors of judgment of the group of Yankees he designated as the forester class. They had pioneered in every part of Wisconsin and had linked their names with every important industry but one. "Though few in numbers," wrote Historian Ellis Usher, in 1899, "the New England men have been a potent factor in shaping this commonwealth, and however the foreign blood may predominate, theirs is the pattern that has been set and must be followed." Usher declared it was a wonder that a population so overwhelmingly German and Scandinavian should be so distinctly American in its institutions of government, in its educational impulse, and in its progress in all lines of endeavor. But he knew the reason. "Wisconsin institutions," cried he, "have been dominated by Americans of the Puritan seed from the beginning."

But the Puritan seed, good as it doubtless was for Wisconsin, could not impose all its flowering on that commonwealth. The Yankees tried hard enough to saddle the new state with their idea of Temperance, but the Germans were too many and too determined. Historian Usher remarked that the Yankees had linked their names with every important industry but one— *"which was brewing,"* he noted in italics. It was in the matter of brewing and alcohol in general that the Yankee met his match, and more. The defeat made him, in time, a more tolerant man. So, if much of the Yankee influence was good for Wisconsin, the influence of the German and Scandinavian influx was good for the Yankee.

The crusade against Rum, which the Yankee commonly set down with a capital letter, began as soon as he arrived. Typical was the town of New

* See John O'Brien, "Vermont Fathers in Wisconsin," in *Vermont Quarterly,* July, 1948.

Berlin, where in 1840 the New England settlers, led by Rufus Cheney of the Freewill Baptists, noted that a Brother L. had been at the dram cup. A committee forthwith called upon Brother L., but he gave them the back of his hand. "He denies having drinked to hurt him," the horrified committee reported, "and seems to think he shall drink as he pleases." The pressure, however, which could have been and probably was exerted on Brother L., in the economic as well as the social field, presently brought him to the pump. He promised to cease his dram taking, whereupon the church "voted to withdraw the labor against him."

It wasn't to be as simple as that all over the state—not with Germans, and then Scandinavians, arriving by the thousand every month. The foreigners put up their breweries as automatically as they put up their churches and started their singing societies. They opened their saloons and beer gardens. Meanwhile they worked just as hard as the Yankees or other native Americans, and often harder. Indeed, no better stock ever came to America to live. But they were to be harassed by every method the Yankees could devise. The most effective, it became apparent, was one founded, characteristically, on a passage in the Old Testament, Exodus 21:28–30: "If an ox gore a man or woman, that they die: then the ox shall be surely stoned, and his flesh shall not be eaten; but the owner of the ox shall be quit. But if the ox were wont to push with his horn in time past, and it hath been testified to his owner, and he hath not kept him in, but that he hath killed a man or a woman; the ox shall be stoned, and his owner shall be put to death." But there was one way by which the owner, scoundrel that he was, could save his life. "If there be laid on him a sum of money, then he shall give for the ransom of his life whatsoever is laid upon him."

Taking this for a text, some forgotten frontier Yankee parson built up what became celebrated as "The Ox Discourse," and it was heard in every pioneer Bethel and village church in Wisconsin where English was the pulpit language. The Ox Discourse was cited as God's own word, his own directions for driving the Demon out of Wisconsin, and in 1849, in spite of vehement protests of German leaders, Wisconsin passed a law providing that every vender of liquor should furnish bond of $1,000 on which he could be sued for damages, either to the community or to an individual, resulting from alleged sale of his liquor.

It seemed at the time like a complete victory over the hosts of darkness; but it was not to last. The law was subsequently repealed, and a greatly modified act took its place. The great breweries of Milwaukee, Madison, and La Crosse, and lesser breweries by the score, were then secure until darkened by national prohibition. But the Yankees' so-called Temperance crusade, by which was meant total abstinence, hardly added to Yankee popularity. The opinion of the average foreign-born citizen in regard to New Englanders was anything but flattering. The Yankee preaches total abstinence, said the German, and drinks his own whisky behind the door.* He is both an enemy of personal liberty and a hypocrite.

Abolition presently took the place of Temperance as the Yankee's first avocation, much to the relief of the foreign-born, and he read the inflaming *American Freeman,* edited at Racine by Sherman Booth, who had migrated from Connecticut. Here in Abolition was something that made sense to the German; and the Germans in Wisconsin, as well as elsewhere in the North, fought and died for the cause. Perhaps the spirit of comrades in arms helped to heal the breach caused by Temperance. In any case, the foreign-born learned in time to appreciate the good qualities of the Yankee. The German saw that the Yankee was enterprising and energetic in business and industry; he created business and gave employment. In fact, said George William Bruce, a Wisconsin native of Yankee and German parentage, "The German would rather work for a Yankee boss than one of his own countrymen. The latter was close-fisted, the Yankee less exacting and more liberal in his dealings with his employe."

How many New Englanders took up permanent homes in Wisconsin is beyond knowing. Joseph Schafer, Wisconsin native who wrote much on the subject, said that in 1850, when the entire population was approximately 305,000, there were "103,000 northeasterners living in the state." He assumed that a slight majority of these came from western New York, but recalled that that region had been settled largely from New England. The same was true of Ohio, from which, by 1850, some 11,000 natives had come to settle in Wisconsin. Many and probably a great majority of these people were sons and daughters of Yankee pioneers on the Western Reserve. It is perhaps safe to assume that at mid-century or thereabout at least two-thirds of the native-born Americans in Wisconsin were Yankees, or born of Yankee parents.

In all the thousands of settlers in Wisconsin, early or late, probably only Luther Parker was the ex-president of a foreign state. This was the fantastic and quite real but now forgotten Republic of Indian Stream, which existed for three years after 1832 in a long disputed region that is now a part of extreme northern New Hampshire. Right after the Revolutionary War, both Canada and the United States claimed the region, but neither did anything

---

* The German could have added that the Yankee often compounded his hypocrisy by taking his dram in the form of any one of a hundred different patent medicines, almost all of which contained from three to ten times as much alcohol as beer.

about it. Squatters from both countries moved in, and there they lived and logged and hunted and fished, undisturbed, for the next forty years, when the State of New Hampshire suddenly discovered and claimed them for its own. This naturally stirred up Canadian interest and claims. As for the stout and far from ignorant residents along wild and beautiful Indian Stream, they wanted neither. So, on July 8, 1832, Luther Parker, a born leader, together with assorted Parkers, Blanchards, Tirells, and others, formally organized the Republic of Indian Stream, adopted a written and reasonable constitution, elected a council and president, set up an assembly and courts, and even authorized a coinage of Indian Stream money.

The Republic's three years of life was a period of alternate serenity and alarums. Catchpolls from Canada and New Hampshire sporadically invaded its sovereignty. There were several clashes with tax collectors and sheriffs' deputies, and at last in 1835 New Hampshire sent its militia, which disbanded the Republic and commanded President Parker and all other officials to cease and desist.

Luther Parker collected his wife, son Charles, and daughters Persis Euseba, Ellen Augusta, and Amanda Marinda, put them into a covered wagon, and on the 16th of April, 1836, drove out of the late Republic, and so to Whitehall, New York, where he sent his family ahead by canal and steamboat to Pleasant Prairie, Wisconsin. He himself stayed with the wagon, arriving three months later, to move his family into Muskego township, and become the first settlers there.

Mr. Parker traveled lightly for an ex-president, but he had his library with him, containing both Blackstone and Cowan's *Treatise,* and he was presently the Muskego justice of the peace. A schoolhouse was erected at once, heated by a little barrel-shaped stove he had brought from the Republic. And when Muskego got around to sending a man to the Wisconsin legislature, it was Luther Parker, and no community could have had a better informed or more alert representative.

Son Charles had something of the father in him. The father had settled in the most remote and by far the wildest section of New Hampshire, two hundred miles beyond the farthest reach Timothy Dwight's travels had taken him. Now the son, after schooling, moved to wild and remote St. Croix County, which was about as far as he could go and still remain in Wisconsin. Charles Parker was twice lieutenant governor of the state, and long a regent of the University. He lived to the age of ninety-eight, dying in 1925, the last living witness to the Republic of Indian Stream.

Just before World War I, I spent more than a year along Indian Stream, scaling timber in company with more Parkers than you would readily believe.

In more recent years, I passed through Muskego and much of St. Croix County, Wisconsin. For reasons I do not pretend to understand, the much-longer settled region is still the wilder. Indeed, there is no aspect at all of wildness in or around Muskego; and St. Croix County has the city of Hudson, and many a goodly town. But the Indian Stream Republic, now Pittsburg, New Hampshire, has a population of less than 600, mainly dependent on logging and the guiding and victualing of city-bred sportsmen. The loon cries on its lakes, in season. Lynx patrol its streams. No more savage, nor primeval-looking, nor lonely country remains in New England. It was immune to the railroads, which never touched it. Even the gasoline age has failed to change it much. As for the Yankee Exodus, so far as I have been able to learn, only Luther Parker heard the call of the West, and so it was Wisconsin that had the honor and the good fortune to receive as a covered-wagon settler, the late head of an independent republic. He was a superb settler, too. I wonder what the Reverend Timothy Dwight would have made of Luther Parker.

CHAPTER X

PILGRIMS IN IOWA

IOWA WAS A NUMBER of things before it got a name of its own. In 1805 it was made a part of the territory of Louisiana; three years later it was in Illinois Territory. From 1812 to 1821 it was declared to be a part of Missouri. In subsequent years it appeared as a part, first, of Michigan, then of Wisconsin, and in 1838 it was set aside as a territory by itself. It became a state in 1846. James Wilson Grimes, resident of Burlington, liked to say that though he had lived in three different territories, under three distinct territorial governments, he had continued to live in the same town.

The name of the town Grimes lived in was probably the first example of Yankee influence in Iowa. The promoters of the new townsite, in 1834, were so anxious to peddle their lots that they permitted one John Gray to name the place on condition that he buy a lot. He did so, and named the future city Burlington for his native town in Vermont.

Otherwise, however, New England influences were remarkably, and often scandalously absent in early Iowa. For instance, there was Dubuque, settled in 1831 by miners who swarmed across the Mississippi from Galena, Illinois. A more irreligious community, said a visitor, could hardly have been conceived of: A gentlemen of that town, anxious to procure a Bible, searched the town in vain and was obliged to return to Galena to obtain one. That he got his Bible, even in Galena, was due to the fact that the Reverend Aratus Kent, "the well known and revered frontier missionary from Connecticut," was in residence there.

Dubuque, in short, was something of a loose and riotous place. In 1834, when it took its present name, it contained some 500 people, most of them from Kentucky, Tennessee, and North Carolina. Groups of Regulators and Vigilantes were organized and tried to take the place of formal law. At least five lynchings marred Dubuque's early years. A correspondent for the New York *Journal* discovered, apparently to his horror, that "the principal amusement of the people seems to be the playing of cards, Sundays and all." Another visitor found that "vice of almost every kind" was practiced openly, leaving one to wonder which vice had been overlooked in such a lively village.

The first wave of genuine settlers poured into Iowa in 1836. They numbered some 10,000, and their influx was termed a "tide of immigration." When the territory was two years old, in 1840, the population was estimated at 43,000. These people were in large part farmers who had entered by ferryboat from the east side of the Mississippi. A majority were natives of Kentucky, Virginia, and Tennessee, and most of the others were from southern Indiana, southern Ohio, and Pennsylvania. In the first territorial legislature, always a good example of the predominating nativity in new regions, only five of the thirty-eight delegates were from New England, while twenty came from the South. The first territorial governor was Robert Lucas, of Virginia. The first territorial delegate to Congress was a Virginian, and so was the first federal judge. The first United States marshal was a native of Kentucky.

Among the settlements other than Burlington and Dubuque, in 1840, were the towns of Keokuk, Montrose, Fort Madison, Bloomington (now Muscatine), Iowa City, and Davenport. Yankees appear to have had less than a modest part in their founding.

Worse, much worse, was that such early influence in Iowa as did stem from Yankee sources was deplorable. It came from that old Yankee rebel Abner Kneeland, long-time editor of the *Investigator,* a periodical published in Boston and usually described as "profane, impious and scandalous." When he moved to Iowa in 1839, with the plan of establishing a town by the improbable name of Salubria on the Des Moines River, Kneeland was one of the best known, or at least most notorious characters in the United States. Born in Gardner, Massachusetts, in 1774, he devised a new method of phonetic spelling, published a spelling book, preached in Baptist churches in Vermont and New Hampshire, turned Universalist and edited that denomination's magazine. His views, however, became too radical for even the liberal Universalists, and so he resigned and went to Boston, there to found and lead the Society of Free Enquirers. In 1831 he started the Boston *Investigator,* the first rationalist journal in the country. A year later he published a pamphlet, quaintly entitled *The Fruits of Philosophy; or, The Private Companion of Young Married People.*

The Fruits of Philosophy was really a treatise on the prevention of conception, the first such in the United States. It made an immediate explosion. For the next five years Kneeland was in and out of jail, but never out of the public eye. After three court trials, which stirred most good Christians to the very depths of abuse, Kneeland was thoroughly convicted. He spent sixty days in jail, and emerged with the plan of going to Iowa.

Acting as Kneeland's agent, Tyler Parsons went ahead to find the site. On June 7, 1839, he was writing to Kneeland, "This wonderful country is destined to outvie everything which can even be imagined in New England." Kneeland and "a few kindred souls" promptly took off from Boston and were "soon establishing their homes in Van Buren County."* It is doubtful that any colonization scheme could have survived the name Kneeland had selected for his Utopia. In any case, Salubria, some two miles from the conventional settlement of Farmington, didn't; and Abner Kneeland, now crowned with white hair but straight and broad-shouldered, went to teaching school and was elected to the Territorial Council. His influence was judged to be the reason that the council dispensed with chaplain and prayer; and one of the Congregational missionaries then at work in Iowa wrote that "Infidelity is presenting a bold front under the leadership of Abner Kneeland."

Kneeland died in what he still stoutly called Salubria, aged seventy-one, in 1844, loved by all those who knew him well, and loathed by most others.† In that year, too, missionaries from New England were making a concerted effort to bring Yankee civilization to the flat lands beyond the Mississippi. These earnest men were to be sorely tried, too; for Congregationalism, as one of its historians remarked, "did not find congenial soil in early Iowa."

The great and concentrated effort was made in 1843–1844 by the Iowa Band—eleven strong, all but one native Yankees, and all classmates at Andover Theological Seminary in Massachusetts—dedicated to founding Congregational churches and schools in the territory. Spadework had been carried on by other Congregational missionaries for a decade, notably by five men called the Patriarchs: Asa Turner and Oliver Emerson of Massachusetts; John C. Holbrook of Vermont; Julius A. Reed and Reuben Gaylord of Connecticut. In ten years their labors had resulted in a total Congregational membership of 300, distributed over fourteen tiny churches. A majority of members were New England natives, and thus the location of the fourteen pioneer societies is of interest in showing where Yankees had settled before 1843. The largest church was in Denmark—of which more presently—with one hundred members. The other societies were in Danville, Fairfield, Lyons, Davenport, Andrew, Bentonport, Brighton, Farmington (near Salubria), Clay, Crawfordsville, De Witt, Mount Pleasant, and Washington.

* Among the kindred souls were Capt. John Kendall, Silas Smith, B. F. Tower, O. Tower, Samuel T. Twombly, Elisha Cutler, and a Mrs. Pratt. "All in the settlement were great readers."

† In *The Pilgrims of Iowa* (1911), Truman O. Douglass reports with no little satisfaction that a child born in Salubria and named Voltaire Paine grew up to be a Congregational deacon; and that one of Kneeland's own daughters joined the church, and that her daughter "was a beautiful little Christian Endeavorer." Thus were the mists of rationalism in Iowa blown away.

Denmark, undoubtedly the first thoroughly Yankee settlement west of the Mississippi, had its inception in a lecture given in New Ipswich, New Hampshire, in 1832, by good Asa Turner, who had just returned to New England from one of his many missionary tours at the West. He stressed the fine and non-stony soils of the prairies and remarked how important it was that this new region be settled by "intelligent and Christian people." He must have been eloquent, too, for after considerable discussion, during which the glorious picture he had held briefly before them did not fade, four New Hampshire families left their homes and, in 1836, for $200, purchased a squatter's claim in what is now Lee County, Iowa. The four families, numbering thirty people, took over their claim, which they soon designated as Big Haystack, by reason of a community pile of hay used by the cattle of all the settlers. The heads of the first families of Haystack, later Denmark, were William Brown, Lewis Epps, Timothy Fox, and Curtiss Shedd.

This invasion of Yankees was doleful news to the sole and original settler in the neighborhood, John O. Smith from South Carolina, and he said plainly he was much discouraged when the New England crew moved in. Guessed he would sell out and move. But he didn't, and after a social call on the new settlers, during which he ate what he swore was his first piece of mince pie, he declared he was going to stay right where he was. The Yankees, said he, were in no manner so bad as they had been painted, which was high praise from John O. Smith from South Carolina.

Although much of the rest of Lee County was settled by families from the South, Denmark grew steadily if slowly. The Congregational church, begun with 32 members, had 130 members in 1846, and later rose to 250. But Iowa was not to be Congregationalized. The young men of the Iowa Band, work as they would, could not compete with the exhorters for Methodism who had been trained by Peter Cartwright—known rightly as "The Primate of All Prairiedom." Elder Cartwright, a robust hillbilly who had preached hell-fire and damnation in the Kentucky backwoods, and then in Illinois, knew the kind of religion suited to the frontier. He chose young men who had not been spoiled by schooling, drilled them in full-gospel style, then sent them out into the newer lands, where they did not disappoint him. He liked to say that his illiterate Methodist preachers "set the American West on fire while the Congregationalists were lighting their matches." By 1860 there were but 71 such churches in Iowa, while the Methodists could count 344; and both the Baptists and the Presbyterians outnumbered the True Yankee church.

But the Yankees of Denmark were more successful in their efforts for education. In 1837, within a year of settlement, Denmark had a school, taught by Miss Eliza Houston of Lyndeborough, New Hampshire, which was attended by the children not only of the Congregationalists but also of the Baptists and Methodists in the neighborhood. In 1843 the Denmark Yankees laid plans for an academy, which was opened in 1845 with the Reverend Albert A. Sturgis, graduate of Yale Divinity School in charge. Later came teachers from Yankee Oberlin in Ohio, others from Amherst in Massachusetts. The school flourished, and by the end of the Civil War had almost 300 pupils, a large majority of them from outside the village. Many Denmark graduates became public- or private-school teachers, and many more became prominent in business and professions in the state.

Denmark Academy, the village of Denmark, and the Reverend Asa Turner, the leader of both, were quite naturally against slavery, against Rum, against "desecration" of the Sabbath; and they had no small effect in making Iowa, at an early date, safe from all three. Mr. Turner was quite as competent a politician as he was preacher, and he is generally credited to have had considerable influence in the election of James W. Grimes, candidate of the antislavery party, as governor of Iowa. But the "Moral Hero" of Abolition in Iowa was another Yankee, Samuel L. Howe, a Vermonter born in 1808, who had taught school in Ohio and wrote and published *The Philotaxian Grammar,* reprinted many times and much used in Ohio and Illinois, and who in 1841 settled in Mount Pleasant, Iowa, and there started Howe's High School and Female Academy. As early as 1849 he began agitating for Abolition. He bought a small, ineffectual newspaper, named it the *Iowa True Democrat,* and made it into an influential weekly in support of Free Soil. This venture cost him dear, for he had to withstand abuse of all kinds, threats, rotten-egging and other violence; but he stood fast and made his paper the Free Soil champion of Iowa. Typically, Abolition was not enough for Howe, and so his paper came out for Temperance, woman suffrage, and against the death penalty in capital cases.

On the whole, however, the early Yankees were neither influential nor numerous, and it seems odd that the first governor of the state of Iowa was a Vermonter, Ansel Briggs, sworn into office in 1846. Briggs was "a modest and humble" man who, on coming west had made his living driving stagecoach, carrying mail, and serving a term as sheriff of Jackson County. He was of little education, said a contemporary, but diligent and honest, and he "had absorbed a great deal of horse sense while driving stagecoaches." The mere fact that a Vermonter was the first governor of Iowa had no great significance, for the state was considered solidly Democratic and proslavery. Not until the middle fifties, when New Englanders and other Northern immigrants came in full flood, was there evidence of change. The little Iowa Band has been given much credit for the overturn of proslavery sentiment; and when Grimes, a native of Deering, New Hampshire, was made governor in 1854 the Yankees were coming into Iowa in greater numbers. "Day by day," said the Dubuque *Reporter,* "the endless procession moves on. . . . They come by the hundreds and thousands from the hills and valleys of New England, bringing with them that same untiring energy and perseverance that made their native states the admiration of the world." This was gross exaggeration. Yorkers and Pennsylvanians were arriving in far greater numbers than the Yankees. But come the Yankees did, in sufficient number when combined with the other Northerners to hold Iowa safely in the Union. But they were not numerous or powerful enough to impose their favorite political subdivision, that of the town meeting. They tried to impose it on Iowa, as on northern Illinois and on Michigan, but Iowa would have none of it. In the later forties and the fifties Europeans were coming in, first the Hollanders, then the Germans, Hungarians, and Scandinavians. Home rule, such as the Yankees were used to, meant nothing to them; nor were they much interested in Temperance, Abolition, or the Puritan idea of the Sabbath.

The fact that in less than a decade Iowa changed from a strong Democratic state sympathetic with the South to a solid Northern bulwark was due, according to one Iowa historian, to "the New England influence exerted by the hundred thousand who came from Ohio, largely from the Western Reserve, and who were of New England stock." And F. I. Herriott, who had no special liking for Yankees or their Congregational church, was quick to cite the Iowa Band. "It is to be doubted," said he, "if any other group of men exerted a tithe of the beneficial influence upon the life of the state that was exerted by this little brotherhood of earnest missionaries and preachers."

The New England immigrants scattered more in early Iowa than in Ohio and Illinois. Only a few groups appear to have been organized for the purpose of colonization. One, mostly Massachusetts and Connecticut people, did drive a wedge westward to the Cedar River in Chickasaw County and founded the village of Bradford, where a Yankee music teacher, one W. S. Pitts, wrote a song, "The Little Brown Church in the Vale" which was long in vogue as a frontier hymn. Disciples of the Yankee Prophet, Joseph Smith, paused in Iowa on their trek to Utah long enough to found a newspaper in what is now Council Bluffs; and to propose and get a law passed to the effect that "no action for adultery can be brought except on complaint of the aggrieved party." And the widow of the Prophet, and her son Joseph Smith, Jr., joined the dissenting group which went no farther west but founded the town of Lamoni, Iowa, where they still call themselves the Reorganized Church of Jesus Christ of the Latter-Day Saints."

The Milford Emigration Society was largely responsible for the organization of Cherokee County where, in 1857, Carlton Corbett, agent for the society, preempted lands for the colony and located the county seat. This group hailed from Milford, Massachusetts, and included the families of Lemuel Parkhurst and Albert Phipps, whose wife was Martha Littlefield. There were also several Yankee families in New Hampton where, in 1856, Harrison Gurley of Mansfield, Connecticut, opened store in a log cabin and Mrs. Gurley started teaching school. Edward P. Greeley, from New Hampshire, built and opened the first store and the first flour mill in Woodbridge and took the liberty to change the name of the settlement to Nashua, honoring, one hopes, his native town. He became one of the big millers of the district. James B. Reeve of Lyme, Connecticut, was the very first settler in Franklin County, near a site that grew into Maysville. Pioneers at Monticello were Moses M. Moulton and family from Sandwich, New Hampshire. The first settlers in Wright County were Sumner B. Hewett, his son of the same name, and an in-law, Nathaniel Paine, all of Northbridge, Massachusetts.

A number of the pioneer hotels were built and operated by Samuel W. Cole, born in Panton, Vermont, who proved, according to his biographer, that "a Christian landlord is neither an anomaly nor a novelty . . . he can conduct his business to the glory of God." A barroom, said Publican Cole, is not a necessary adjunct to a hotel. No liquors were to be had in the Cole hotels at Fort Dodge, Vinton, and Ackley; and, more, Publican Cole organized many Bands of Hope throughout the state and these fought the Demon at every turn.*

Many a settler, Yankee or other, always had an eye open for an opportunity to get in on the ground floor somewhere. Ground floors were often found to collapse, but Suel Foster, from Hillsboro, New Hampshire, had better luck. In 1836, for the sum of $500, he bought one-sixth of a newly surveyed townsite that grew into Muscatine. He prospered from his investment, prospered again from the nursery business he established, and also fought a good fight for the founding of an agricultural college, which is said to have been the second in the United States. Charles Hendrie, from Stamford Connecticut, fitted well in pioneer Burlington, where in 1842 he started the first iron foundry; later he specialized in the manufacture and transportation of heavy mining machinery, as well as the carrying of large numbers of passengers to the mining region of Colorado, and back. In spite of difficulties, such as once being obliged to "pay $80 for enough firewood to cook breakfast" for his passengers, he did very well and was rated one of the big businessmen of the region. It was in Burlington, too, that Yankee Elbridge

---

* Perhaps this partial confining of Demon Rum was responsible for the excellent material welfare of early Iowans. In 1849, the state auditor reported that citizens possessed "28,-000 horses, 5,298 pleasure carriages, 3,112 watches, and 33 piano fortes."

D. Rand made a fortune from his pioneer meat-packing business; he made another from his lumberyards throughout the state.

From the first, Iowa was a country of small mills, both saw and grist, that were turned by water power. More than seven hundred of them were built, and one of the earliest was that of Benjamin Nye, put up in 1833 on Pine Creek in Muscatine County. In the neighborhood at the time were other "sturdy Vermont pioneers like Nye," so that the settlement was named Montpelier, from the Green Mountain capital. William Larrabee, Connecticut native and future governor of Iowa, had a pioneer gristmill in Fayette County. A Vermonter named John D. Parmalee had a mill in Warren County that sawed lumber for the Army barracks at Fort Des Moines, and also ground a deal of grain; but he heeded neither the teachings of the Iowa Band nor the warnings of the Bands of Hope. He fell into sottish ways, and "his business suffered from that fact." Other mills had names that would indicate Yankee ownership, like Bunker's Mill in Washington County, Lowell Mills in Henry County, and the Merrimac Mill in Jefferson County.

Probably the most effective Yankee in all Iowa was the Vermont lad to whom, directly and explicitly, Horace Greeley had directed his famous command. This was Josiah Bushnell Grinnell, born at New Haven, Vermont, in 1821. Almost the only boast Grinnell ever was heard to make was of Greeley's remark to him. "It was a remark that has been shot at thousands of dullards since my day," he liked to say; "but I was the young man to whom Greeley first said it, and I went." Horace Greeley not only advised Grinnell to go west but gave him an assignment to report the Illinois State Fair of 1853 for the New York *Tribune*.

Josiah Grinnell arrived in Iowa with a complete stock of carefully tended Yankee notions of the intellectual sort. After teaching school in Middlebury, Vermont, he had set out for Yale, but was dissuaded by the Reverend Erastus Ripley, a devout Abolitionist of Meriden, Connecticut, who told him that "Latin and Greek will amount to nothing in the next twenty years." What he should do, said the old gentleman, was to prepare for the coming battle with Satan in the form of slavery. The church must be expurgated and made bold; Texas must be kept out of the Republic; brave speakers were to be more in demand than bookworms. "Therefore," cried old Erastus Ripley, "give us a race of students with backbone and courage for the coming great days." The right place to prepare for the coming great days was Oneida Institute, at Whitesboro, New York; and there went young Grinnell, to study under Beriah Green, one of the founders of the American Anti-Slavery Society. "The church and the nation are asleep," President Green shouted at his young men. "Go wake them!"

In 1851 the Reverend Josiah Grinnell opened the first Congregational church the city of Washington had ever known, and delivered the first Abolition sermon. He got what was coming to him, too—a request for his resignation. He was also too radical for New York City. Then his good friend Mr. Greeley suggested the West.

After pausing in Illinois to report the state fair, Grinnell went into Missouri and saw that the place "was clinging to barbarism," and that "no grass grows where the Devil dances." Iowa was much better. Here he became acquainted with Henry Farnam, just then preparing to build an extension of his Chicago & Rock Island Railroad into Iowa; and met Grenville M. Dodge, soon to be noted as an engineer. Dodge marked with a flag the spot on the projected railroad which he thought would make a good townsite for the village Grinnell planned to establish. This was in Poweshiek County on the divide between the Iowa and Des Moines rivers. With three other men, including Dr. Thomas Holyoke, of Searsport, Maine, Grinnell purchased 5,000 acres and put up a long house for temporary shelter. This was to be Grinnell, Iowa.

Founder Grinnell hung a lantern on a tall pole to guide travelers at night, and a bit later brought in a thousand-pound bell to summon settlers to divine services, even before a Congregational society had been organized. In laying out the town, the founding fathers reserved a goodly block for the village green, and several lots to be sold for the purpose of starting a Literary Society. No liquor, naturally, could be sold within the town.

Colonizer Grinnell did not have to pay for newspaper space to sing of the town of Grinnell in Iowa. For the New York *Tribune* he wrote descriptive articles about the state, and naturally took occasion to mention the advantages of his own neighborhood. The Yankees started to come, among them a numerous group from Searsport on the Penobscot. By the autumn of 1856 there were more than two hundred houses—not cabins—in the village. A lyceum and a literary society were organized. Grinnell Academy was opened, and a young radical from Oberlin College named L. F. Parker came to run it. Josiah Grinnell planned a college for his town, too, and doubtless would have accomplished it, except that Iowa College, then a feeble school, was moved to the village and Josiah Grinnell became president of its board of regents. (In 1909 the name was changed to Grinnell College.)

In 1859 Josiah Grinnell, and his town, became a great scandal to much of Iowa, when Mr. Grinnell welcomed the madman, John Brown, who just then was taking a band of escaped slaves through the state, not long before the raid on Harper's Ferry. After the raid, Brown, dead, was a hero to the North, and Iowa changed its mind and sent Grinnell to Congress. Both here and at home he continued to have an immense influence on Iowa. From first to last he talked and wrote about his adopted state. More than one writer has called him Iowa's best and greatest publicist. He died in 1891.

One of the surveyors who helped Grinnell lay out his town was Gideon Gardner, of Plainfield, Massachusetts. Gardner soon laid out another called New Hampton, of which he owned much of the site; and he lived to see it "bloom like a prairie flower."

It seems probable that the group from Searsport in the Grinnell settlement attracted another native of the Penobscot village. He was Coker F. Clarkson who went to farming in Grundy County and did so well that he and two sons purchased the *Iowa State Register* at Des Moines. The senior Clarkson became agricultural editor and for the next two decades pioneered in agricultural education. He was much thought of and came to be called Father Clarkson. He was the leading spirit in the battle of the farmers against the Barbed Wire Syndicate, which was a combination of manufacturers seeking to keep prices just as high as the market could bear. He organized the Farmers' Protective Association, which established a factory for barbed-wire manufacture. A great deal of war followed in the courts; but the farmers won, and the syndicate was broken. Clarkson lived to ripe old age, a sort of patriarch and hero of the farmers. "His morals were rigid," wrote a biographer, "and his opinions were held with great tenacity." Few obituaries have contained so much of the essence of New England character in one short sentence. . . .

Other Yankee newspapermen were showing up in Iowa. Jesse Clement from New Hampshire was one of the founders of the *Daily Times* in Dubuque. David W. Richardson, native of Orange, Vermont, moved to Davenport, bought a printing outfit on credit, and established the *Daily Democrat*. One is glad to know that even at that early time Editor Richardson met and married in Iowa "Miss Jeanette Darling, daughter of a thrifty New England farmer." Another Vermonter, Azor Hildreth of Chelsea, was one of the pioneers in Charles City, where he established the *Intelligencer,* a weekly, and waged a long and successful battle to permit females to enter the state university. A fellow townsman from Chelsea, George S. Shaw, followed him West, to Davenport, to make his fortune in no less than three Shaw's Additions to the city's area, and died "one of the most wealthy, enterprising and useful citizens of Davenport." Its mayor in 1874, the Honorable Jacob Stewart, born in Danbury, Connecticut, had gone to Iowa in 1852 to teach school and practice law. One of the most notable farmers in all Iowa was Tristram Dow, native of Canterbury, New Hampshire, who tilled better than 15,000 acres and had large milling interests. It was no more than natural that he was elected president of Davenport's First National Bank.

One is pleased to know that a marvelous lightning-rod salesman was in one of the waves to Iowa. He was Charles E. Witham, native of that restless New Sharon, Maine, which sent its sons everywhere. Witham went to Ohio in 1848 and was soon most successful in a calling the very name of which is a byword in the American language. But he had ambitions for something better. Between trips to place rods on every barn and most houses in Ohio, he used his profits to take a course in medicine, at Cincinnati, and when he got his diploma, he struck out for Wilton, Iowa, where he became a revered country doctor in the best tradition.

Although most of the backwash from the rush of '49 to California was to the mines of Colorado, this did not hold with William T. Shaw, a native of Steuben, Maine. Shaw worked his way east overland to Iowa and stopped in new Anamosa, where he performed prodigies, building the Iowa Midland Railroad, promoting industry and commerce, and earning the name of town father. Sumner B. Chase, also a Maine native, was then laying out the town of Osage, where Nathaniel Deering, of Denmark, Maine, made a pile of money in land and lumber and in 1876 was elected to Congress.

The sons of Maine continued to leave their mark on Iowa. Charles C. Gilman of Brooks founded the town of Earlville, promoted and built the Central Railroad of Iowa, and had interests in almost everything, including lumber, coal, terra cotta, and farm produce. Henry O. Pratt, of Foxcroft, Maine, settled in Charles City, from which he was sent to Congress in 1873.*

One of the few Yankees to gain prominence in early Sioux City was Asahel Hubbard, native of Haddam, Connecticut, who practiced law and was sent to Congress in 1862. Eldora appears to have attracted a number of Yankees in early days, one of whom, Enoch Eastman of Deerfield, New Hampshire, was elected lieutenant governor of the state in 1863. Alvin Adams of Weston, Vermont, sat for many years as a judge of the state supreme court. He made his home in Dubuque and was perhaps of some influence in bringing more of his townsmen—the Pease and Cragin and related Adams families—to Dubuque.

The historians of Iowa generally consider that the pioneer period of the state came to an end in 1860. No doubt many a settler who came later held a different opinion; but as of 1860 the so-called pioneers included 25,040 natives of New England and amounted to only 4.4 per cent of all native Americans in the state. They were not in sufficient number to eradicate wholly the influence of the early dominant Southern immigration. They could not, for one thing, eliminate the southerners' lack of interest in education. In 1843

---

* Vermont's long tradition of having native sons in Congress from almost if not all the states was upheld in Iowa by John Adams Kasson, born in Charlotte, and Martin Joseph Wade, born in Burlington.

Governor John Chambers, expressing his mortification to the territorial legislature, cried, "How little interest the important subject of education excites
among us!" Nor did conditions change for a long time. In the fifties, wrote
one of Iowa's leading historians who obviously had no keen liking for
Yankees, the conditions in Iowa's rural schools were a scandal, especially compared to rural schools "in the states north and east of us."* For thirty years,
or until well into the eighties, Iowa continued "very slow in progress in
education, in the promotion of libraries, in the improvement of city governments . . . and in public provision for art and culture." Governor Grimes,
himself a Yankee, constantly urged establishment of libraries in country
and town, but nothing came of it.

The infant University had hard times until the eighties, when the
"vigorous opposition to its enlargement ceased." No, the Yankees in Iowa
were not numerous enough to prevent "an attitude of constant hostility and
bush-whacking opposition" to all forward movements, which prevailed generally until after 1880. Yet, the first governor of the state was Ansel Briggs
from Vermont; the second, Stephen Hempstead from Connecticut. And in
1868 Governor Samuel Merrill, a native of Maine who had emigrated to
Iowa in 1856, was of the opinion that the state" had been settled mainly from
Ohio, Indiana, and Pennsylvania, with a large admixture from New England." Judge Francis Springer, also from Maine, held that the first settlers in
Iowa came from *southern* Ohio, Indiana, and Illinois. The pioneer schoolmaster, Professor L. F. Parker, agreed with Judge Springer, but added that
many of the first settlers were "from the more northerly of the *Southern*
states."

But these opinions could not obviate the first census, which found only
5,535 Yankee residents in Iowa, or a mere 3 per cent of the total population.
Natives of southern states accounted for some 60 per cent. Thus, wrote
Herriott, as late as 1906 one "may discern a sharp cleavage among the
people of Iowa that in general typifies the traditional conflict between the
Cavalier and the Puritan."† He was glad of this "Cavalier" influence, for
he thought the Yankees had always "been much given to Socialism, and
turned naturally to the state and communal authorities to secure civic or social
improvements and popular culture"; but the southerner preferred to "improve things chiefly by the individualistic route." Herriott discovered in the
Iowan's character "a noticeable trait that we may designate Languor—not to
worry or fuss if things do not satisfy." As for the New Englander in Iowa,

* F. I. Herriott, *Did Emigrants from New England First Settle Iowa?* (Des Moines, 1906),
—a careful and detailed study.
  † He was still bemused with the illusion that the first settlers in the American South
were blue-blooded Cavaliers. In reality, they were of the same stock and class as those who
settled at Plymouth and on Massachusetts Bay. Climate formed their differing characteristics.

he "is alert, aggressive, eager in the furtherance of any business or culture in which he is interested . . . is ardent, disputatious, relentless. He agitates, educates, and preaches reformation." And Herriott added, "This is not the characteristic disposition of the Iowan"—for which he was patently thankful.

Intermarrige of southern and New England stocks naturally took place in Iowa before, during, and after the Civil War; and in lesser degree both of these stocks intermarried with immigrants from Holland, Germany, Scandinava, and other foreign countries. If Historian Herriott believed there was a "characteristic Iowan" by 1900, so, too, did Rollin Lynde Hartt, who in that year went to consider them on their farms and in their cities and villages. He found Iowa to be "a huge overflow meeting, thronged with second-generation middle-westerners." He thought Iowans "so uniformly respectable that they will attempt nothing quixotic or piratical." They had progressed from prairie grass to wheat, from wheat to clover, from clover to corn. Such, said he, were the short and simple annals of the Iowans.

Contentment had brought complacency. Happy the people who have no history. "The sober truth," wrote Mr. Hartt in the *Atlantic Monthly,* "The sober truth is that the Iowans are an effect in drabs and grays. The state is too young for quaintness, too old for romance. They have founded a great agricultural state, not remarkable in any particular."

A quarter of a century later Ruth Suckow, native Iowan, reflected upon the region and its people. She said that Iowa was a "meek state," on the fence geographically, religiously, and aesthetically. She thought it could do with a little of the bumptiousness and boosterism of Kansas and Minnesota. But it was self-conscious, and timid. It was torn in its allegiances; the thin grasp of New England had weakened; the sons and daughters of immigrants from Europe wanted no part of their parents' native language or customs. Yet, a genuinely Iowa culture had begun to show, even if humbly, tentatively. At its worst this was colorless, wishy-washy. But at its best "it is innocently ingenuous, fresh and sincere, unpretentious, and essentially ample, with a certain quality of pure loveliness—held together by the simplicity and severity of its hard-working farmer people."

The great seal of Iowa displays a homesteader's cabin, a plow in the furrow, and a field of corn; but it is the motto that tells something of the founders of Iowa: *Our liberties we prize and our rights we will Maintain.* It expresses equally well the sentiments of Iowa settlers from South Carolina, and from Vermont. One may well judge that the state of Iowa has been perhaps the most efficient of all of our so-called melting pots.

CHAPTER XI

THE LAND OF GOLD AND CLIMATE

AT THE WINTER TERM of school that began late in 1837, New England boys and girls were offered a new textbook entitled *Atlas Designed to Illustrate the Malte-Brun Geography,* which was "up to date" and contained, in addition to "Tabular Views of Extent of Population &c," the "Latest Maps and Charts," all in handsome colors. It was the work, and gorgeous work, too, of S. Griswold Goodrich, a Connecticut Yankee widely known as Peter Parley.

The two center pages of the atlas were devoted to a map of the United States, with the various commonwealths and territories appearing in the brightest of greens, yellows, and blues, and a startling cerise, the whole composing as eye-arresting a piece of cartography as any Yankee youngster could have wished. The eastern half of the United States fairly scintillated with clashing colors; but, except for a square green block in the extreme northwest corner, designated as Oregon Territory, almost all the remaining western half of the map was buff-colored and labeled Mexico. This vast region of buff was studded with vague and even sinister legends, such as "Unexplored Region," and "Great American Desert," the latter of which was "Traversed by numerous herds of Buffaloes & Wild Horses and Inhabited by roving Tribes of Indians." In small type along the very bottom of the buff area appeared what were said to be names of the Mexican provinces of Durango, Sonora, and California. Not one city or village was shown in all the buff area.

There is always, of course, a lag in the preparing and the publishing of maps; and in this particular case of Mexico more than one far-ranging Yankee could have corrected Mr. Goodrich's somewhat dim view of the country. By 1837, New Englanders had long been established at Monterey and Los Angeles and other places in Mexico, none of which, as said, appeared on Mr. Goodrich's map. By 1837, in fact, several of these Yankees had lived in the buff wastes of "Unexplored Region" so long, and had come to like

144]

it so well, that they were even then thinking of suitable ways by which it could best be brought within the United States.

The continuity of Yankee arrivals who settled in what is now the state of California seems remarkable. The first, the Nestor of them all, was a Bostonian, Thomas W. Doak, who jumped ship from the *Albatross* in 1816, was baptized Felipe Santiago Doc the same year, married a daughter of Mariano Castro, and settled down to propagate children. Doak or Doc was not long the only Yankee in this paradise, for in 1823 Daniel A. Hill of Massachusetts left a ship, married a local girl, settled in Santa Barbara, and received a grant of fine land from the Mexican governor.

Between them, Doak and Hill started something of a trend, for now came Henry Delano Fitch, born in New Bedford, Massachusetts. He too married a Californian, was granted a ranch, and went into cattle raising and trade. At about the same time Nathan Spear of Boston opened a store in Monterey, the provincial capital. In 1826 two more Bostonians arrived, Thomas B. Park, who became a trader in hides at Santa Barbara, and William G. Dana. The latter married an Indian, fathered twenty-one children several shades darker than the Boston Danas, and also did very well with a ranch. When young Alfred Robinson came ashore at Monterey in 1829 as agent for Bryant, Sturgis & Company of Boston, he found "several N. E. merchants married to Spanish señoritas and settled in the vicinity."

All these men had come to California by way of the sea. In 1826 a man proved that the region could be reached on foot from the United States. This was Jedediah Strong Smith, the son of New Hampshire emigrants to York State, who had entered the fur trade at St. Louis to become the oddest and one of the ablest of that company of frontier characters known to history as the Mountain Men. Jedediah Smith was a devout Christian, a Methodist, could read Latin and English, and kept a journal, yet withal was accepted as a leader among the generally wild crew who ranged the plains and the Rockies.

In 1826, then, this paragon of Mountain Men led a party of traders overland from the Mississippi to the Pacific coast and was thus "the first Smith in California." He wintered in the Sacramento valley, then walked up into Oregon country, moved over the Cascades and on to the Spokane River, and so back to St. Louis. His was the first party to reach California other than by sea.

Smith met several of the Yankees who had gone native. Their number continued to increase, as John Bradshaw from Beverly, Massachusetts, settled comfortably down to a life of trading interspersed with smuggling; and Robert J. Elwell, also from Massachusetts, arrived to marry a native girl and establish trading at Santa Barbara. There was also Henry A. Peirce of

Boston, who traded in hides and tallow, and much later was appointed United States minister to Hawaii. A year after Peirce, came a Yankee who spoke Spanish most fluently, for he had lived in Mexico some years and was already a naturalized citizen. This was "Don" Abel Stearns, late of Lunenburg, Massachusetts, who married a native beauty and began to deal in hides and liquor in the adobe settlement of Los Angeles. Don Abel acquired a ranch, entertained lavishly, and in a little came to operate an immense estate.

Up to this point, what surely was not yet known as the New England colony in California was composed wholly of Bay Staters. In 1831 they were joined by a Connecticut man, Jonathan Trumbull Warner, who was naturalized and received a land grant at San Diego. Within a few months came a second Nutmegger, Daniel Sill, who hunted sea otter for the China trade, and later brought out his family and settled in the Sacramento valley.

Thus, as early as 1832, what might well be termed the infiltration of Americans into the Mexican province of California was in considerable volume; for in addition to the New Englanders there were many Americans from other parts of the United States who had come and gone native. But in that year came a Yankee who was to have more effect on California than any who had come before. This was Thomas O. Larkin, of Charlestown, Massachusetts, later appointed United States consul at Monterey.

Being consul in the sleepy and pleasant settlement of Monterey was the least of Larkin's activities. He built a flour mill, he traded in hides and tallow, he speculated in lands. He claimed, apparently with justification, that his children were the first born in California of parents from the United States. More important than any of these things was the fact that Larkin was himself the first of a distinguished line; namely, the California boosters. Throughout the decade of his arrival, and for many years more, he was the chief correspondent of newspapers and periodicals in eastern United States; nor did the land or the climate of California suffer at his hands. Here, said he, was the nearest to heaven on earth any Yankee had ever known. Larkin's inspired prose painted lovely pictures of his adopted home and everything connected with it. Gilead was running full and over with balm. Fruits and grains grew enormously, and quickly. Neither snow nor ice was known. The sun shone gloriously and continuously. It was inconceivable, to Thomas O. Larkin from windy Charlestown, Massachusetts, that anybody who once saw California could desire to live anywhere else in Christendom.

Mr. Larkin was something more than the first booster. He was also a secret agent for the United States government, and his private reports kept Washington well and accurately informed as to events and attitudes in the Mexican provinces of California. In the light of subsequent history, it is not too much

to say that Larkin was the competent head of a fifth-column infiltration—one
that boded no good for Mexico.

Thus so early did this wonderful foreign land have a Yankee explorer
by land, a Yankee—Don Abel Stearns—leading businessman, and a Yankee
who was the granddaddy of all California boosters to come. New England influence in California was felt from the beginning.

The effects of Larkins's letters and articles in the eastern press were soon
apparent. What had been a trickle of Americans rose steadily through the
years, and in it were always a few sons of New England. In 1836 he who
may have been the first Harvard graduate to settle in California arrived
in the crotchety person of John Marsh, a doctor of medicine, who had
already trekked through Wisconsin, Missouri, and Mexico. In California
Marsh chose a spot at the base of Mount Diablo and there built a cabin in
which he lived pretty much as a hermit. Yet, though "a peculiar and generally
disagreeable man, of notorious parsimony," he was a great writer of letters to
newspapers and public men in the East. He bombarded them with descriptions
of this land of milk and honey, constantly urged Americans to leave their
abysmal homes, and said without any folderol that California should be "in
possession of the United States." Perhaps Dr. Marsh could be termed the
second California booster.

The infiltration of Yankees continued, and Francis and Harry Mellus,
brothers, with William D. M. Howard, all of Boston, set up a successful
trading concern, dealing in the usual hides, tallow, otter skins, and of course
whisky. Other Bay State arrivals included Eliab Grimes, who settled in the
Sacramento valley to become a noted character and trader; William Sturgis
Hinckley, a most successful smuggler; Faxon Dean Atherton, who went into
banking, married a native, and in time was one of the most prominent
citizens of San Mateo; and the Temple brothers, Pliny and John, who later
built the grand Temple Block in Los Angeles as an indication of their
prosperity.

The man who was to lay out the pretty town of Napa on his fine ranch
arrived from Massachusetts in 1843, in the person of Nathan Coombs, aged
eighteen. And now the other New England states began to show an interest in
the Unexplored Region. From Maine came Robert Hasty Thomas, who
worked as a carpenter at Monterey and San Francisco, obtained a land grant,
and rose to wealth. In this period the head bookkeeper for General John
Sutter, the noted Swiss immigrant, was William F. Swasey of Maine. George
H. Card from Rhode Island was one of the earliest settlers at Stockton, and a
fellow Rhode Islander, Richard M. Sherman went into San Francisco real
estate and later erected the fine Sherman Building there. From Connecticut
to work for Consul Larkin came Josiah Belden. Belden made his pile and

was the first mayor of San Jose. Other early arrivals from Connecticut included Kimball H. Dimmick, to achieve success at the bar in Los Angeles; Andrew Goodyear who came overland and settled in Benicia; and Dr. Thaddeus Leavenworth, who had the good sense to buy several lots in San Francisco, where a street still bears his name.

In 1845, when James K. Polk became President of the United States, the American interest in California quickened, partly because there was some reason for believing Great Britain was planning to take over the Mexican province. Polk sent John Slidell to Mexico to offer as high as forty million dollars for cession of the province to the United States. It was refused. Then, American Consul Larkin at Monterey was secretly informed by the administration, in a somewhat mealy-mouthed manner, that "whilst the President will make no effort . . . to induce California to become one of the free and independent States of this Union, yet if the people should desire to unite their destiny with ours, they would be received as brethren."

Larkin busied himself, enlisting the help of a number of the most influential native and foreign-born citizens of the province, including Don Abel Stearns, the former Bostonian who had become one of the most prominent ranchers and businessmen of the Los Angeles area. Plans for bringing California into the American Union were getting under way when John C. Frémont led a party of pretty tough men into the province on what he said was a mere scientific exploration for the United States government. Whether or not Frémont was acting on secret orders for his government has never been determined. In any case, American settlers in the Sacramento valley staged an insurrection and proclaimed the Republic of California. William Brown Ide, a new settler from Massachusetts, wrote and signed the fantastic proclamation, which called "all peaceable & good citizens of California" to aid in establishing and perpetuating "a Republican government which shall secure to us all Civil & religious liberty, which shall encourage virtue and literature, which shall leave unshackled by fetters Agriculture, Commerce & Mechanism." Ide went on to greater heights of oratory, saying that he relied on Heaven and on the bravery of those associated with him in the affair, and declared his "hatred of tyranny"— an odd thing to mention in a region that had been as casually governed as California.

Ide was patently a man who must also have a flag, and his gang quickly raised a standard on which appeared an alleged representation of a grizzly bear. They also mustered a battalion of ex-scouts and trappers and assorted settlers to fight under John Frémont's personal command. They drilled a good deal, made considerable noise, fought a skirmish in which they routed a force of Mexicans, and became, one and all, heroes without compare to the future state of California. All told, the Bear Flag revolt resulted in six killed, and a few more wounded.

The revolt was soon ended, when the United States declared war on Mexico and an American naval force took possession of the provincial capital of Monterey. The Bear Flag men were sworn in as volunteers in the United States Army. San Diego and Los Angeles were occupied without resistance. The Mexican troops were disbanded. Kit Carson was sent overland to inform President Polk that Californians were prepared to be welcomed as brethren. That wasn't quite true, for considerable fighting and "pacification" remained. Yet, on February 2, 1848, California was formally ceded to the United States by treaty. Without passing through the usual territorial status, it was admitted as a state on September 9, 1850. Long before then, California had become an unprecedented sensation as a goal of emigrants, including several thousands of Yankees.

The man commonly credited with letting the world know of the discovery of gold at Sutter's mill was a Yankee, Sam Brannan, born in 1819 in that same Saco valley of Maine where the first Mormon missionaries had found a welcome and made many converts. At the age of fourteen Brannan had become a printer. He joined the Mormon church in 1842, and was sent to New York City to edit and publish the New York *Prophet*. His abilities must have been apparent, for he was quickly made an elder and placed in charge of a Mormon expedition to California, to explore possibilities for a permanent colony.

In July of 1846, Brannan's ship, containing seventy women, twenty-eight men, and perhaps a hundred children, anchored in San Francisco Bay, to find the American flag flying over what had been a Mexican city when the voyage began, and was now occupied by American troops. This was a bad beginning, for the whole idea of the Mormon expedition had been to get outside the jurisdiction of the United States. Brannan was sorely disappointed. But he was no man to quit just because the whole region seemed overrun with loathsome gentiles. He led his group to a spot on the Stanislaus River, near its junction with the San Joaquin, and there founded New Hope, strictly for Mormons.

Brannan was a tremendous man, deep-chested, shaggy-headed, with broad shoulders and flashing black eyes. He was also energetic and fearless. His manners were rough; but he was genial and generous, and his whole personality has been described more than once as brilliant. So, too, were his talents. Within a year after arrival he had founded San Francisco's first newspaper, the *California Star*. He preached the first sermon in English, and performed the first non-Catholic marriage ceremony in the city. He spoke up for a public school. Late in 1847 he moved to John Sutter's fort and opened a store. He was there on the 24th of January, 1848, when men, including several of Brannan's Mormons, engaged in deepening the tailrace of a saw-mill, discovered gold. General Sutter asked that the discovery be kept quiet until after the sawmill was finished; so the workmen continued their labors, and spent Sundays washing more gold in the branch of the American River that supplied power to the mill.

Sutter charged later that Elder Brannan collected one-third of the gold the Mormons brought in, saying that such was the tithe of the Lord and that it should be used to erect a suitable temple. This is unimportant compared to Brannan's next move: Early in May of '48 he disappeared from his store, to turn up a few days later in San Francisco. There he rushed, wild and un-kempt in his travel-stained clothes, to the Plaza, holding aloft a bottle of gleaming dust, shouting in his full-throated bellow: "Gold! Gold from the American River!" Up to then, it was probably the most important announce-ment that had been made in California, of greater significance even than the "proclamation" of Brannan's fellow-Yankee Ide.

Although it was going to take an unconscionably long time to make the eastern United States comprehend the truly momentous event, the citizens of San Francisco were ready to believe Sam Brannan at once. Within a week after his wild announcement on the Plaza, the city was being rapidly de-populated. Even crews of ships in harbor deserted. All hands headed for the American River.

Many years before the strike at Sutter's mill gold had been known to abound in California. As early as 1842 Don Abel Stearns had sent twenty ounces of it, taken from placers, to the United States mint at Philadelphia. Mexicans, Indians, Americans, all had found it accidentally in both the north-ern and southern portions of the region. But it had nowhere created any-thing like excitement. This time, however, it was different. San Francisco lost two-thirds of its population immediately. At Monterey, wrote Walter Colton,* the blacksmiths, the doctor, and the carpenters upped stakes; even the Yankee woman who kept a boarding house was away to the golden river, without waiting for her lodgers to pay, "I have only a gang of prisoners," said Colton, "and a community of women left." The news quickly traveled north in a lumber schooner to Oregon City, and the saw-mill hands there and many another took off, some by ship, others pellmell overland through the Siskiyou Mountains, on foot. In Oregon the mania is still known as the rush of '48.

---

* Born in Georgia, Vt., in 1797; a graduate of Yale and of Andover Theological Seminary; chaplain with the U.S. Naval forces in California; founder of the first newspaper there, the *Californian;* builder of the first school in the region; in 1846 appointed chief judge at Monterey. Colton was a notable example of New England influence.

Yet, what to most of the world became the rush of '49 was a long time getting started. Casual items about gold on the Pacific coast appeared in newspapers in the East as early as August of 1848, being run under small general headings such as "California Correspondence" and "California Intelligence." Papers in New York, Philadelphia, and Boston had them first, and smaller papers copied the items. Yet they had little or no effect. It was President Polk's message to Congress early in December that touched off the mania—that, plus a small chest of fine gold which was displayed in the War Office in Washington.

President Polk was anything but sensational. "Recent discoveries render it probable," said he with the windy care of the politician, "that these mines are more extensive and valuable than was anticipated." It was easily the understatement of the decade. But it was, certainly, official; and there, too, was that chest of yellow metal in the War Office. Delirium, said one observer, seized upon the community of the District of Columbia.

In New England, the chest of gold plus the President's statement revised opinion of the "California country." The great majority of Yankees at home had previously paid little if any heed either to news of the gold discovery, or to the letters and articles from those early boosters of the region. Now, however, the impact was sudden and powerful. The alleged hardheadedness of the Yankees, who had ignored the news from Ophir, and who in any case were just then interested in Michigan, Illinois, and Wisconsin, turned quickly to extreme credulity. They were ready and anxious to believe that fine gold clustered around the root of every blade of grass that grew in California, that the streams there were clogged with it, that it bulged from the very hills and mountains.

These illusions were approximately the ones held by other residents of eastern United States. Within a few weeks after Polk's message to Congress even the name of California was a symbol, an effulgent golden symbol, radiating the light that stemmed from Ophir on the darkest days—a promise of the metal that would unlock all doors, that would knit and break religions, make leprosy adored, that could crash the strongest barriers more easily than the lightning's bolt.

The Yankees girded their loins. On January 13, 1849, the first organized company, one hundred and fifty strong, marched aboard the 700-ton *Edward Everett* and set sail for the Horn and San Francisco. This company was probably typical of the swarming New England groups that took off for El Dorado in organized bands. Indicative of the typical Yankee notion of having eggs in not one but two baskets was the title of the group. It was the Boston & California Joint Mining & Trading Company. Note the "& Trading." If

Ophir did not immediately produce its gold, then Yankees would sell, to those fools who insisted on seeking it, a considerable cargo of trade goods taken along expressly for that purpose. The *Edward Everett's* hold contained provisions and supplies estimated to be sufficient for the company's use over a period of two years, plus enough more to stock a store. All contingencies were considered; the ship had lightning rods and two brass cannon. On deck was a knock-down house complete, to be erected in San Francisco as the Hanover House, thus honoring the Boston hotel where the company had been organized. The Hanover House was to serve as company headquarters.

The personnel of the Boston & California company was both varied and of a high order. In it were eight sea captains, four doctors, a parson, a mineralogist, a geologist, several merchants, manufacturers, farmers, artisans, and medical and divinity students. The genius of the Yankee for organization is to be seen in the details of the company's regulations: The clergymen aboard were to preach a sermon on each Sunday; there would also be a midweek prayer meeting; amateur musicians were to bring their instruments and form a ship's band; professional men of the group were to deliver lectures on various intellectual and scientific matters. (A well stocked library was taken aboard.) The four M.D.'s constituted a board of health; at their disposal was a room fitted up as a dispensary, complete with drugs and "twenty-five gallons of whiskey for medicinal purposes only." Just in case any member of the company should, for any reason, get out of hand, a police force was appointed and a brig provided.

So, away to Golconda went the brave young men of the Boston & California Joint Mining & Trading Company.

Massachusetts and Maine, both with a long maritime tradition, supplied the greatest part of New England's participation in the Rush of Forty-Nine. Vermont was the third in number of emigrants, ranking just above Connecticut.

Perhaps half of the Yankees leaving for California in 1849 were in organized companies such as that on the *Edward Everett*. No fewer than 102 joint-stock companies sailed from Massachusetts alone in the year of excitement. Following the *Edward Everett* in the *Pauline* was the Bunker Hill Mining & Trading Company, with paid-up capital of $15,000, all its members pledged to "abstain from all the vices and temptations incident to the expedition." In January the old whaling town of New Bedford sent eleven ships, all heavily loaded with incipient miners *and* traders.

Maine was away, too. Out of the mouth of the Penobscot went the *James W. Paige,* its company containing at least one excellent reporter, J. Lamson, who noted among other things on the voyage that the company's spiritual adviser, the Reverend John Johnson, was a man of unclerical temper.

By February the Green Mountain Boys were in the van, when the Rutland California Company sailed out of New York harbor in the brig *Empire*. In March what appears to have been the first formally organized group from Connecticut sailed as the New Haven Joint Stock Mining Company. Why "& Trading" was omitted from the corporate title is hard to explain. It was followed closely, however, by the more explicitly titled Hartford Union Mining & Trading Company. Most of these New England outfits prohibited the use of liquor on the voyage but carried, for sale to other gold seekers, large stocks of New England rum. One exception was the group from Nantucket which sailed "without a drop of intoxicating liquor on board."

One member of the Old Harvard Company, leaving Boston in February, was of the opinion there was altogether "too much praying on the ship." This particular group seems, even for Yankees, to have been uncommonly bedeviled by seagoing divinity authorities. The Reverend Mr. Brierly not only offered a prayer every morning but also delivered what he called "a brief sermon" daily. On Wednesdays he held a prayer meeting, and on Sunday gave out with "a full length sermon." Not even the boredom of ship's life could support such a program, and long before the end of the voyage all religious instruction ceased.

One of the fanciest bands to leave New England was the North Western Mining & Trading Company, which bought a bark and fitted and supplied her without regard to cost. It was a select group, twenty-two in all, and every member put in one thousand dollars. Many Brahmin families had representatives on board, among them being Charles Francis Adams, Jr. This was probably the only organized party whose members wore identical uniforms. Their bark made a slow passage and did not reach San Francisco for nearly seven months.

Ships continued to leave Beverly and Newburyport as fast as they could be chartered, or built. In almost every case the company gathered in church to hear a farewell sermon, to sing a hymn or two, before going up the gangplank. One of the largest passenger lists in the entire rush was that of the *Sweden*, which left Boston in March with three companies aboard. Before shipping they were supplied with a good long sermon in the Seamen's Bethel, and then their commander was presented "by a citizen of Brookline" with a splendid banner of pure white satin, fringed with gold, on which, one is not wholly astonished to know, appeared the single word "Excelsior." Mr. Longfellow did not write poems for nothing. . . .

You may be sure that Yankee merchants rose to the occasion of the exodus to El Dorado. The stores of Boston, Providence, New Haven, Portland, and Bangor hurriedly put on sale what they said were absolute "necessaries" for prospectors; and as early as April were advertising their wares in country newspapers in inland Vermont and New Hampshire. The merchants were quick to attach California names to their merchandise; hence, Dr. Isaac Roswell, a Dartmouth graduate practicing in remote Coos County, New Hampshire, who was leaving for the gold fields, could read in the Concord *Monitor* that he had best take along either a Feather River Overcoat or a California Cloak. Kimball Webster of New Hampshire, preparing to leave with the Granite State & California Mining & Trading Company, could read that among his needs was an El Dorado Cap, an Isthmus Bag for Pack Mule, and one of the superior Sutter's Long Mining Waistcoats.

At least one of the New England companies had a different idea about going to California. This was the Boston & Newton Joint Stock Association, which bought a bark, the *Helen Augusta,* crammed her with her supplies, then sent her around the Horn, while her twenty-six owners went overland by wagon train. In this company were two brothers, David and Fred Staples of Medway, Massachusetts, whose activities during the rush were possibly typical of many of the higher grade New England emigrants. The Staples brothers had a very brief fling at actual mining, and saw quickly enough that this was no business for an intelligent Yankee. They started packing supplies from Stockton to the southern mines and made a small fortune, sufficient for David to return east and bring out his wife and daughter and buy land where Lodi now stands. He operated a ferry and toll bridge there, became a leading citizen, and in time was drafted to run against Leland Stanford for governor.

It would be interesting to know how many Yankees who came in the '49 rush got rich panning gold. The number surely was not large, for one finds them, within a few weeks after their arrival in the new El Dorado, busy at almost everything else than prospecting or operating sluice or rocker. These, in large part, were the Argonauts who remained in California to settle and raise families; to found towns, build railroads, establish schools, colleges, and churches; to ranch and farm; to peddle patent medicines and daguerreotypes; to become bandits; to start newspapers, shipping lines, and wildcat and blue-sky companies allegedly to exploit gold and silver and diamond and oil lands, but really to exploit other Americans, including Yankees. Whatever they did, good or bad, New Englanders left their impress on California, occasionally on all of the West.

There was, for instance, Hubert Howe Bancroft, born in Granville, Ohio, in 1832, the son of a Yankee Forty-niner named Azariah Ashley Bancroft, native of Granville, Massachusetts. The elder Bancroft was followed to California in 1852 by his son. Together they worked a claim above Sacramento; then the son went to San Francisco to found a publishing concern. Out of this astonishing literary mill came Bancroft's vast history of the West in twenty-eight volumes, along with several more volumes of essays. Since that day, no historian of the old West has performed without the aid of H. H. Bancroft and his crew of workers, for he spoke only justly when he remarked, "He who shall come after me will scarcely undermine my work by laying another and deeper foundation."

Bancroft was unique. More typical of the better grade of Yankees who came to pan gold but soon turned to other things was Benjamin Dore, born in Athens, Maine, in 1825. He was one of the fifty-six men who in 1849 bought the bark *Cantero,* loaded her with lumber, and sailed around the Horn. Dore sought gold but briefly, then started for Oregon in the first steamship to enter Humboldt Bay, where the young man noted a new settlement he spelled "Ureca"; continuing to Portland, he helped build a ship or two, then returned to San Francisco and went immediately into the business of lumber. In later years he moved to West Park Colony, Fresno, to be the first settler. He plowed the first furrow in the colony, built the first house, and, incidentally, married Jane Amanda, widow of Hiland Hall, Jr., of Bennington, Vermont.

Whether or not Dore's company of adventurers in '49 were typical of the New England groups cannot be known, but they did leave a partial record. Ten of the fifty-six "Maineites" returned home during 1850–1851. Two "died at the mines." As for the others, a majority seem to have remained in California, where many founded families with names long familiar in the Pine Tree States—like the Wingates of Sebec, the Nortons of Corinth, the Towles of Bangor, the Woodburys and Colbirths of Oldtown, the Bradburys of Buxton.

Disease, usually described either as cholera or as typhoid, and accidents took a fearful toll. Of the Rutland California Company of seventeen members, one died while crossing Panama, two died "at the Mercedes Diggings" in 1849 (one of them by drowning), two more died in 1850 at San Francisco, and four others died in California between 1853 and 1865.*

College men were among the Argonauts. Stephen J. Field of Haddam, Connecticut (Williams, 1843), began his ascent to the heights when he was elected the first mayor of Marysville, California. While his brother Cyrus was busy in other fields, such as laying the transatlantic cable, he helped to frame the state's judiciary act, became chief justice of California, and was called by President Lincoln to the United States Supreme Court, where he sat for many years. Judge Fields was a doctrinaire, and in California was known, if none too favorably, for his Yankee notion of trying to uphold a most drastic Sunday-closing law.

* Information supplied in 1946 by Mrs. Charles C. Ward of South Pasadena, Calif., *Vermont Quarterly,* Vol. XIV, No. 4.

Many of the incoming New Englanders seem never even to have had a gold pan in hand. Frederick Billings, born in the Vermont hills at Royalton, a graduate of the University of Vermont in law, came through the Golden Gate with the Forty-niners, and immediately opened a law office. His firm became the most sought after in the wild and contentious city. He made much money, some of which he invested in real estate that doubled his fortune. It was he that named charming Berkeley, though his own name is borne by a city in Montana, through which he later pushed the tracks of the Northern Pacific Railroad as its president. The mines never saw James A. Folger, of Boston, who stopped in San Francisco to sell coffee, and founded the firm that bears his name.

The celebrated California town of Folsom took its name from a New Hampshire man, Joseph L. Folsom, who made his pile in San Francisco lots, then operated a huge ranch on which Folsom and its prison were built. One of the first music stores in San Francisco was opened by Joseph T. Atwill, from Boston, who did very well with music supplies, and even better in real estate. Yankees were so thick in San Francisco that early in 1850 one of those numerous New England societies was formed, with a library and reading room for members. Its officers were chosen, one each, from the six Yankee states: Charles Gilman, New Hampshire; J. C. Derby, Massachusetts; W. H. Clark, Maine; John A. Collins, Vermont; G. V. S. Gibbs, Rhode Island, and Theodore Dimond, Connecticut. Prominent among the members were William A. Dana, Louis R. Lull, Henry L. Dodge, Robert Hopkins, and O. N. Bush.*

In 1850 came the Reverend Samuel H. Willey of Campton, New Hampshire, but more recently of San Jose, California, where he already had organized the First Presbyterian Church, to build a fine church in San Francisco, for which William A. Palmer, a lumberman from Maine operating in California, donated a whole cargo of boards and timbers. He was soon preaching to three hundred of the faithful every Sunday, and among his most prominent parishioners was Captain Ebenezer Knight, native of Corinth, Vermont, now managing the great Atlantic & Pacific Mail Company's operations. Dr. Willey thought that the frantically busy San Franciscans ought to do something about a school. He marshaled all the kids he could find, formed them into a column, and at the busiest hour of the day marched them through the main streets, thus to show the crying need. Samuel Newton, a new Yankee arrival, thereupon was encouraged to open the first day school in the city.

* Even six years earlier, or 1844, the city could muster enough native New Englanders to stage a Thanskgiving feast "at the home of Mr. Lincoln."

When the frantic year of '49 had played out, records of the port of San Francisco showed that 275 vessels had docked there from the ports of the United States. Of this number, 121 came from New England. The total number of immigrants in California in that period is beyond knowing, for they came from all parts of the world; but the census of 1850 shows that native-born Americans numbered 69,610. The native Yankees discovered by the census takers were as follows: Massachusetts, 4,760 (which may have included those numerous men from the Bay State who had become naturalized citizens of Mexico in order to receive grants of land) Maine, 2,700; Vermont, 1,194; Connecticut, 1,317; New Hampshire, 904, and Rhode Island, 861. Incidentally, the New England natives increased steadily and their relative proportions, as by states, remained the same in 1870 as in 1850.

It seemed to many Argonauts that an unhealthy proportion of all the immigrants of '49 had taken up residence in San Francisco. The city was overrun with assorted thugs; and though there were a plenty of lawyers in the town there was little respect for the law. Hence, the Vigilantes, among whom at least one Yankee played a leading part—none other than the redoubtable Sam Brannan of Saco, Maine, who had brought the first gold from the American River to the city in '48. Brannan had closed his store at Sutter's fort and moved into San Francisco, where he bought all the real estate he could get. The Vigilantes were organized in his office, and he was elected their first president. They proceeded to take care of the worst of the city's thugs with dispatch; and Brannan gladly lent a hand to hang them higher than Haman of old.

Yankee Brannan appears to have lent a hand in almost everything in his adopted town. He was elected a member of the first city council. He was active in promoting the first banks, telegraph and express companies. He was active in promoting agriculture in the Bay region. He helped to organize the Society of California Pioneers, for he decided to remain in the state, having apostatized from the Latter-Day Saints. His greatest mistake was in establishing a distillery, for his need of the product became greater than that of his best customers. His wealth melted away, says one of his many biographers, and he died in poverty and obscurity in 1889. "But," said Hubert Howe Bancroft, "Brannan did more for San Francisco and for other places in California than was effected by the combined efforts of scores of other men."

Yet, Thomas Starr King could not be included in those scores of other men. This brilliant young preacher from the Hollis Street Church, Boston, was surely of the greatest influence in and on California. Having the grace of God in his heart and the gift of tongues, as Theodore Parker said of him,

King had preached to Universalist and Unitarian congregations, taught school, and in a book still celebrated had taught New Englanders something about their own White Mountains of New Hampshire. Now, in 1860, the struggling Unitarian parish in San Francisco asked him to come to help them. The young man came, and so did the Civil War. The thousands of Southerners in California were as hot for secession as their brothers in South Carolina. They organized and joined, almost to a man, subversive groups with such names as Knights of the Golden Circle, Knights of the Columbian Star, and openly supported a program to leave the Union. Incidentally, the commander of federal troops in California in 1861 was General Albert Sidney Johnston, who soon left to accept a high command in the Confederate army. Thus, when young Starr King arrived in 1860, he found the newest state torn with bitterly contending interests.

With a furious energy that unquestionably shortened his life, King threw himself into the fight to keep California for the Union. In San Francisco, in Sacramento, in all the settlements, and also in the mine diggings, he raised his eloquent voice to hold and charm city dwellers no less than the lads at the placers; and went on to raise more than a million dollars for the United States Sanitary Commission, while some 15,000 Californians volunteered for service in the Union army. Then, in 1864, he died, barely forty. He is remembered, too. Grateful Californians erected a monument to him which stands in Golden Gate Park, and sent a statue which is to be seen in the Capitol at Washington.*

New Englanders continued arriving in California right up to the outbreak of war. The census of 1860 showed that 32,269 of them, or almost triple the number in 1850, had remained in one place long enough to be enumerated. The relative proportions were about the same. Massachusetts still led with 12,165, and was followed by Maine, 9,864; Vermont, 3,419; Connecticut, 2,950; New Hampshire, 2,552, and Rhode Island, 1,319. In the meantime, the whole population of Californians born in the United States had risen from 69,610 to 233,466—which astounded everybody in the United States except good Californians.

With the end of the war, a new exodus to California began; and it was soon stimulated and simplified by completion of the first transcontinental railroad, which was the combined effort of the Union Pacific and the Central Pacific lines. Yankees had a great deal to do with both of these roads. Incidentally, completion of the Central Pacific left stranded several thousand Chinese laborers, who in a short time were considered as a menace to the state. But they had at least one champion, the Reverend William Chauncy

* Two mountain peaks are named for Starr King—in New Hampshire, and in Yosemite National Park.

Pond of Cambridgeport, Massachusetts, who migrated to found and super-intend the California Oriental Mission. Pond was a hero. At a time when feeling against Chinese on the West Coast ran tragically high, and American politicians were using the poor orientals as a Peril, bringing on murders and even massacres of Chinese and destruction of their property, Pond stood up and fought courageously, himself undergoing social boycott and even threats against his person.

Both before and after arrival of the railroad a great deal of transportation within California was by the New Hampshire, Concord-made stages of Wells, Fargo & Company, itself a Yankee-founded institution. Henry Wells, native of Thetford, Vermont, established Wells, Fargo specifically to do business in the West. In California another early stage and express line was already doing business as Adams & Company, and had as its president Alvin Adams, born in Andover, Vermont. Both concerns also did a large amount of banking; but in 1855, during a sudden panic, Wells, Fargo did and Adams did not continue to pay all obligations, and the former emerged as one of the great and classic institutions of the state and of the West generally. Wells, Fargo hired the most reliable drivers and guards possible and bought the best equipment, notably coaches and harnesses made in Concord, New Hampshire—of which more later.

Communication between California and the East had already been established by a company formed for that purpose by another New Englander, Hiram Sibley, of North Adams, Massachusetts, first president of the Western Union Telegraph Company; and the first transcontinental telegram was dispatched on October 24, 1861, by Yankee Stephen J. Field, chief justice of California. The New England influence was continuing even when it obviated an earlier New England influence, such as that of the Pony Express, which was put into operation by William Hepburn Russell, a native of Burlington, Vermont, who conjured up the idea of fast mail by relays of swift horses and good riders as a method of advertising his freighting and express company known everywhere on the Plains as Russell, Majors & Waddell.

In 1863 California elected a Yankee Forty-niner as governor. He was Frederick F. Low, born in Winterport, Maine who after seeking gold briefly had thrown away his pan and gone into business, as a banker in Marysville. The widow of another Maine Forty-niner, Mrs. Eliza Farnham, thought what California needed most of all was more marriageable females; and with that thought in mind she sailed for the eastern seaboard and went up and down it in an attempt to recruit two hundred unmarried or widowed women to go with her to the land of gold and climate and unattached males. In spite of the endorsement of Henry Ward Beecher, William Cullen Bryant,

Horace Greeley, and other prominent Yankees, she failed, and arrived back in San Francisco with one maiden and two widows. It was a noble try, however, and the California press hailed Mrs. Farnham, "who so warmly exerted herself to bring a few spareribs to this market."

Yet, Yankee males and females streamed into California throughout the sixties, and when the census of 1870 was taken it found 37,210 New Englanders scattered in all parts of the state. The ratios remained as before. Massachusetts was first with 15,334; then Maine, 11,261; Vermont, 3,500; Connecticut, 2,977; New Hampshire, 2,720; and Rhode Island, 1,418. By 1870 the total population was approximately 560,000, and well over half was native American. In that same year, most of them too late for the census, 32,000 more immigrants entered the state by the new railroad, while 20,000 others came by sea.

Among those arriving by railroad was a Maine man who was to become as notorious in California as he had been in New England and in Kansas— none other than the Reverend Isaac Kalloch, genius of Boston's White Temple, until a charge of adultery drove him forth and so to New York City, then to Kansas where, as this chronicle will be obliged to report later, he founded the town of Ottawa. Now, in the 1870's, he left Kansas for San Francisco, a city, said he, that "contains more wicked people of both sexes than I ever met in my life." His reputation as a preacher of great power had preceded him, but the newspaper reporters of San Francisco were astonished to find him a huge man of more than 240 pounds, whose rich, virile voice was like a musical foghorn. Nor was his garb clerical; he wore "a slouch hat with dressy clothes, smoked choice Havana cigars and looked like a prosperous Rocky Mountain stock-raiser."

No matter how he looked, the Reverend Isaac Kalloch prevailed on local Baptists to erect a huge Tabernacle for his church; and this he filled to overflowing at every service, or performance. He took an interest in local politics, ran for mayor in a hot campaign, and was shot and seriously wounded by Charles De Young, one of the publishers of the San Francisco *Chronicle*. Thereupon, Kalloch's son Milton purchased a revolver and without any loose talk proceeded to shoot De Young dead in his own office. Kalloch Senior was elected mayor. His term was most turbulent, and included an effort by his enemies to unseat him. He rode out this storm and many another, including circulation of a juicy and highly scandalous pamphlet relating to his trial on adultery charges in Boston thirty years before.

It would be difficult, probably impossible, to discover any lasting influence Kalloch had on California; but he was a good example of a restless and highly talented Yankee at large. He had left Maine for Boston, Boston for New York, New York for Kansas, Kansas for San Francisco; and now, in

1883, he left California for Washington Territory. He was fifty-one years of age when he started what was to be the last lap of his migration.

But, if Kalloch left no mark on the Golden State, that was not true of another immigrant from Maine, whose influence on much of California was to be very great—much greater, surely, than has generally been accorded him. Luther Calvin Tibbetts, a native of South Berwick in the Pine Tree State, was, in the capitals that are due him, the SEEDLESS ORANGE MAN, no less; and by all rights he should rate a statue or monument not only in the town of Riverside, where he settled and worked his magic, but in every city, town, and hamlet in the vast orange-growing region of the state.

Tibbetts was no youthful adventurer in 1870 when, in Washington, D.C., he met John W. North, one of the founders of Northfield, Minnesota, who was promoting something he called the Southern California Colony association. Tibbetts was fifty when he joined this group and settled on 160 acres in what is now Riverside, California, set out a few grapes and oranges, and ran a few cattle. He was a great reader, and had brought a considerable library with him; and now that he was a man of the soil he concentrated on agricultural subjects, including all the pamphlets and bulletins of the commissioner of agriculture in Washington. He was a great one for sending samples of soil for analysis. He continuously asked the commissioner as to what shrubs and trees were most suitable to his land. His letters and comments were so intelligent that the commissioner, William Saunders—one of the founders of the Grange—came to take considerable interest in the affairs of Luther Tibbetts. One day he sent three small orange shoots which had come to him from an unknown woman in Bahia, Brazil.

These strange plants, Saunders wrote, were reputedly of a seedless kind —if there was such a thing—and perhaps Tibbetts would like to experiment with them. Tibbetts would. He was elated. One day late in 1873 he hitched up and drove sixty-five miles to the nearest express office and returned home with the plants, which he set out, in March of 1874, close to his house in Riverside. He was careful to put a fence around each little tree. He acquired and read everything he could lay hands on about the cultivation of oranges. This turned out to be meager enough; so he went ahead pretty much by trial and error. No rules for irrigation were known. Suggestions for care were vague and conflicting. Most of his neighbors thought the idea of a seedless orange was preposterous, anyway. Orange trees had been set out in California as early as 1804, by the Spanish padres, and had done well enough, though the fruit was not particularly good—and was filled with seeds.

Tibbetts tended his three trees like children. Even so, a cow got through the fence and trampled one of them. He then put up a fence that would have stopped a shorthorn bull in full charge, with a padlocked gate to keep out inquisitive neighbors. He seems to have been a man of the greatest faith, and henceforth much of his thought centered around the remaining two orphans from Bahia, Brazil. To insure long life, the roots must first be well developed, and so Tibbetts nipped the buds to prevent flowering and fruiting. Meanwhile, news of his foolish experiment got around. Neighbors joked about "seedless" oranges, and had a grand time poking fun at this curious eccentric from Maine.

In their fourth year, Tibbetts decided the time had come to let the trees produce and see what the fruit was like. So, in 1878, he permitted each tree to bear two oranges. When ripe, he made something of an occasion of it, inviting many people of the settlement to his home. The four oranges, all sliced, were passed around, and lo—it was seen they contained not one seed. This in itself was most astonishing, probably as astonishing an event as southern California had witnessed, and surely, as things turned out, the most momentous. The fruit, moreover, was of superb quality. The skeptics who had come to laugh now sampled the bright slices and vowed they had never tasted the like in an orange, in California or elsewhere. The town of Riverside rejoiced exceedingly and promptly held a Citrus Fair, the first in the state.

Next season Tibbetts permitted the two trees to bear half a bushel of fruit each. The fruit was as good as before, or better, and wholly seedless. Tibbetts sent samples of the great, golden, juicy globes to one of his admirations, Senator James G. Blaine of Maine, who wrote enthusiastically of the fruit in the *American Agriculturist*.

These Washington Navels, as Tibbetts called them, naturally could not be propagated by seed, but only by grafting. Tibbetts was offered $10,000 apiece for his two trees. He refused, and for the next several years sold buds from them. Sales rose to $600 a month for this budwood. In 1880 a grove of seventy-five acres was set out to Tibbetts's Seedless by grafting buds to the stumps of the former trees. Within a year an English syndicate planted an even greater tract, all from Tibbetts's buds. The mania was in full swing.

Thousands of enthusiastic growers came to visit the Tibbetts home, to see the old master of magic and his two trees from which stemmed all this wondrous wealth. Southern California went into a boom of orange growing, as well as many other activities, which continues into the second half of the twentieth century. Land that could be had in 1880 for $20 an acre, sold five years later for $1,000 an acre. Luther Tibbetts, now known and without derision as the Seedless Orange Man, enlarged his home, bought a rubber-tired buggy and even a brougham.

As though her husband had not contributed enough to southern California, Mrs. Tibbetts now sought to give it something that would to become just

as typical of the region as seedless oranges. Mrs. Tibbetts, in short, set up as
a seeress and mystic prophet along the lines established elsewhere by Mother
Ann Lee, the Shaker leader, only she improved matters by giving séances and
founding a cult of her own. It was her custom, in the Tibbetts home at Riverside, to don "a ceremonial robe, reclining on a couch in a semi-darkened
room, Mr. T standing behind, gently waving a fan, while she passed into a
trance to await the arrival of a desired spirit." Believers came from round
about and overran the house and grounds, while the Seeress peered beyond
the veil and brought messages from the country of shades. It appears to have
been the first esoteric cult in a region since become famous for cults.

Luther Tibbetts himself was no cultist, yet he was no conventional man.
Because of lawsuits over lands and water, he felt called upon to erect a small
fort on his place, with portholes all around—to protect, he said, his interests
and person. Even then, he was shot and seriously wounded by the farm hand
of a neighbor. Litigations drained his wealth. He lost his home and property.
His end came in 1902, in the county hospital at Riverside, a melancholy end
indeed for the man who had done so much to set off the boom by which
southern California caught up with and passed the northern section of the
state. No other American appears to have contributed so much to his adopted
home. Yet, less than fifty years after Seedless Orange Tibbetts's death, he
is largely forgotten.*

Another migrant to southern California was to have an immense influence
in building up the orange-and-climate country. This was Harrison Gray Otis
—born of New England parents of old stock at Yankee Marietta, Ohio,
in 1837—who arrived in California at about the time Luther Tibbetts began
selling buds from his two precious trees. Otis bought an interest in the Los
Angeles *Times,* no great shakes of a newspaper, got control of it a bit later,
and for the next thirty years made that journal into the Voice, so far as the
boosters of southern California were concerned. Otis also operated in real
estate and built up one of the great fortunes in the entire state. His paper was
read by all, hated by more than a few, and in 1910 was thoroughly dyn-
amited. It came up out of the rubble bigger and noisier than ever, and lost
nothing by his death when it was taken over by his son-in-law Harry
Chandler, a native of Landaff, New Hampshire.

Beginning in the eighties, about the time the Seedless Orange came into
its own, and helped immeasurably by the clarion, not to say strident, voice

* Luther Calvin Tibbetts's daughter by his *first* wife—who does not enter this story—
made a significant remark about her father and her stepmother: "For many years the real
founder of this great California industry has been ignored, while his second wife, Eliza T.,
who had nothing to do with the event, except as an eyewitness, has been given almost whole
credit in various books and many magazine articles."

of the Los Angeles *Times,* a wholly new tide of immigration flowed into the southern counties of the state, among them Yankees, and among the Yankees Russell Judson Waters, a true man of vision, born in Halifax, Vermont, who had taught school, practiced law, and worked as a machinist. In 1886 he promoted the successful town of Redlands in southern California. Involved on the highest levels in banking, in cattle, water, and real estate, he also went to Congress and somehow found time to write a novel and a book of verses entitled *Lyric Echoes.*

The Yankees in southern California turned out to be great ones for forming state societies, to hold meetings and picnics; and one of the earliest of these groups was of people from Maine. A member of the Maine Society of Southern California, Mrs. Sarah B. Chapman Ensign, is probably a fair example of these transplanted New Englanders. Born in Stroudwater, Maine, in 1836, she was married in Massachusetts in 1861, settled in Algona, Iowa, right after the Civil War, and in 1893 came at last to the Elysian fields of southern California, forgetting, said she, "all past hardships and rejoicing in the beauties and warmth of the Golden West of southern California."*

Incidentally, it could have been the same Mrs. Ensign that came by way of Maine *and* Iowa who was the leader of the hegira out of the latter state to southern California, a phenomenon that appears to be without end. In mid-twentieth century there are said to be more Iowans in southern California than natives of any other state, including California. Also, there are doubtless more New Englanders than in the northern counties, so many, indeed, that it would be pointless to attempt to assess their influence in later years.

Yet, a fair example of the better grade of Yankee businessmen who did a good deal to build up the magic land might be in order. Such, surely, was William B. Staats, born in Glastonbury, Connecticut who came in 1886 to "improve his health." At that period the climate was becoming widely known, and many physicians recommended it on both general and specific reasons of thaumaturgy. Staats chose Pasadena, finding it chiefly a settlement in tents less than six months old; yet many Yankees were there, including his old preceptor at Williston Academy, C. M. Parker. Staats looked

* In 1913 what in the trade is vulgarly known as a mug book was published in Los Angeles under the title *Maine Men and Women in Southern California.* This contains many portraits and is careful to state the very year in which each Pine Tree Stater arrived. The examples here listed indicate that all parts of Maine heard the call of the Golden Land: Dr. William B. Bullard of Turner, and Lydia Bullard of Limerick; L. W. Blinn, Dresden; N. B. Blackstone, Livermore; Walter Trask, Jefferson; Jonathan Bixby, Norridgewock; Frank E. Trask, Industry; Addie Mitchell, Bangor; Frank S. Forbes, Brooks; Edwin Hutchinson, Rumford; Charles F. Abner Johnson, Sullivan, who "became first mayor Long Beach"; Mercios and Colin Whittier, Caribou; Hannah Judkins Starbird, Skowhegan; Micah and Andrew Croswell, Farmington; Everett Blanchard, Cumberland; Chester W. Brown, Washburn; and Mark T. Berry, who promptly planted his acres to Tibbetts's Seedless Oranges. Most of these Yankees came in the eighties, a few in the nineties.

around and with unerring judgment went into the real estate business. When he died, four decades later, he was still in real estate and was also a high official in the Pasadena Ice Co., the Union Oil Company of California, the Los Angeles Trust Co., the Home Telegraph & Telephone Co., the Ventura Water, Light & Power Co., the Mount Wilson Toll Road Co., and many another, including the Pasadena Country and Hunt clubs. Long before he had passed on, the city of Pasadena was known across the country and marveled at as the Millionaire Settlement of California. As late as 1927 the state elected a Yankee as chief executive. He was Clement Calhoun Young, born in Lisbon, New Hampshire, properly enough a Congregationalist and a Republican, but oddly enough, for a governor, a member of the society of Phi Beta Kappa.

As of 1910, California mustered an imposing number (50,873) of New England natives in residence, almost as many who were born there of New England parents, and at least 27,000 Californians who said their grandparents were Yankees. More, many more, have since followed them; and their chauvinism, or boosterism, for their adopted state is so quick and so deadly serious as to have long since become a byword. One can hope that they one and all know of and honor the first of their kind, good Booster Larkin, the Yankee immigrant from Massachusetts who composed his paeans as early as 1832; and honor energetic Sam Brannan of Maine, who in 1848 brought the first dust out from the original diggings; and honor, too, Maine's Luther Calvin Tibbetts, whose seedless oranges accounted for more wealth than the Mother Lode ever produced, and his spouse, Eliza T., founder of the first cult in the region of cults.

No matter where one goes to live in California, one will find, whether or not one knows it, a land in which New Englanders played notable parts.

CHAPTER XII

PIONEERS IN MINNESOTA

JAMES MADISON GOODHUE, a native of Hebron, New Hampshire, arrived in April of 1849 at the assortment of shacks and cabins called St. Paul and immediately started publication of the *Minnesota Pioneer*, the first newspaper in the territory. Goodhue was a large and stately man possessed of a keen mind as critical as it was sound, and for the next three years he and his brilliant *Pioneer* were the finest things a new region could have. His able writing soon brought the paper an audience as far afield as the Atlantic seaboard. He described eloquently the advantages of Minnesota and attracted many a good settler, but he was no mere booster; he condemned speculation in townships and town lots and was savagely critical of the casual and only too often loose government of the frontier hamlets. For he was pure Yankee and naturally believed in order.

Goodhue also held a profound belief that Minnesota was the ideal place to nourish New England virtues and to become a source and reservoir from which Yankee influence should spread into all the newer states, one after another as they were formed, until "the teeming millions of the West" were well indoctrinated with the ethics and general morality considered proper at Amherst College, from which Goodhue had been graduated in 1833. "We regard this Territory," he wrote with grim complacency, "to become the New England of the West."

Goodhue died in 1852, and a grateful legislature named a county in his honor. But his idea of a Yankee Minnesota did not die. Five years later, in the settlement of St. Anthony's Falls that was just beginning to be Minneapolis, a New England Society of the Northwest had been organized long enough to call for an anniversary banquet, a thumping and elegant affair, held in the new Cataract Hotel, which shook with the gorgeous oratory of the assembled Yankees. It was strictly cold-water oratory, too, for intoxicating liquors were rather pointedly absent from the tables.

But mere thoughts of the original Pilgrims of Plymouth were sufficient to mellow the orators and put them into high gear. And they reached the peaks and soared beyond. One hoped that Minnesota might imitate the heroic virtues of her foster mother, meaning New England. Another vowed that Yankee Thrift and Industry and Enterprise should build here a glorious superstructure of Education and Gospel Truth. . . . Aye, and the Sabbath bells of Yankee churches should echo, cried another who could not have seen much of Minnesota, should echo from hill to hill; and the still untrodden wastes of white pine be filled with the murmur of the common school. These things, agreed the congregated Yankees, would ensure the intelligence and integrity of our people, and "make the land we live in like the land we left."

It was all as noble and inspiring as it was smug. Yet it was far from idle or futile talk. The Yankees *were* to have an influence in and on Minnesota. Just how much is difficult, perhaps impossible to know, for racial influence is a subtle thing. It is not to be measured, like so much Lowell calico over the counter of a sutler's store at Fort Snelling, or the number of Mr. Colt's Patent Revolving Pistols needed to liquidate the recalcitrant Sioux along the Minnesota River. The influence on a region of a large but always minority group is to be sensed, to be felt, perhaps on occasion even seen with the naked eye; but it defies all the yardsticks of the professors of the social sciences, no matter their imposing graphs, their means and medians, their cabalistic improvisations which they cite as truths and call by such wondrous terms as the coefficient of acculturation.

Who, in God's world or without, could get his teeth into the coefficient of acculturation? Better, far, to consider the life and times of Northfield, a town of Rice County, Minnesota, where Yankee influence could be sensed, seen, heard, *and* measured most accurately as long ago as 1876, and where it flourishes notably to this day. Moreover, the Yankee influence emanating from Northfield spread, as James Goodhue had hoped and believed it would, far beyond Minnesota's borders, to be felt in all the West, even in darkest Missouri.

Northfield, in the county named for Minnesota's territorial delegate in Washington, Henry M. Rice, who was born in Waitsfield, Vermont, was settled in 1855 by a group composed almost wholly of Yankees. The town was named for two eminent early citizens, John W. North, a graduate of Wesleyan College, Middletown, Connecticut, and Ira Stratton Field, a native of Orange, Massachusetts. Thus was Northfield's genealogy pure from the first cabin.

More Yankees followed closely on the heels of the founding fathers, and by the time they all had time to put down their roots, they set about, typically enough, to found a Yankee college. To head this school presently came James W. Strong, late of Brownington, Vermont, educated at Yankee Beloit College in Wisconsin, a slightly built but sinewy Congregational clergyman who was possessed of strong character and great energy. For the next third of a century Strong gradually molded the feeble school into a small yet outstanding college worthy the name, and by reason of a large gift from a Yankee donor, named it Carleton. Carleton is one of the reasons why Northfield retains, after almost a century of dilution, a good deal of its primeval New England character.

That character prevailed in even greater degree in 1876, and because of it, on that year's 7th of September, Northfield became a town in the American legend, a place fit to compare with Lexington and Concord, Massachusetts, with Harper's Ferry, Virginia, or Johnstown, Pennsylvania, in that the towns themselves live in the shadows of the tremendous events that have taken place within their borders.

It was at Northfield that the celebrated James-Younger gang broke, as the saying has it, their pick. They broke it on the flinty character of the Yankees in residence, men who would not permit their First National Bank to be robbed with impunity. Nor was it robbed. In six or seven seething minutes that clouded the street and village square with the blue haze of exploding powder, the enraged Yankees made western history in true western style. Aghast at the effrontery of strangers who should attempt to steal *their* thrifty dollars, they shot all hell out of the raiders.

And, lest present-day descendants of the First National's defenders grow effete and forgetful, there reposes in a fine plush-lined case in a Northfield museum, a relic that would jog anybody's mind. It is the authenticated right ear of one of the raiders, now desiccated and brown as an autumn leaf, but patently an ear, warning enough, surely, to leave Northfield institutions alone.

The story of the frustrated raid has been told many times.* Eight horsemen, including Frank and Jesse James, and Cole, Bob, and Jim Younger, met resistance at every turn, *and* aggression. Josiah Allen, native Vermonter, Northfield hardware merchant, was the first to note what the strangers were up to. He ran like mad for his shop shouting, "Get your guns, boys," then started passing out his stock of fine new rifles and shotguns to the embattled townsmen, who rallied like their forebears at Lexington. Young Henry Wheeler, native of Newport, New Hampshire, took up the cry at about the same time, ducked into a hotel across Division Street from the bank, picked up a handy Army carbine, and went into action.

* See the author's *Little Annie Oakley and Other Rugged People*, published by The Macmillan Company, New York, 1948.

Captain Henry Sumner French, Northfield postmaster, looked out upon the astounding scene. He had never seen anything like it in his native Sandy Point, Maine. He first locked his front door, then started looking for a weapon. None was at hand. So, Captain French stepped briskly out into the alley behind the post office, picked up an armful of sizable rocks, then began bouncing them off the astonished two-gun men in the street and their irritated horses.*

The robbers inside the First National were not doing very well either. The acting cashier, Joseph Lee Heywood, late of Fitzwilliam, New Hampshire, refused to open the safe. Nor would the bookkeeper, a Mr. Wilcox from Westminster, Vermont, nor Teller Alonzo E. Bunker, from Littleton, New Hampshire. One and all, they answered "No" to everything. One of the bandits wantonly shot and killed brave Heywood.

Out in the street, where the rest of the gang were attempting to terrorize the town, the Northfield Yankees were rallying with the firearms from Merchant Allen's store. And the other hardware merchant, Anselm Manning, a good marksman, had fetched a gun and started shooting. A few moments later, while smoke still curled in the street, six of the raiders were in flight, two of them badly wounded. Two more of the gang lay dead in the dust of Division Street.

Three of the fleeing men were presently caught, another killed. Only two, the James brothers, escaped; and they were never quite the same after. Northfield had cured them completely of any hankering for banks. They did stage one train robbery in 1879, two more in 1881; for the rest, they remained quiescent. Northfield had been their supreme disaster. The Yankees there had been too much for them. They had robbed banks with impunity all over the West. But not the First National of Northfield, the funds of which, as the local historian remarked with grim satisfaction, remained intact.†

The breaking up of the James-Younger gangs was the most spectacular instance of New England influence in Minnesota. Whether or not learned men would consider it in determining their coefficient of acculturation is

---

* I immensely enjoy contemplating doughty Captain French, probably the first man ever to attack the James-Younger gang with an armful of stones; and hope that when Northfield gets around to having a mural painted of the affair, as surely it will, one of the scenes will show State-of-Mainer French with his neolithic artillery, ably supported by his fellow citizens Truman H. Streeter, late of Rowe, Massachusetts, and Elias Hobbs, both of whom heaved Rice County rocks at the bandits.

† In the museum-home of William Schilling, at Northfield, reposed in 1949, just as it had for years, the right ear of bandit Charlie Pitts. The body of bandit Pitts was probably dissected at Michigan University's medical college. Young Henry Wheeler, who did such noble work in the Northfield defense, was at the time a medical student at Ann Arbor. In a recent letter to the author Frederick H. Whitfield, now of Los Angeles, recalled that during his boyhood in Ann Arbor "the body of one of the Northfield raiders was brought to the college and was worked over by the doctors and students, who reserved several small portions as relics."

doubtful. It is too simple, too easy of comprehension, to figure in the means and medians of academic mumbo-jumbo. But it will serve here as one indication of Yankee influence in the region, and a better example of the display of certain characteristics which are generally held to be typical of Yankees might be difficult to discover. The New Englanders of Northfield surely showed great courage and savage determination in defense of *Thrift*, which to them was represented in their First National Bank.

By 1876, the year of the Raid, there were approximately 29,000 native Yankees in a total population of approximately 450,000 people in Minnesota. They were thus a tiny minority group, and steadily their number became smaller in relation to the whole population; yet their influence was all out of proportion to their number. One reason stemmed unquestionably from the Yankee character. Another, just as unquestionably, came from the fact that uncommonly able Yankees in all lines of endeavor, both intellectual and other, were in the vanguard of settlers, and thus had the advantages, as well as the risks and the difficulties, of all pioneers. The whole map of Minnesota is covered with their names.

Minnesota became a territory in 1849, a time when the main stream of migration out of New England was still, if the sudden rush to California be excepted, into Iowa. Yet a small number of highly influential Yankees were already busy in the region which Henry Hastings Sibley, the son of New England parents, suggested could well be called Minnesota. This name came from the Sioux dialect and had been handsomely translated by the Reverend Gideon H. Pond, missionary and pioneer settler from Connecticut, as the Land of Sky-Tinted Water. It was and is a beautiful name, indicating that the good and revered Mr. Pond had a feeling for poetry in his kindly soul.

Anticipating the organization of the new territory, James M. Goodhue began publishing Minnesota's first newspaper a few weeks before. Two years before that, Miss Harriet Bishop, tall, angular, and spinster, the perfect symbol of the Yankee schoolmarm, who had been born in Panton, Vermont, and drilled under the stern and inspired Catharine Beecher, also a Yankee, had opened the first school in St. Paul, with two white and five Indian pupils.

The convention called to take preliminary steps toward territorial status was held in still raw Stillwater, named for the native town of some of its founders in Penobscot County, Maine. Nine of the twenty-seven members of the first state legislature were born in New England, and they were men filled with both ideas and energy. Incidentally, the Army post which played so important a part in Minnesota's earliest days was named for Colonel Josiah Snelling, a soldier born in Boston.

Stillwater was the first genuine white settlement in Minnesota. John Mc-

Kusick proposed the name in 1853. He had come there three years before, to log and to build the first sawmill in the region. Jonathan McKusick had arrived in 1846, and a year later came more men of the family, named Ivory and William. The McKusick migration formed a pattern that became common in the movement from New England to Minnesota and endured to the end of the century. The pattern went like this: First, a father or an adventurous son took off to see what was "at the West." Once he had found a place to his liking, he wrote home and related the wonders and beauties of his particular piece of ground in Minnesota. Then, and usually soon, came another brother, or perhaps two, often with wives and families, to be followed at intervals by more brothers, sisters, cousins, uncles, aunts, and in-laws.

This sort of migration also had occurred to western New York, to Ohio, and the other new states in turn; but the record indicates Minnesota as the first state where the continuous movement of the members of whole families became so numerous as to make a pattern. It had begun early, in missionary times. Gideon and Samuel Pond began it. Soon came the Hobarts from St. Albans, Vermont—Chauncy, who preached all over the pine woods and was chaplain to the territorial legislature, and Morris, who came in 1850 to expound the Methodist Word in early Hastings and Farmington and to die at last in Mankato.

There was almost a mass migration of the Staples family from Maine. Isaac appears to have been the first to venture into Minnesota. He left his native Topsham in 1853 to settle and log in Stillwater and to found the First National Bank in that town. Samuel followed Isaac in 1854. Josiah reached Stillwater in 1858. William had come in 1855, and was one of the founders of Grow, in Anoka County. George L. came in 1856 and settled and named Brunswick, Kanabec County. Charles A. came with his parents in 1854 and later farmed in Meeker County. Franklin, fresh from the College of Physicians and Surgeons in New York City, hung out his shingle in 1862, in Winona. Another Staples doctor of medicine, Henry L., continued the migration into 1888, when he came to practice in Minneapolis. Not all these Staples men were brothers; but all were of the same family, and with their wives and progeny probably numbered a full thirty persons, to say nothing of the natural increase after they arrived. It is only fitting that a town in Todd County should bear the name of Staples.

When John Sargent Pillsbury left Sutton, New Hampshire, in 1855 to look at the West, he started one of the most influential migrations of all. He himself became in due time governor of Minnesota, and long before that other Pillsburys, all from in and around Concord, New Hampshire, were in his wake. Charles A. came in 1869 and was responsible for putting the Pillsburys into the flour-milling business. Fred C. came in 1871; George A., in 1878.

The Pillsburys knew how to prosper in a new country, and they made a great deal of money in timberlands, in banking, and in railroads; but their name became indelibly identified with flour. In the Pillsburys, along with their energy and shrewdness, were also virtually all of the Yankee characteristics. It was only typical that as governor of Minnesota, John S. Pillsbury often called upon his New England God for help in trying times, and not in vain. During Minnesota's worst grasshopper epidemic in 1877, he made an eloquent plea for divine interposition, and in almost no time at all the hordes of insects disappeared. . . .

Composing another flouring family were two of the remarkable Washburns of Livermore, Maine; namely, Cadwallader C. and brother William D. who, with partner John Crosby of Hampden in Maine, became as well known as the Pillsburys. The great success of these Granite State and Pine Tree State Yankees had the effect of attracting many more from their home regions to Minnesota. And it also had an even more direct bearing on migration. All three families—Pillsburys, Washburns, Crosbys—were patently of the opinion that the best possible help they could have in their various enterprises was in Maine and New Hampshire. So, in the last third of the century they brought to Minneapolis a large number of energetic young men who were immediately engaged in the manufacture, sale, and shipping of flour.

In the 1830's and before, a goodly portion of New England migration had been, as shown before, by formally organized companies, such as those that founded Marietta, many villages in Illinois and Michigan, and Beloit, Wisconsin. In Minnesota, however, with two or three none-too-successful exceptions, the new towns were pioneered by one or more maverick settlers, or perhaps one and at most two families, who had little idea where they would drive their stakes until they arrived on the ground. Then, and not before, they attracted others from their native villages by the basic and excellent medium of letters home. This pattern appears again and again in Minnesota. Consider Stillwater, a fair example, and the flow of State-of-Mainers:

Pioneering at Stillwater with the McCusick and Staples families were the Stimsons, Charles F. and Albert, from York County. John Benson was an early Methodist pastor there. John Goodrich from Somerset County was deputy surveyor of logs, a most important job in Stillwater. Next, came Aquila Greeley, from Greeley, who did much of the town's early surveying. The best hotel in the new village was built and run by William Stanchfield, born in Maine. A Maine Congressman Samuel F. Hersey, with many relatives, established large sawmills in Stillwater, not long after the McKusick mill started running. A bit later came Jacob Bean, from old Stillwater, to team in lumber with the Herseys, whom he had known back home. The movement continued to the end of the century bringing, in the 1860's the Merrys from Bath, the Sticakneys from Wilton, the Francis Joys from Clinton; bringing, in the 1870's, the William Lowells from Concord, and more Herseys from Bangor. The 1880's saw the arrival of still others, including the George Atwoods from Waterville. But the pioneer Congregational minister in this largely Maine settlement, who came early in 1847, was a New Hampshire man, the noted William Boutwell, missionary from Lyndeboro.

Men and women of both Maine and New Hampshire were pioneers of Anoka. Before either the village or the county had a name John R. Bean of Salmon Falls—on the line between New Hampshire and Maine—had broken the first land and made a farm, in 1849. Two years later James Frost from Rumford, Maine, had settled another farm, and Maine-Stater Silas Farnham had opened a crossroads store. When the village of Anoka was organized in 1853, the Millers of Waterford, Maine, moved in, to be followed by more Maine families—the Josiah Clarkes of China, the Martin Beans of Dexter, the Daniel McLaughlins of New Sharon, and the Cutter brothers of Westbrook—Ammi, who came first to log along the Rum River, and Oscar, who went into banking. The Robbins family of Phillips—a Maine town which, with New Sharon and Corinna appears to have sent forth to various states far more than its share of migrants—came to Anoka in the fifties, and their son, Daniel M., became prominent in the important grain elevator business. The sixties, seventies, and eighties all witnessed a steady flow from Maine to Anoka, among them being Marcus Q. Butterfield from Farmington, Benjamin McCann from Aroostook, which even then was itself hardly settled, the George Wymans from Chester, the Everett Hammonds from Cornish, and Alvah Eastman from Lovell Center, who published the Anoka *Herald* in the town where his brother Job had erected the first hotel.

And that was the way in which the Yankees came to Anoka.

The mores of Maine appeared in Anoka at an early period, when a vigilante group attacked the Empire saloon operated by Daniel D. Dudley— likely a Yankee too—broke door and windows, then poured his stocks of liquor into the street. Dudley promptly reopened, and this time his place was destroyed by fire "of undetermined origin." It was possibly a coincidence, but the First Methodist Church of Anoka was presently destroyed by fire, the origin of which was as mysterious as that of the disaster to Dudley's dramshop.*

---

* The first Temperance agitation in Minnesota arrived in the person of the aforementioned Miss Harriet Bishop, an inveterate foe of dramtaking. When in 1852 the territory enacted a strong antiliquor law, patterned after the Maine statute, she saw to it that the bells of Protestant churches in the city "rang with many a simultaneous peal of joy." A sensible chief justice of the territorial court said the act was unconstitutional.

Quakers and others from Maine settled Bethel in Anoka County, and Moses Twitchell named it for his home town on the Androscoggin. And the town of Blaine, which came into being as late as 1877, was named to honor the Plumed Knight and senior senator from Maine.

Although the town of Zumbrota was settled by the Strafford Western Emigration Company, mostly from Massachusetts, families from Maine were there as soon or sooner than the organized group. The Joseph Thachers of Lubec, the Mullikens of Orneville, and later the Frank Welds of Skowhegan were Zumbrota pioneers. So was Heman Palmer, of Orford, New Hampshire, who set up as a merchant. A Goodhue County history says that Withian Fisher, from Maine, was the first Zumbrota settler of all.

The village of Marine on St. Croix got its name by honoring the Yankee sea captains who founded Marine in Illinois, several of whose enterprising citizens soon heard of the great white pines of Minnesota, and forthwith moved there, to found the new Marine and speculate in lands. Among them were Lewis and George Judd from Connecticut, and Orange Walker from St. Albans, Vermont, who was soon joined by a brother, P. E. Walker, also from St. Albans. A pioneer lumberman of Marine was Levi Stratton from Chester, Maine.

Without a doubt the most casual, and perhaps the most improbable settlement in Minnesota was Hutchinson, founded after a fashion, and named, by three of the Singing Hutchinsons of New Hampshire. For half a century this remarkable group of brothers and sisters sang their way up and down and across the United States—and took England into camp, too. They sang not only for cash but for Causes. First, it was Abolition; then in turn came Dr. Graham's foods, Amelia Bloomer's clothing, Susan Anthony's rights for women; and always they raised their voices against Rum, nicotine, calomel, playing cards, pool halls, and bowling alleys. They were born, all twelve, in Milford, children of Jesse and Polly Hutchinson, who would not permit a musical instrument in the house.

But the Hutchinson children could not help singing. By 1842 a group of them were touring New England. Ten years later the Singing Hutchinsons were a national institution. There was nothing before, nor since, quite to compare with these natural, wholly untrained vocalists, who wrote most of their numbers, but also did very well with a song composed by their friend, a New Hampshire lad named Walter Kittredge. This was "Tenting Tonight," and the Hutchinsons made it one of the great songs of the Civil War period.*

* The author's maternal grandmother heard a group of Hutchinsons sing several times in Boston, and more than half a century later she could recall the vital alto of Abby, throbbing like the low notes of an organ, while brothers Asa, John, and Judson sang all around the melody.

The Hutchinsons simply could not say No to any "good" Cause. So, in 1855, when all New England was stirred by the plight of Bleeding Kansas, and was being urged to go and settle there, to keep it Free-State, the Hutchinsons heard the call. In August of 1855, Asa, John, and Judson Hutchinson suddenly decided to sing their way across country to Kansas and found a stout Abolition town there.

September saw them singing sweetly on a Lake Erie steamer bound for Cleveland. But at Milwaukee, they happened upon an old acquaintance, William Wirt Pendergast from Durham, New Hampshire, who persuaded them to take a look at Minnesota before going to Kansas. The desolate fate that hung over Bleeding Kansas could not have weighed too heavily on the brothers, for they changed their route overnight and struck out for St. Paul.

After a concert or two, the three brothers with Roswell Pendergast, cousin of William, and a party of guides loaded two wagons and drove west along the Minnesota River. They paused briefly at the new, and mostly Yankee, settlement of Glencoe, then went on another seventeen miles up the tributary Hassan River. A spot on the bend of the stream looked pretty good. Without more ado, they set up their tent, made a big fire—it was well below zero—and then the three brothers put their heads together and let go with a familiar hymn, "Thus Far the Lord Has Led Us On." And thus, too, was the blame properly placed for leaving Kansas to the Enemy.

Come evening, the matter of formal organization of the town of Hutchinson was cared for. In the frosted tent, with a log fire at the flap, officers were elected to plat and to govern the place. Land for a village green was voted. Twelve lots were to be set aside for schools and churches, and fifteen acres for public parks. The trees along the Hassan River were snapping with cold as the Yankee brothers went on with their plans. Judson suggested that five acres be marked off for what he called Humanity's Church, a nonsectarian house of worship (which incidentally, and early in its life, developed a powerful tinge of Methodism). And the founders were explicit on the uses to which the land of Hutchinson, Minnesota, could *not* be put. "Resolved," they vowed in the drafty tent, "that as a company or as individuals we will not sell, lease or give away any lot or a part of a lot . . . to any person or persons who shall under any circumstances sell, or keep for sale or give away, any *alcoholic* or intoxicating liquor whatsoever except for *medicinal purposes,* or who shall keep . . . any Bowling Alley, Billiard Table or a gambling house of any description whatsoever."

On the next day the Hutchinsons paid a surveyor for marking off a townsite and commissioned another man to build a community log cabin, to be ready by April 1, 1856. Then the brothers departed, singing their way down the

Mississippi, and at St. Croix Falls paid Judge Charles E. Flandrau $75 to register the townsite of Hutchinson.

For the next thirty years various Hutchinsons came to the town to spend weeks, or months. Asa actually settled there in his later years, and his son Oliver opened a drugstore in which, one feels certain, no alcoholic liquors labeled as such were sold. In the early years of its life, a number of New Hampshire people went there to settle and stay, among them Ellen, sister of the Pendergast boys, who showed great courage and resolution when the village was attacked and partially burned by Sioux. After the village was incorporated, women were permitted to vote on all local questions. But more Germans than Yankees settled in Hutchinson.

The Yankee settlers of Hutchinson were not to be an isolated group in McLeod County. Glencoe, where the singers paused before choosing their townsite, proved to be a New Canaan for a continuous trek from New England. Gideon Gilbert from New Haven, Connecticut, founded the Bank of Glencoe. Liberty Hall from Peru, Maine, established the Glencoe *Register,* which had occasion often to chronicle the arrival of more Yankees, including Dr. Albert McWright who came from Whiting, Vermont, and Aubry Knight from Editor Hall's own home town of Peru, who established the McLeod County Bank, and another banker, Franklin Dean from Windsor, Vermont. There came, too, Benjamin Buck from Bethel, Vermont, to set up as a hotel keeper in Glencoe; Henry Wadsworth, from New Haven, Connecticut, to open a hardware store; and Sylvanus Holbrook Kellogg, born in Franklin, Vermont, and trained at Bangor Theological Seminary, to preach a while before going on to distant Hoquiam, Washington, on the west coast. H. A. Child, lawyer of Paris, Maine, came to practice in Glencoe, and his letters home brought his younger brother Elisha, to go into the farm machinery business.

Elsewhere in the county Eli F. Lewis founded Winsted and named it for his native town in Connecticut. Settlers from Maine prevailed in naming Hale township for the New Hampshire senator and noted Abolitionist, John Parker Hale.

It was in Sherburne County, however, that the Yankees were almost as numerous as in the counties they had come from in New England. The county itself was named for Moses Sherburne, born in Mount Vernon, Maine, in 1808, who served as United States judge in Minnesota territory and took an important part in writing the state constitution. The good judge must have liked the county, too, for he moved there and built him a nice home in Orono, which had been named by Ard Godfrey, a native of the Maine

Orono. Into Sherburne County presently moved the Houlton families, from Houlton, Maine, to establish a new Houlton. They arrived in Minnesota in the pattern that was becoming common. Horatio Houlton came in 1864. Dwight followed a year later, and in 1866 came William. Their combined energies were very great, for they engaged at one and the same time in logging, sawmilling, farming, and banking, and appear to have been successful in each field.

Another group of brothers from Maine came to log the timber along Sherburne County's Elk River. Nathaniel Tibbetts came first, in 1850, then came younger brothers Joshua, Benjamin, and James. All had been born in small New Sharon, on Maine's Sandy River, from which, after about 1840, young men, and whole families, left in what in retrospect seems an interminable procession. One wonders what and who began the movement. Were New Sharon's people uncommonly restless? or amibitious? Was the town, as one said, played out? Or was it overpopulated? Whatever the cause, emigrants from New Sharon dispersed to all parts of the American West. One finds records of them as early settlers in virtually every county in Minnesota. More often than not, like the Tibbetts brothers, they were energetic people of good judgment, quick to see a chance and just as quick to grab it. Opportunity was not obliged to knock more than once, nor very loudly, to be heard by New Sharon men, once they had left Maine.

Perhaps the most influential Yankee to settle in all Sherburne County, however, was a Bostonian, a human dynamo named Oliver Hudson Kelley, who took a section of land in Elk River township as early as 1849 and made himself a farm. He had already roved through Illinois and Iowa, working as a tramp newspaperman or as a telegrapher. He was intelligent and was a forceful writer. From his new farm on Elk River, its stumps still smoking from clearing fires, he sent several articles on farming conditions in the West to the Bureau of Agriculture in Washington. The Bureau, astonished at such valuable reports coming from a backwoods farm, asked Kelley to come to Washington. This he did, in good time, and at the end of the Civil War the Bureau sent him into the South, where he reported conditions in the rural districts. Then, in 1867, he and six other men organized the National Grange of the Patrons of Husbandry. Kelley himself was the first chief organizer; he went through the Midwest like a tornado, sweeping the farmers into the Grange, which became one of the great influences on life in the United States. The idea of the Grange had come to Kelley, a big-city man, while clearing his lonely farm in Sherburne County.

On the western bank of the Mississippi, across from Sherburne County, was another political division named for a New Englander—Charles Thomas

Stearns, born in Pittsfield, Massachusetts. He served on the territorial council, and in 1855 settled in St. Cloud, which had been pioneered and named in 1851 by John L. Wilson from Columbia Falls, Maine, the "Father of St. Cloud," who was presently joined by his younger brother Joseph. John liked to read history, especially that of Napoleon's time, and was much taken with the name of the French palace where the Empress Josephine spent only too much of her time. Hence a St. Cloud in the wilds of Minnesota Territory.

Men from Maine were not to dominate primeval Stearns County, for the settlers seem to have been largely from other parts of New England. Thomas Alden of Hartford, Connecticut, owned part of the site of St. Cloud. The first lumberman was Charles Bridgman from Amherst, and one of the first merchants was Nehemiah Clarke from Hubbardston—both Massachusetts towns. An early farmer was Oscar Taylor from Lisbon, high in the New Hampshire hills. Alphonso Barto, born in Hinesburg, Vermont, settled in St. Cloud at the end of the Civil War and in 1874 was elected lieutenant governor of Minnesota. One of his neighbors in St. Cloud was Christopher C. Andrews, from Hillsborough, New Hampshire, who became United States Minister to Sweden. But Maine was well represented by a lumberman, Thomas McClure from Waldo, and by Josiah Haywood from Mechanics Falls, who built both a hotel and a flour mill.

In neighboring Benton County, the Gilmans from Gilmanton, New Hampshire, established a new Gilmanton and were pioneer settlers, too, in the village of Sauk Rapids; Charles Gilman was elected lieutenant governor in 1880. George Brott of Tolland, Connecticut, was a founding father of Sauk Rapids, and to it came William H. Wood and wife Eliza of Loudon, New Hampshire, to found and edit the *New Era*. Lorenzo A Babcock, born in Sheldon, Vermont, who was attorney general of the territory, lived in Sauk Rapids before removing to St. Paul to practice law.

In Stearns County the rising village of Sauk Center did not attract as many Yankees as St. Cloud, though Elliott Bridgman from Amherst, Massachusetts, was a pioneer miller, and Edward Phelps Barnum of Stonington, Connecticut, became a hotel keeper and later established a newspaper, the tremendously named Sauk Center *Avalanche*. Then, in 1866, came Dr. E. J. Lewis, born in Westfield, Connecticut. To Dr. Lewis and wife, says one of the histories of Minnesota, "three children were born: Fred, a miller at Bertha; Claude, a physician at St. Cloud; and Harry Sinclair, author of the famous book *Main Street*."*

* Son Sinclair wrote some other books, too, and in 1930 received the Nobel Prize in Literature. In 1949 his first historical novel, *The God Seeker* appeared, its scene set in early Minnesota.

ALLEGED OPPORTUNITY AWAITED THE YANKEE IN BOTH MINNESOTA AND COLORADO

THE GOAL OF MANY YANKEES WAS STILLWATER, MINNESOTA

MINNEAPOLIS WAS NAMED BY A CLASSICAL-MINDED YANKEE

"Harps in the Wind"

Arthur French

Left: CAPTAIN JOHN FRENCH ATTACKED THE JAMES-YOUNGER OUTLAW GANG WITH AN ARMFUL OF STONES. Right: JOHN, JUDSON, AND ASA OF THE SINGING HUTCHINSONS FOUNDED A MINNESOTA TOWN

THE EVENING HYMN

THE DEPARTURE

THIS IS HOW THE CARGO OF MERCER'S MAIDENS APPEAR

TO AN IMAGINATIVE ARTIST OF HARPER'S WEEKLY IN 1865

CARTOON USED TO OFFSET LIBEL ON KANSAS CLIMATE (*c.* 1870)

BUSY BLAKE STREET IN ENERGETIC DENVER IN 1865

Oregon Historical Society

DREAMER HALL J. KELLEY
OF NEW HAMPSHIRE

New Hampshire Historical Society

KELLEY'S CIRCULAR
OF 1831 PROPOSING
A MIGHTY EMIGRATION

THE
OREGON COUNTRY.
A CIRCULAR
TO THE CITIZENS OF THE U. STATES.

PORTLAND, OREGON, IN 1852; FOUNDED BY YANKEES

The first permanent settler at Faribault was Luke Hulett, from Walling-ford, Vermont, and he was little more than established when other Green Mountain people arrived: Edward Leach of Waitsfield, George W. Batchel-der of Danville, Horace Barron of Bradford, Thomas Scott Buckham of Chelsea, and Nathan Bemis of Whitingham. Hard on their heels came William H. Dyke, from Pittsford, to make and ship the first Minnesota flour sold in the eastern states. A part of the farm of Levi Nutting from Amherst, Massachusetts, went into the site of Faribault, and so did the acres of G. L. Gilmore, a pioneer from New Hampshire. Nutting may have had a hand in bringing Lauren Armsby from Amherst to preach at Faribault.

In the neighboring village of Northfield, the very same where the Jameses and Youngers were put to rout and disaster, Benaiah James from New Hampshire owned part of the townsite. Henry Lawrence, born in Claremont, New Hampshire, established the Northfield *News,* its run now (1950) un-broken for almost three-quarters of a century. John Scofield from Stamford, Connecticut, was probably the first physician to practice in Northfield. Jesse Ames, retired deep-sea skipper of Vinalhaven, Maine, came early with his sons to build a flour mill on the Cannon River in Northfield. Solomon P. Stewart from Williamstown, Massachusetts, was a pioneer merchant.

One senses a tragedy connected with the founding of one Rice County village, Walcott, now no longer on the map. Says the county historian: "It was named in honor of Samuel Walcott, from Massachusetts, who was a very able, energetic and talented man, but after a time his mind became distraught, and he found an abiding place in an insane asylum in his native state."

Olmsted County in Minnesota took its name from a most notable man in the pioneering line, David Olmsted, born in Fairfax, Vermont, in 1822. At sixteen he was working in the lead mines of Wisconsin. At eighteen he was a pioneer at Monona, Iowa. At twenty-four he helped to frame the state constitution for Iowa. Two years later he established a trading post in Min-nesota, and was elected president of the first territorial legislature. In 1861 he returned to his old home in the Green Mountains, to die.[*]

The county named for James Madison Goodhue, who came from Hebron, New Hampshire, to establish Minnesota's first newspaper, was also attract-ing a whole raft of Yankees, among them William Stanton and family, who founded Stanton. Cannon Falls had an influential pioneer in William D. Hale, from Norridgewock, Maine, who became a partner with W. D.

[*] This remarkable young man also took time out to edit the *Minnesota Democrat,* and to be elected, in 1854, the first mayor of St. Paul.

Washburn in lumber and flour. But the prettily named Red Wing drew them early and late, with Vermonters the most numerous. Here from Williamstown came Silas Bolles to preach, and Sidney Grannis, from Orleans, to build the big sawmill on the Bluff, and Charles K. Davis, from Chester, to publish the *Argus,* and Edward L. Baker, from Hubbardston, with his surveying tools, and Dr. Charles N. Hewitt from Vergennes; and Elijah Blodgett, from Weathersfield, to operate a grain elevator. A native of small Hartland, Jesse M. Hodgman, was without difficulty twice elected mayor of the new city. One of the first teachers was Orrin Dinsmore, from New Hampshire, who may well have selected Red Wing because of Daniel C. Hill, from New Hampshire's Hillsborough, who was its pioneer manufacturer of doors and sash.*

No matter what Minnesota needed, the farms and villages of New England could supply it. Steamboats were important before railroads came to Minnesota, and so Captain Russell Blakely migrated from North Adams, Massachusetts, and ran a line in opposition to Captain George Houghton from Brandon, Vermont, and Captain Edwin B. Lowell from Abbott, Maine. Amherst Willoughy from Rutland, Vermont, started a pioneer stage and express line in St. Paul. Alonzo Whitney, an intelligent husbandman of Rindge, New Hampshire, migrated to Wadena and there established an influential periodical, the *Northern Pacific Farmer.* But it was Horatio Lillibridge from Connecticut that filled a really gnawing need; in 1856 he started a cracker factory, the first in Minnesota and perhaps the first west of the Mississippi, much to the delight of New Englanders, who were not quite whole without a supply of crackers.

Roswell Russell of Vermont opened the first store of any sort in what soon became Minneapolis. He had walked through deep snow all the way from Prairie du Chien, in Wisconsin, to do it; and he was also groom at the first wedding.

New England, of course, sent missionaries beyond numbering, and probably almost as many schoolteachers. It also sent Edmund McIntyre from dry Orange County, Vermont, to start the first distillery in Houston County. And from Pawtucket, Rhode Island, to Minneapolis came William A. Tanner, who was most successful in his line of goods. Tanner was, says an early biographer of the community, "head of the syndicate that conducted the gambling houses of Minneapolis."

It took, as they said, all kinds to make prairie land and dense timber into

---

* Yankees were present in the newer counties, such as Redwood, where the towns of North Hero, New Avon, and Waterbury were named by settlers, respectively, from Vermont, Maine, and Connecticut. In Pine County, a famous village was named for Isaac Hinckley, native of North Adams, Mass., and Nickerson for John Quincy Adams Nickerson, born in New Salem, Me.

a territory, then a state. So, the migration continued from New England to Minnesota, and it held true in large part to the pattern early formed, that of brothers and families. There were the Sanborns, all native to Epsom, New Hampshire, and all or nearly all graduates of Dartmouth College, who started moving to St. Paul as early as 1854 and continued into the late 1870's; and the Soules of Brownville, Maine, who settled in Princeton, Minnesota, and more Soules, from Avon, Maine, who pioneered one of the first towns in Grant County; and the Reverend William Soule from Palermo, Maine, who came to preach at Paynesville. The Paines of Anson, Maine, led by Parker who went to Minnesota in 1853, continued to migrate one after another, throughout the fifties and sixties, and went into occupations as varied as railroading, lumbering, and preaching. . . . Aye, they were coming: Mankato attracted the Keenes from Clinton, Maine, the Waites from Wardsborough, New Hampshire, the Shepards from New London, Connecticut, the Charles Chapmans from Cambridge, Massachusetts, and the Dickinsons from Hartford, Vermont.

One could marvel at the many members of the Keyes family, all of tiny Chelsea, Vermont, who set up as doctors, lawyers, and merchants in Winona, a town, incidentally, much favored by Green Mountain migrants. To Winona from Vermont also went Harvey Hull Johnson, to promote and become president of the pioneer Winona & St. Peter Railroad; and the Henderson Morse family from Milton, the George F. Hubbards of Swanton, the William A. Allens of Burlington, and a large delegation of Moreys from Vershire, probably relatives of the doughty Captain Samuel Morey, who made and ran a steamboat on the Connecticut years before Fulton's *Clermont* churned up the Hudson.

Now and then a lone settler founded and named a new town and, naturally, wrote letters home to New England to induce others to migrate to the finest village in all Minnesota. George Hitchcock left Claremont, New Hampshire, in 1855, built a home on his claim in Dodge County, and said it was Claremont, Minnesota. For neighbors he soon had the Edwin F. Ways from Lempster, the George O. Ways from Sullivan, and the Joseph H. Clarkes from Gilmanton, all in New Hampshire. Before long the Reverend A. H. Tebbets from New Hampton came to preach in the thriving settlement.

George B. Wright, a surveyor born in Williston, Vermont, laid claim to being the founder of Fergus Falls, Minnesota, as he well may have been; and before it was little more than platted Elmer E. Adams of Vermont's Waterbury arrived to establish the Fergus Falls *Journal*. John Metcalf of Vermont's Glover came to open a dentist's office, and Judge Luther L. Baxter of Vermont's Cornwall came to sit on the bench.

Joshua Lovejoy Taylor, born in Sanbornton, New Hampshire, gave his name to the lively village of Taylors Falls. A town in Mower County was named for William Z. Clayton from Freeman, Maine. Delano village honored Francis R. Delano from Braintree, Massachusetts; and Verndale was named by its founder, Lucius Smith from Caledonia County, Vermont, for his pretty daughter, who was Verna.

Charles Hoag, of Sandwich, New Hampshire, did not found Minneapolis, but he moved there in 1852, when it was St. Anthony, and concocted its new and immediately popular name, which he swore meant "water city" in the Chippewa tongue, with a little help from classic Greek. Lyman P. White, from Whiting, Vermont, laid out the town of Brainerd and christened it for Ann Eliza Brainerd Smith, wife of a governor of Vermont and president of the Northern Pacific Railway. Josiah P. Mooers from Deerfield, New Hampshire, was the first settler and postmaster at Cokato. Abner Tibbits from Maine owned much of the site of Lake City. One of the founders of Brockway was Nathaniel Getchell, late of Wesley, Maine. Other Maine men are said to have been the first settlers elsewhere: George McComber of Durham, at Great Bend; Levi Griffin of Vassalborough, at Carver; C. H. Whitney of Cumberland County, at Marshall; and Henry Stoddard of Farmington, at Verona. One of the first counties set off in Minnesota was named for a Maine man, John W. Mower of Bangor.

Until the end of the Civil War there seems to have been no great effort by the state of Minnesota to attract settlers from New England or elsewhere in the United States; but, for all that, the Yankees had gone there in great number. In 1860, so said the First Annual Report of the Commission of Statistics, some 20,000 native New Englanders were living in the new state, along with some 20,000 natives of New York, Pennsylvania, and New Jersey, and 27,000 more from the "Northwestern Free States."

The region had seen a truly phenomenal growth in the decade of the fifties, chiefly during the latter half. In 1840 the total population, "whites and half-breeds," was estimated at 700. By the end of 1855 it had risen to 40,000. A year later this figure had doubled. By 1860 Minnesota contained 172,000 persons.

In 1866 the state began officially to talk about its "Advantages to Settlers," in a pamphlet which apparently ran through many editions and was only slightly more trammeled in claims than were the primeval realtors, who were wild men indeed. The state's pamphlet said that its land exemption laws were "more liberal than those of any other state." It listed a large number of local railroads, several of which operated solely on paper, lines like the Minnesota Valley, the Minnesota Central, the Hastings & Dakota, the Mc-Gregor & Western, and called them, collectively but none too accurately, a NETWORK OF STEEL. In the matter of wheat, it appeared, Minnesota was at the top with an average yield of 22 bushels to the acre, whereas Michigan could grow but 19 bushels, Ohio 17.3 bushels, and Massachusetts 16 bushels. There were other advantages, too, such as the "cheapness of opening farms," and the climate, which was discussed "by a Physician." The good if unnamed doctor claimed to be privy to statistics that showed people lived much longer in Minnesota than elsewhere, and it also had "no equal as a resort for Invalids."

But it was in its "social status" that Minnesota stood preeminent. This was proved by a morass of statistics to the effect that while Massachusetts got one conviction in every 841 criminal indictments, Minnesota managed one conviction for every 3,854 indictments. This reasoning seems cloudy at best, but the State of Minnesota thought it pretty convincing.

Three years later the St. Paul & Pacific Railroad came out with a booklet which, compared with the state's effort, fairly glittered. The railroad obviously had engaged a poet. "The whole surface of the state," cried he, "is literally begemmed with innumerable lakes. . . . Their picturesque beauty and loveliness, with their pebbly bottoms, transparent waters, wooded shores and sylvan associations, must be seen to be fully appreciated. . . . The assertion that the climate is one of the healthiest in the world may be broadly and confidently made." And so it *was*—made.

It was the practice of the St. Paul & Pacific and other railroads to refund the cost of a land-prospecting trip if land was purchased. The railroads also promised to buy all fuel wood cut by settlers along their lines. They established "immigrant houses" at division points for the reception of the lucky customers. The Lake Superior & Mississippi line, for instance, had one such house at Duluth, and several more along the road to St. Paul. The Northern Pacific had houses at Duluth, Brainerd, and Glyndon; the St. Paul & Pacific, at Litchfield, Benson, Morris, Willmar, and Breckenridge.

Nor did the sweet singers in the railroad pamphlets sing in vain. In 1880 the population of the state reached 780,773. It had quadrupled since 1860; in population the state had risen from thirtieth to twenty-sixth place. Five years later Minnesota had passed the million mark, with 117,798 souls to spare. Significantly, there were by then 5,000 miles of actual railroad within the state. The coming of the steel rails was what served to settle the back-counties, of which Minnesota, larger than the six New England states combined, had a great many.

A large majority of the Yankees who came to Minnesota in pioneer days were unquestionably of old Timothy Dwight's so-called forester class. They sought the farm lands and the timber. They plowed and cut and sawed and burned and planted and harvested. They developed, among their thousands, a few hundred shrewd and aggressive—and ruthless—industrialists who, once their piles were made, moved into the larger cities. "Removed to St. Paul" or "went to live in Minneapolis"—so read the biographical sketches of these worthies who may never have read Herbert Spencer, but would have understood him. They built large and often quite horrible mansions and otherwise displayed varying degrees of both the wealth and the vulgarity which were common in late nineteenth century America, East and West. They bought gold-headed canes and plug hats. They used gold-mounted toothpicks. Their elegant cuspidors were of gold plate, at least. Some of them ran for and occasionally got into Congress, or became governor. They paid to have their steel-engraved likenesses embalmed in gorgeous volumes cynically called mug books by the Yankee operators who conducted these biographical monstrosities.

There was a credit side too, for these barons and princes of this-and-that gave or bequeathed vast sums of money for educational or municipal improvements. Hospitals, academies, colleges, parks, libraries, and churches arose from the dust of wheat flour and iron ore, and from the rotting piles of sawdust along the logging streams.

A small but potent group of New Englanders paid no heed to the future possibilities of a Sauk Rapids, a Zumbrota, a Litchfield, or a Cannon Falls, but moved direct to St. Paul or Minneapolis and made them into hives of furious activity. Chauncy W. Griggs from Tolland, Connecticut, will do for a sample. He arrived in St. Paul in 1856, teamed up with James J. Hill, then a nobody, in fuel and other lines, then made a couple of fortunes by founding, with others, the whosesale grocery firm of Griggs, Cooper & Company, and the St. Paul & Tacoma Lumber Company, both as prosperous in 1949 as they are venerable. Horace and James E. Thompson, brothers from Poultney, Vermont, set up as money-lenders, and out of their efforts emerged St. Paul's pioneer First National Bank. The Noyes brothers, natives of Lyme, Connecticut, arrived in St. Paul in 1868 to find the place lacking in one respect; so, with Edward H. Cutler from Boston, they founded Noyes Bros. & Cutler, wholesale drugs.

The Prince brothers, all of Amherst, Massachusetts, formed almost a migration of Yankee bankers—Walter, George, and Frank—setting up in Stillwater and in both of the Twin Cities. James D. Humphrey, who had manufactured soap in his native Connecticut, and in Illinois and Wisconsin, found Minneapolis just the right place for his business. Frank Clark Brooks, a native of Taunton, Massachusetts, moved to Ohio with his parents, was schooled in the proper Yankee college at Beloit, Wisconsin, then went on to Minneapolis

to become one of the most noted lawyers in the state; though he was nowhere so colorful as Attorney—and Congressman—Frank Mellen Nye, called
the Tall Pine, who came from Shirley, Maine, and was probably Hennepin
County's most famous prosecutor.

Possibly the largest fortune of the time in Minneapolis was that of Levi
M. Stewart, a realtor of the first mark, who was born in that same tiny
Corinna, Maine, from which so many adventurous men went forth to far
places. Charles M. Loring, merchant and miller, from Portland, Maine, left
his name on a fine park in Minneapolis; while the Maine lumberman Samuel
A. Jewett, born in Gardiner, not only made a mint of money from Minnesota
logs, but wrote books, one of them entitled *Elements of Science, Moral and
Religious.* Jewett would have been still another of the forester class to dum-
found Dr. Dwight. So, too, would have been an idealist named George W.
Higgins, of Rockland, Maine, who was as Dry as General Neal Dow and set
up in Minneapolis as Prohibition candidate for governor of Minnesota.

There was always something an energetic man could find to do. Francis
Bachelor of Union, Maine, took one look at the primeval flouring mills rising
at St. Anthony Falls, and promptly started a barrel factory. Elias Connor,
born in New Sharon, Maine, built the first suspension bridge across the river
at Minneapolis. Josiah Chase of Kingston, New Hampshire, opened the first
store on the west side of the river at a time when John C. Bohanon, from
Maine, was logging part of his claim to make room for Minneapolis streets.
Charles E. Babb, from Portland, Maine, who knew his business before he
left home, founded the Cedar Lake Ice Company in the Twin Cities. Jacob
Bass Wales, native of Braintree, Vermont, opened the pioneer St. Paul House,
and William E. Brimhall of Hardwick, Massachusetts, operated the first fruit
nursery in St. Paul and probably the first in the state.

Yankee migrants worked at both ends of an era: Lyman Dayton, from
Southington, Connecticut, was organizer and president of the Lake Superior
& Mississippi Railroad at a time when Abram H. Cavender, from Hancock,
Maine, was setting up in St. Paul as a maker of freighting wagons.

In the profession of law Yankees seem to have been particularly notable
in Minnesota. Up to 1890, of the twenty-three chief and associate justices
of the territorial and supreme courts, nine, or almost 40 per cent, were of
New England birth; and of the remaining fourteen, seven were of whole or
part New England ancestry. When in 1904 somebody got out a book on the
bench and bar in Minnesota, which contained sketches of two hundred
twenty prominent attorneys, fifty-three, or one-fourth, turned out to be
Yankees. Vermont contributed a majority.

Of eleven Minnesota state governors between 1858 and 1890, only two,

Austin and Pillsbury, were born in New England.* But five others, says
Theodore Blegen, naming Sibley, Swift, Davis, Hubbard, and Merriam, were
of New England parents or grandparents. In the same period no fewer than
twenty, or nearly one-third, of the lieutenant governors, secretaries of state,
treasurers, and attorneys general were of New England birth.

James Madison Goodhue's wish, and prophecy, that Minnesota would
become the New England of the West was not to be fulfilled. Since 1893,
ten of her fourteen governors have been of Scandinavian stock. The same
doubtless holds true of other state officers, and her delegation in Congress.
But it would be incorrect to infer that Minnesota was the scene of a racial
war for supremacy in politics, or in anything else. It does mean, surely, that
the original Yankees—and other native Americans—were swamped in the
great migration from the Scandinavian countries. But in no other part of the
United States, perhaps, have a new and an old group become so well inte-
grated and happily fused as in Minnesota. The so-called melting pot, which
in Chicago, in New York City, and also in New England has melted so
slowly, was more precipitous in Minnesota. This was due chiefly to racial
inheritance. The Norse pioneer and the New England pioneer were both
essentially Puritan. The Lutheran church was merely a more strict Congregational or Presbyterian group, perhaps comparable to the Methodist. It is
quite likely the Yankee who liberalized, in many things, the Norse rather
than the other way about. Both believed in economy, in hard work, in education, and in the "true" religion, the latter in this case being not too difficult
to live with, if not to accept in a formal manner.

Today, ninety years after the main migration from New England to Minnesota, and seventy years after the height of the Scandinavian arrivals there,
it would require more than a professor of the social sciences to assess the
two migrations and to say whether the more numerous immigrants from
abroad had been of greater influence on Minnesota than the earlier and far
fewer immigrants from New England. To weigh the coefficient of acculturation would call for necromancy.

* David M. Clough, of Lyme, New Hampshire, became governor in 1895.

CHAPTER XIII

KANSAS—BLOODY BUT SAFE

ON the 19th of May in 1856 the gentleman from Massachusetts, who was Charles Sumner, arose in the United States Senate to pass a few remarks on what he said was the Crime Against Kansas. He was forty-five years old, six feet four, strikingly handsome, and possessed of a voice of great power. He had few if any peers in invective.

As the tall senator arose, the chamber was tense, charged with emotion; the battle between the advocates of slavery and the Free State men had become increasingly bitter since the passage of a bill, two years previously, which opened the new territory of Kansas to slavery. Mr. Sumner went to the point at once. "To lay bare this enormity," said he to the packed chamber and the galleries, which included the aged Webster making his last visit, "to lay bare this enormity, I now proceed."

And so he did. He called, naturally enough, upon God Almighty to witness the Crime. He charged that the President of the United States, together with his minions in the Slavocracy, had conspired to introduce the Abomination into Kansas. He mentioned Catiline. He quoted Latin phrases of great resonance. He brought in the campaigns in the Crimea and the siege of Sebastopol. He said that an armed multitude of the Slavocracy from Missouri had invaded Kansas in larger numbers than General Taylor had commanded at Buena Vista—much larger than our noble forefathers had rallied at Bunker Hill to defend the Nation. He charged that the Administration had aided and abetted these thugs and assassins, whom he happily characterized as "hirelings picked from the drunken spew and vomit of an uneasy civilization, having the form of men."

(The manner in which he said *form of men* was singularly maddening— yet more and worse was to come.)

It had originally been the foul plan of these hirelings—said Mr. Sumner —to introduce slavery into Kansas quietly, so "that the crocodile egg might be stealthily dropped on the sunburnt soil, there to be hatched, unobserved, until it sent forth its reptile monster."

He was an extremely able man on his feet, was Mr. Sumner, and the way in which he ejaculated *reptile monster* made men shudder; it carried with it all the venom he had secreted during the many months when southern senators had applied to him the worst epithets of their wondrous oratory. He was now engaged in passing back a few of his own devising, each barbed with his quick, sure, and curious genius for incomparable invective.

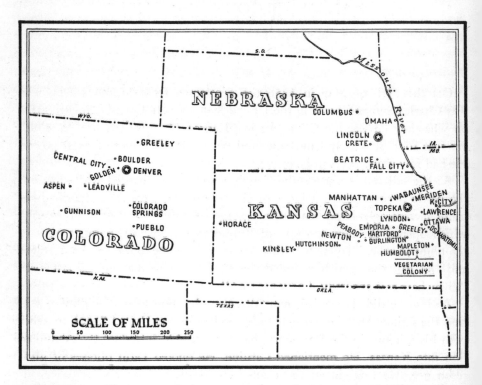

SCALE OF MILES
0   50   100   150   200   250

Now, as to Kansas—and the great voice rolled out to enthrall or inflame the ear of the most distant of his listeners—as to Kansas, sir, while the act opened the door of the new territory to slavery, it opened it also to emigrants from the North. And the North, said he, stung by sense of outrage and inspired by a noble cause, was pouring into the debatable land and promised soon to establish a supremacy there, involving, naturally, a just supremacy of Freedom. On and on went the voice. Southern senators writhed in their seats, and even northern men were astonished, and a few alarmed, at the concentrated venom which Sumner poured forth upon the heads of all proponents of slavery.

Then, as though he were God's district attorney, he summed up this Crime of Crimes and indicted the South, the President of the United States, and all his catchpolls on a charge of barbarism as horrifying as it was complete. In closing he felt the need of support from the classics to express his revulsion, and so he called upon the majestic Milton, to show how this Crime of Crimes "ended foul in many a scaly fold," while "a cry of hell-hounds never ceasing barked with wide Cerberean mouths full loud, and rung a hideous peal."

Then, the Senator from Massachusetts sat down.

Two days later the Free State settlement of Lawrence, Kansas Territory, was raided by a proslavery mob; houses and places of business were burned, the newspaper office destroyed. Two days after the speech, too, he himself was attacked, while seated at his desk in the Senate, by a southern gentleman named Brooks, who represented South Carolina in Congress and South Carolina's idea of a gentleman anywhere. The defenseless Sumner was beaten nearly to death with a heavy cane. And though it was almost three years before he recovered, his words meanwhile were being read all over the North and in Kansas. The speech, as well as the attack on Sumner and the raid at Lawrence, roused much of the North as nothing before. In New England, the attack on the Yankee senator was followed by indignation meetings of protest at which leading preachers and other orators took the platform.* Perhaps only Mrs. Stowe's novel had a more inflaming effect in the New England states than the attack on Sumner and the meetings it inspired.

Sumner's speech had of course contained no little hyperbole—a custom of the day—and several untruths. It had also contained a great deal that was quite true and most unpalatable, especially to southerners. Incidentally, Senator Sumner had not exaggerated when he declared that the North "were pouring into the debatable land." He could well have stressed that the source of this pouring was New England, where the Yankees had been set in motion by as curious a private organization as ever had a hand in making history. This was the New England Emigrant Aid Company.

What became the New England Emigrant Aid Company first took form in the mind of a Massachusetts man, Eli Thayer, born in Mendon in 1819, as a strictly business opportunity, a chance for astute Yankees to invest idle dollars and see them multiply, quickly and manifestly, in the new territory of Kansas; and at the same time prevent the spread of slavery. It was a two-headed chance, or so Thayer devoutly believed, to serve both God and Mammon at one and the same time.

Thayer himself was a strange mixture of commercial and intellectual in-

---

* Faneuil Hall in Boston was packed two nights running to hear about the Crime Against Charles Sumner, and hence against all Yankees, as discussed by Theodore Parker, Wendell Phillips, James Freeman Clarke, and Peleg Chandler.

terests. After graduation from Brown University he had taught at Worcester Academy, then had established on Goat Hill, in an undeveloped part of Worcester, Oread Collegiate Institute for Young Ladies. In 1852 he was elected to the state legislature as a Free Soiler, though his efforts here were directed chiefly to a reform of the Massachusetts banking system. He also read the papers, just then filled with discussions of the Kansas-Nebraska bill, and came to the conclusion that the unholy spread of slavery could be best contained, and at last stopped and sent into decay, by a colonization of all debatable lands. He was convinced that even the border states could be shown, by free colonies transplanted from the North, the advantages of free labor. He was also convinced, and never failed to state his conviction, that all such colonizing schemes could be made to pay their way and leave substantial profits for the investors. It was a perfect example of the perfect enterprise—for the glory of God and 10 per cent. . . .

Thayer must also have been a man of force and personality. The debate on the Kansas-Nebraska bill was still going on when he set out to raise capital. His idea of capital was five million dollars, and this was the staggering sum stated in the organization papers of the Massachusetts Emigrant Aid Company, chartered in April, 1854. He approached Amos Adams Lawrence of Boston, one of the whales of New England capital; then John Carter Brown of Providence, and J. M. S. Williams of Cambridge, all men of money and, one is prepared to believe, of ideals. The first charter was found faulty and was discarded, while a new group, the New England Emigrant Aid Company, was formed. Lawrence was elected president, with Brown and Williams as officers, and Thomas H. Webb, secretary. Edward Everett Hale, though never an officer, was one of the moving spirits of the group.

Amos Lawrence never considered the company as anything but a philanthropy, a patriotic thing that might preserve Kansas for the North; nor does it seem likely that Brown, Williams, and others who made substantial donations ever considered their interests in the light of speculation or business.

While the company was being organized, Thayer circulated throughout New England, discussing the white-hot subject of Kansas and expounding his plan to make Kansas free soil. He must have been quite eloquent. "In December of 1854," related Isaac T. Goodnow, a professor at Providence Conference Seminary, "I heard Eli Thayer speak in Providence. I resigned my professorship, and spent three months writing and talking, to organize a group of two hundred to go to Kansas."

Thayer also engaged several paid agents, the most active of whom were Charles Robinson, a physician of Fitchburg; Samuel Clarke Pomeroy, schoolteacher and politician of Southampton; and Charles H. Branscomb of Holyoke. They, too, busied themselves with the coming crusade. Thayer, no man to overlook the arts, told the press that the Emigrant Aid Company wanted a rousing poem on the subject of keeping Kansas free, and instituted a prize contest, the winning poem to receive $50. He also called upon as many Yankee preachers as possible and urged them to deliver sermons on Kansas.

So fast did Thayer and company work that a party of twenty-nine took off from Boston on July 17, 1854. In it were eighteen from Massachusetts, including Architect Ferdinand Fuller of Worcester—later to plan the first college building in Kansas—and five Vermonters, all from West Randolph. The group contained eight mechanics, five farmers, two who admitted to pure speculation, and one journalist. Agents were already on the ground at the West. This pioneer party of the Emigrant Aid Company was met at St. Louis by Dr. Robinson of the company, who was escort and guide as far as Kansas City, where Agent Branscomb took over. On the voyage up the Missouri the Yankees had company: "several Potawatomie Indians . . . and six slaves with their masters going to work hemp at Lexington. Some of them appear happy in their midnight ignorance." The Yankees aboard also got warning of what lay ahead; the slave owners present talked loud about the use of tar and feathers.

Branscomb had already chosen a townsite—which became Lawrence. The party arrived on the spot on August 1, and immediately got a taste of Kansas in summer. A copper sun was pouring down its beams with intense ferocity, and all nature, said a member of the party, shrank under the infliction. True, a high wind swept the prairie, but it reminded the Yankees of the blast of a furnace.

Back in New England a second party was being prepared, and John Greenleaf Whittier, his eyes and his pen both smoldering, was writing the song of "The Kansas Emigrants":

> We cross the prairie as of old
> The pilgrims crossed the sea,
> To make the West, as they the East,
> The homestead of the free!

Children declaimed the lines. Preachers found their congregations larger when they let it be known that the subject of the discourse was to be Kansas. The editors of daily and weekly papers, and of the many religious periodicals, were stirred as seldom before. Here was a crusade, the first since the days of 1775.

The second party was ready in late August. Members assembled in the ladies' waiting room of the Boston & Albany depot at Boston a little after noon on the 29th. An immense crowd was there to wish them well. Among the emigrants an observer noted five young men with band instruments, all from Hartford, Vermont. They carried rifles, too, and so did other men. Few in the party were more than thirty-five years old. Present also was Agent Pomeroy, the future senator from Kansas, and Agent Robinson, soon to be governor of that commonwealth. Emigrants and their friends stood up to sing Mr. Whittier's poem, already set to music; then the crusaders marched to the train shed and so into the cars.

Where in New England had the Kansas excitement taken root at this early stage? In the whole party there were sixty-eight persons from Massachusetts. Worcester, Lynn, Boston, and Fitchburg led in that order. Vermont sent seven, from Hartford and West Randolph. The other New England states were not represented. Additions to this second party who boarded the train en route brought the total to one hundred thirty five. Yankee families included Willard and five more Colburns, Wilder and four other Knights, all from Massachusetts. The Lewis Litchfields of Cambridge were aboard. Among the musicians and riflemen from Vermont were the Savage brothers, Forrest and Joseph. There was a trained civil engineer, Albert Dwight Searle, from Brookfield, Massachusetts; and Jerome B. Taft of Boston. Among the members from Worcester was young Levi Gates. He was later to become a Free Soil martyr, dying in defense of Lawrence, Kansas, against the unspeakable raider, Quantrill.

While the first and second parties, which had joined hands on the prairie of Kansas late in September, were organizing their town of Lawrence, a third and even larger party left Boston. It was also indicative of the spread of the mania in New England; in this group all sections but Rhode Island were represented. Worcester and Fitchburg, home towns of two of the Aid Company's agents, were, as usual throughout the crusade, well represented. Whittier's town of Haverhill showed for the first time on the list, seven coming from there, leading much larger towns such as Boston, Salem, and Springfield. More significant was that distant Bangor on the Penobscot had heard the call: Charles and Ralph Grindall of that lumber city were possibly the first from eastern Maine to go to Kansas. And elsewhere in Maine were stirrings—men joined the third party from Cumberland, and there were also some Thaxters from Portland. Down from Londonderry, New Hampshire, came six of the many Pillsburys. For the first time, too, Connecticut sent a goodly delegation, from Bridgeport, Unionville, Eastford, Waterbury, and "ancient Woodbury." The whole party numbered one hundred sixty one persons, but there were several who were not suitable for pioneers, for, after their arrival in Kansas, Agent Branscomb dropped a discreet note to the Aid Company at home suggesting that "more circumspection be exercised in regard to the character of the emigrants selected." At least one of the migrants in this party never reached Kansas at all; he was sent back from Chicago to his home in Fitchburg as "a confirmed drunkard."

There were others, too, who took one long look at the endless sea of the prairie, saw their first dust storm, saw their first rattlesnake, felt a tropical sun such as they had never known, felt their first wind that seemed to blow straight out of hell—and returned at once to the native land of the Yankees. But a large majority remained, and they appear to have been as capable pioneers as New England ever lost to the West. They had to work swiftly, for not only was winter coming but the Border Ruffians of Missouri were coming too. These people had been aroused to an even higher pitch than the Yankees.

The rousing had been instigated by David R. Atchison, a shrewd politician who weighed more than two hundred pounds and could and did swear and drink like a trooper, which, indeed, he was, being a major general of the Missouri militia. Atchison was also, until 1855, a United States senator and aided in framing the Kansas-Nebraska bill, that Crime of Crimes. Now he turned his simple eloquence loose on western Missouri.

A large majority of the natives there were not given to much reading, even of the newspapers; but General Atchison told them what was afoot: A gang of rich Yankees had raised *five million dollars* for the express purpose of taking twenty thousand paupers and criminals from the slums of Boston and the textile cities, giving them each a rifle, and shipping them into Kansas, all costs paid. These yahoos, said General Atchison, were already pouring in by the thousand; every boat up the Missouri carried them; they were settling in "military colonies" and were going to vote Free State.

To aid his campaign, Atchison engaged one B. F. Stringfellow, an adventurer of considerable forensic ability. Stringfellow spoke feelingly of these hirelings, these Hessian Mercenaries, who were stealing Kansas, and called upon all patriotic Missourians to go to meet them, on the battleground of Kansas. He promised—it was charged—that two Missouri requisites, namely food and liquor, would be supplied free of cost to all who would go and vote Kansas into the ranks of slave states.

The local press took up the song. "We now," said the *Democratic Platform* of Liberty, Missouri, as early as June 1, 1854, "we now have two new territories to colonize—with *Southern citizens*. . . . We must make Kansas a slave state, else we have no security for our property."

General Atchison was tireless, and also effective. "Now," said he in November of 1854, "if a set of fanatics and demagogues a thousand miles off can afford to advance their money and exert every nerve to abolitionize the territory and exclude the slaveholder, when they have not the least personal interest, then what is your duty?"

Their duty was clear. In no time at all gangs of footloose men, all armed, were roving into Kansas from Missouri. Within a short time they would come head-on into the Yankee fanatics.

For the present, however, the citadel of Yankees in Kansas, which was Lawrence, was doing famously. By August 1 it had been given its name. A "hotel" made of logs and thatched hay had been erected as a receiving station. Two steam sawmills sent by the Emigrant Aid Company were running. A printing press bought with company funds was turning out the *Herald of Freedom.* A school was in operation. Religious services were being held. A lyceum had been organized. Civil Engineer Searle had supervised laying out the streets, the principal one named Massachusetts. When a visitor from Ohio, the Reverend Mr. Boynton of Cincinnati, visited Lawrence late in 1854, he was amazed at the progress. He called the town "the advance guard of freedom's hosts which is taking possession of the lands and dominion of slavery in the name of God and humanity." He reported the village to contain nearly one thousand persons, and hoped other northern immigrants would emulate the noble work of the Yankees at Lawrence. He was not wholly content, for he had noted that the second party from Boston had reached St. Louis on a Saturday, and instead of resting there over the Sabbath had proceeded immediately upriver, thus "trampling down one law of God, in a mission professedly undertaken to vindicate another." But then, the Reverend Mr. Boynton doubtless did not understand the urgency with which the Yankees felt they should work to colonize Kansas before the hosts of evil should block them by numbers.

Before returning east to bring out another party, Agent Pomeroy purchased for the company what had been the Union Hotel in Kansas City, to be used as a way station for future parties. This was renamed the American House and leased to Shalor W. Eldridge of Southampton, Massachusetts, who operated it with the help of his mother.*

In October, Agent Branscomb was back in Boston, ready to start with the fourth party, the largest to date, numbering two hundred thirty persons. In it, incidentally, were Jonathan F. Tabor and wife, formerly of Vermont but more recently of Quincy, Massachusetts. Jonathan was a brother of H. A. W. Tabor, still a stonecutter in his native Holland, Vermont, and was to influence him in coming west. Horace Tabor, in turn, was to have some influence on the West.

Maine people were strong in this fourth party. They came from Corinth, Auburn, Deer Isle, Topsham, and St. Albans. Rhode Island had at last

---

* The Eldridges later operated the famous Eldridge House in Lawrence; and in subsequent generations the Eldridges continued to move westward. Shalor C. Eldridge, grandnephew of Shalor W., is a well known Oregonian.

caught fire: the entire Titus family, of Foster, joined up. So did Mr. and Mrs. Charles Yeomans of Norwich, Connecticut. And there were more from faithful Worcester and Fitchburg. The group arrived at Kansas City on October 23, being less than a week on the road. This big party taxed Lawrence to the limit. Many had to sleep in close ranks on the floor of the "Free State Hotel"; but there was sufficient food. Several families moved on a bit farther, into present Wabaunsee County, where they settled on claims, among them Calvin Sawin of Fitchburg, George Hill and wife of Charlestown, Massachusetts, and George Lewis of Salem. Schoolmaster Morse of Derry, New Hampshire, joined this group, as did Sam Tay of Corinth, Maine.

It was now getting late in the season, yet two more parties were on the way from Boston. The fifth of the year, numbering fifty-five, and the sixth, with some thirty members, arrived late in November. Members of these two parties were the founders of Topeka, the future capital. They were directed to the site by Agent Robinson and got quickly to work, raising shelter against approaching winter. These founding fathers came from four Yankee states. There were Milton Dickey and George Davis from Vermont, Enoch Chase and Jacob Chase from Newburyport, and William Kinker from Boston; Fry Giles, Daniel Horne, and Timothy McIntyre from New Hampshire; and one Maine man, Jonas Greenwood, from North Turner Bridge. As winter closed down on Kansas, two Free State settlements had been firmly established; and there were scattered communities of Yankees mixed with people from York State, Ohio, and Pennsylvania.

Throughout the winter months of 1854–1855, men of Missouri, Alabama, Tennessee, Georgia, and the Carolinas moved across the Kansas line for the purpose of voting proslavery politicians into territorial office. Their headquarters were at Lecompton, a new settlement set down fair between Lawrence and Topeka, and to which all proslavery men referred as the territorial capital. Atchison's propaganda had been working fabulously well, stirring, yeasting, maddening those who had become known as Border Ruffians, preparing them to vote and shoot, and if necessary to die for the right of their betters to keep slaves in Kansas, a region wholly unfit for slave labor. Atchison continued to use the New England Emigrant Aid Company as the chief exhibit in his gallery of northern horrors, stressing the five million dollars it "was spending lavishly to ship 20,000 armed paupers and thugs" into the territory.*

In New England, as the maples ran with sap in the spring of 1855, excitement mounted to a new and higher pitch. Eli Thayer and his company men had been active all winter. Yankee newspapers were filled with com-

* The company raised and spent approximately $140,000 during its life, 1854–1862.

pany propaganda. Even more came in the form of letters from Kansas, most of them written under stress of the emotion of Gideons fighting the battle of the Lord. Thayer's regiment of preachers were in the best of form, and their sermons were recruiting efforts for the Kansas crusade.* The Aid Company's poetry contest for a $50 prize had brought in much drivel and some verse. It was announced that Miss Lucy Larcom, who had worked in the mills at Lowell, but was now teaching school in Norton, Massachusetts, had won the prize with strophes entitled "The Call to Kansas." Agent Pomeroy had been traveling extensively in New England, speaking before the Maine legislature and large audiences elsewhere.

On March 13 the Kansas crusade of 1855 opened with a bang; one hundred and eighty-two people left Boston in the first party. Miss Larcom's ballad was sung to them in the Boston depot. At stops at Leominster, Fitchburg, and Keene, the emigrants were greeted with cheers from imposingly large crowds, and sent on their way with massed voices singing Miss Larcom's and Mr. Whittier's stirring numbers. One of the emigrants estimated the depot crowd at Fitchburg at well over a thousand.

There was even one Whittier, a young man from Lawrence, Massachusetts, in the first party. As usual, both Fitchburg and Worcester were represented. There were also aboard several citizens of Saco, the Maine town that had been quick to listen to the Mormon missionaries two decades earlier but had not, until now, joined the movement to Kansas. There were other Maineites aboard from Buxton and Brunswick, and Samuel Grey from Biddeford. Only four Vermonters had joined this party; but one of them was to make a great name and fortune at the West, though in Colorado instead of Kansas. This young man was Horace A. W. Tabor, the stonecutter from Holland on the Canadian border, whose brother, as noted, was already in Kansas. But the surprise of this first party of 1855 was the representation from Rhode Island, where the Reverend Isaac Goodnow, who had been converted by Thayer, had been propagandizing all winter. The fruits were apparent, for men and women were leaving their homes in Providence, Wakefield, Pawtucket, Coventry, and East Greenwich.

Goodnow himself had gone ahead, in company with Luke Lincoln and others, to seek out a site for a new Free State colony. With them were the Reverend Charles Lovejoy from New Hampshire and his energetic and competent wife, who had been Louisa Julia Hardy of Lebanon, to see that the souls of Methodist Yankees in Kansas were properly cared for. Mrs. Lovejoy turned out to be an excellent reporter. She wrote that the party

* Thayer thus followed the example of Sam Adams of Revolutionary days, who was careful to keep his Black Regiment, as he called the preachers, informed of the alleged horrors perpetrated by the King's officials.

traveled by train to Chicago; then "our noble steed bore us impetuously on over the far-famed prairies of Illinois, with almost lightning speed to Alton." Then, to the river boat. She said the party was made up mostly of Massachusetts and Rhode Island people.

It is through Mrs. Lovejoy's eyes that one is permitted to know how the first sight of the land of slavery seemed to Yankees. On the way up the Missouri River she noted neglect and decay and indolence everywhere. It made her most melancholy. Near Jefferson she saw her first slave, a female, spreading manure on a field while a husky overseer watched. She was thoroughly shocked, and permitted herself a cry: "O slavery, thou unsexing demon, how art thou accursed of God and humanity." This was the kind of people New England was sending out. At Kansas City, Mrs. Lovejoy, from neat and orderly Lebanon, found but one church, unpainted, uncarpeted, and "as filthy as any incorrigible tobacco chewer would wish to have it." The whole town was indescribably repulsive to her. It was high time, she thought, that the hosts of the Lord did gather in this benighted land, lest Evil become wholly triumphant.

Goodnow, Lovejoy, Lincoln, and a few more went out from Kansas City to find a good site. "On Saturday evening, March 24, 1855," wrote Goodnow, "I stood on a mound at sunset and there was the most beautiful townsite ever beheld. . . . We named it Boston." This became Manhattan—another citadel, as the crusaders liked to call it, of the Free State ranks.

Not all the Free Staters were happy with what they found in Kansas. Several in the first party of 1855 were disgruntled; and Samuel Grey, he of Biddeford, was disgusted with them—naïve souls who seemed to think they would find farms all fenced, houses ready, every advantage they had left behind, including "all the luxuries of the East." Well, let them tarry, or let them return whence they came, he said—let them by all means go back "well content, I suppose, to pick rocks and dig out stumps and raise their scanty crops from the barren soil of Maine." As for Sam Grey, he took a farm near Topeka, where there were no stumps and few rocks such as he had known in his native Biddeford.

One week after the first party left Boston, another was ready, one hundred and seventy strong, with John T. Farwell of Fitchburg in charge. The roster shows that Rhode Island was now well in the moving stream. Beatleys, Burrowses, Cowees, and seven Pearces, all from Providence; the Ed Turners of Olneyville, and Fullers, Davises, and Douglases from Pawtucket. Significant was that a number of emigrants from the Massachusetts industrial towns of Lowell and Dedham gave their occupations as "mill operatives." Perhaps the new Yankee industrial heaven did not please everyone. There was also a Nathan Hackett of Lowell who described himself as a manufacturer. From New Hampshire the effects of the Reverend Charles Lovejoy's preaching were becoming apparent: the Peter Bartons of Croydon were going; so were John and Samuel Colby of Springfield, and several families from Walpole. Across the river in Vermont, Brattleboro sent a delegation of eight, and there were a couple of families from Randolph, which seemed to be particularly susceptible to the Kansas crusade. On arrival in the territory, a large number of this second party of 1855 settled in Lawrence and surrounding Douglas County; but the George Nichols family of Brattleboro took a claim in Osawatomie—soon to be in the news.

The Emigrant Aid Company was much better organized in this second year of the exodus, and parties continued to leave at weekly intervals from Boston. That the Yankees were carrying *all* their notions with them is to be seen in the leader of the third party of 1855, the Reverend Dr. Amory Hunting, "one of the firmest, self-sacrificing *Temperance* men in Rhode Island." In his party was a William Goodnow, printer from Norway, Maine, bound for his brother Isaac's new town of Manhattan.*

The fourth party of the season was destined to have a tragic experience. This had been especially organized to found a Hampden colony in Kansas, named for the Massachusetts county from which many of the party came. It was led by the Reverend Richard Knight of Holyoke. It numbered one hundred and sixty-five people, but well before the end of the summer the ranks had been woefully reduced by ague. This was a complaint common in new country, but the Hampden colony appears to have been particularly susceptible to it. On the roster one notes again and again the brief remark: "Died in Hampden Colony of ague 1855."

Elijah Porter, an editor of Westfield, Massachusetts, did not like anything he saw in Kansas. For one thing the soil was tough. After some of the group had broken two plows in one day, they fashioned one "mammoth plow" which required five yoke of oxen and three men to operate, yet the best it could turn over was one acre "of adamant turf a day." Porter got out of there quickly, and returned home to report that "Hampden Colony was laid out as handsome a *paper* town as one could wish." That was the best he could say for it.

In this spring of 1855 there was at least one party of Kansas crusaders not mentioned in the Emigrant Aid Company rosters. They were young men, brothers, five of the twenty children of John Brown, a native of Torrington,

* A study of the party rosters of 1855 indicates that a much larger number of urban, or industrial town, people were leaving than in 1854. For instance, Taunton was the home of Benjamin Booram and sons and of Asher Peckham and three children; out of Warren came the Joseph Wetherbees; out of Willimansett came a sizable group of woolen workers; out of Lowell, Lawrence, and Milford came other textile people. There were William Blaisdell and George Church of Chicopee; and glass blowers from celebrated Sandwich, down on the Cape.

Connecticut, who had spent much of his fifty-odd years in moving around in Ohio, Pennsylvania, and New York. The five brothers, like their father, were stout abolitionists; and now they were taking up farms along the Osawatomie River. They discovered hostility at once; and one of them sat down and wrote their father, telling him arms were needed to hold the Osawatomite region for Free Soil.

John Brown was fifty-five years old. Without a word he collected and filled a one-horse wagon with assorted rifles, carbines, revolvers, and sabers, and struck out alone for Kansas. Nobody sang Miss Larcom's song for him, nor Whittier's. He needed neither, for his ears were filled with whisperings and roarings like those that came forth from a conch shell, and their source was just as mysterious, though he himself was certain they came from his Lord Jehovah. . . .

And on came more parties of the Emigrant Aid, one after another, leaving Boston at regular intervals through April, May, June, July, August. The last of record left Boston on the 11th of September, 1855.*

The total number of Yankees in the Aid parties of 1855 was approximately nine hundred, or one hundred and fifty more than the number sent out in 1854. The exodus was carried on under great excitement; but now that the movement was beginning to fall off many stay-at-homes reflected on the state of affairs and wondered if New England were not being drained of its people. This impression was so general that Yankee newspapers looked into the business, trying to estimate the total number of emigrants to Kansas, including those who had gone out in parties having no connection with the Emigrant Aid Company. The Boston *Advertiser* found no reason for worry:

There is a very general impression that New England has been drained of a considerable number of her people to settle Kanzas. It is entirely false. It is not probable that more than 3,000 New Englanders, men, women, and children, are now in that Territory. They form about one-tenth part of its present population. The character of the emigration, after the homesick boys came back, was of the very best, for culture, discipline, and morals. The New England settlers, therefore, take a prominent part in the affairs of the Territory, but in numbers they are in as small a proportion as we have stated.

What the Yankee settlers needed most in that period were courage and

* Farmers were probably and properly in the majority, such as the Asa Whites, the George Risings, the John Drummers, all of Keene, N.H.; two families of Killams from Pembroke, N.H.; two families of Bushees of Warren, R.I.; the Weston Humphreys of Waterbury and the Durkees of Brookfield, Vt. There were also such artisans as Calvin H. Bacon, chair-maker from the noted furniture town of Gardner, Mass.; tin worker Isaiah Loring of Hingham; teachers like Lydia Hall and William K. Vaill of Lowell and Salem, Mass., and James O. Hale of Temple, N.H.; from Newburyport's maritime families five Coffins and five Comers; a whaling man, Abe Atkins, from New Bedford; plus the only person from Billerica, Mass., to figure in the Aid Company rosters, Simon O. Hareis.

discipline. The pro-slavery men, aided and abetted by the federal administration, and using threats and violence to prevent voting by Free Soilers, staged an "election," choosing a legislature, a governor, judges, sheriffs. The Free State farms and settlements were harassed. Free State farmers worked in the fields with guns strapped to their backs. And Free Staters, though still in the minority, retaliated. Partisanship aside, the situation was most uncomfortable all around.

The town of Lawrence, spearhead of Free Soil, lived in constant fear of attack. During the summer of 1855 townsmen formed a militia company, the Lawrence Rifles, and drilled daily under Captain Joseph Cracklin, late of Boston. A new Free State hotel was being built—of brick and stone. Pro-slavery men termed it a fort. Old John Brown had arrived on the Osawatomie to join his sons, his wagon a rolling arsenal. Brown said he was a surveyor, and went immediately to work, ranging the district, taking stock of the pro-slavery forces there, considering the lay of the land, listening ever to the whispering and roaring voices in his ear that never failed to guide him.

The preliminary skirmishes went on—a barn burned here, a haystack fired, a settler shot dead by an unknown hand. Then, on April 14, 1855, a pro-slavery mob attacked the offices of the Parkville *Luminary*, on the Missouri side of the big river, and destroyed it. Editor George Shepard Park moved over into Kansas and bought an interest in the Manhattan City Company, a Free State enterprise.

These events, and many more clashes between the contending forces, were promptly reported, with exaggerations, in the New England press. Meanwhile, Eli Thayer had at last interested Horace Greeley in the Kansas struggle, and now the great editor lent a hand in his *Tribune* in New York, a favorite paper all over the North. The Reverend Henry Ward Beecher, who may possibly have been something of an opportunist, also became convinced that Kansas could be saved only by Yankee settlers in number. A practical man always, Beecher said from the pulpit that every emigrant to the new territory should have a Bible in one hand, a Sharps breechloading rifle in the other.

So, on the last day of March, 1856, a group of seventy men, calling themselves the Beecher Bible and Rifle Colony, paraded in the streets of New Haven to band music, while thousands of spectators lined the way to cheer, weep, laugh, and applaud. Dr. Beecher was in the reviewing stand, and so were other eminent men. The emigrant party included farmers, tradesmen, politicians, and ministers, and a few tutors from Yale College. Each carried a Sharps. Within a month they were founding the town of Wabaunsee on a hilltop above the Kaw River.

The older Yankee settlements, uneasy though they were, had yet found time to display Yankee notions. In Lawrence, otherwise a town of orderly habits, some wicked men of "the frontier element" had opened a Liquor Den "across the ravine" from the village and were peddling strong drink to all who would buy. Then, one day in 1856, and most suddenly, a group of a dozen women led by Mrs. Helen Hutchinson, late of Randolph, Vermont, attacked the Den with hatchets, hammers, big axes, and vigor. They broke glass and bottle, and poured every drop of RUM into the dust and stubble of Bleeding Kansas. Thus did the much later Carry Nation, a Kansas woman, have an example for her lone-handed operations against the rum-sellers.

But the Hutchinsons tired of the constant vigil of living in Lawrence. "For nearly two years," wrote William Hutchinson, who had once edited the *Green Mountain Herald* in his native state, "we kept a light burning every night in our sleeping rooms, with firearms within reach." So, with Jonathan C. Burnett, a fellow Vermonter, and some twenty others, the Hutchinsons moved into Bourbon County, Kansas, and all took claims in what became Mapleton, so named by Hutchinson for the only grove of sugar maples he had seen in the territory.

In the spring of 1856 the town of Lawrence, and other Yankee settlements, lighted up. Said an official report of the New England Emigrant Aid Company:

On the 21st of May, the United States marshal of Kanzas, acting on orders from Washington, D.C., entered the city of Lawrence, in command of companies of South Carolinians and Georgians, whome he had sworn into service as an armed posse of the United States government, and burned to the ground the Free State Hotel, just finished.

The mob also burned the offices of the *Herald of Freedom* and the *Free State* newspapers. There was some shooting, as the Lawrence Rifles turned out, and a number of homes were burned. The marshal informed Lawrence that the (proslavery and pseudo) grand jury at the proslavery settlement of Lecompton had indicted the hotel and newspapers as common nuisances, and that the court had ordered them destroyed.

This was two days after Senator Sumner's speech in the national Capital.

In near-by Osawatomie, God's angry man, John Brown, knew that the time had come. The Voice had told him. With four of his stalwart sons and two other men, they fell upon a proslavery farmhouse in the middle of the night of May 24, took forth six of the men therein, and hacked them to death with sabers, in cold blood and upon orders direct from Jehovah.

Revenge came quickly, and Mrs. Louisa Lovejoy, living in the new settlement of Palmyra, in the troubled section, wrote home to the *Democrat* of Concord, New Hampshire, to say that the horizon was alight with the

flames of Free State homes and haystacks, as the Ruffians put Osawatomie to
the Torch of Slavery. They also burned the Free State saw and grist mill at
Franklin. They shot and killed four settlers, including "the Gallant Brown,
who was shot dead in the street." Here Mrs. Lovejoy referred not to the
Angry Man but to Orville C. Brown, a Free State pioneer settler of the
Osawatomie. She reported, in September, that fifty families of the neighborhood were shelterless and were living in their wagons in the woods, en-
deavoring to escape "from these fiends in human form." There were only
Heaven and Elijah's ravens to feed them, she said, and called earnestly upon
people of the old Granite State to send clothing.*

The quickened bitterness in Kansas naturally got prominence in newspapers all over the North, and one effect was a falling off in the numbers of
emigrants. Another was the sudden increase in cash contributions to the New
England Emigrant Aid Company. Eminent men like Lyman Beecher, Leonard
Bacon, and Thomas Starr King were aiding in founding Kansas Leagues in
scores of Yankee towns and cities. Henry D. Thoreau of Concord and
Walden, however, was not moved. "I had thought the *house* was on fire,
not the prairie," he said. Kansas, to Thoreau, was of less importance than
the fact that the citizens of Boston had not prevented—though some few
had tried—the taking of an escaped slave there and returning him to his
master.

There were presently two state governments in the Territory, for the
Yankees and other northerners had drawn up what they called the Topeka
Constitution and had elected Dr. Charles Robinson of the Aid company as
governor.†

Small parties organized by the Aid Company continued to arrive in 1857.
So did a group of young missionaries, the Kansas Band, from Andover
Theological Seminary, carrying on the tradition of the bands that previously
had gone to Iowa and Illinois. Sylvester Storrs helped to found a church at
Quindaro; another—now the First Congregational Church of Kansas City—

* Mrs. Lovejoy had some ideas how her sisters in New Hampshire could help the Free
State cause: "Let the little misses and young ladies in their ornamental work for the parlor,
have the names 'Fremont & Jessie' wrought in choicest colors; let the matrons in the dairy
room make a mammoth 'Fremont Cheese,' to be eaten with a zest, at their annual State
or County Fair." But to no avail. Frémont was defeated by proslavery Buchanan, and Kansas
continued to bleed. But Mrs. Lovejoy's letters to New England newspapers resulted in a
generous response of clothing for the desolate people of the Osawatomie.

† At least seven Yankees—there may well have been others—were in the Topeka territorial
legislature, three of them in the upper chamber or Council: Carmi Babcock, from Franklin
County, Vt., Oscar E. Learnard, Fairfax, Vt., and Joseph P. Root, of Greenwich, Mass., a
member of the Beecher Bible and Rifle colony; and in the house, Hiram Appleman, Groton,
Conn., William P. Bodager, Tamworth, N.H., Addison Danford, Laconia, N.H., and Edmund
N. Morrill, Westbrook, Me.

at Wyandotte; still another in Atchison. Grosvenor Morse went to Emporia, where soon he was helping to establish a state normal school. Roswell D. Parker went to Leavenworth, and Richard Cordley to Lawrence, where for the next thirty-eight years he was pastor of Plymouth Church. Lewis Bodwell, a native of New Haven, had come before, in 1856, and had been arrested and held prisoner for a time on the suspicion that he was an ardent Free State man, which was true. Bodwell preached all over the territory, and was one of the few who ventured to help old Brown out of the region with his last batch of escaped slaves.

Old Brown returned to New England after the troubles of 1856. There he called upon Thomas W. Higginson, Theodore Parker, G. L. Stearns, Frank Sanborn, and Samuel Gridley Howe (who had married Julia Ward), and from them and others secured supplies of arms, which he informed them were to be used expressly to protect Free State settlements in Kansas. In the autumn of 1857, Brown was on the way back to Osawatomie, a traveling arsenal, his blue-gray eyes aglitter, the Voice in his ear. There were plenty of the grapes of wrath stored in Kansas. Brown would trample them.

But the Angry Man discovered that Kansas had tired of bullets. Both sides were in a mood to go ahead with a legal, or at least a more conventional, state government. Well, let the fools doze if they would. As for John Brown, he stowed away his guns for the present and started to recruit men for a new enterprise—the founding of an inner-state in the mountains of Maryland and Virginia to which escaped slaves should come and be protected by Brown's army until the whole South should be free of the Abomination, by insurrection. He remained quiet until late in 1858 when, under the style of Shubel Morgan, he and his party of madmen raided plantations across the border in Missouri, killed one planter, and escaped with a dozen Negroes. In less than a year he was at Harpers Ferry.

Long before that the people of Kansas, both proslavery and antislavery, were glad to be rid of him. But on the second day of December, 1859, John Brown became a piece of American History, no matter what Kansas wanted.

As for Kansas, it had its own Free State martyrs, one of the best known being David Starr Hoyt of Greenfield, Massachusetts, who in 1856 led a company raised by Dr. Calvin Cutter to Kansas. With them they had no fewer than four cannon, one hundred brand-new Sharps rifles, and much ammunition. Coming up the river, the arms were discovered, though the rifles were without magazines, these having carefully been sent in another manner to Dr. Cutler. The ordnance was put ashore at Lexington, Missouri; but Hoyt managed to secure it and eventually took it to Lawrence. But he was a marked man, and his end came suddenly. "In August, 1856, David Hoyt was murdered by Border Ruffians."

In the sack of Lawrence and the violence at Osawatomie, Manhattan, and Palmyra, Free State settlers suffered more than the proslavery people. But the Yankees continued to come. In 1858, by a vote of 11,300 to 1,788, Kansas rejected a proslavery constitution. In 1860 Kansas, still bloody, was admitted as a state in which slavery was prohibited.

In the migration of 1857 from New England was a curious theological freak, the Reverend Isaac Kalloch, pastor of Tremont Temple in Boston, and Exhibit A in New England's most celebrated adultery case in generations. In his Temple, Kalloch had spoken well for the Emigrant Aid Company, and now he led one of its parties to Kansas. He already knew Dr. Robinson, the Aid Company agent who became governor; and he also became acquainted with a young adventurer from Vermont named Clinton Carver Hutchinson. Kalloch prevailed on Hutchinson to become a Baptist preacher and secured him a pulpit in Topeka, then returned east. But he was a man seeking new opportunities, and he thought he saw one in Kansas. Early in 1864 he came back to the prairies and with Hutchinson and others founded the town of Ottawa. Fifty settlers, mostly friends of Kalloch from New England, moved in immediately. He got the legislature to name Ottawa the seat of Franklin County. He established a Baptist church, founded a newspaper, and projected a mighty seat of education to be called Roger Williams University. He took time out to build a toll bridge, established a cemetery association, and began to organize a railroad company. He was a man who liked to have things hum, to have many sources of income.

The railroad was actually built, and Kalloch arranged for the shops, employing some two hundred men, to be erected in Ottawa. He started to raise stock, imported Essex pigs, Jersey cows, and Kentucky horses, for he was a notable sporting man—for a Baptist. He was elected president of the state agricultural society. He got into the legislature. He bought the Eldridge House in Lawrence and thus became a seller of liquor. He dabbled in much else, too, and the panic of 1873 broke him. He came out of it with little more than clothes on his back—and his still unquenchable energy. He returned to the church and to the Baptist pulpit in Lawrence, where for two years he enthralled his congregation with the old magic. In 1875, without warning, he packed up and left for California—but not for obscurity.

Kalloch had managed, with little room to spare, to keep free of criminal indictments in Kansas; but this was not the case with his partner, C. C. Hutchinson. This gentleman escaped prison, however, and was so pleased that he moved to the very center of Kansas and there founded a town named for himself, a native of the Green Mountain State, which flourished from the first.

By late 1857 it was apparent to the New England Emigrant Aid Company that Kansas was certain to be Free Soil. It then ceased sending more organized parties, though until 1860 it continued to offer advice and low-rate tickets to settlers. The company had never paid the fare of emigrants, anyway. It simply offered them a guide, and tickets at greatly reduced cost, somewhat the same as a travel agency. The ten or more steam sawmills it sent out were of the greatest help to settlers. Its two hotels, in Kansas City and Lawrence, were also of aid and comfort. But unquestionably the company's importance as a free-state builder rests upon its superb propaganda. By organized groups it sent no more than three thousand people to Kansas; but the attendant publicity probably induced three or four times as many to go to the debatable ground.

The Aid Company also brought to Kansas many active men who were very able as town founders, as witness Lawrence, Topeka, Osawatomie, and Manhattan. And many another Kansas community was founded in whole or in part by people from New England, without company aid.* An emigrant from Middleton, Massachusetts, who needed no aid from anyone was John James Ingalls. He arrived in 1858 and presently settled in Atchison. He went promptly into politics, to follow Yankee Pomeroy into the United States Senate and to serve two more terms, becoming the idol of the G.A.R., if nobody else, because of his bloody-shirt and pension activities.

Incidentally, the officers chosen to govern and to represent the new state of Kansas included Governor Robinson, Senator Pomeroy, and Representative Conway, all former agents of the Aid Company. In assessing the effect of Yankees on Kansas, one careful historian has said that they exercised "an influence out of all proportion to their numbers," and that, even though Kansas might well have become Free State in any case, "certainly it would not have developed the way it did, and would not be exactly the same today" had it not been for the Emigrant Aid Company and its New England emigrants.†

One is prepared to believe, too, that correspondence from such ebullient Yankees as the aforementioned Mrs. Lovejoy of Palmyra and Manhattan, Kansas, was of effect in attracting new settlers who may have cared less for

* For instance: Baldwin, named for Yankee John Baldwin, who previously had founded Berea, Ohio; Burlington, named for the Vermont city; Greeley, for Yankee Horace Greeley; Haddam, by Connecticut settlers; Hartford, the same; Horace, for Mr. Greeley; Lyndon, by Vermont settlers; Meriden, by Newel Colby of Meriden, N.H.; Newton, from the Massachusetts city; Peabody, for F. H. Peabody of Boston; and Whiting, for Mrs. Whiting, last wife of Senator Pomeroy. Mr. Greeley also had a county named for him; and so did Charles Sumner. In the seventies the town of Kinsley, Edwards County, was named for the Hon. Edward Kinsley of Boston.

† Samuel A. Johnson, in *Kansas Historical Quarterly*, Nov., 1932. Another view is that of W. E. Connelley, *An Appeal to the Record* (Topeka, 1903). Mr. Connelley argues that the Aid Company did Kansas more harm than good in the Free State cause.

Abolition than for other things. Take the remarkable case of E. M. Thruston of Maine—she wrote to her papers—who had been in the last stages of consumption when he arrived in Kansas. By wrapping himself in a buffalo robe and sleeping outdoors on the rich prairie, he was cured quickly and manifestly. Such were the noble air and soil of Kansas. Mrs. Lovejoy had other attractive items to report: She had green corn to eat on July 1, two months before corn was ripe in New Hampshire. The Kansas grapes were of the most wonderful flavor. As for grain crops, why, a Yankee could scarce believe his eyes. She was blunt, too, and warned that drones were not wanted, nor those who could not live on coarse fare. And she never failed to sound the great Moral Objective: "A mighty work is to be done, and Kanzas is the great battlefield where a conflict is to be waged with the monster Slavery. He will be routed and slain. Amen, amen."

After the Civil War, the movement of Yankees continued.* In later years William Allen White of Emporia was of the opinion that Yankees in Kansas had been a mixed blessing.† They had, said he, set up their own kind of commonwealth, dominated by the Political Puritan. They builded townships, cities, and counties upon a belief in the moral government of the universe. In their yearnings they fabricated their own kind of Utopias. Thus they attempted to establish a sort of theocracy. For thirty years, said Mr. White, they dominated Kansas politics. They kept the state a plutocracy with benevolent aspirations. One of its early and persistent manifestations was prohibition.

In White's opinion prohibition, which arrived in Kansas in 1880, had kept many good European settlers out of the state. Kansas had not grown in numbers much, he said, and the stagnation of the state was largely the result of prohibition. The Yankees were surely to blame for that, for "we got whatever population we had from New England and from the Middle States, who were out of New England," thus stemming directly or indirectly from the Puritans. He was of the opinion that this puritanical longing for the Kingdom of God upon earth accounted for what might be called the ethnological difference of Kansas from the rest of the Missouri River states. Many Bohemians lived in Nebraska, he pointed out, while Minnesota was filled with Scandinavians.‡ Kansas did get large colonies of Mennonites; but

* It included George Porterfield Gates, of Lunenburg, Vt., who settled in Independence in 1865, and made a success of his flourmilling business. A granddaughter became Mrs. Harry Truman.

† In an address to the Kansas Historical Society, published in the *Kansas Historical Quarterly,* Feb., 1939.

‡ Mr. White did not say so, but Scandinavians were often quite as puritanical as the Yankees. One found the perfect example of this phenomenon in Northfield, Minn., where, in the days when Carleton College was dominated by the Congregational clergy, it and the near-by St. Olaf's College, Norwegian, were of one mind in the matter of "morals" as concerning liquor, tobacco, sex, and the keeping holy of the Sabbath.

they too believed in a moral government of their universe, differing from the Puritans only in that they spoke German. The Mennonites gave Kansas what the Yankees had already brought there; namely, "thrift, diligence, and a strong tinge of religious feeling."

"So," summed up Mr. White, "we Kansans remain essentially New Englanders—essentially a Puritanical type." As for Populism, the radical movement that took Kansas by storm in the 1890's, it was "merely a left-wing Puritanical revolt." Even in its revolutions, Kansas thus remained pure Yankee.

Once, and apparently only once, was there a temporary weakening of the general moral structure in Kansas. In 1874 Kansans were enjoying a feeling of great security from economic worries. Times were good, getting better. The legislature voted to dispense with the services of a chaplain, who for many years had received three dollars a day to open the sessions with prayer. The lawmakers had scarcely completed their unholy labors at Topeka when a visitation was called down upon the whole region. Locusts in unbelievable numbers came out of the sky to darken the bright Kansas sun and to devour "every green thing from the sagebrush lands of Colorado to the turgid flood waters of the Missouri River." Nor did any sea gulls put in an appearance, as they did in Utah, to destroy the horde, which proceeded to eat Kansas alive. At the next sitting of the legislature, one of the first pieces of business was the restoration of the office of chaplain, which survives to this day.

CHAPTER XIV

YANKEE INFLUENCE IN COLORADO

THE MOVEMENT OF genuine settlers into Colorado did not begin until the spring of 1870. The region had become a territory nine years before, but so uncertain seemed its future that people seeking land for farms passed it by. Its population was little larger in 1870 than in 1860, when the census men had counted 34,277 men, women, and children.

If a count had been made in, say, the middle of 1859, it would unquestionably have reached 120,000, perhaps even more; for the sudden madness called the Pikes Peak gold rush had brought into the region an army of adventurers second in number only to that of the Forty-niners to California. The Pikes Peak rush was touched off, in no small part, by a crew of Yankee prospectors from the Yankee town of Lawrence, Kansas, led by John Easter, local butcher, who had been shown a quill of gold dust by some Delaware Indians. Easter could not get much information from the Delawares, other than that the gold country was "two sleeps from Pikes Peak"; but he appears to have thought of himself as something of a diviner, anyway, and in the spring of 1858, with some thirty other Kansans, he struck out for what is now Colorado. In that unknown country the Easter party presently staked out a town on Cherry Creek they called St. Charles, later a part of Denver, the name of which sought to honor a governor of Kansas Territory.

One of the Easter party, John King, did not remain long in Denver City. He returned home to Lawrence and there displayed a small amount of fine gold which he had panned on Cherry Creek. The news got around, and within a few days a company of optimists pulled out of Leavenworth for the diggings. From Kansas the word spread to the East, and even to golden California. It spread even more quickly than the news of Sam Brannan's bright bottle from the Mother Lode; and the result was all but instantaneous. In the next twelve months at least one hundred thousand people left their homes in the Midwest, the South, and the East, and managed somehow to get to Colorado—which still did not have a name.

A contributing factor to the sudden rush was the panic of 1857, which was felt throughout '58 and later. The cities were filled with unemployed. Farmers were bankrupt. The rush to California was a whole decade in the past, and its countless disappointments were forgotten; only those few who had struck it rich were remembered. And now, in '58 and '59, men who had been too young to join the Forty-niners, or had merely failed to go and now suddenly recalled the fantastic stories of the free gold of the Mother Lode, resolved that this time they would not wait at all, but go in the advance guard.

The St. Louis Chamber of Commerce egged on the Pikes Peak business by memorializing Congress, demanding of that body nothing less than establishment of a United States mint at St. Louis, a handy spot to "the headwaters of the Platte and Arkansas rivers" which, said the Chamber, was a country "richly covered with gold deposits of great purity and fineness." Every border town along the Platte and the Arkansas, stagnating in the hard times, added to the din set going by the St. Louis men of vision. Even a transient population would necessarily leave some cash behind along the route to the new gold fields, and the towns needed it. So, out of these hamlets presently flowed thousands of copies of cheaply printed and quickly compiled guidebooks to the Pikes Peak country, composed by people who had never so much as seen either the Peak or the country round about. These compilers troubled themselves not at all with facts; they merely set down their utmost dreams in type. A typical and highly popular sample of guidebook information instructed prospectors how to mine gold: The best method was to fashion a heavy wooden drag, its bottom studded with iron rasps. Take this rig to the top of Pikes Peak, get aboard, then slide down to the bottom. The rasps simply ripped the surface gold free, which accommodatingly rolled down in the wake of the drag, and the rich harvest arrived at the base of the golden mountain along with the drag. Occasionally—so the guidebooks said—one such drag "yielded a ton of metal in a single slide."

Grown men believed it, and grown men started for Pikes Peak. This was the most prominent and dramatic mountain in the region, and its alliterative name was almost as alluring; hence it became a symbol. Many of the hundred thousand or more madmen traveled up the rivers or across the barrens under banners that proclaimed "Pikes Peak or Bust."

Mostly, so it turned out, it was bust. Perhaps never has a tide of migration so quickly turned to ebb as the Pikes Peak rush. The ebb seems to have its genesis among the would-be miners who had little more than arrived at the diggings on Cherry Creek. They had found little gold, or anything that looked like gold. They were hungry and destitute. They were far from home. One can imagine how the exodus began; probably, on some dolorous morning, a completely discouraged young Kansan looked up once more at the hard, towering peaks, again at the goldless sands, said the hell with it in so many words, and offered for sale, at Denver City's thriving secondhand market, his pick and shovel, his pan and boots—and a drag if he had one. Then, another young man did the same, and so on and on until, within a few days there, had developed an enormous stampede back to the States—a head-long, maniacal surge of bitter humanity, as wild and heedless as had been the incoming. The street of Denver City was a babel of auctioneers, buying the cast-off paraphernalia of the mobs seeking to get away. The Platte River itself, and every trail, was crowded with the returning stampede, which carried all before it, stopping in their tracks and hurling back thousands who were still trying to get to the alleged diggings. The wagons of the exodus now had legends on their canvas sides, "Busted, by God!" and "Bound for America." There was still gold in Colorado hills, and a wealth of still un-suspected silver, but neither was to be taken by panning or sliding down a mountain. The rush to Pikes Peak was in powerful reverse even before the urge to get there had petered out.

Thus a year later the federal men, in their first count of the Territory, could find only 34,277 souls.

How many New Englanders had set out for Pikes Peak is now beyond knowing, if it was ever known. Probably they were not many. In 1860 the census reported 1,400 natives of Massachusetts and 980 natives of Con-necticut in Colorado. Natives of the other New England states were too few to warrant separate categories. Nor did many of these early Yankees remain. The next census, that of 1870, found only 618 from Massachusetts, indicating a loss of more than half during the decade, while no other Yankee state showed at all. Yet, a small number of determined Yankees went to Colorado in the first rush and remained, to exert no little influence there.

There was, for instance, the remarkable John Quincy Adams Rollins, born in the hamlet of Gilmanton, New Hampshire, which was singularly sus-ceptible to migrating fevers. Rollins had left home while young, made money in wholesale groceries in Boston and Chicago, even more money in trading in cattle along the Mississippi River. At almost the last gasp of the Pikes Peak rush he arrived in Denver City driving a nineteen-yoke ox team, surely even in that day something to see. He started prospecting in the Boulder district and did very well, then lost what he had made in a stagecoach venture and an attempt to found a salt works in South Park. But his mining ventures con-tinued to prosper, and in Rollinsville he built up a community unique among the Colorado towns of the period. Rollinsville harbored no saloons, no gambling houses, no rouged women. He erected a stamp mill, to reduce his ore on the spot; and also built what local historians say was the first wagon road over the Continental Divide, through properly named Rollins Pass, to Hot Sulphur Springs in Middle Park.

George A. Patten, of Surrey, Maine, was in the middle of the Pikes Peak rush, and was wise enough to set up as merchant at Idaho Springs, then to buy into mining ventures and to operate the best of them, to such purpose that on his death, forty years later, he was "reputed to be the wealthiest man in Clear Creek County."

Apparently the first Yankee of political influence in the new territory was Lewis Ledyard Weld of Hartford, Connecticut, a nephew of the great abolitionist Theodore Weld. Young Weld was practicing law in Kansas City when the Pikes Peak excitement broke out. He went to Denver City, and was appointed secretary of the territory, for which he designed Colorado's great seal, with its motto *Nil sine Numine* (officially translated by Colorado as "Nothing without the Deity") taken direct from the Weld escutcheon. But Weld did not live to see Colorado a state. He died in 1864, a colonel in the Union Army; not forgotten, however, for Weld County honors his name.

In all of the Pikes Peak rush, however, the Yankee who was surely to have the greatest influence on Colorado was Horace Greeley, the New Hampshire lad who had founded the *Tribune* in New York City and was already, in 1859, an institution. In that summer Greeley made a trip to the new diggings. He saw, as was his custom, a great deal, and reported what he saw in his paper. What interested him more than the search for gold were the agricultural possibilities of the high plains country which he crossed on the way to the mountains. This interest was to bear fruit a decade later in the first successful effort to get farming under way in a region that until then was pretty much absorbed with minerals.

In the same year, a few months in advance of Greeley, came he who was to be Colorado's first great Bonanza King, Horace Austin Warner Tabor, a native of Holland, Vermont, looking for the fortune he had not been able to make at stone-cutting in New England or in squatting on an abandoned homestead in Kansas, where he had followed a brother in the migration inspired by the New England Emigrant Aid Company. With him, moving toward Pikes Peak, were his wife Augusta, of Portland, Maine, and a year-old baby, huddled in the wagon, both ailing.

Tabor had failed at everything. What little money the Tabors had known on their forlorn homestead in Zeandale, Kansas, came from boarders Augusta had cooked meals for and from the butter she had made.* Nor did

---

* Mrs. Tabor belied her looks. She had poetry in her soul, one of the few people in the Colorado rush who gathered wild flowers along the way because she loved them, who saw more in the prairies than so much real estate, and who did not "look upon the mountains merely as heaps of rock perversely piled up by the gods to hide gold and silver treasure." See George Willison's fine tribute to her in *Here They Dug the Gold*.

Tabor succeed as a miner. He opened a transient store first at one diggings, then another, made a little money, and grubstaked prospectors in the silver excitement that followed the first rush for gold. The grubstakes were to pay off.

Yankees of varied talents were in the first rush, and in the sixties their heads were appearing above the surface of the still limited population. Wilbur Fisk Stone was an experienced emigrant long before he went to Colorado. Born in old Litchfield, Connecticut, in 1833, he moved with his parents first to York State, then in turn to Michigan, Indiana, and Iowa. When he was twenty-seven years old, he quit his law practice in Omaha, bought an ox team and drove overland to Denver. He followed the rush into South Park, spent a winter in roaring Canon City, where he drafted the code for the People's Court, set up in lieu of more formal government. A bit later he went to Pueblo, became editor of the *Chieftain*, first newspaper in the area, and was active in promoting the Denver & Rio Grande Western Railroad. He had a leading part in drafting the state constitution; and was elected without opposition to the Colorado supreme court. More important than any of these things was that he was the consulting editor of an excellent four-volume history of his adopted state, monument enough for any man.

In the Pikes Peak rush were a number of Forty-niners who had failed to strike it rich in California. One of these was William Austin Hamilton Loveland, native of Chatham on Cape Cod, who had mined the Mother Lode at Grass Valley and got nothing for his pains. He came to Denver City in '59. He opened a store in Golden, bought considerable real estate at low prices, some of which turned out to be fine mining property. He purchased the *Rocky Mountain News*, which he operated for a decade, and never failed to say a good word for the proposed Colorado Central Railroad, which eventually was built. One of the towns along its tracks became Loveland. Another disappointed Forty-niner was Hammond Gilbert, a New Hampshire man, who, after fifteen years of seeking hit it at last in Colorado, where he discovered the rich silver mine he called the Clifford, then opened several more rich lodes, including Clifford No. 2, War Eagle, Little Chief, and Rosita.

In the sixties one of the most successful properties was that of the Boston & Colorado Smelting Company, perhaps the first large amount of Yankee capital to be invested in the territory. This outfit built the first successful smelter in the region, established and operated under direction of Nathaniel P. Hill, professor of chemistry at Brown University, in Rhode Island; and improved, as was many another venture of its kind, by the expert touch of Nathaniel S. Keith of Boston, who held degrees in both science and medicine.

Keith was master of the refractory ores, and for almost a decade he applied his knowledge to the extremely tough ores of the Rockies, being later called because of his understanding of electromagnetism to advise Thomas Edison himself in such matters. He was the Keith who in 1884 built the first electric lighting plant in California.

When Pikes Peak rush had run its course, and subsequent strikes of the sixties had settled down to the business of smelting, Colorado contained only a few more residents than it had had before the rush of '59. Its admission as a territory in 1861 had no effect on immigration. The first indication that it would ever be else than a mining region came in December of 1869, when the Union Colony of Colorado was formally organized in Cooper Institute, New York City, through the efforts of Horace Greeley.

This group, which was to have a great effect on Colorado, was the outcome of Greeley's visit in 1859 and of his long-held and strong notions about the proper way to farm. He always fancied himself a farm boy, anyway, and in the *Tribune* he wrote as often about farming as he did about politics. But he might never have founded Union Colony had it not been for his agricultural editor, a strange character named Nathan Cook Meeker. Born on the Western Reserve in Ohio, Meeker got his schooling at Yankee Oberlin, then wandered over New York, Pennsylvania, and New Jersey, seeking a Utopia. He became enamored of the cooperative theories of Fourier and joined the Trumbull Phalanx in Ohio. When this visionary experiment played out in 1848, Meeker went on the move again. He operated a cooperative store at Hiram, Ohio, where Campbellites were planning to open a college. He visited Oneida Community. In 1865 he became Greeley's agricultural editor and was sent to the West, to see how farming went in those parts. He noted the same possibilities in high and dry Colorado that Greeley had remarked. Union Colony was the result of the discussions of the two men.

Greeley announced the venture late in 1869 in his immensely influential paper. The response was immediate and showed, he felt, that a considerable number of American farmers believed as he did; namely, that agricultural pursuits could be carried on without the isolation and inconveniences common to farms. He outlined his plan at the first meeting, to a room filled and overflowing. Farmers, he said, had just as much right as anybody to the opportunity for intellectual and cultural development. But the cooperative colonies of Fourier had proved failures; free riders took advantage of the real workers. Nor was Greeley a believer in Socialism, or in the so-called Christian Communism of the followers of Noyes. But he did believe that a carefully selected group of genuine farmers could make a success of living in a village of their own making and at the same time carry on their farms.

Both Greeley and Meeker stressed the low price at which land could be purchased in the high arid plains of Colorado; and how this land could be made into the most fertile of soil by irrigation. Greeley's admiration for Brigham Young and what he and his Saints had done in the Utah desert was of the highest. Behold the Mormons, Greeley told his group in Cooper Institute, had they not watered the desert and made it rejoice? The meeting agreed with Greeley, and an executive committee was named, which included Nathaniel Paul of Wakefield, New Hampshire, and General George C. Shelton, of Seymour, Connecticut; Meeker being instructed to go forth and seek out the land. Greeley was elected treasurer of the company.

Meeker set forth. Early in April of 1870 he selected a site on the Platte River, fifty-odd miles north of Denver on the Denver Pacific Railroad, which was just completing its line from Cheyenne, on the main line of the Union Pacific, to Denver. Here he obtained 12,000 acres from the railroad's land department and a few individual owners, and made arrangements to obtain some 100,000 acres more, from the government.

At a second meeting of Union Colony in New York, memberships were sold and cash paid into the treasury to the total of $60,000. More memberships were promised. Greeley's own strong convictions were apparent in the rules and regulations of the colony. First of all, membership was open only to "men of good character, who are Temperance Men." Membership cost $155. For this fee each member or family was entitled to a parcel of land outside the colony village, and the right to purchase a town lot for from $25 to $50. Deeds would not be issued unless the land were improved within one year from time of purchase. Union Colony was to be a town, perhap a city, but it was not to be a speculation.

No religious tests of any sort were required of members; but let it be understood, the antiliquor clause was in every deed, and violation of it meant loss of the land involved.

Greeley and Meeker took considerable pains to make clear that, although Union Colony certainly had aspects of cooperative living, it was not to be thought of as anything like Onedia Community, which at the time was as widely as it was scandalously known. Even so, the press both East and West had a wonderful time of it poking fun at Uncle Horace's farmers as a pack of eccentrics, if not worse, who were going out into the Great American Desert, to starve.

Possibly they were eccentrics, but they were not going to starve in the desert. In the advance party to Colorado went Edwin Nettleton, the son of Connecticut parents, Oberlin-educated, to survey the site of what it was agreed should be the town of Greeley, and to lay out the irrigation ditches. Nettleton did both jobs to perfection; and in Greeley for the first time in the United States, to anticipate a bit, water rights were transferred to the water-using farmers on what an agricultural writer has called "a truly practical and cooperative basis."*

In April of 1870 the first of Union Colony settlers arrived on the ground, their last lap by the new Denver Pacific. In late May some four hundred of them had come; and on the 22nd, a Sunday, two hundred and fifteen persons attended church. Tents and temporary board shacks were up. So was a rambling old building which had been bought in Cheyenne, taken apart, brought to the new town of Greeley and set up as Hotel de Comfort, a lodging house for new arrivals.

So well was the transportation arranged, and the departures, that virtually all the orginial members of Union Colony were on the site by the last of June. They numbered all told approximately fourteen hundred people, of whom between two hundred and three hundred came direct from New England. These Yankee shareholders—and their families—came from sixty-seven widely scattered communities in the six Yankee states, indicative of the wide influence of Greeley and his *Tribune*. The only concentration of Colony shareholders appears to have been in Waltham, Massachusetts, where the heads of six families—including Atkinsons, Russells, Wareings, and Waddingtons—signed up. In the town of Hopedale, Massachusetts, which had itself been an experimental colony of sorts, the call to Colorado must have been feeble; only one person went from there. Both Dexter, Maine, and Poultney, Vermont, sent members to Greeley, for no villages in all New England contained more mobile people. Again and again, in the exodus to almost every western state, both Dexter and Poultney were represented. So, too, was Showhegan, Maine, and Putney, Vermont, the latter of which was the home ground of the original Perfectionists.

Union Colony was a most methodical organization. It had been carefully planned from the first; even its prospectus was such as to discourage Utopians —all of them, including the lunatics who wanted settlements for vegetarians only, who wanted lands laid out in octagonal form, who wanted free meals or free love, who wanted to live in phalanxes and build phalansteries, who wanted a Christ to lead them, who wanted to make fun of Christ and defy Jehovah, who wanted buttonless clothing, bloomered women, long-haired men, or who wanted no medium of exchange except "time books" in which was recorded the labor of each Utopian. These people were all loose in

---

* From Greeley, Edwin Nettleton went on to become one of the greatest figures in irrigation in the United States. He laid out the vast systems for an English syndicate which began farming on a huge scale near Fort Collins; then surveyed the sites of Colorado Springs, Manitou, and other towns. He established the weather bureau on Pikes Peak. He went to Spain to study irrigation, and returned to lay out immense systems in Idaho and Wyoming. In the dry parts of the old West, he was easily the most influential pioneer.

nineteenth century America and the members of Union Colony wanted no part of them in Greeley, Colorado.

There was nothing, indeed, in the prospectus of Union Colony that could offend the sensibilities of the most confirmed hill farmer in Vermont—unless it was parting with the $155 membership fee; for despite his many crotchets, Horace Greeley was a man of great, good, common sense. He believed most devoutly that hard work directed by intelligence could build a successful community on the neglected high plains of Colorado; and the original colonists of the town of Greeley were probably of a quality well above that of the general run of settlers at the West.* Certainly, no village ever rose on the plains more quickly than Greeley and in such a well ordered manner.

When in May a reporter from the Denver *Tribune* "stepped from the cars at Greeley" he was greeted by the din of the hammer and the merry hum of the laborer building his future home. "Were you to see an example of the energy and pluck" of these people, said the man from Denver, you would be astonished. Many houses were all but completed; ditches had been dug, and wells; one man was planting fruit trees. There were a post office, a grocery, a boot and shoe shop, and a hotel. Two weeks later a man from the *Rocky Mountain News* counted three provision stores, two bakeries, a meat market, a sash, blind, and paint shop, a bank of exchange, and a railroad depot. What was more, and startling, was that he counted thirty-four frame houses, in one of which was "a landscape and portrait painter at work." It was not true, then, that the Puritan tradition denied Art. . . .

The Union Colonists, who incidentally included a few Yankees who had already helped to settle the New England Emigrant Aid Company's town of Lawrence in Kansas, were up with the sun, or before, and they hammered and sawed and dug and planted until the shadows fell across the flat land. By mid-June their irrigation system had a tremendous start—a ditch fifteen inches deep, eight feet wide, and *ten miles long*. This was working with a will. Good will and good health both prevailed, according to one visitor, who remarked that "the moth consumes the lawyer's volumes here while rust and mildew play havoc with the doctor's lancet and pills." On June 21 the first child was born and named Horace Greeley Meeker Cameron Dickinson. In July a Methodist church and a Congregational society were formed. A public school was open. In September the Masons organized a lodge, while

---

* In the New England delegation were, from MAINE: five of the James Armstrong family, Calais; S. M. McDermid, Skowhegan; George A. Pease, Appleton. NEW HAMPSHIRE: Nathaniel Paul, Wakefield; J. W. Titcomb, Farmington. VERMONT: "Dyer & Hoslett," Fairhaven; Herbert Jones, Putney; Victor A. Howe, East Middlebury. MASSACHUSETTS: Moses Ellor and family, Dracut; H. N. Rogerson and family, Haydenville; Elisha C. Monk, Stoughton. CONNECTICUT: Francis Francher and C. W. Devine, New Haven; D. W. Olis, Franklin; W. S. Starr and family, East Hampton; Samuel Linn, Bridgeport. RHODE ISLAND: A. W. Banker and C. Bardill, described as "old Bachelor," Providence.

the Good Templars were meeting also, one hundred strong. By then two brick blocks were up and occupied. And one great day there stepped from the cars the rustic and fanastic figure of Mr. Greeley himself, beaver hat, linen duster and all, his long white hair and shorter fringe whiskers blowing free in the wind, benign blue eyes alive behind the severe square spectacles, umbrella in hand, come to see for himself how things were going. They were going pretty well, and he was elated.

By October the settlers had planted "several thousand" maple trees around their houses, which were 4,740 feet above sea level. By this time the town of Greeley's character was obvious even to casual visitors, one of whom remarked, "The Sabbath is observed here with Puritanic scrupulousness." Yet, a minor crisis was at hand. A man of more daring than brains dared to "open a billiard saloon." He was promptly "bundled out of town, and the shop burned down during the melee." It was more irrigation ditch and not billiard games that Greeley needed. There was not room for both, or so the colonists thought.

It was in October, too, that an incredibly stupid person sought to establish what colonists referred to as a "liquor den," on a site outside the village but still within the town limits. News of this obscene attempt was whispered to several of the town fathers during church services. Then, "before the benediction had been pronounced, a committee was appointed to interview" the saloonkeeper. It must have been quite a committee, too, for a newspaper account of the affair says that "about 200 persons gathered around the liquor establishment." The poor publican's key was taken, and the door locked. Just then "the den was discovered to be on fire"—apparently a common occurrence which the Lord or some other agency prepared for all dens of booze or billiards in Union Colony. The numerous committee rescued the liquid curse, however, loaded it into a wagon, and had both it and its owner taken out of town. When Greeley citizens learned that the rum seller had paid $200 rent on the property, they paid him that amount in cash.

On November 16—it was still 1870—the first issue of the Greeley *Tribune* appeared, to be added to the "115 copies of the New York *Tribune*, 62 copies of the *Rocky Mountain News*, 35 copies of the weekly *Colorado Tribune*, and over 200 miscellaneous publications" to which townsmen already subscribed. Greeley citizens were as literate as they were energetic. A man from the Boulder *News* wrote in his paper that "Greeley contains a larger per cent of intelligence, refinement and industry than almost any other Western town of its size and age."

Now that the town of Greeley had a local spokesman in its own *Tribune*, citizens and the rest of the known world were told that "our Eastern people testify to this climate's superiority over New England's." As for the local

antiliquor laws, which aroused so much mirth in most other western communities, the *Tribune* remarked that the citizens of Greeley had enjoyed
an emancipation as great as that of the former slaves. "No young men
growing red and bloated. We breathe freer. The day of Jubilee has come."
One Greeley citizen paraphrased, with smug satisfaction, the Union Colony's
antiliquor clause as "Thou shalt not sell liquid damnation within the lines of
our Colony." Another, in replying to criticism by a visitor, vowed that "when
saloons are opened and drunkards seen around here, then perhaps I will be
ready to admit we are a miserable failure."

During the winter months there were few arrivals, and settlers devoted
some of their remarkable energies to improving still more the tone of their
village. In December an event was the opening of the Free Reading Room,
which was well lighted and was provided with a fire. In January of 1871
the Greeley Dramatic Association put on its first play, which—naturally—
was the triumph of Timothy Shay Arthur's art, *Ten Nights in a Barroom.*
In the same month two Lyceums were going full tilt, discussing everything
from Liquid Damnation to Irrigation.

By early spring the Greeley ditch was twenty-seven miles long and all but
completed; and in April water was let into it, apparently without cannon
or oratory. It was the first organized irrigation on a large scale in Colorado.
In April, too, new members of Union Colony were "arriving each day by
the dozens," probably an exaggeration, though not much. The town grew
steadily.

It was now spring, and sap was running in the newly planted maples;
and perhaps running elsewhere, for the town now had its first scandal.
Not the Greeley paper but the Denver *Tribune* reported that she who was
described merely and curtly as "a woman" had made some sort of confession
implicating at least ten local worthies, among whom "Dame Rumor mentions
some of our married men." More important in April were preparations for
what the local paper spoke of, in capitals, as Our Grand Fence. Ten thousand
fence posts had been delivered, more than half of which had been placed
and driven; tons of wire had been purchased, and the whole rigging came to
$20,000. While water gurgled through the long ditches, Greeley's citizens
turned out to drive the remaining posts and string wire to enclose some
35,000 acres of their land. They did it, too, to the marvel and the disgust of
cattlemen in the region.

On May 1, 1871, the town of Greeley was said to have a population of
more than fifteen hundred persons, including seven hundred actual shareholders in the Union Colony. This was all well enough and doubtless worth
bragging about; but the town of Greeley was then and after of immensely
greater influence on Colorado than even its citizens were aware; and the

first season of irrigated crops proved beyond any doubt that the high plains could be made as fertile as any land in the whole West.

The settlement soon started its first industry, that of tanning buffalo hides. Like almost everything else in connection with Greeley, this proved most successful. A little later the enterprise was turning out twelve finished robes a day, and the aggregate sales "fetched from $20,000 to $30,000 monthly."

The subsequent history of Greeley's success is to be found in almost any respectable volume that treats of agriculture in the pioneer West. Suffice here to remark that the town flourished from that day to this, first on potatoes, then on sugar beets. Its irrigation and fencing work continued. Greeley, in short, started what until then had been a mining region on the way to agriculture, and its success was responsible for attracting many more people to the state than mining alone would have done. Even without the New York *Tribune,* which survives in altered form, Greeley, Colorado, would be a suitable monument for the Yankee who perhaps more than any other— either Yankee or "foreigner"—had a lasting influence on all the American West. Incidentally, the great editor's name survives in four other Greeleys, in Iowa, Kansas, Missouri, and Nebraska; in three Horaces, in Kansas, Nebraska, and North Dakota; and in Greeley's paper's name, in Tribune, Kansas.

In the 1870's, with silver strikes at Leadville, Aspen, and elsewhere, and also with the success and example of Union Colony, the population of Colorado increased almost fivefold; and in 1880 it counted 194,327 for the census.

One of the silver strikes started Yankee H. A. W. Tabor, of the many failures, on the way to becoming Colorado's first great Bonanza King. One can doubt that so-called Yankee energy and shrewdness had anything to do with it. Stonecutter Tabor from Holland, Vermont, was merely lucky. Two of the many prospectors he had grubstaked, neither of them experienced and both given to liquor, struck their picks into a mountain side of boulders and discovered the Little Pittsburgh mine, one of the greatest. For his $17 grubstake he received one-third interest, which quickly amounted to half a million dollars. Slickers promptly sold him a mine they had salted—that is, planted with rich ore—and he sent men to work it, amid ribald merriment of those who knew of the hoax. Tabor's men almost immediately found something besides the salted ore; they hit the great Chrysolite Lode, one of the region's richest. He sold out for an even million dollars.

The middle-aged Vermonter invested in even more remunerative ventures, including the immensely rich Matchless mine, which produced more millions. He was elected the first mayor of whooping Leadville. He drank heavily, gambled prodigiously, built gaudy opera houses in Leadville and Denver; and always passed out money lavishly to moochers of every degree. He was elected lieutenant governor of Colorado; and he virtually bought his way into the United States Senate, to fill an unexpired term of thirty days. He divorced Augusta, who by her hard work had supported the Tabors in earlier days, and married a pretty divorcée known as Baby Doe, in a spectacularly lavish ceremony at which a guest was Chester Alan Arthur, President of the United States and fellow Vermonter.

Tabor's fall was as sudden as his rise. He bought into every worthless enterprise that was offered him, and the panic of 1893 finished him off. When he died six years later, he was holding the postmaster's job in Denver. His widow, Baby Doe Tabor, as every reader of Sunday supplements ought to know, lived on to die in 1935, in a tumble-down shack at the minehead of the Matchless, by then merely a hole in the ground, surrounded by a miscellany of unopened gifts sent to her by unknown friends.

Silver Dollar Tabor accomplished little or nothing of lasting influence, but he did leave Colorado its favorite legend. The folklore of old Silver Dollar is almost without end, but none of it indicates that the man had any influence whatever on his adopted state.

It was different with Edward P. Tenney, born in Concord, New Hampshire, who was graduated from the Bangor Theological Seminary in 1858 and became pastor of the First Congregational Church in Central City, Colorado. In 1876 he assumed the presidency of the all but destitute Colorado College at Colorado Springs, at no salary. Here he wrote the book that fairly put the region into the cure-and-health business.

Tenney had never been robust, but he noted a quick improvement in his health after living for a time in the mountains. He poured his own enthusiasm into a booklet that immediately became famous, *Colorado: and Homes in the New West*. First published in 1878, and reprinted in 1880 and after, Tenney's eloquent volume gave hope to thousands of invalids and near-invalids in eastern states, particularly those given to "consumption" as it was generally called. These people were quick to respond, and in a little the chief business of Colorado Springs and its neighborhood was the supplying of accommodations to and care for the "lungers" who came from every state in the Union and from many foreign countries. In time, too, various organizations, including labor unions and fraternal orders, established sanitariums in Colorado. Tenney was largely responsible for starting the trend. Good Mr. Tenney was also responsible for saving Colorado College. In fact, next only to Horace Greeley's influence was that of Edward Tenney.

It is melancholy that, though almost any native Coloradan can talk endlessly on the celebrity of Silver Dollar Tabor, few seem to have heard of

the man who really did something for the state, as well as for many dis-
pirited human beings who found new health and life in Edward Tenney's
beloved mountains.*

Among the many who came to Colorado seeking health was Frederick
Walker Pitkin, a native of Manchester, Connecticut, who in 1879 was elected
governor of the three-year-old state, the first Yankee to hold that office and
reputedly one of the strongest chief officials Colorado has had the good
fortune and sense to elect. Meanwhile, the infant University of Colorado
got its first president in Joseph Addison Sewall, born in Scarboro, Maine, who
also wrote a good volume on the botany of the region.

Early and late, of course, Maine's celebrated town of Skowhegan was
sending her sons to Colorado, just as she had sent them, in turn, to every
other western state; and in Colorado, true to Skowhegan traditions, they did
not settle in a group but scattered widely.†

Women were scarce in Colorado in early days, yet in 1860 Maria and
Miranda, the twin-sister wives of, respectively, Jonathan Tourtellote and
Fred Squires, were in Boulder, running a busy boarding house in the rear
of the log-cabin store kept by their husbands, serving the meals "on two
boards brought from New England" and covering their household goods
with horse blankets, when rain came through the roof of split shakes.

Only a few communities appear to have been named for or by New Englanders. There is Brighton, laid out by D. F. Carmichael and named for the
home town of his wife in Massachusetts, now a part of Boston. Holyoke,
too, still appears on the map, telling of settlers from the old Bay State.
Gunnison is for gallant Captain John W. Gunnison, a native of Goshen,
New Hampshire, who was killed by Indians in 1853, while exploring the
region. There is also Littleton, named for Richard S. Little, a settler from
New Hampshire and possibly from the Granite State's own Littleton.

Two Maine men who found Colorado to their liking were John B. Ballard,
from Vassalboro, who became a successful contractor in Blackhawk and
held a profitable interest in the Gunnell Lode there; and William Fullerton,
who had mine interests in Blackhawk and Central City and was described
as "a prominent banker." At Blackhawk for a time was a schoolmaster,
Edward O. Wolcott, born in Longmeadow, Massachusetts, who practiced

---

* I term this fact melancholy, and so it is; but it is not astonishing, for genuine accomplishment is only too often forgotten, while notoriety, if sufficiently spectacular, is remembered and embellished. Old Tabor's notoriety was sufficiently spectacular, and it is
celebrated in books, pamphlets, and newspapers beyond knowing.

† Skowhegan emigrants seemingly never went in for colonizing plans by themselves. From
the Maine town went Coburn Ireland and Ebenezer Weston to Canon City, Colo.; Sidney
Weston to Leadville; William Lumsden and Dr. Charles W. Judkins to Aspen; Charles
B. Folsom to Durango; Thomas E. Emery to Boulder; Ezra Staples and Albert Dyer to
Denver; while William R. McClellan and Harry Neil settled in Greeley.

law in Georgetown and was sent to the United States Senate in 1889. Fullerton, who was described as "a large man of sporting tendencies," died in 1905, properly enough, at Monte Carlo, where he had gone "in search of health and diversion."

In the latter years of the exodus from New England were a future governor of Colorado, James H. Peabody, born in Topsham, Vermont; a future chief justice of the state, John Henry Royalton, born in Royalton, Vermont; and the founder of the *Daily Press* of Pueblo, John Alexander Hill of Bennington, Vermont. One of the state's great moguls of public utilities, George H. Walbridge, was also a native of Bennington.

There was at least one influential woman immigrant from New England whom Colorado claims, and rightly. She was best known as Helen Hunt Jackson, author of the fabulously successful novel *Ramona*. Born Helen Maria Fiske in Amherst, Massachusetts, she went to Colorado Springs in the seventies "because of bronchial trouble," and there she lived and wrote during the last decade of her life, though the scene of *Ramona* was California, and though she wrote her famous report *A Century of Dishonor* in New York City. This document concerned government chicanery, and worse, in dealing with the Indians; and so, indeed, did *Ramona,* though it was accepted and read as a wonderful romance by an audience which did not give a whoop about Indian affairs. Mrs. Jackson's was perhaps the most eloquent of all the many American voices raised in protest against the treachery of governmental dealings with the red men, of which Colorado itself had a local example of great clarity and unparalleled ferocity in the Sand Creek Massacre, perpetrated by Colorado militia under command of Colonel John M. Chivington—in his spare hours a frontier-type preacher of few if any ideas but of vast stentorian powers.

Of native Yankees, there is no knowing how many went to Colorado, which became the Centennial State in 1876; or how many of them died there, or how many tarried awhile, then sought new mountains or new pastures. The census of 1900 declared their number to total almost 12,000. At that time neither Rhode Island nor New Hampshire was given as a separate source. The natives of Massachusetts then numbered 4,589; Maine, 2,847; Vermont, 2,057, and Connecticut, 1,641. The Yankees were thus, at the turn of the century, scarcely a seasoning in the more than half a million population. Of them all—dead or living—two seemed secure in Colorado memories: Horace Tabor in legend; Horace Greeley's name in the fourth city of the state, on whose development, it should be repeated, he had an incalculable influence.

CHAPTER XV

THE OREGON COUNTRY

HALL JACKSON KELLEY, a strange and consecrated character out of small Northwood, New Hampshire, and Middlebury College in Vermont, was the Lord's own messenger to New England in respect to the settlement of God's own country in the Pacific Northwest. The visitation occurred in 1831 when Kelley, who had never been nearer the region than the eastern shore of Lake Champlain, felt called upon to organize in Boston, where he had been teaching school, and to incorporate under Massachusetts laws, the American Society for Encouraging the Settlement of the Oregon Country.

Until then, the few Yankees who had seen that distant region were mostly trading sea captains. The general public in New England had never heard of it, save as a doubtful river mentioned in verses by Yankee William Cullen Bryant—a poet, and therefore suspect in regard to such practical matters as geography, anyway. Bryant was lyrical enough, and said that the river Oregon rolled through continuous woods and heard no sound save its own dashings; but this could have had but little appeal to Yankees, other than a few romantics and perhaps here and there a lumberman out of timber.

As a matter of fact, Kelley's Society was a dismal failure; yet from it stemmed a remarkable succession of men and events which were to have an overwhelming effect in the founding and shaping of the state of Oregon, and no little effect in founding and shaping the state of Washington—which, in his day, was a part of the Oregon country, at best a vague enough region.

Hall Kelley was two things—a good fanatic, a poor businessman. When he started to talk and write about Oregon, he had just lost what money he had in a manufacturing venture at Palmer, Massachusetts. He somehow raised cash or credit enough to permit publication of an eighty page booklet he composed about Oregon and the printing of circulars. The circulars described his colonization company and displayed him at his fanatical best. Here was to be no little group such as the Ohio Company which went away to establish Marietta on the Ohio River. Kelley's original Oregonians were to number *five thousand,* including a "regular army" of five hundred men, two hundred of whom were to be mounted and armed with "light rifles, pistols, and sabres." As to the quality of his colonizers, he minced no words. There must be no vicious characters among them, nor drones, nor even "cunning persons possessing talents without virtuous principles." Ironically, too, he said the group would not tolerate "idle dreamers," which in all truth would surely have prevented his own presence in the colony.

Up went Kelley's posters in the crossroads stores all over New England, while his pamphlets went out from headquarters at 18 Cornhill, Boston. He petitioned Congress for aid, and while waiting for that tardy body to act, went ahead with recruiting, for which he appointed agents in Frankfort and Northport, Maine, in Gilmanton, Lee, and New Hampton, New Hampshire, and in Palmer, Massachusetts. The Oregon country was pictured in pretty fine colors, but with considerably more truth than could have been expected under the circumstances. Kelley also sought to make capital of the fact that "thousands who have settled in Ohio, Indiana & c" had been shipwrecked because they could not sell the produce of their farms. Things would be different in the Oregon country, for there the farmers in Kelley's horde of grangers would find "ready markets in the East Indies."

Although in all his writing and talk Kelley referred to "that portion of the American Republic called Oregon," the sovereignty of the region was to be doubtful for another fifteen years, or until 1846. In 1831, when he prepared to move in, such government as existed there came from the Hudson's Bay Company, the able spearhead of empire of Great Britain. Kelley's huge colony never got off the paper of its plans. His recruiting campaign, however, created an immense interest in New England and seems to have started with a large tentative membership. But Congress delayed offering any help, and meanwhile Editor William J. Snelling, of the Boston *Journal,* a satirist of unequaled bitterness, attacked Kelley's scheme with telling ridicule; and the companies of prospective emigrants from Maine, New Hampshire and Massachusetts disintegrated. The American Society for Encouraging the Settlement of the Oregon Country blew away in the mists and was never heard of again, or not heard seriously.

But Kelley had succeeded in touching off a sequence, a sort of apostolic succession, which began with young and energetic Nathaniel Jarvis Wyeth, manager and production genius for Frederic Tudor's blooming ice business, the first such in the United States or for that matter in the world.* When Kelley's emigrating scheme failed to materialize, Wyeth fitted out a ship and cargo and sent it around the Horn, headed for the Oregon, or Columbia,

* For an account of Wyeth's work, with his beginning of the ice-making industry, see the author's *Lost Men of American History* (New York, 1946).

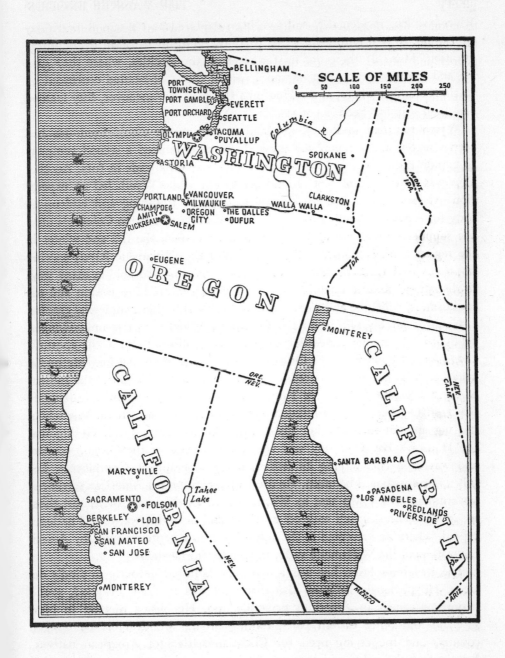

River—which, incidentally, had first been explored by Captain Robert Gray of Boston. Wyeth enrolled a small party of young men for an overland expedition. Many of these got no farther than the Rockies, where they gave up and returned home. But he and a few of the stout-hearted continued on to the Columbia where, at the Hudson's Bay post at Vancouver, they learned that their ship had been lost at sea.

Wyeth returned to Boston overland in no manner discouraged. He had seen Oregon, and Oregon was good. Now he organized a second company to exploit the Columbia River fisheries and carry on a trade in furs. Another ship was outfitted and sent around the Horn, while Wyeth led an expedition overland. This time his ship was struck by lightning and laid up so long for repairs in South America that it did not arrive at the Columbia until the summer salmon run of 1834 was done. He spent the fall and winter in the region, built a small fort at the mouth of the Willamette River, another known as Fort Hall. But the Hudson's Bay Company was able in many ways to discourage Yankee establishment, and Wyeth returned to Boston and the ice business, which he and Tudor made into a world-wide commercial empire.

Yet, for all his failure on the Columbia, Wyeth, even if unknowingly, brought in his second expedition the man who followed him in the apostolic succession of Yankees in the Oregon country. This was Jason Lee, Methodist preacher, who had been ordered to go forth and take the Light to the Indians of the Far West.* With three Yankees Lee founded on Oregon's Willamette River, in October, 1834, a mission settlement and Indian school. The school did not amount to much, but his extracurricular activities did. Noting that the Hudson's Bay Company was virtually the ruler of the Oregon country and was even encouraging its settlement by superannuated employees, Lee felt that steps should be taken. He drew up a petition for American territorial government which was sent to Washington. Nothing came of it, just then; so, in 1838, Lee himself took off overland and made his way to the national capital, where he presented to the administration a petition signed by American settlers of the Willamette valley urging territorial status.

The Reverend Jason Lee was a man who believed devoutly in God's designs. He obviously believed also that God was in favor of good, sound majorities—truly an American principle, too. He busied himself in New England and other eastern parts, talking up the wonders of the Oregon country, and the crying need for Christian settlers of American nativity. Late in 1839 he sailed with a party of fifty men and women, which he called

---

* Technically a Canadian, Lee was born in 1803 in the town of Stanstead, Quebec, which at the time was believed to be in Vermont. His father was a veteran of the Revolutionary army. His ancestors on both sides had lived in New England since 1641. It seems proper to consider him the essence of Yankee stock.

the Great Reenforcement. Meanwhile and soon other Americans, most of them sparked by Lee's eloquence, were coming across the plains to Oregon.

So, in 1841 Lee presided over a preliminary meeting of settlers, at Champoeg, seeking territorial organization. Nothing happened; but a second meeting, in 1843, resulted in a provisional government. Of the four principal officers elected, only one was not of New England birth. A. E. Wilson of Massachusetts was named "supreme judge"; G. W. LeBreton of Massachusetts, clerk of the court; and W. H. Willson of New Hampshire, treasurer. Oregon City was declared the capital; a code of laws was drawn up, and an executive governing committee appointed. Two years later a provisional governor was elected. In 1846 the United States obtained title to the Oregon country by treaty with Great Britain. Oregon Territory was established in 1848.

While the region was still of doubtful sovereignty, many Yankees arrived in the wake of Apostles Kelley, Wyeth, and Lee, to display no little ability in the business of infiltration and empire building. Quite a number of Americans, both Yankees and others, were attracted to Oregon by a book, *The Far West,* which was written by the Reverend Samuel Parker of Ashfield, Massachusetts, Congregational missionary who returned to New England after more than two years in Oregon, which he found an excellent place for God's own children.

An early one was the William H. Willson who was elected treasurer in the provisional government. He founded Salem—later to become the Oregon capital—and married Chloe Aurelia Clark, a Connecticut native who taught school at the Jason Lee mission. Others who came as missionaries and remained as permanent settlers were the Reverend John Griffin Smith of Castleton, Vermont, and the Reverend David Leslie from New Hampshire. But the so-called Great Migration of 1843 did not contain many New Englanders, though the adjutant of the wagon train was James W. Nesmith, born of Maine parents in New Brunswick, where all three had narrow escapes in the tremendous Miramichi forest fire of 1825, which took many lives. Nesmith was a good man to have in any pioneering company. He served ably as adjutant of the train, was elected a judge in the provisional government, and led local militia in the Indian wars of the fifties. He settled at Rickreall in the Willamette valley and took a prominent part in founding the state of Oregon, in 1860, which later sent him to Congress.

One of the many migrating Lovejoys of New England was in the 1843 migration, returning to Oregon where he had already spent several months in the previous year. He was Asa Lawrence Lovejoy, born in Groton, Massachusetts, and on his way from Fort Vancouver to Oregon City noted a fine piece of land for a townsite. He forthwith took a claim of six hundred and forty acres, giving a share of it to his hired man, one William Overton. Overton sold his share to Francis W. Pettygrove, from Calais, Maine, looking for a chance to turn an honest dollar in this new country; and Pettygrove and Lovejoy laid out some sixteen blocks of streets and called the place Portland, from the Maine city, thus abetting confusion which a century later is more profound and irritating than it was when committed. Still, it could have been worse, for Lovejoy, who had no more originality than Pettygrove, wanted to name the place Boston.

The future metropolis of Oregon had a few difficult years fighting for dominance, and it was another Yankee that turned the tide in its favor. He was Captain John Couch, born in Newburyport, Massachusetts, who wore gold earrings and had been trading for years along the Oregon coast. Captain Couch settled in Portland in 1845, and often remarked that any ship which could cross the Columbia bar could come upriver as far as Portland and no farther. He spoke with such authority that the town was all but assured of success. It quickly passed Oregon City and Milwaukie.

Cofounder Pettygrove presently moved out and north, to establish Port Townsend on Puget Sound. Asa Lovejoy remained to play an important part in shaping Oregon, serving as adjutant general in the wars against the redskins, for which he pledged his personal fortune to supply the troops; was elected a judge, and was speaker in the first territorial legislature. He died in Portland in 1882, which by then was far and away the largest city in all the Northwest.*

One of Portland's contenders was the settlement of Milwaukie, laid out by Joseph Kellogg, the son of immigrants from St. Albans, Vermont, who came in 1847. With his partners in the township enterprise, Captain Kellogg also built the first steamboat of any size to ply Oregon rivers, and many another craft. The type for Milwaukie's first newspaper was set by young William D. Carter of South Barre, Vermont, who acquired half-ownership, moved the paper to Portland, and later started publication of the *Oregon Farmer,* first periodical of its kind in the Northwest.

A veteran of the War of 1812, Joseph C. Geer, was in the Yankee emigration of 1847, bringing wife and ten children, one of whom, Theodore T., was to be elected a governor of Oregon. Three other immigrants from New England were to hold that office, too: La Fayette Grover, a genial though often stormy man from Bethel, Maine; Stephen Fowler Chadwick from Connecticut; and Zenas Moody from Massachusettts. He who was to be the great and revered patriarch of Oregon law arrived from Blandford, Massa-

---

* The author is happy as well as honored to live on Lovejoy Street in Portland, which is near thoroughfares named for other Yankees, including Capt. Couch and his brother-in-law Mr. Flanders, Mr. Pettygrove, and Mr. Hoyt.

chusetts, in 1851: Reuben P. Boise, a graduate of Williams College, helped to prepare the first state code of laws and sat for many years upon the supreme court bench with another immigrant from Massachusetts, Aaron Wait of Whately (who fought Indians in Oregon, edited for a time the *Oregon Spectator,* and at last became chief justice of that court), and with the grave and learned Judge Erasmus Shattuck, from Vermont.

So far as yearly migrations were concerned, that of 1850 appears to have brought several extremely competent pioneers from New England. William Starkweather of Preston, Connecticut, settled a large claim in Clackamas County, and Cyrus A. Reed from New Hampshire helped to start what was to be Portland's chief industry for a century, by erecting a steam sawmill which had a whopping-fine whistle that came near frightening out of their wits the few Indians who were clinging to the fringe of Portland.

Ephraim Cranston of Rhode Island started west in the migration of 1850 but did not arrive until two years later. The delay was largely because of the large herd of heifers which he bought in Ohio and drove ahead of him all the interminable way to Salem, in Oregon. One can believe that Cranston had the patience of Job. But he arrived with a small herd of cows that must have been able to survive with great ease in the lush Waldo hills where he took a farm and started raising stock.

One of the state's great newspapermen, who also became a notable banker, arrived in young Asahel Bush from Massachusetts. He edited and later was publisher of the *Oregon Statesman,* a success from the day of its founding to the present.

In 1850 Oregon Territory counted a population of 13,294, of whom almost 12,000 were living in the Willamette valley. The New England contingent was small, probably not more than 6 per cent, but it had been and continued to be highly effective. It also attracted and paved the way for a small and continuing Yankee migration of the apostles of business, several of whom were of quite astonishing abilities in commerce and business generally. They appear in retrospect to have actually been tireless, men who wrote and spoke the word with a capital letter thus, Industry.

When he was twenty-five years old, in 1851, William S. Ladd arrived in Portland on a ship that docked late at night. Next morning he rented a shack near the water front, moved into it a stock of merchandise he had brought, and well before noon was doing business as a merchant. He was born in that same remote and tiny and remarkable village of Holland, Vermont, that gave Silver Dollar Tabor to Colorado. Ladd went to work in his boyhood for the Boston, Concord & Montreal Railroad as station agent at Tilton, New Hampshire, where he once met Dan'l Webster and heard that eminence make a none-too-original remark which Ladd ever after liked to quote. "There is," rumbled old Dan'l, "always room at the top." So, William Ladd took off for Portland—and the top.

Although his store prospered from the start, Ladd kept his spare capital for reinvestment; to pay his first taxes he grubbed two huge fir stumps for the municipality. The doors of his little store were opened every morning at four o'clock, for in his youth he had lived on a Vermont farm where the custom was to rise and shine not long after midnight. Eight years after his arrival, Ladd was recognized as Portland's leading merchant. He had already built the first brick structure, had been elected mayor, and had married Caroline Elliott, a native of New Hampshire. Now he opened the Ladd & Tilton Bank. He became the chief promoter of the Oregon Steam Navigation Company, a river-boat monopoly as hard-boiled as it was successful; and went on to be an organizer and heavy investor in concerns dealing with the telegraph, with flouring, lumbering, cordage, furniture, iron and steel, and much else. He continued to answer much of his business and personal mail by replying on slit-open envelopes, or by turning letters received upside down and writing between the lines. In 1887 he formed a company to take over the Hotel Portland, which Henry Villard had failed to finish, and completed it. Better still, better than all else he did, Ladd devoted much time and money to the founding and support of the Library Association of Portland. (The Library received more aid, and so, too, the Portland Museum of Art, from a later arrival, William B. Ayer of Bangor, Maine, who founded the Eastern & Western Lumber Company, and also liked to read books.)

Ladd was not the only Yankee immigrant who understood the importance of the rivers to early Oregon. Simeon Gannett Reed and wife arrived in Portland in 1852. Six years later this young man from Abington, Massachusetts, and partners, who included William Ladd, were operating three fast river steamers and were making fortunes; Reed also made another fortune in railroad promotion and construction, still another by developing the famous Bunker Hill and Sullivan mines in Idaho. Faithful to his stewardship, as Vernon Parrington remarked was characteristic of the better-grade Yankee businessman, Reed gave much of his fortune to the establishment of the college that bears his name in Portland.*

A Yankee from Mercer, Maine, who designed the river boats for the

* The acting president of which, as this is written, is a Yankee in the true apostolic succession, Ernest Boyd MacNaughton, born in Cambridge, Mass., who on his first day in Portland, in 1903, attended services at the First Congregational Church and had baked pork and beans at the home of an established Yankee. Forty-five years later he was board chairman of Oregon's largest bank, president of the Oregonian Publishing Co., president of Reed College, treasurer of a hospital, and a director in more corporations than would be convenient to list here. MacNaughton has added much to the tradition of Yankee businessmen by having the courage to paint in water color and the ability to paint extremely well.

monopoly and improved them steadily, including their spark arrestors, steering apparatus, and some twenty more gadgets important enough to patent, was John Gates. He had learned the trade of machinist in Worcester, Massachusetts, where machinists were trained as carefully as lawyers were trained at Harvard. He went to California in '49, but did not tarry long for gold. A year later he was helping to build Cyrus Reed's steam sawmill in Portland. But his great contribution was designing the swift, graceful boats of the Oregon Steam Navigation Company, among them the remembered *Emma Hayward, Harvest Queen, Mountain Queen,* and one appropriately named the *John Gates.* If there is a "typical" Columbia River steamer, then it was Gates who was responsible.

To run the many boats designed by Gates were a number of men from New England, including the several Hoyts from New Hampshire and Massachusetts, among them Henry La Fayette Hoyt and Richard Hoyt, for whom a Portland street is named; and Captain Josiah Myrick, of Newcastle, Maine.

Henry Winslow Corbett, immigrant from Westboro, Massachusetts, also looked purposefully at the rivers of Oregon, and was one of the syndicate-monopoly. He also put up more good buildings in Portland than anybody else, and promoted banks and railroads. As a merchant, he was the first to close his doors on the Sabbath. Though he made donations to all religious and charitable organizations, he played no favorites; nor was he, as only too many Yankees have been, a Temperance crank. Corbett refused to run for governor, but he was elected by the legislature to fill an unexpired term in the United States Senate.*

Not all the Yankees were concentrated in Portland. Wilder W. Parker, born in Washington, Vermont, stopped off in 1852, in the much older settlement of Astoria, where, though he "used neither tobacco nor intoxicants," both favorite vices of the lumber industry, he engaged in the trade of shingles and boards, served as mayor and postmaster, promoted the city water system, and at the time of his death was hailed as the town's leading citizen.

The Willamette Valley continued to receive Yankee farmers and businessmen, a majority of whom came across the plains. Polk County, for instance, looked like promising land to the McLenches from Maine, the James Rowells from New Hampshire, and the T. W. Waits from Massachusetts. Here in Oregon there were no genuinely Yankee farming communities, such as were known in Iowa and Kansas, probably for the reason that settlers from

* Early Vermonters who helped to develop Portland and Oregon, and did themselves good in the process, included Lot Quimby, Ira Powers, Samuel W. King, Josiah Atkinson, and Samuel Swift. The Connecticut group contained Justin Millard, J. Henry Page, and Maurice Wakeman. In the Maine contingent were Bushrod Wilson of Columbia, Phineas Hanson, and John G. Porter. John Ward and Franklin O. Fuller came from Rhode Island. New Hampshire does not appear to have been attracted by the Oregon metropolis, although James E. Hazeltine and Edward P. Rogers came.

Missouri and Tennessee were in much greater number than New Englanders. Marion County was filled with the former, though the Stephen Clarks from Connecticut and the J. S. Hawkins family from New Hampshire managed to find room. J. B. Riley from Vermont opened the first hotel in the town of Dayton; and after "settling" in three other states, William G. Buffum, native of Vermont, came to rest in Amity, Oregon.

What must have been something of a champion migrating family was represented in Oregon as early as 1855 by John Quincy Adams Worth, born in Starksborough, Vermont, a small and wild hamlet in the middle of Green Mountain peaks. The Worths migrated first to York State, then to Ohio, where the father died. Of the sons and daughters, Lionel died in Illinois, Guy in Iowa, William in San Francisco, Richard while "on the way to the mines," Eliza in Ohio, Martha in Florida, Harriet in Wisconsin; while Arthur and John both died in the Willamette valley of Oregon.

A large majority of immigrants of covered wagon days settled somewhere in the "west-side" counties, between the Cascade Range and the sea. A few, however, stopped short of the mountains, and three of them were Smith French and two brothers from Orleans County, Vermont, who settled at The Dalles, at the head of navigation on the Columbia, and proceeded to do a lot for it and for themselves. The Frenches had a hand in everything—mining, banking, stock raising, transportation. Another notable Vermont family in eastern Oregon was the Dufurs, of Williamstown, whose head, Andrew, Sr., came over the plains in '59, then sent for his family. They were pioneer ranchers with both cattle and sheep. Andrew, Jr., laid out the town of Dufur.

The Dufurs had as a neighboring rancher, only some eighty miles distant, which in that region was considered neighborly, Charles Hilton from Cornville, Maine, who came to operate an eight-thousand-acre ranch and run some twelve thousand sheep. Perhaps Hilton's great success inspired another man from his native county in Maine, Edward F. Day, who came to eastern Oregon in 1879, and in Morrow County ran thousands of sheep into prosperity.

This migration of the seventies brought Joseph Wood Hill, Yale '78, to Oregon from his native Westport, Connecticut, to found Hill Military Academy, which still flourishes. This period also brought the young man who was to perform wonders with the chaotic and all but bankrupt flour-milling industry, Theodore Burney Wilcox of Agawam, Massachusetts, who took over several small mills, built others, and organized the Portland Flour Mills Company, at that time one of the largest concerns of its kind in the United States.

Large-scale logging did not begin in Oregon until the eighties, when the steam donkey engine came into use. To build these engines on the spot was Joseph F. Watson, recently arrived from Westfield, Massachusetts, who with a partner became Smith & Watson Iron Works and proceeded to fashion steam yarding and loading engines of great merit.

Yankee lawyers, naturally, were in the migrations to Oregon, as they were everywhere. What became one of the most successful law firms in Oregon was that of two brothers from Milford, Connecticut, and Yale—Harrison Gray Platt, Phi Beta Kappa, and Robert T. Platt—who were very proficient in corporation law and were just in time to aid the organization of the timber, banking, railroad, steamboat, and other interests.

For some now inexplicable reason, the great fisheries of the Columbia River lay dormant for many years, until William Hume, late of Waterville, Maine, came to look at the big stream in 1865. He was a most self-contained and reticent man; but he could and did ask questions, always to the point, and he saw much with his noncommittal eyes. He had already tried canning salmon in tin boxes on the Sacramento River in California. He and brothers John and George had set up a pioneer cannery there and had induced Andrew Hapgood, a Maine friend and tinsmith who had done some canning of lobster, to join them. In 1864 they formed Hapgood, Hume & Company, in Yolo County, California, and while Hapgood soldered the tins by hand, the Hume boys peddled the product from door to door.

But the Sacramento runs had been disappointingly small. After his reconnoitering trip to the Columbia, William Hume returned to California, told his partners what he had learned, and they shut up shop and moved to Eagle Cliff, on the Washington side of the Columbia, and established the first commercial cannery in the Northwest. In the first season they produced 4,000 cans, in the second, 18,000 cans. The Humes were most conservative; everything, even the soldering, continued to be done by hand, and they seem to have attempted no improvements. They simply hired a lot of men and got all the work possible out of their crews. Much of their first product was sold far afield, in Australia. In less than twenty years the Humes were operating twenty of the thirty-five canneries on the Columbia, and their output was enormous; the industry for two decades or more was second in importance only to that of wheat. The Humes were energetic and hard-working men. They also were typical industrialists of their era; to his death in 1902, when the salmon runs in the Columbia were greatly depleted, William Hume stoutly opposed establishment of hatcheries or any other attempt that sought to keep the runs equal to the catch.

The land sharks and boosters of real estate along the Columbia River and its tributaries made much of the "fact" that the big stream never flooded. In a pamphlet of the Oregon Land Company, issued in 1889, it was declared that "in his annual rage the dirty Missouri overflows his muddy banks,

while the Columbia moves forward serenely for his encounter with the
Pacific and gives battle behind barricades of his own creation." Five years
later, the combined floods of the Columbia and the Willamette almost
drowned Portland and Vancouver; and in 1948 occurred the flood that
centered on Vanport, a huge housing project, and resulted in much loss of
life. It also wreaked destruction for hundreds of miles along the Columbia.*

The Columbia River bisected, east and west, the region known as Oregon
Terrritory. On the Columbia at Vancouver was the Hudson's Bay post; and
Chief Factor McLoughlin and his men were careful to advise prospective
settlers that the country south of the river was the more suitable. The
British still hoped to establish the boundary line along the Columbia and
thus retain all the region that is now the state of Washington. Hence, the
Bay men told immigrants that north of the stream lay little but wilderness.
Mr. McLoughlin was a kindly and courteous man, but he was also a man of
Empire who believed in diplomacy. Despite his talk of wilderness north of
the Columbia, his men were already raising hay and hogs and cattle on
Puget Sound and were even exporting their products to Alaska and California
through a subsidiary known as the Puget Sound Agricultural Company. It
was not all wilderness, but for many years this harmless fiction of the astute
Hudson's Bay men proved effective in keeping new settlers to the south
of the Columbia, chiefly in the Willamette valley.

Beginning in 1844, however, a few skeptical and determined people who
had crossed the plains were not to be stayed. They pushed on northward,
even as far as Puget Sound, to establish farming communities and small
villages. Edmund Sylvester, from Deer Isle, Maine, was among them. He
was one of three partners who founded Tumwater, which grew into Olympia,
the state capital.

In 1850 the settlement named Seattle was coming into existence, one of
its three founders being Dr. David S. Maynard of Castleton, Vermont, a
great favorite of Chief Seattle, leader of the tribe around Elliott Bay, who
guided Maynard in his trips on Puget Sound looking for a good site. Two
years later, forty-four residents north of the big river met and voted to
petition for separation from Oregon as the Territory of Columbia. In 1853
Congress acted favorably, merely changing the name to Washington.

To be the first governor of the new territory President Pierce appointed

---

* For many years federal dam projects have been going forward in the Pacific Northwest,
and for some reason or other a large number of the engineers are natives either of Scotland
or of New England. R. J. Newell, long in charge of these flood control, irrigation, and
power dams, has a theory about this. He remarks that the Scotch and the Yankees are ex-
ceptionally good men in any field of endeavor chiefly because "they want to make good
wherever they go because of fear that otherwise they might have to return to their native
lands."

a Yankee, Isaac Ingalls Stevens, born in Andover, Massachusetts, in 1818. After brief schooling at Phillips Academy, Stevens entered West Point and was graduated in 1839 at the head of his class. He served well and bravely in the Mexican War, then entered the United States Coast survey, and in 1853 resigned from the Army to accept the post of governor of the new territory. He took up residence at Olympia, to face the nightmare of opening some hundred thousand square miles to white settlement, meanwhile directing for the federal government the survey for a northern transcontinental railroad.

Governor Stevens was a good man and able, though he probably lacked patience, especially in dealing with the Indians. In any case, his administration was marked by many troubles with the aborigines and complicated by a singular lack of aid from the United States Army. But the people of Washington trusted him, and they sent him to Congress as their delegate. On the outbreak of the Civil War, Stevens took command of a regiment of New York volunteers, and in 1862, as a major general, was killed while leading a charge at Chantilly. His character as governor is still a matter of debate among Washington historians.

Settlement of Washington Territory was no doubt delayed by the long continued wars with the tribes. In 1860 the total white population was less than 12,000. By 1880 it had risen only to 75,000. Long-settled Oregon was still getting a majority of the immigrants who came to the northern Pacific coast. But Francis Pettygrove, he who had once owned half of Portland, had moved to Puget Sound, as related, and founded Port Townsend, which for several years seemed destined to be the northern metropolis, though the Popes and Talbots from Maine, instigators of what was perhaps the longest continued organized migration in history—of which more presently —had established two lively sawmill settlements at Port Gamble and Port Ludlow. One of their early employees, Daniel B. Jackson of Maine, did not work long in the sawmill, but founded on less than a shoestring the successful Washington Steamboat Company, and later the Puget Sound & Alaska Steamship Company, a pioneer in the northern trade.

Lewis Solomon Rowe, a native of Madison, Maine, who had built Concord coaches in New Hampshire and had done some pioneering in Kansas and California, came to look over the Puget Sound situation, bought a piece of water-front land and promoted the town of Port Orchard, a handsome and successful enterprise. The great battle for business and population growth, however, was that between Tacoma and Seattle; and what all western Washington was waiting for was the railroad. In 1887 the Northern Pacific went up and over the Cascades and so down the western slope to tidewater at Tacoma. This was naturally a great advantage to that city, and men of vision were not lacking to make the most of it. David D. Clarke from South Hadley, Massachusetts, who was associated with the Northern Pacific's engineering department, had a hand in laying out the Tacoma townsite and organizing the Tacoma Land Company. On the first train into the new town were William B. Blackwell and wife from Milford, Connecticut. With them were several carloads of furniture for the settlement's first genuine hotel, which they forthwith built and operated.

Newspapermen, who doubtless possess certain instincts, flocked to Tacoma to tell the Tacoma story with a passing regard for facts and an immense regard for enthusiastic rumors, all to the end that hated and feared Seattle might be obliterated. Edward N. Fuller of Boston set up the *News,* Ralph Metcalf started publication of the *Morning Globe.* Tacoma's pioneer bookstore was opened by Charles W. Morrill from Farmington, Maine and Elisha Vaughan from New Vineyard, Maine. A leader in starting the local Y.M.C.A. was Eric Rosling, from Cambridge on the Charles. Surprisingly enough, for Yankees were not often found in police work, one of Tacoma's first patrolmen, who later became chief of the department, was Delmont O. Smith of Blue Hill, Maine.*

But Seattle managed to grow, and went into a boom with the discovery of gold in the Klondike in 1897, outstripping Tacoma and all other hopefuls in the state, and passing Portland in Oregon. Washington became a state in 1889. A year later the federal census showed the population to be 337,232.

For many years, the all-dominant industry of the West Side was lumber. Nearly every settlement on Grays Harbor, on Puget Sound, and many an inland community as well, grew up around sawmills. An exception was Everett which, though it at last did come to depend on lumber, was originally planned as a smelting city for the gold and silver ore that was to come from the neighboring Monte Cristo mines, the very name of which was indicative of splendid expectations. Rockefeller and other eastern capital was invested both in the mines and in Everett; and a Yankee born in Bennington, Vermont, Horace C. Henry, was given the contract to build the golden railroad. It was built, too, though it never hauled much ore to the hulking great smelting works erected in Everett, for the mining venture soon faded,

---

* Among Tacoma's other Yankee pioneers were a number of Massachusetts men: Stephen M. Collins from North Truro on the Cape; Thomas W. Hammond from Plymouth; Eben Pierce from Royalston; Franklin S. Poole from New Bedford; Zebulon B. Taylor from Ashfield, and James F. Mylan from Boston. Most of Tacoma's men from Maine were in the lumber business, and are treated elsewhere, but others from the Pine Tree State engaged in less typical pursuits. Among them were Charles Sumner Fogg from Stetson; Robert M. Mountfort from Brunswick; Daniel E. Gilkey from Waldoboro; and Edwin J. McNeeley from Skowhegan.

and Everett turned to lumber and shingles. But the Monte Cristo railroad job set Horace C. Henry up in fine shape; he went on from there, to build more railroads, engage in banking and real estate and for many years was called the leading businessman of Seattle.

One of the horde of Maine lumbermen who converged on Puget Sound and the Columbia River did not remain long in lumber. This was Warren W. Philbrick, born in Pittston, a master at making cutter heads of an improved kind. These are a part of planing-mill machinery, and so good was the Philbrick product that his one-man business expanded and half a century later is busy and prosperous.

The early concentration of Yankee lumbermen in both Oregon and Washington was often the final lap in a cross-continent migration that was broken for a decade, or even a generation, by pauses in one of the Lake states. The Merrills had logged in their native Maine. They logged again in Michigan, then on Puget Sound and in British Columbia. It was much the same with the Wentworths, though their terminus was on the Columbia River, like that of the Bradleys who had begun in Massachusetts. The Blackwells of Maine came from Maine directly to Snohomish County, to log with a home-made railroad. Charles H. Cobb of Lincoln, Maine, did his first work on Puget Sound as a common logger. He was soon on the way up, and left the tall Cobb Building in Seattle to mark his success. Gary B. Peavey of the famous Penobscot family which invented and manufactured the tool called the peavey migrated first to Minnesota's pine, again in the eighties to Puget Sound, where he was noted for the uncanny accuracy of his timber cruises, or estimates. If Gary Peavey said that a tract contained one hundred and sixty-two million board feet of timber, one could buy it in perfect confidence that it would cut that amount, and no more. John W. Stanchfield from Maine's Washington County had also spent much time in the Minnesota pineries before coming to Puget Sound. Here he turned contractor to build many of Seattle's business blocks.

Arriving late in the continuous Pope & Talbot migration from Machias, Maine, was Edwin G. Ames, who took the helm when the great Cyrus Walker dropped it, and soon was a force in formulating the operating policies of logging and sawmilling in Oregon and Washington.

Tacoma received a large delegation of Yankee lumbermen. These included George Browne of Boston, Charles H. Jones of East Randolph, Vermont, and Percy D. Norton of Portland, Maine, all of whom joined with Chauncy Griggs of Connecticut to organize the highly successful St. Paul & Tacoma Lumber Company. William C. Wheeler, born in Fitchburg, Massachusetts, established the Wheeler, Osgood Company, one of the largest makers of lumber on Puget Sound, in which the Ripley brothers of Rutland, Vermont,

—Thomas E. and William T.—were partners. Tacoma's North End Lumber Company was founded by George Henry Reed from Nashua, New Hampshire.

New Bangors had appeared in Michigan and Wisconsin; and now this old name, classic in the world of lumber since the eighteenth century, was applied to sawmill communities in both Oregon and Washington. A Machias, Washington, budded around a sawmill. Mark Draham from Maine didn't care a great deal what a town was named; he was content to whack away at a township named Shelton, Washington, and for forty years had a custom of sending back to the Pine Tree State, once a season, for a thumping-big box of spruce gum.

Not all the men of Maine worked in lumber. Alden J. Blethen, born in that state's Knox County, arrived in Seattle after having owned and published newspapers in Kansas and Minnesota. With him he had a quarter of a million dollars, which he used to purchase and rehabilitate a bankrupt daily and make it into the enormously profitable Seattle *Times*. Sidney Albert Perkins, born in Boston, first saw Washington Territory as a traveling salesman. He stayed, went into politics, and became private secretary to Senator Marcus Alonzo Hanna, the gentleman from Ohio. He may also have gained some if his astuteness from Senator Hanna, for when he returned to the west coast, he quickly built up a small but effective newspaper empire in Washington and got into many industries as a capitalist. In 1949, at the age of eighty-four, Yankee Perkins was still active, one of the last of his generation of migrated New Englanders.

Yankees of every degree still migrated. At the other pole from Capitalist Perkins was James Ferdinand Morton, native of Littleton, Massachusetts. A graduate of Harvard, he emerged from under the Cambridge elms as a devout Single Taxer. Later he called himself an anarchist, and went to Home Colony, Washington, where he founded *Discontent, Mother of Progress,* a periodical of violent opinions that was suppressed shortly after the assassination of President William McKinley; and Home Colony itself was threatened with the torch. Morton later wandered off, to lecture all over the United States in the interest of Esperanto, an international language; to edit freethought papers; and at last to act as curator of a museum in Paterson, New Jersey. What Morton was seeking apparently did not exist, except in the visions given to poets and dreamers of all sorts. But Morton's *Discontent* made more noise than any paper in Washington, before or since.

The first electric streetcar line in Washington was organized and built by a New Hampshire man, Frank Hines Osgood of Charlestown, who went on to build lines in Tacoma, Spokane, and Bellingham. M. Harwood Young, of Groton, Massachusetts, promoted a number of short-line railroads, including the Seattle-Tacoma interurban. Herman Chapin of Brookline, Massachusetts, organized the Boston National Bank and built many of Seattle's larger business blocks. William Henry Lord from Maine laid out the town of Tolt, where he operated a store and hotel.

Washington's governor elected in 1892 was John Harte McGraw, born on the Penobscot in Maine, who first went to work in Seattle's Occidental Hotel, built by Amos Brown of Bristol, New Hampshire, and later became one of the town's four policemen. A most unusual cop he was, for he spent most of his pay buying books which he gave to Seattle's struggling public library. He meanwhile studied for the bar and went into practice. His term as governor came at a period of great stress, with strikes and Coxey's army to contend with; but he was a strong man, equal to the task. Governor McGraw also took the trouble to improve the status of both the University of Washington and Whitman College.

McGraw was soon followed in the governor's chair by another son of Maine, tall, bold-featured John Rankin Rogers, born in Brunswick, who had established himself as a storekeeper in Puyallup. In Kansas, Rogers had aided in promoting the Farmers' Alliance and become a red-hot Populist, founding the "radical" *Kansas Commoner*. He wrote books about the money question, and even one novel; but in spite of this handicap Washington elected him governor only six years after he came to live in the state. One of his pet laws, the Barefoot Schoolboy Act, sought equal per capita distribution of state school funds, and the provision of free textbooks; and he also tried to establish state control of the railroads. Even though neither his school nor his railroad legislation was wholly successful, they did improve matters; and Rogers was reelected in 1900 and died in office.

If there was any community in Washington that stood out in the number of Yankee immigrants it attracted, it was Walla Walla, both county and town. Here Dr. Marcus Whitman, a Yankee once removed, had established his tragic mission in 1836. Eleven years later he, his wife, and twelve others at the mission were victims of a massacre by Indians. Yankee settlers started coming into the Walla Walla valley in numbers during 1858, among them E. B. Whitman and Stephen G. Whitman from Massachusetts, and the Reverend P. B. Chamberlain of Barre, Vermont, and the Bangor Theological Seminary, who with his own hands erected the first Congregational church in the region.

This Yankee settlement of the Walla Walla country was to be a continuous

one.* One of the most remarkable settlers arrived in 1869. He was Dr.
Dorsey S. Baker, "of Puritan stock, numbering among his ancestors General
Ethan Allen, of Ticonderoga fame," who practiced medicine for many years
but took time out to construct the long-since celebrated Walla Walla &
Columbia River Railroad and to found the first bank in Washington
Territory. Dr. Baker's railroad, the subject of much mythology which even
a few historians have swallowed as fact, was certainly a line as jerry-built
as could be imagined; but when it was completed from Walla Walla to
Walulla on the Columbia River his fellow Yankees, who had been raising
wheat but could not ship it anywhere, were able to do business with England.
From that day to this, the Walla Walla country has been one of the great
wheat-raising and shipping districts of the Northwest.

Another Yankee remembered in the eastern part of the state was Daniel
C. Corbin of Newport, New Hampshire who moved to Spokane and soon
hooked that city by rail with the rich mining region of the Coeur d'Alenes
in Idaho; and also with the Canadian Pacific in Canada. Corbin was also
interested in many other ventures in this Inland Empire country, most of
them highly successful. He had, said one of his biographers, "the shrewdness, sound judgment, tenacity of purpose, and integrity characterizing many
New England businessmen in the unprecedented growth of the West." His
hand came in time to show in nearly everything in the eastern portion of
Washington and in the Idaho Panhandle as well.

Considerable Boston capital went into the promotion of the town now
called Clarkston. This seems to have been the idea of Charles Francis Adams
the second when president of the Union Pacific Railway, a line he had
brought up from the depths by excellent management only to have it wrecked
by the Jay Gould wrecking crew. About 1890 Adams planned to start an
irrigated area in Washington which should be served by a line of the railroad down the Snake River. Construction of the line was begun, then
abandoned when Gould took over. But the Adams group went ahead with
the town idea, laying it out as Concord, later Vineland, bringing in water
from Asotin Creek. Settlers, including several Yankee families, came in and
the place boomed, though it did not become the metropolis of the district.

But, railroads or not, the young men of Yale Divinity School at New
Haven, Connecticut believed, as late as 1890, that the state of Washington
needed instruction in spiritual matters, as no doubt it did; and six of them

* In the sixties, seventies and eighties came, from Maine, George W. Bradbury, Daniel
Burr, James S. Barrett, John H. Foster, Charles B. Richardson, Alvin Boston, and Dr.
Ellsworth Shaw; from Vermont, William C. Townsend and Samuel A. Ash; from Massa-
chusetts, Le F. A. Shaw and Benjamin W. Marcy; and from Rhode Island, George W.
Babcock, a man who left his mark by designing and erecting the state penitentiary at
Walla Walla.

forthwith organized the Washington Band, similar to the little bands that had gone out of Yale in times past into Illinois and Iowa, and moved into eastern Washington, where five of them remained for long periods, teaching and preaching in the Yankee manner.

In 1900, the population of Washington topped half a million. Of this number a mere 12,527 were natives of New England. Here, in timber country, Maine immigrants naturally led the other Yankee states with 5,821 arrivals. In turn came Massachusetts, 3,714; Vermont, 1,962; and Connecticut, 1,030. Natives of Rhode Island and New Hampshire were too few for separate listing.

By 1900, much longer settled Oregon could show but 413,536 population. Of these people, only 5,160 were Yankees, almost a half of them from Maine.

Of all the communities in the two states, in mid-twentieth century, Portland and Walla Walla probably display more of the characteristics of New England than any other. Neither is given to wild "progress"; neither is easily excited; both have a leisurely gait which is generally considered to be due to one of two things—either a Yankee failing, or good New England common sense and decency. One may take one's choice about it.

In the long look backward, however, there can be little doubt that a comparatively small number of men from New England exercised a vast influence in acquiring Oregon from the de facto English government of the Hudson's Bay Company, and of making it into two commonwealths of the United States.

In all the migration of Yankees to Oregon and Washington, there seem to have been but three organized groups; and because in the whole history of New England migration there has been nothing else even remotely resembling them—two quaintly amusing, the other most efficient—they are set apart in the following chapter.

CHAPTER XVI

CARGOES OF MAIDENS

WHEN young Asa Mercer arrived early in 1861 at the new port of Seattle in Washington Territory, he found a region occupied largely, so far as white people were concerned, by young and unmarried males. Conditions were no better than they had been two years before, when Charles Prosch, the observant editor of the *Puget Sound Herald* in Steilacoom, had remarked plaintively there were in his little village alone some fifty bachelors, all of whom, he vowed, were "eager to put their necks in the matrimonial noose."

The ratio of men to women, regardless of marital status, was estimated at 9 to 1, and virtually all females of fourteen and over already were married. This was due chiefly to stipulations in the Land Donation Act which gave 320 acres to each man, another 320 acres to his wife. Being like all pioneers hungry for land, the males of Puget Sound were avid to marry almost any white woman who was, as the saying went, between six and sixty. More than one child as young as thirteen had been given as wife, with parental blessing, to a man of forty or more.

The few white women arriving in Washington Territory of the fifties and sixties were mostly married, wives of the loggers and sawmill workers whom the firm of Pope & Talbot was importing under contract from East Machias, Maine, to operate its camps and mills at Port Gamble, commonly called Teekalet Mills, on Puget Sound.

Thus, the lack of unmarried females was much on Editor Prosch's mind. He had brought the subject to public notice first in 1858. A year later he reverted to it, brooding in an editorial entitled "The Scarcity of White Women" that at least two-thirds of the three thousand voters in the territory wanted to get married, right then. The editor did not approve of Indian-white marriage. "Half-breeds," said he in print, "carrying in their veins the blood of men now historic are known to all pioneers." But he thought the products of mixed marriages did not add luster to either line, and perhaps he knew what he was talking about.

Editor Prosch's brooding at last resulted in a meeting. On a Tuesday evening in February of 1860, the bachelors of Steilacoom rallied in the Delin & Shorey Building to discuss their deplorable condition. They admitted that their "only chance for a realization of the benefits and early attainments of matrimonial alliances depends on the arrival in our midst of a number of the fair sex from the Atlantic states," and sought "to devise ways and means to secure this much-needed and desirable emigration to our shore."

All these noble words, however, were as the sound of the wind in the tall firs that hemmed Steilacoom on three sides. Nothing came of them. Then, almost a year after the abortive meeting, Asa S. Mercer arrived in the near-by and newer settlement of Seattle. He came from Illinois. A student of Franklin College, Wilmington, Ohio, he was good-looking, of attractive manners and, as it turned out, had no lack of confidence in his own abilities. It seems certain, too, that he possessed more imagination than any other unmarried male in Washington Territory, for he practically alone did something about the dreary condition of Puget Sound bachelors.

Judge Thomas Mercer, who was already an old and respected pioneer, got his younger brother a job helping to clear a site for the University of Washington, and Asa went on to work as a carpenter on the lone building. In the autumn of 1862 he became the first president of the university, teaching a small class, the only class, of students.

Judge Mercer, like Editor Prosch, often spoke of the lack of decent white women and proposed, only half jocosely, that territorial funds should be used to bring a party of young women "of unblemished character" to Puget Sound. The idea took fire in the mind of young Asa, who may well himself have felt the mating urge. In any case, he went to Governor William Pickering and talked the matter over. The governor was most favorable to the plan but said, doubtless with truth, there was no money in the territorial treasury.

Asa Mercer was patently a dreamer of wondrous dreams and possessed of all the faults common to dreamers. But he was also a man of action. He promptly went about Seattle in a private crusade to raise money and seems to have had little trouble getting donations from young male citizens. Then he took ship to Boston.

Near Boston was the industrial town of Lowell, a Yankee textile heaven where the morals of female mill operatives were carefully guarded and guaranteed. Mercer went there at once, to find the town in abject depression. Its population of 40,000 depended almost wholly on the cotton mills. Little cotton was to be had from the embattled South. More than a thousand female operatives were out of work. It looked to Asa Mercer, who certainly wasn't interested in the war that was raging, as if Lowell were the spot God had chosen for him.

He lost no time. He engaged Mechanics' Hall and called a meeting for the purpose of telling "girls and young women who are war orphans" about the attractions of Washington Territory. There was a good turnout. One who was present, a young girl named Flora Pearson, said that Mercer pictured in glowing terms the "wonderful financial advantage that without doubt would accrue to any and all young ladies of good character" who would leave New England with him for the delights of Puget Sound and Washington Territory. The subject of possible matrimony was carefully not mentioned, but Mercer bore down heavily on the astonishingly good pay the girls could earn teaching school.

Charming and eloquent as he was, Mercer must have lacked what high-powered sales people term "the ability to close with the prospect": only eleven young women of the large gathering "found courage to leave their friends and make a journey of seven thousand miles into a wilderness." He was somewhat disappointed in the results. Right after the meeting, he related in later years, a "large number of the audience" had come forward and expressed a desire to see Puget Sound. But all except the eleven stanch girls soon "lost courage."

With Mercer in charge, the eleven Yankee and Irish girls took ship in New York in March of 1864 and crossed the Isthmus of Panama; so on to San Francisco, where the barge *Torrent* took them to Port Gamble, to be transferred to still another ship. In this they arrived at Seattle about midnight, May 16, 1864, and even at that hour were given a royal reception.* One who was present recalled that the welcoming males, which is to say a majority of Seattle's population, looked something like grizzlies in store clothes—which may, of course, have been a piece of smug condescension. But they meant business, these single young men of Pugget Sound. Ten of the girls were soon wives. The other young woman died, unmarried.

As for Asa Mercer, he became a local hero and prophet at almost the same moment his cargo of virgins set foot on the Seattle dock. The appreciative voters of Puget Sound elected him, seemingly on the strength of his importations, without an opposing vote, to a seat in the upper house of the territorial legislature. The *Puget Sound Gazette* praised him without stint. Fellow legislators were honored to shake his hand. His name was known in Olympia, in Steilacoom, Nisqually, Port Gamble, Port Townsend. He basked in celebrity, which can be just as dazzling in a backwoods settlement as in a metropolis.

As young Asa Mercer basked in this happy and disturbing new light, which had made an obscurity into a personage overnight, he dreamed up

* In the Pacific Northwest almost everybody seems to know everything about the "Mercer Girls" except their names. For the sake of the record, here is a list of the first cargo: Georgie and Josephine Pearson, Annie May Adams, Maria Murphy, Kate Stickney, Sarah J. Gallagher, Kate Stevens, Lizzie Ordway, and the Misses Cheney, Coffman, and Baker.

a bigger and better importation of females, a stupendous cargo of five hundred, perhaps seven hundred, war orphans, "daughters of those brave, heroic sons of liberty," of whom Mercer was patently not one. It could be made an event of the first magnitude, one of national significance. Much good would be accomplished for all concerned—female war orphans and widows would be removed from their woeful condition in New England and become happy housewives on Puget Sound. Puget Sound would gain even more. Its bachelors would no longer spend their mights in Madame Damnable's place on the water front, but would go to work at the production of children and the support of families. The infusion of the blood of old New England stock, into the cosmopolitan and perhaps doubtful stream common to frontier settlements would make for solidity of character. The well known New England Conscience would temper and refine the careless ways of adventurous men. Aye, and Asa Mercer would be a bigger man than before.

Being a celebrity is all very well, but it pays no bills. In March of 1865, just before he left again for the East to carry out his tremendous plan, Mercer drew up a contract which was not publicized but was circulated among those who might be interested. There were a number of such. The contract read as follows:

I, Asa Mercer, of Seattle, Washington Territory, hereby agree to bring a suitable wife, of good moral character and reputation from the East to Seattle on or before September 1865, for each of the parties whose signatures are hereunto attached, they first paying me or my agent the sum of three hundred dollars, with which to pay the passage of said ladies from the East and to compensate me for my trouble.

If poor Asa could have known the troubles he was to undergo on this expedition, then three times three hundred dollars per maiden would not have begun to compensate him. But he didn't know; and, being an optimist of the highest power, he wouldn't have believed the difficulties ahead, even if an authentic Sibyl had warned him. How many of the single men of Puget Sound signed the $300 contract is not known.*

Asa Mercer, bubbling over with enthusiasm for his great project, arrived in New York City just in time to buy a newspaper announcing the assassination of President Lincoln. This tragedy was not only bad for the United States, but bad for Mercer as well; for, having sat on Lincoln's knee as a boy in Illinois, he had counted on the President to help him. Lincoln, he was sure, would be glad to give him a government ship for transporting "war orphans and widows" to Puget Sound.

This was the first blow. More were to come, with discouraging regularity.

---

* Clarence Bagley, Seattle historian, who in 1901 got Mercer to talk—a little—for publication, had seen the contract and copied it, but deleted all names and did not say how many there were.

But Mercer was resilient in the face of his first tragedy. He bounded up to Boston, where he had no trouble getting an audience with Governor John A. Andrew. His Excellency professed to be much taken with Mercer's idea, and he knew the man, the very man, to help. This turned out to be Edward Everett Hale. What help, if any, the author of "The Man Without a Country" gave Mercer, I can't learn. I imagine Hale quickly introduced the young man to somebody else, for no matter how worthy the scheme, the very idea of moving several hundred unattached girls to a wild and little known part of the West unquestionably struck conservative people as of doubtful propriety. And, too, there was the danger of public ridicule. Prominent men must be careful.

But Mercer was doing very well with the recruiting part of his project. He ranged from Maryland into New Hampshire, talking up his idea. On July 23 he wrote to the *Puget Sound Gazette* from Lowell, Massachusetts— apparently his stronghold—that he would sail from New York City "with upwards of 300 war orphans" and asked that Seattle be ready to give them a fine welcome. The *Gazette* and all Puget Sound were delighted. The paper ran the communication and sent marked copies to brother editors in all parts of the territory.

But still Mercer had no ship. He went to Washington, and after weeks of a sort of chain-introduction, being shunted from one catchpoll to another, he at last got the ear of General U. S. Grant. Now Grant had soldiered in the Oregon country before the war, and understood thoroughly what Mercer meant when he said the great need on Puget Sound was for single women of good character. As soon as he had heard the young man's story, the first hero in the United States went into action. "Mercer," said he, "sit down and read the morning paper until my return. I am going over to the White House to meet the President and his cabinet and will bring your matter to a head one way or the other."

Mercer was understandingly pleased, even elated. After weeks of the Washington treatment, he had at last found the man who would act.

Half an hour later Grant returned, and as he entered the room he spoke briskly to his aide: "Captain Crosby, make out an order for a steamship, coaled and manned, with capacity to carry five hundred women from New York to Seattle, for A. S. Mercer. I will sign it." Sign it he did, and sent the delirious young man of Puget Sound on his way to Montgomery Cunningham Meigs, quartermaster general of the Army, who like Grant was a man of quick decision. "No," said Meigs as soon as he had read Grant's note. "I will not accept this order." He remarked that the order was illegal, as probably it was.

But though Meigs was extremely watchful of government property he was not adverse to selling surplus goods. He told Mercer he would sell him a fine ship of 1,600 tons for $80,000, in cash; it would be a bargain, too, for the steamship *Continental* had cost $240,000 to build just two years before, and was in excellent shape. The price might as well have been one million dollars. Mercer possessed the price of little more than a lifeboat. He told General Meigs he would think it over. Then he went to New York to think.

Now an amazing thing happened. While Mercer was glooming in his room in the Merchants' Hotel a card was brought from a caller in the lobby. The visitor was Ben Holladay, a man of many parts who had made considerable money supplying food to troops in the Mexican War and more recently had been doing very well with freighting and government mail contracts in the West. He had also organized a ship line. He was looking for more ships—cheap. Mercer was astonished that a big man of affairs, nationally known, should look him up. He had the magnate shown to his room.

In later years Mercer came to realize what a lamb he must have seemed to Ben Holladay, one of the shrewdest and most ruthless operators in the United States. But Holladay could be genial, and now he told Mercer he would advance the money to purchase the *Continental*—for Holladay, of course—and said he would be happy to carry the war orphans to Seattle "at a nominal sum."

While this wasn't exactly the way Mercer had envisioned the outcome of the expedition, still it seemed the only way. He met later with Holladay and that sharp trader's attorneys, who drew up a contract. This instrument said Holladay should have the ship at the price offered to Mercer, and that the ship would transport "500 passengers at a minimum price" to the Pacific coast. Whether or not Mercer read the contract, I do not know. If he did, it did not mean anything to him. He signed it, proud to collaborate with the great Holladay. The first part of the deal went through.

Now that the ship was ready—as Mercer thought—he sent out his call for the war orphans to assemble in New York, ready for the voyage to the promised land. Just then, according to Mercer, the New York *Herald* got wind of the project and promptly came out with a story strongly intimating that the five hundred female orphans were being shipped to Seattle for the express purpose of becoming inmates of Puget Sound brothels—a fate, allegedly, worse than death. The *Herald,* said Mercer, also termed Puget Sound males a pack of lecherous louts.

The Massachusetts legislature had also been discussing the migration of women from Lowell, and an official committee had made its report, saying, among other things:

In the polygamous realm of Brigham Young, it seems that the numbers of male and female were nearly equal, and this, too, when the chief magnates of the so-called latter day saints have harems which are but little inferior to that of a Mahometan Shah of Persia. . . . There are, or were, Massachusetts women in those same households of abomination; and it is painful to believe that the class from which they went would be the first to offer candidates for emigration to Oregon [*sic*] and other parts of the remote West.

The implications of that report are obvious and may well have reached the ears of the maidens. But Mercer always claimed it was the New York *Herald's* remarks which had the most effect. In any case, the results were immediate and lamentable. "More than two thirds of the ladies wrote me," Mercer recalled wistfully in later years, "and inclosed clippings of the *Herald* story." They also inclosed their resignations from this proposed voyage into a land of venery. The *Continental's* passenger list dwindled.

One can appreciate the feelings of Asa Mercer, the great dreamer from Puget Sound, to see his public-spirited project turned into a monstrous scheme of commercialized lechery. It was a blow to fell the stoutest. Consider these innocent and alluring maidens—one could almost see them arriving at Seattle. One could see also those profligate characters with which all Puget Sound was infested, slavering, pawing dirt, avid to lay their obscene hands on these tender flowers from the land of the arbutus. Was Christian New England to supply women whose lips dropped as an honeycomb, and whose mouths were smoother than oil? . . . Was Yankeeland to be the source of the kiss that had poison and was as a pernicious drug?

To make matters worse, indescribably worse, the report of the Massachusetts legislative committee spelled Mercer's name "Mercier," thus making him a Frenchman and hence almost automatically a procurer of the most subtle and dangerous sort. It was easy to see, even at a distance of three thousand miles, the wicked gleam and glow of red lights along the Seattle waterfront. . . .

It was, surely, a blow to fell the stoutest. And now Mercer, the great procurer, suddenly thought of his contract with Ben Holladay. With an armful of the letters and clippings received from the girls who did not wish to engage in the profession of trollop, thus indicating why he could not now carry out the 500-passenger stipulation of the contract, the naïve young man went to the prince of commerce for understanding and sympathy. Holladay had his faults, but they did not include the shedding of crocodile tears. He displayed a modicum of sympathy, accompanied by a brisk, business-like notice that, though it was too bad about the cancellations, a contract was a contract: Mr. Mercer certainly would understand that he would have to charge "regular rates" for the lesser number of passengers. Dizzy from one blow after another, and virtually penniless, Mr. Mercer went away with a new understanding of the manner in which business was carried on in his native country by experts.

The faithful were already gathering at a New York dock, ready for the voyage to Puget Sound—and possible perdition—and they numbered something less than one hundred female war orphans and widows. The total passenger list, including several married couples and a reporter from the New York *Times,* totaled two hundred. Mercer thought that others might be on the way, but Mr. Holladay could wait no longer; they must be off.

The passengers found the ex-troopship in anything but shipshape order. Little had been done to improve it since it had carried its last contingent of soldiers—men who are not ordinarily careful of United States property. Nor had Mercer done anything about assignment of quarters. Nobody knew where he or she was to sleep. Angry men and weeping girls sought everywhere aboard to find the man responsible, but he could not be located. Thus, on January 6, 1866, the steamship *Continental* pulled out of New York harbor in a state of wild chaos, with Mercer safely hidden in an obscure coal bunker. He emerged, somewhat later, to find himself not the most popular person on deck.

Flora Pearson, whose two older sisters had gone to Seattle in the first Mercer expedition, was on the second, and kept her eyes open. She reported the vessel was in such terrible shape that tidy New England girls went to work scrubbing the decks and walls. The food was a disgrace—so bad, indeed, that Mr. Mercer himself started taking his meals at the captain's table, where the provender was of the finest. Not for long, though. The sharp tongues of Yankee maidens quickly brought him to book and to share with them the Spartan fare Ben Holladay thought good enough for New England war orphans. And for the next ninety-odd days Mercer relished the salt beef and tea steeped in salt water which appears to have been the basic ration; that is, except for one period of two weeks when parboiled—not baked— beans were the main course.

There was one good meal during the entire trip, and that was when one of the Yankee girls somehow prevailed on the ship's cook to permit her in the galley, where she made and baked a rousing-fine batch of gingerbread. Then, back to the salt beef. But the sparse diet probably was the reason that no case of seasickness was reported.

An artist for *Harper's Weekly* depicted life aboard the *Continental* as ideal. He drew handsome sketches showing hundreds of young and beautiful girls in the "grand salon" of the old trooper—playing the organ, singing, writing letters, or improving their minds with literature. The heading above the pictures said, "Emigration to Washington Territory of Four Hundred

Women on the Steamer *Continental.*" The brief text termed Mr. Mercer "The Moses of the Exodus from New England" and said he had induced "about 750 to enter the expedition, but that many had returned to their homes"—probably with a clipping from the New York *Herald* in hand, their virginity still intact.

Ninety-six days brought the ship to San Francisco, where the newspapers had a wonderful time with the party, which by then was reputed to number seven hundred beauties. All hands had to go ashore, for Ben Holladay had other plans for his new vessel. A number of the girls never took ship again but disappeared into the life of California. "What inducements some of them found to remain in California," remarked the tart Flora Pearson, "I do not pretend to say." I can imagine Flora sniffed. But perhaps the deserters suspected that Mercer had got to the end of his rope, that he would be unable to take the party to Puget Sound. If so, they were not without reason. Mercer was all but penniless. He couldn't have bought himself passage to Seattle, to say nothing of his brood of maidens. But there was his friend, good Governor Pickering of Washington Territory. Just before Mercer had left Seattle, Pickering came to him and said, in the grand free-handed manner suitable to pioneers, to count on him, Pickering, should Mercer need financial aid.

Mercer did need aid, and so with the last two dollars to his name he went to the telegraph office in San Francisco and dispatched a wire to Pickering. It was simple, and clear: "Send two thousand dollars quick to get party to Seattle." Then he sat back to wait for good old Governor Pickering, a friend to count on in any emergency. Next day the telegraph company notified him they had a message for him. He could have it by paying the $7.50 charge. Puzzled and worried, Mercer went to the telegraph office manager to explain he was without a cent. But the message, said he brightly, contained two thousand dollars; and if the company would let him have it, he would of course pay the collect charge.

The manager, I can imagine, wearily eyed Mercer, then let him have the telegram. It was from good old Governor Pickering of Washington Territory —one hundred windy, gorgeous words of congratulations on the "success" of the expedition, and not one word about money.

Well, there he was—still a thousand miles from snug harbor, with no money, no ship, no credit, a pack of irritated females waiting for the next move, and not with patience. But many a lumber schooner plied between California and Puget Sound. Somehow Mercer had enough spirit left to talk several schooner captains into taking portions of his feminine cargo to Seattle, and there they finally arrived, not in one exuberant and overpowering party, but in batches of half a dozen or more. It was a pale ending to such a dream as Mercer's had been; nor was the popularity of the business enhanced by the fact that the Puget Sounders, then as now hospitable people, had taken Mercer at his word and had prepared a truly gigantic welcome for the seven hundred maidens, or the four hundred, or the three hundred, whichever they turned out to be. Instead, the welcome had to be cut down to size, to fit less than a hundred persons who, moreover, arrived at odd times and in small parties over a period of days.

But the Mercer girls began to fulfill their destiny as soon as they landed. On May 27, Sarah Robison married David H. Webster. On July 15, Mercer himself took as wife one of his charges, the charming Miss Annie Stephens. Other marriages followed in quick succession.*

Asa Mercer did not remain in Seattle, or even Washington Territory, but removed to the Middle West, where he lived and died. Estimates of his character have varied. Mr. Bagley, the Seattle historian, believed that his great trouble was his proneness to take whatever he urgently hoped for as certain of accomplishment, which, in view of the record, seems fair appraisal. He was also careless. Large sums of money had been put into his hands when he went east the second time. These sums were given to him by relatives and friends for various and specific purposes and had nothing to do with getting a bride or with the emigration scheme in any way. Mercer diverted most or all of this money into his great dream, and could never pay it back. Bagley remarked that he "broke up several of his best friends and financially crippled others." He was also "made the subject of ugly charges by many of those whom he had injured. But that he used these monies for his personal benefit no one claimed."

After commenting on Mercer's contract with the unnamed Puget Sound bachelors, Bagley remarks that, though he "did not lose sight of the financial profit that might be obtained" from his scheme, "his every action, his whole attitude toward those who had entrusted themselves to his guidance and care was that of a chivalrous, pure-minded American gentleman."

Bagley also thought that Mercer had done both the Yankee maidens and Washington Territory a good turn. The immigrants themselves received "far-reaching and beneficial effects," and they "proved a blessing to every community from the Cowlitz River northward to the Canadian line."

The Mercer Girls, as they are always referred to, have long since gone into the folklore of the Pacific Northwest where, because of their unorthodox

---

* I have been unable to find a complete passenger list of the second Mercer migration. Family names of the maidens, however, included Grinnold (two different spellings), Wakeman, Chase, Stephens, Stewart, Davidson, Lord, Bacon, Manning, Peebles, Guthrie, Barlow, Robison, Rhodes, Atkinson, Lawrence, Connor, and Miss Pearson, who soon became Mrs. Engle. A majority of the girls were from Lowell and Boston, Mass., and from Portland, Maine. A few hailed from New York, New Jersey, and Maryland.

manner of immigrating, they occupy a peculiar position. There is as yet no organized group called the Sons and Daughters of Mercer Girls. As one after another of the original Girls died, Seattle and other papers printed obituaries which mentioned the fact of their being Mercer Girls. It seemed to be some sort of distinction, as assuredly it was.* In time, naturally enough, a play was locally written and produced as *Petticoat Cargo*. It showed the Mercer Girls as they had allegedly lived in New England, in what appeared to represent superb mansions, the darlings being waited upon by maids and other servants. The playwright either had never seen the rambling old boarding houses of Lowell, or decided to ignore them.

Although the Mercer immigrations got all the publicity, the constant immigration from eastern Maine to Port Ludlow and Port Gamble, over a period of seventy years, had a greater influence on Puget Sound. The contract between the lumber firm of Pope & Talbot and the men—and sometimes women—of East Machias, Maine, has been mentioned. The contract was first offered in 1856, after a spearheading cruise of Popes, Talbots, and Kellers from Maine had noted the "great pines" that grew right down to tidewater on Puget Sound. They returned to Maine, erected a complete sawmill on the dock at East Machias, carefully putting it all together, to make certain the parts fitted, then took it to pieces and stowed it away in a ship. They sailed again and planted the mill at Port Gamble. For the next seven decades the Port Gamble mill and another at Port Ludlow were manned by crews composed of local Indians and of Yankees imported from eastern Maine.†

Even before the outbreak of the Civil War the Huntleys of East Machias had gone to Puget Sound, and so had Wilsons, Hoveys, Burralls, Pierces, Fosters, Blackmans, Harmons, and members of the Gaddis, Keller, and Weston families, all from the same village in Maine. They were followed by hundreds more, needed to fill the ranks at Ludlow and Gamble depleted by death and by the moving to other communities of restless Yankees, looking still for the other side of the mountain. Their descendants today are to be found in almost every community on Puget Sound, and in many another sawmill town in Washington and Oregon.

The contract-bound employees of Pope & Talbot worked out their fares,

* An old friend of mine, a native of Sweden who had lived for many years in Seattle and read the papers, once asked me if this here Mercer family "vas Mormons." I explained the matter, and he seemed much relieved.
† Port Ludlow's big mill and most of the village has now disappeared, along with the Yankee-type mansion built there by Cyrus Walker, late of Skowhegan, Me., who liked rock maples and a white picket fence around his house, and baked beans of a Saturday night. Port Gamble carries on, with first and second generations born there of New England forebears.

which ran from $125 upward, by wage deductions of so much per month. In 1944, being then in East Machias, I had the pleasure of talking with George Hoyt, then aged ninety, who had gone to Port Gamble on contract right after the Civil War and worked there for many years before returning to his old home. "Port Gamble was a fine place," he said. "It was filled with State-of-Mainers, not just common Yankees. Always cousins, uncles, sons working there, and often, too, married sisters and aunts. It seemed that everybody there came from East Machias, or his father did. I suppose Pope & Talbot was old-fashioned. They were reckoned to be so, on the west coast. But that was the way we liked it. We always had baked beans and johnny bread at Gamble, and plenty of codfish. One of my sisters married one of the Thompsons at Gamble. Thompsons have filed saws there for three generations."

I talked with many other older people in East Machias. Without exception they were sad that Pope & Talbot had constantly taken their young folk for seventy years past; but they did not resent it. If it hadn't been Pope & Talbot, I was told, then it would have been somebody or something else. . . .

The past hangs heavy over East Machias village. Along both banks above the river are rows of stately houses, mostly in straight colonial style, but here and there a mansion with mansard roof, denoting a much later period. Many of these homes once belonged to families named Albee (of vaudeville fame), Sanborn, Whittier, Wiswell, Keller, and of course Pope and Talbot. Two church spires rise from among the elms and maples. A general store, the post office, Masonic hall (the charter was signed by P. Revere, grand-master), and power house cluster at the upper bridge across the river, now a piddling stream of water. A score of sawmills once lined this stretch of river, and they sawed and sawed until the pine and spruce was gone. Even before the mills had ceased, the Popes and Talbots had discovered the big fir on Puget Sound, which they called Oregon Pine, and had moved there. Their lodestones of Gamble and Ludlow proved strong and enduring. I can think of no two towns so closely allied by blood and tradition today as East Machias in Maine, and Port Gamble, Washington—three thousand miles apart as crows might fly it, but sixteen thousand miles as the winged ships came.

CHAPTER XVII

INTERLUDE: THE SHADOWS FORM

THE SHADOWS grew longer. It was afternoon, late afternoon, in New England, and the old men who sat endlessly in the crossroads stores wondered aloud to each other: Was there some truth in the theory that man in his migrations always moved with the sun, westward? It might be true and it might not; but, still and all, this country of the Green Mountains was settled by people who moved *north,* from Connecticut. Who was it that settled New Hampshire if not Old Colony and Massachusetts Bay people? And they certainly moved north to do it. If a man wanted to make anything of it, then how was the great province of Maine populated if not by men who came into it from the west and the south?

True, but the land had not been able to bear them all, all the Yankees, that they might dwell together, even as the Book had told it; and the people of Abram and the people of Lot, had they not gone away, the one into Canaan, the other to the cities of the plain of Jordan? Yet, the Book or no, the tribes of the Yankees were committing self-destruction by leaving their homes for the West, whilst multitudes of foreigners were coming in on every ship, bringing Babel with them, bringing not only a confusion of tongues, but of religions, of customs. . . .

The shadows grew longer, and the old men at the crossroads talked on without end, talked for months and for years, calculating time, warning of the dusk, crying night. They could tell that the old order was passing; in fact, in these backwashes of New England the passing of that order was seen more plainly than elsewhere, for here there was less to distract reflection. You could see that the old cocked-hat men were now pitifully few, the survivors who wore small-clothes and hose and shoes with big buckles—the men who still took snuff, who preferred that their women use the fireplace instead of the new and loathsome cooking stoves, and cursed the new steel pens in paragraphs of protest written with quills and sent to the editor of the *Vermont Watchman* or the *New Hampshire Patriot*. These were the men

254]

who in spite of Portland Star matches still lighted their fires, and often their very pipes, with flint and steel, who were, regrettably, Deists or worse; or, if they held to a personal God, held to that of the Old Testament exactly as he was revealed in Genesis. These old men could not be made to realize, though more than one Universalist attempted to explain, that even God changed His style every few millenniums. . . .

They talked on, these immensely ancient men, and they were listened to, for they had *seen* with their own eyes Colonel Ethan Allen in his latter days on Onion River, or had shaken the hand of General Stark, or might even have been with Old Put in Mr. Bunker's pasture at Charlestown. God save us, you *listened* to such men, for they came from a world as far removed from the present, for all practical purposes, as the time of Mordecai, and they were believed somehow to have a wisdom that had not been given to the other sons of men. In the name of the great Jehovah and the Continental Congress they had performed prodigies. They had told the King's men in their day, if a war was wanted, then let it begin here and now. They had known too that, if they did not beat the Redcoats, then Molly Stark would sleep a widow. . . .

Aye, you listened to men such as these, sitting with their canes in the crossroads stores, while a bluebottle fly beat again and again on a dusty window, and outside a horse stamped at the hitching post. They spoke in an aroma of coffee that emanated from the new grinder, as red and gaudy as any fire engine, to mix with the smells of spice and tea and kerosene and tobacco. Some of these ancient men had mellowed since Yorktown; others had merely dried and toughened, and these latter spat at the cold box stove and said they would be goddamned and double goddamned if they would so much as raise a finger to prevent all the younger generations of Yankees—man and maid together—from trooping out to this Ohio or Ioway or Californy. Let them go. They were a poor lot, anyway, who had long since deserted the ways of their fathers. Let them go.

The pious old men saw the hand of God in the business. The Lord their God was a jealous God—and had not the younger generations of Yankees gone a-whoring after false gods? The authority of the Congregational clergy had broken down. Many a descendant of the Pilgrim Fathers was now preaching some form of the Arminian Heresy; or was shouting for the Baptists or the Methodists; or, worse, was speaking up for the Universalists and the Unitarians who really were not Christians at all. Or, worse still, had gone away to Illinois—and hell—with the imps of Moroni. All was confusion; and if you needed to know what came in confusion's wake, then consider the fact that the Harlot of Rome was already among us. There were half a dozen Papist churches in Massachusetts. Little wonder desolation stalked New England. Why, the fine old stagecoach towns were moldering even now, while the new steamcars did nothing but set fire to barns and fields with their hellish sparks, and mangle and kill man and beast. Oh, it was piteous, it was scandalous, but it was also just and according to Holy Writ. Yankees had defied the Decalogue, and now they should pay, without end.

Every stray wolf seen or killed, or merely rumored, was evidence— wasn't it?—that the packs were returning from the far north, where they had been driven in your grandfather's day. Every abandoned hill farm in the six states showed patently that the wilderness was returning, and Chaos and Old Night were riding the wilderness. Indeed, cried the ancient men, any-body could see that the shadows had formed, and that they grew longer and darker, even as one watched. It was not noon any more, nor afternoon, in the Yankee kingdom. It was night. It might well be close to midnight, and, if the clock ever struck again, it would strike thirteen. Time—you'd best believe, sir—was running out. . . .

Dust blew in an open window. Outside, an unheard wind fluttered the leaves on the great old elms; and on the wind came the godless chatter of a mowing machine, a device direct from the Pit, which a few thoughtless men—praise be, there were few such thoughtless men in New England— called an "improvement" over the hand scythe. But even this machine could not cut the wiry worthless grass in these fields. The tough stalks bent but refused to be cut down. Perhaps the Yankees who remained on their native farms amidst all this confusion of tongues and emigration and hard times— perhaps they were like the grass. They bent but did not break. Come to think of it, how many native Yankees were still where they ought to be, at home?

Nobody could guess, because things were in such flux. But one had a pretty good idea how many had gone away. One of the ancient men said that he see in the Hartford *Courant,* awhile back, that sixty-seven thousand natives of Connecticut had gone to live in York State, another ten thousand to Pennsylvania, three thousand to New Jersey, and—if you could believe it— still another twenty-three thousand deluded Nutmeggers had gone to Ohio. Nor was this quite all. Another twenty thousand—the old man said—were scattered around in other parts of what he stoutly, using an obsolete term, designated as Northwest Territory. He was right, too. These old men did not read much, but they remembered what they read with an exactness that was fantastic and even mysterious to younger people who read a great deal and remembered almost nothing of what they read. He was right about Con-necticut's emigrants, right also about those from Massachusetts, which he said were almost as numerous. But, he went on—his high dry old voice charged with emotion—but these figures paled to nothing compared to what had been going on in the Green Mountains. That is, in proportion. Almost a half of the living natives of Vermont—he was citing the census of 1850—

were living elsewhere than at home: fifty-three thousand in York State, fifteen thousand in Ohio, twelve thousand each in Illinois and Michigan, almost as many in Wisconsin. God alone, he went on, and certainly not the immigration authorities of Canada, knew how many Vermont people and New Hampshire people had moved into the provinces of Quebec and Ontario.

(A decade later, in 1860, more than half a million New Englanders had gone away—and *new* old men talked on.)

One read in the papers how curious professors were digging into strange mounds at the West, in Ohio, digging into lava beds in Italy, plumbing the earth in other foreign parts, all for the sake of learning something of ancient peoples whom Time had buried deep and then forgotten. Better far they came to New England and paused at this cellar hole on what had been a hill farm—this excavation fringed with brush in which ancient apples trees were being choked to death and lilacs struggled feebly to put forth a few wan blossoms. Here, my good professors of archaeology, was a relic, a fossil, a memoir of an extinct people. Dig into it. You'll find a spoon or two of pewter, perhaps a latch of hand-wrought iron and a bullet mold, a candle mold, a bee-runner's trap. Those spikes came from a hatchel, used in preparing flax. That great slab of pure granite was the doorstep; to move it a hair, would call for a yoke of the oxen of Job and a goad like unto Shamgar's. That rotting hulk of cedar, moss-grown and a lodging house for hordes of pismires, was once a noble trough, fashioned by untold hours of hand work and charring, to hold water that was carried for half a mile in logs that had been bored end to end and most painfully slow with a monstrous auger.

Work? They knew little else, the people who built and built well on these hills. They built believing that they and generations of their children would live here. Though they worked in an age of iron and wood, they continued to work much in stone, too. Follow through the jealous and protesting brush that now guards the mile or more of stone fence, the units of which were piled one upon another, just so, by men and boys who grew in time to have something of a neolithic look about them, and a neolithic quality of character, too. Even their women came to have the same look and quality.

You wonder what power could have driven these determined and patient people from their hard-won hills. Well, there were any number of things that conspired to drive them; but mostly when they left, it was to the tune of bells, the pretty, mellow, tinkling bells of a hundred and more thousands of sheep, more sheep, indeed, than the Midianities of old had known— Merino sheep. That was their knell, no matter what they thought or believed or said. To raise sheep in vast numbers required a lot of land, and the hill farms were the first to supply the extra pasturage. No man could actually farm where sheep ran in number. So, the hill farmers sold out to the Merino men. They then piled a few things into a wagon and struck out for the eastern end of the Erie Canal, leaving their lands to the Merinos, their houses to wood-borers and wasps, their barns to the bats and the owls. . . .

The Merinos, in turn, disappeared into mutton when wool fell to forty cents a pound, and when most of the wool for the Boston market was coming from Ohio, anyway. When the Merinos had gone, then the birch and the balsam took over their pastures; and raspberries and sumac and hazel combined to guard the graves of the house and barn and to throttle the apples and the lilacs, which were the result of culture. When a hill wilderness took over a place, it consumed it entire, covering everything man had made or planted, putting forth every effort to blot out completely the shame of man's industry and cultivation.

Desolation, the old men noted, was creeping down the hills, invading the villages and the hamlets. The little bethels of these communities were the first to feel the chill, the chill of the Merino bells that came through the open windows in summer, an undertone or background music, an accompaniment to warmed-over sermons delivered by bemused pastors—good men, too, who had been trained at Middlebury, or perhaps at Bangor, but worried now as they preached to the ghostly pews, wherein sat a meager few old men and women. And who could blame them too much if while they preached they wondered and held secret hope of quick response to the letters they had written to former parishioners now living at the West—asking to know how went the work of the Lord in such far places, asking boldly if help were not needed in the vineyards of Cleveland and Beloit, of Stillwater and Grinnell, of Rockford and Lawrence.

The desolation that began on the hills spread almost everywhere in the rural districts. The local industries which for generations had been supplying almost all local needs—the tanneries, the sawmills, the gristmills, and such—felt it; their vats molded and their water wheels ground to a halt, while the untended dams gave way or filled with silt, and alder and willow grew high in the millrace—all to the music of the Merino bells. The once bright clapboards on the old stage taverns weathered to mellow patina, then started molting like Plymouth Rocks in autumn, while deep green moss climbed the shingled roofs from eaves to ridgepole, where a bent and mangled weathervane pointed, no matter the quarter of the wind, straight down to hell.

The crossroads stores hung on awhile longer, though they faded perceptibly by the year, and around their stoves, summer and winter, the old men talked on; and on the shelves mice nested and brought forth their young, and the spots of flies grew so thick they were no longer distinguishable from the paint, which had been last applied in the year John Quincy Adams died, which was 1848, and may God give peace to the great man's noble if puckered soul.

Time here at the crossroads did not stand still, nor did it move forward. It actually moved backward. On a wall in the store, over the molasses barrel, was still a sign, faded out perfectly legible, which announced the goings and comings of the splendid coaches of the Eastern Stage Company, whose wheels had long since ceased to roll. Time here moved backward; in the town hall was a poster, once a handsome thing in four colors, bidding Welcome to New England to the great and popular but aged General Lafayette. The First Selectman of the town had tacked it on that wall in the summer of 1824. . . . The Town Clerk still compared each new season as it came and went to the Year of No Summer, which he remembered well, and which had been in the year of our Lord One Thousand Eight Hundred and Sixteen.

Digging in mounds and buried cities, were they? They need never have gone outside the limits of their native towns to discover a way of living as dead as anything in Pompeii. Why, sir, hardly a man is now alive who . . .

Yes, the shadows were longer, and much deeper. Night was settling down on the hills, on the remote villages. Nor could the state church, the church of the Founding Fathers, the one true and Congregational church, do much to dispel the gathering gloom. Strange rings were seen around the sun. Crosses appeared in the skies. So did an ominous comet which for days on end hung over the earth—even over New England—like a huge sword threatening a guilty world, or at least a guilty people. The Last Days were nigh; but neither the Congregational pastors, nor the Unitarians, nor the Universalists paid any heed. It was left for an ignorant Yankee farmer, a reformed atheist named Miller, to give warning. So, Miller stood forth out in the open and gave cry: *Behold, the bridegroom cometh, go ye out to meet him!*

Why not? Doom hung heavily over everything. It seemed no more than reasonable that Time itself had run out. Prophet Miller said that exactly one hundred and forty thousand souls, and not one more, could hope for salvation. It was thus obviously time to prepare. So they came out of their churches and flocked, as many as could, to the Great Tent, set up first at Concord in New Hampshire, then elsewhere, to listen to Miller's awful warning and to gape at the Prophet's frightening Advent Chart, in six colors, a horrendous nightmare depicting men with bellies of brass, showing the fearful beasts of the Old Testament's *Daniel,* and proving beyond all doubt that the Trump should sound tomorrow noon, next week at latest. When the Trump did not sound, and the Bridegroom came not, the disappointment was appalling, and many sank into the dismal swamps of Infidelity.

But Prophet Miller had been right—almost. In 1861 came the very Apocalypse, four grim, bloody years of it; and when it was over, the Yankees started leaving their native homes in larger numbers than ever before, going away not to such now well known places as York State and Ohio, but to outlandish regions called Dakotah and Colorado and Nebraska.

Meanwhile, still newer old men took their seats in the surviving crossroads stores in what had once been the kingdom of the Yankees, and talked on, much as the preceding generations of old men had talked—but to less attentive audiences, now composed largely of strangers who had been born in French Canada or in Ireland, who thought that the Pope was a greater man than John Quincy Adams, greater even—God forgive their ignorance—than Mr. Webster.

At last the shadows had closed in. It was night.

CHAPTER XVIII

WAS IT NIGHT—OR NOON?

IN SPITE OF the continuing exodus to the West, God Almighty was going to take care of His own people who remained faithfully in the land—in the very land to which, in 1620, He had specifically guided them. It said so in almost all their newspapers. The Yankees who stayed at home could read it, as plain as noon on a sunny day, in the august *Courant* of Hartford, which told how the new railroads and expanding industries were making New England into a hive—a mechanical, power-driven, all but automatic hive of manufacture and transportation.

They could read it in elegant phrases in the *Evening Transcript* of Boston, which said that the new rail line to Albany would carry good Yankee goods quickly and cheaply into the West and thus civilize that barbarous region.

They could tell how things were going in Rhode Island by the columns of the *Journal* of Providence: Hundreds of mill hands wanted in Pawtucket; hundreds more wanted in Central Falls.

The *Daily Express* of Portland was certain that the shipping of Canadian wheat over the half-Maine-owned Grand Trunk and thus to Europe by way of Portland's year-round harbor would make the city an immense place of commerce.

Up in New Hampshire the Concord *Monitor* vowed that nothing had ever been seen to compare with the incredible expansion of the textile industry along the Merrimack; and the making of harnesses and stagecoaches for the West. Words, indeed, were inadequate to describe the "one hundred monster cotton and woolen mills, whose massive walls, towering toward the clouds, enclose gems of humanity as well as of intricate, delicate, and almost intelligent machinery." But words *tried* to describe them, with their "ring and pleasant hum which form a cheerful and melodious diapason of prosperity." Even the mill towns, mostly ugly as sin, seemed to most observers to be beautiful cities "teeming with industrious and intelligent populations."

261]

Did it really matter too much, then, if half a million Yankees had gone away?

It depended a good deal on where you lived in New England, and what your business was, whether or not the Exodus mattered very much, or not at all. But it seemed to many that the railroads and new industries, to say nothing of the immigration from the British Isles and Europe, would more than make up for the going-away. Even in basically rural Vermont there were spots of throbbing optimism. One could read of them in the Rutland *Herald*, which told how the inexaustible supply of Vermont marble and slate was at last finding new markets by way of the steamcars. One could read it in the *Free Press* of Burlington, now a flourishing city with two railroads, several lake shipping lines, and a big industry in timbers, boards, and shingles. Even Windsor, known chiefly because it harbored the state prison, had made thousands of guns for the Crimean War in its new factories. Some of the fine Windsor carbines may have been carried in the charge of the six hundred at Balaclava, so recently immortalized by an English poet. It was astonishing.

Doubtless, the Lord was their shepherd still. Had He not brought their fathers out of bondage? Perhaps, even, His goodness and mercy had followed those of His people who had gone seeking green pastures and still waters at the West. It was well so, too, for the West was a dangerous country, where a man might easily lose his soul, a place where the strong bulls of Bashan could beset one, where the Harlot walked in the dark wood, and the Fourth Beast stamped and hideous noises issued from his slavering jaws. . . .

Yet, the Lord has not forsaken those who stayed at home. The God of New England had many peculiar and unfathomable ways, but the Yankees never forgot for a moment that His was a heaven that favored most those who helped themselves. Theirs was a God who knew what evils could be charged rightly to idle hands. He was a God who admired Industry—and so, when Yankees had occasion to mention the word in writing, they wrote it thus, Industry. So, too, when a Yankee parson spoke it from the pulpit, his congregation knew that he spoke it with a capital letter. Cleanliness might well be near unto godliness, but Industry was a step nearer than that. It had been so from the first, when old Bradford, at Plymouth Plantation, had laid down the law with great firmness: Idle hands caused the house to drop through; only those who labored should have victuals and lodging. And when printing became common, the Yankee almanac makers continued the indoctrination by suggesting—almost demanding—what decent God-fearing folks should do with their time. Harken to old Nathan Wild, of Chesterfield, New Hampshire, a noted almanac writer of northern New England, who knew his public as only successful almanac makers could:

Good morning, my neighbor, this new year [1820] is happy indeed, for each of us is possessed of a good farm, a neat tidy house, with a contented wife, buxom girls, and fat boys; comfortable barn, well stocked with hay, and cattle bright and trim; our cellars well stocked with meat, sauce, butter and cheese; and our garrets with grain, beans, wool and flax. Ah! these, my old neighbor, are the reward of Industry and prudence.

From that point on, old Wild kept after his readers, permitting them never an idle moment. When it snowed in February they were to make the most of this Fleecy Bounty, for winter was the time to prepare for spring; and he suggested enough work to outlast the longest February. As for the winter evenings:

you call occasionally upon your minister. . . . I take it for granted that he is a sensible and discreet man, and that you take delight in preparing for the *after-harvest*.

Did it blow and storm in March? So much the better. See again that your buildings are all tight and warm. This is the time to test your work. Look to your pigs; give them bedding. And in this dull weather gird your loins and get out there to split your posts and rails. Then, too, it would be best at this season to keep a close eye on the family:

Don't let them be running after fickle, ever-changing Fashion. See that your children have dress that is neat; give them as good an education as you can afford; but do not let them think much of painting landscapes, for such arts are trifling when compared with the substantial knowledge required to make them useful and happy.*

In April, Wild pointed out that the man who sticks close to his business is the one who makes money; but idleness, said he, is in the end poverty. In May, he brought home the fearful and undeniable fact that Time once gone was gone forever. Therefore, plant ye now, for it will soon be too late; be glad you are out in the fields, and do not "drag out your existence within the confines of a city"—a hellish place given much to fashion and all sorts of trumpery, and idleness. The months of June and July should call you from your pallets well before daylight, so that you may work while the dew lingers. You had best be cautious how you drink cold water these hot days, and even more cautious with your rum. And so on through the remaining months, each filled with countless tasks, rising to a veritable fury of activity

* Fortunately, not all of old Wild's public took his advice in this matter. Among those rejecting it were the parents of Larkin G. Mead, Hiram Powers, and Daniel Chester French, sculptors; of William R. Mead and Richard Morris Hunt, architects; and of painters William Morris Hunt and Thomas Waterman Wood. All were born in New Hampshire or Vermont, in the era of Wild's Almanacs.

in October, for which period Wild outlined sufficient labor to keep every member of the largest and strongest family imaginable busy from before peep of day until bedtime.

Wild was only one of the many makers of local almanacs in New England; and almanacs were but one of the countless methods of indoctrinating the young with one immutable and inescapable fact: *Man prospers best in the sight of the Lord by Industry.* That was the message. It was considered probable, too, that the Lord somewhat favored piety, but this was secondary, except with preachers and schoolmasters.

It was good that for generations the sons and daughters of New England had been given a continuous dose of this special kind of religion, for now, with the hill farms played out, and the river farms unable to compete with products from the West, they were going to need not only all the plain, hard Industry they could muster but also some ingenuity.

Money had never been easy to come by for most New Englanders; and now a greater part of the entire region, which was rural or forested, was being doubly drained of its cash. Every family that took off for the West, took with them at least a modest amount of cash; and the swiftly rising manufacturing centers attracted, retained, and thus concentrated far more money than had been the case before.

Incidentally, emigration to the West combined with the new textile cities to bring into being one Yankee tragedy that has never received proper consideration—the making of the New England spinster. The great majority of Yankee emigrants were men and boys. So much so that by 1850, or thereabout, the native population at home was grievously overweighted with females. Then, in the 1820's, began the rise of the textile centers. These came to be operated, except for a few overseers and mechanics, by women and girls, many of whom had reached the age of ten before they went to work, as doffers, at eighty cents a week and found. Competition for cheap help was established early, as the mills arose at Waltham, at Lowell, Haverhill, Lawrence, Pawtucket, and Manchester; and great long wagons, drawn by six and eight horses, trundled into rural Massachusetts, into Vermont and New Hampshire, even into Maine, while genial and smooth-talking men expounded the wonderful opportunities offered young women—even young women six years old—in the mills.

The conditions in rural New England were exactly right, and away went Yankee maidens to work in the great brick factories and to live in the great brick boarding houses. They went by the hundred, then by the thousand, and their morals, just as had been advertised to their parents, were watched over by their employers. They might lose a finger or two in the unprotected machinery, but their chastity was seldom impaired in the mill towns; nor was it likely to be when they at least left the looms at the advanced age of thirty-five or forty, to return to their native and rural regions, now so bereft of marriageable males.

A great many of those Yankee girls who did not go to work in the mills found no mates at home either; so they went to teaching school. Between them, the teachers and the girls of the mills numbered many thousands; and they formed the style and character of the New England Spinster, or Yankee Old Maid, long a favorite butt of ridicule in story or play, a character as formalized and as recognizable as that of the standard Villain, or Cruel Banker. That she was easily ridiculed by exaggerating her peculiarities made her into a comic instead of a tragic character. From the ranks of the Yankee Old Maid came largely the schoolmarms of the American West, for the old maids, often in sheer desperation, joined the migration even before the railroads had appeared to remove the uglier aspects of travel west of the Berkshires and Lake Champlain.

Certainly the new railroads gave new life to many a New England town and neighborhood. Just as surely they brought decay to many another. One autumn day in the 1870's, my mother's father stood on the steps of what had been Brownington Academy, a four-and-a-half story building of great stone blocks which in its day had been the wonder and the pride of all northeastern Vermont. He was not a moody man, Edward Amherst Stewart, though a contemplative one, and how he reflected upon the rise and fall of small empires.

Brownington village had been a small empire, an important stopping place on the stage route from Wells River to Canada, a lively center of inns, stores, a church, and tanneries, with other small home industries—so important, indeed, that in 1820 it was made a half-shire town for the county of Orleans, and court was holden there. The proud villagers, with little enough aid from county or state, presently erected the great stone building to house their Academy, whence soon came the Reverend Alexander Twilight, a graduate of Middlebury College, to teach in what he, a man of classical tastes, liked to speak of as Athenian Hall but what the villagers continued to describe as the Stone House.

For four decades and more Brownington Academy was a beacon, shining in remote and timbered Orleans County with a luster as fine as that of Harvard in its greater sphere. Then, the Iron Horse—mused my grandfather—had at last penetrated northern Vermont, passing to the west of Brownington. People moved away to live somewhere along the tracks that were somehow to bring prosperity. The village industries ceased. The Academy closed its doors. The town became in large part a range for sheep.

Though my grandfather found it a bit sad to stand here by the old Stone House, its doors sagging, its windows broken, its empty rooms ready to echo and mock the sound of voice or step—though it brought nostalgia to one who had studied his Latin grammar here, nevertheless it was good, and gave one a proud feeling, to reflect how this isolated and moss-grown structure erected so far from the cities and from the main arteries of Industry and culture, this pile of native stone, had radiated influences "wide-spreading and more interesting than romance."* Here, from this one school, at best a tiny font of learning, one might clearly see the varied trails of the Yankee Exodus and estimate, in a modest way, the influence which the Exodus had exercised, both on Brownington and on far places as well. The male graduates of the Academy, and no few of its alumnae, were now scattered throughout the Republic, and beyond its borders. Brownington Academy was an epitome of a hundred or more similar schools in New England which were closed primarily by emigration.

But, for the moment, consider only the graduates of small Brownington Academy. Outstanding among them, my grandfather said, were the sons of Elijah Gridley Strong, who had been a merchant in Brownington village's prosperous days. His son Henry had gone away to become a physician, had performed noble work during the late Rebellion, and since the end of the war had achieved a fine medical practice in Beloit, Wisconsin, where fellow citizens had elected him mayor.

James Strong was in Minnesota, building with sure hand the small Congregational school at Northfield into Carleton College, making it an outstanding institution of the prairies. As for William, his success had been perhaps the most spectacular of all; he had gone to work for a railroad, and recently had become head-man of the Santa Fe, which he was expanding into a system to cover the whole Southwest.

Indeed, the Lord had scattered us among the heathen. Charles Stimpson was a merchant in Leavenworth, Kansas. Samuel Eaton had an insurance agency in St. Paul. Walgrave Eaton had a good hardware business in Cedar Rapids, a city of Iowa. But brother Charles Eaton had not done so well; he had "led a wild, roving life" and was thought to have been killed by Indians. William Grow had been a colonel in the Mexican army, but of late had gone on to further adventures in South America. Charlie Brigham had gone off to superintend a New-York-owned plantation at Commerce, Mississippi. His brother Fred was in business near Memphis, Tennessee. Charles Walker was living near Chicago. Charles Remick, after getting a degree in

---

* I know what my grandfather mused because he set down his musings on this subject for a weekly paper of which he was a part owner, the *Express & Standard* of Newport, Vt.

law at Dartmouth, was practicing in Iowa. Lester Bigelow had gone away into Canada somewhere.

In Sparta, Wisconsin, lived my grandfather's sister, who had remarked in letters home that pioneering in Wisconsin had been easy compared to making a living on a Brownington farm. In near-by Baraboo, William Kelly had cleared and settled a nice place. Alvin Howard, Henry Newcomb, and L. H. Bisbee were in business in Chicago. Away out in the Napa valley of California Jerre Mansfield had established himself as one of the most prosperous farmers in the region. He owned, if one could believe it, some five thousand acres of fine land. In San Francisco another former Academy boy named Gilman had done very well—if that term could be applied to such a business—as a *dealer in Rum.* . . .

There they were—the old Academy boys, scattered throughout the great West, overflowing into Canada, into Mexico, South America. As for the others, mostly they had gone to Boston and so into some business or profession. My grandfather's own brother Tyler had got as far as the District of Columbia, where he entered the consular service and even now was in Spain, a wicked country given over to idolatry and bullfighting. Even Grandfather himself had left Brownington and was long since settled, ten miles away, in the new railroad town of Newport.

But the West had never tempted him. He often wondered why, and came to the conclusion that it probably was because he had inherited more of his forebears' characteristics than his brother and sister who had left New England. In some two and one-half centuries his forebears in New England had moved, all told, less than three hundred miles from Rowley in Massachusetts, where the first of his paternal line in America, Duncan Stewart, had settled. Duncan had lived and died in Rowley. So had his son James. But the third of the line, Solomon, had died in Lunenburg, some forty-five miles west of Rowley. The fourth, Daniel, had died in Fitchburg, a good five miles from Lunenburg. Daniel's son Amherst, however, caught the Green Mountain Fever and made a tremendous move, two hundred miles in extent, to clear and settle a farm in Brownington before it had a name, and to become one of the founders of the Academy. His son, Thomas Carlisle, born in 1804 at a period when two given names were coming into common use, remained in the village, and there my grandfather was born.

Thus in two hundred and sixty years, through seven generations, the family had migrated all told about two hundred and sixty miles. Seemingly, neither the Genesee Fever nor the Ohio Fever—mused my grandfather—had even tempted them. But now his own sister was living in Wisconsin and liking it, and his own brother was in Spain. As for himself, he should live and die in the Green Mountains. He had come to the opinion that is was usually the bolder, more adventurous people who went away, chiefly to the West; but not necessarily the more able or intelligent. Nor was it poverty, as so many held, that made emigrants of Yankees. No, it was rather something in one's inheritance—some unnamed thing in the blood—that either kept them in their native country, or sent them over the mountain, into that vague region called the West.*

Middlebury College of early days turned out a large and continuous supply of emigrants. Consider for example its class of 1822, the members of which were mostly natives of Vermont or Massachusetts. The graduates totaled twenty-seven. No fewer than twenty-one of them died outside New England —died in Texas, Illinois, Georgia, Missouri, Florida, South Carolina, Alabama, New York, New Jersey, Iowa, California, and Michigan. It seems not unlikely that, in the same era, the sons of Amherst, of Williams, Bowdoin, Dartmouth, Brown, and surely of Yale, did much the same.

Whether the urge was in the blood, or stemmed from discontent or poverty or ambition, the urge played Old Ned with the towns by-passed by the railroads; and also with many a village that the railroads did touch but did not transform into the vast mart of trade which the promoters had promised. And of course many had not even waited for the railroads; they had gone west on foot, in carts, in wagons.

A family notably possessed of the urge to scatter were the descendents of David Evans, who had settled in Fryeburg, Maine, in 1763. Little more than a century later David's kinsmen were living in New York City, Philadelphia, Chicago; in the Illinois towns of Waukegan, La Clede, Newman and DuQuoin; in Columbus, Ohio; in the Wisconsin communities of Kenosha, Anthony, and Eau Claire; in Stillwater, Minnesota; in St. Louis; in Kinsley, Kansas; in Sykeston, North Dakota; in Freehold, New Jersey; in Leesburg, Florida; and in California at San Francisco, Sacramento, Little River, and Marysville.

It was odd how this or that emigrating fever found one village so ripe, the next one immune. Neither the rush to the Genesee country of New York, nor the later Ohio fever made an impression on Skowhegan, Maine. But Illinois started the exodus, in 1850, when William McLellan left his native Skowhegan to pioneer at Geneseo, to pioneer all over again in Wisconsin, and not to settle down for good until he started raising stock as a Union Colonist at Greeley, Colorado. McLellan broke the dam: the Amasa Pratts

* My grandfather may well have been wrong in all his conclusions, but he did not speculate out of mere ignorance. He made a transcontinental trip, visiting such far places as Topeka, San Antonio, Los Angeles, San Francisco, and many another, then returned to Vermont, refreshed and quite content to finish his days there.

soon moved to Ripon, Wisconsin; Henry Pratt to St. Paul, Frank Hartwell to Minneapolis, Lyman Linnell to Duluth. Miss Fidelia Coburn went out to Queen's Bush, Upper Canada, an "almost unbroken forest," as missionary and later, with her husband, John S. Brooks, to sinister Sierra Leone in Africa.

The Skowhegan exodus had fairly begun. It was going to outlast the century. Joseph Locke went, oddly enough, to Georgia, where he became editor of the Savannah *Republican*. Hiram Swain settled near, at Atlanta. Augustus Hills tried Arkansas, before deciding on Bryan, Texas, as his permanent home. Henry Weston went to Mississippi, where with six sons he founded and carried on a mighty lumber business. And when the War Between the States came along, Skowhegan's sons named Weston, Hartwell, White, and Steward fought in the Confederate ranks, much to the scandal of the folks back home.

John Tufts and family of Skowhegan moved straight to Grinnell, Iowa, a sound Yankee town where the children could attend the new Congregational college. Erastus McIntire went to Newton, Charles White to Humboldt, and Fred F. Coffin, to Osage, all in Iowa. Charles and Frank Hilton and Ulysses Burrill migrated to Wimbledon, North Dakota. Henry Simmons stopped near Emporia, Kansas, and there struck a thumping-big gusher of oil on his acres. Myron C. Jacobs had the same good fortune near Tulsa, Oklahoma. Frank A. Leavitt opened a dentist's office in Decatur, Nebraska. Clifton W. Arnold went to Bland, New Mexico, where he was postmaster. Carroll F. Morrill settled in Reno, Nevada, and Captain A. G. Manley in Elko.

They were as the leaves of autumn. The Egyptians had scattered, the Ammonites had scattered, and now the tribes of Skowhegan in Maine were scattering. . . .

The Emery boys, Philander and Thomas, pioneered in Montana, where an old friend of Skowhegan days, William Spearin, was in the express business at Dillon; where Charles Wilson and wife were living at Deer Lodge.

Pious men of Skowhegan wondered if it were a Devil's whirlwind that was whisking away so many of their townsmen. Or, was it some lightning that shone, as the Book said, unto the west? Were these the plains of Jericho that so many went to seek?

If it was a wind, it blew them far. Joseph White had reached Idaho as early as 1863, and there he died. Stephen C. Steward did not stop until he had reached the Pacific shore at Coquille, Oregon. In the same state Fred Farrington and Charles Tobey had settled in Eugene. James Currier was at Heppner, William H. Garland at Portland. Dr. William F. Robinson was a dentist at The Dalles, near the great falls of the Columbia River.

In Goldendale, Washington, in 1880, citizens elected Dr. J. S. Houghton,

late of Skowhegan, their mayor. Perley T. Kendall had come to live in Spokane, Billings O. Hall at Snohomish. W. Guy Pennell and wife, who was
Estora Jewett, went to Seattle, where their four children attended the University of Washington. As mentioned elsewhere, Cyrus Walker of Skowhegan
shipped west with the Popes and Talbots of the eastern Maine shore, to
take charge of logging and sawmilling on Puget Sound, and at Port Ludlow
in the wilderness built a splendid mansion of Douglas fir and lived like a
Yankee grandee, remaining, however, true to Yankee form in small economies, such as picking up nails that his millwrights carelessly dropped, to
shame them with this wicked waste.

The Reverend George Hathaway was perhaps the earliest from Skowhegan
to penetrate the paradise of southern California, blazing the way for others
from his native town—the Sherman Smiths, the John Gages, the Walter
Robinses, the Thomas Farrands. Stockton attracted Harry Washburn. Josiah
Field went to Santa Cruz. William Nash opened a drugstore in Covina.
Urban Parkman favored Pasadena.

The Florida country had never been, in Skowhegan, more than a name on
a box of cigars until 1875, when Robert Williams moved his family there
and planted a big grove of orange trees. He was successful, and his letters
home started something of a migration, bringing to lush Florida families
named Bean, Baxter, Downing, Owen, Foss, and Chase.

Nor were those all, or even half, of the emigrants from one village along
the Kennebec in Maine.

In near-by Livermore there was evidence that not all Yankee maidens
were content to remain at home as spinsters, or to go to the mills at Biddeford and be spinsters there. As early as 1873 the charming daughters of
Francis F. Haines of Livermore village were all living at the West and in
a state of matrimony. Emeline was wife of Earl S. Goodrich, a St. Paul
businessman; Linda Ann was wife of the Honorable Timothy O. Howe,
United States Senator from Wisconsin; Mary was already the widow of Dr.
E. P. Eastman, late of Platteville, Wisconsin; Sophia had married Joseph Lee
who lived in Minnesota. A brother of these girls, Silas Haines, was a successful lawyer in Colorado.

Although Maine was known above all for the ability and ingenuity of
its boss lumbermen, who followed the timber line west like hounds on a
hot scent, the state exported talents in other lines, for example, three of the
eight children of Isaac Maxim of small Sangerville. Isaac himself was a
local character, an eccentric who spent only too much of his time puttering
with a flying machine and an automatic gun. His son Hiram left home as
a young man and went away to perfect the machine gun that bears his name.
Hiram's brother Hudson puttered, too, and out of his puttering came an ex-

plosive, maximite, which by comparison made dynamite seem mild. Brother
Samuel left home also, to experiment with this and that, and eventually to
contribute much to the improvement of metals. The tradition continued into
another generation. Hiram's son, Hiram Percy, invented the Maxim silencer,
for firearms.

It was odd, the endless patterns in which migration showed itself in New
England. If Sangerville, Maine, exported inventors, then the chief export
of Chester, New Hampshire, was probably missionary teachers. Chester was
one of the numerous towns which had been busy centers in stagecoach days
and began to fade with the first wail of the locomotive. Let it fade. Chester's
young women were not going to fade with it—at least, not at home in
Chester. So, as missionary teachers to the heathen in India went Ann Hazelton and Harriet Atwood. Clarissa Emerson went to Ceylon. Mary Eliza
Tenney and Helen Eliza Melvin departed for Turkey. Mary Kelly, Celestia
Goldsmith, and Grace Eaton left for the no less benighted region of
Tennessee; and Martha A. Forsaith went to Hiltonhead, South Carolina.
Emma Pearl Goldsmith drew a post at a missionary school in Austin, Texas,
and Emily Hazelton at another in Iowa. Perhaps this movement out of a
hamlet like Chester was sparked in the first place by the Reverend John
S. Emerson, pioneer of 1831 in the Sandwich Islands, who spent the rest of
his life there. In addition to the missionaries, Chester also exported a large
number of "regular" or lay teachers.

If the Lord called forth missionaries without number from New England,
then who or what accounted for the endless procession of lawyers moving
westward? They moved, surely, without divine sanction, for the Good Book
said that lawyers rejected the counsel of God, that they loaded men with
burthens grievous to be borne, yet themselves did not touch the burthens
with one of their fingers. Whatever the cause, Yankee lawyers were exceedingly prone to the urge; and the urge could hardly have been stronger than in
small Newport, New Hampshire. As early as the mid-seventies natives of
Newport were practicing law in Santa Fe, New Mexico, in Austin, Texas;
in Glens Falls, Rochester, Brooklyn, Lockport, and New York, New York;
in Illinois, Ohio, Pennsylvania, Missouri, Alabama, Minnesota, Virginia,
and Michigan. The Corbin brothers of Newport—Austin, a lawyer, and
Daniel, a surveyor—turned out to be a great combination in the business of
railroads and banking; and when they had made their piles they did not
forget their native state, but bought 24,000 acres of it, which was made into
one of the finest game refuges in all the eastern states.

In Windham, Connecticut, it was a common saying, and perhaps even a
boast, a vicarious wanderlust of the stay-at-homes, that no matter where one
might go, there "he would find the sons of Windham bearing her impress

and her institutions." The states of New York, Ohio, and Wyoming, said a local historian, had received large colonies from Windham, while "Edmund and George Badger won success and honor in North Carolina, and New Orleans still [1888] bears witness to the eloquence of Sylvester Larned and Chief Justice Bradford." Some fifteen other states had also benefited by the abilities exported from Windham with her sons. "Let a son of Windham rove where he will, he finds a brother to welcome him."

Here and there, for reasons not often easy to explain today, the migration from a Yankee town was not to the west but to the north. Littleton in New Hampshire seems to have been such a town. During the early years of the nineteenth century many large families moved out of Littleton in a body and into the Eastern Townships of the province of Quebec, a region which the English conquerors hoped to build into an Anglo-Saxon island in the midst of almost solid French territory. Possibly the Littleton colonists were given special inducements to go there to settle; and it is barely possible that the Littleton people had become irked with a village where the Sabbath was kept even more austerely than was common in New England, for this was the very place where one week in 1802 the postboy was delayed by a midwinter storm and had to deliver the mail on Sunday. At the home of Deacon James Rankin, an influential townsman, he tossed a newspaper, along with a jolly greeting, through the open door. Without a word Mrs. Rankin fetched the tongs from the fireplace, picked up the hideous sheet which had become vile because of its arrival on the Sabbath, and still without a word dropped it into the fire blazing in the open hearth. Whether such an attitude tended to be, as seems possible, of no little aid to emigration, is not to be known; but the citizens of Littleton were soon moving in great numbers into Quebec—among them the families of Caswell, Larned, Hopkinson, Williams, Aldrich, and even some Rankins. The numerous Websters also took off for the Eastern Townships, numbering the four families of Henry, William, James, and Nathaniel. The descendants of most of them are to be found to this day in the townships, of which Sherbrooke is the principal city.

Quite often the migration of Yankees from a specific neighborhood in New England to a specific region in the West or South was something of a chain affair, touched off by the early success of an emigrant. The affinity between Connecticut and Mobile, Alabama, for instance, was perhaps due in no small part to Lewis Judson, who left his home in Stratford, about 1795, and founded a trading business in the southern city. He was followed in 1806 by Josiah Blakely of New Haven, and still later by Joseph E. Sheffield of Southport, who became a leading cotton merchant and in later years gave money to establish Yale's Sheffield School.

Once in a while the influx of Yankees into a foreign neighborhood was of such magnitude and influence that the natives resented them and attempted to get the situation in hand by founding exclusive clubs or societies to keep the newcomers in their place. No less a personage than Washington Irving, a hardshell New Yorker, was the founding spirit, in 1835, of the St. Nicholas Society of New York City, which had the avowed purpose of "combating the social influence of New Englanders in the City."

When Yankees were leaving home in such multitudes as to call for repressive measures in the big city of New York, it was little wonder that here and there, and especially in rural New England, many an editor, preacher, storekeeper, and farmer looked around and came to the conclusion that his native region, or neighborhood, was fast becoming a deserted country. The free land of New England had long since disappeared. There was no opportunity to move and squat and remain. Somebody or other, individual or corporation, *owned* the land and would stand for no trespass. Not only was free land no longer to be had at home, but the villages and most of the cities were now supplied with all the professional men they could support, and more. It was with good reason that doctors, lawyers, and ministers of the gospel were commonly among the first to leave their native towns to settle at the West. Too, the ranks of the skilled laborers and mechanics were filled to overflowing. Only unskilled jobs—the jobs of hired men on the farms, of ditch diggers, of pick-and-shovel men—were left. No intelligent and ambitious Yankee, not even those with a minimum of schooling, wanted such work. Leave it to the hordes coming in from unhappy Ireland, from the province of Quebec. So, they went away and left it. . . .

It was not always easy to know where to go. As early as 1834, when young Richard Emerson Ela of Lebanon, New Hampshire, made up his mind to leave it, he discovered that one might "read Flint's Geography till he is blind, and then must have an uncommonly grasping mind to combine all the circumstances of every place and compare them so as to make a selection." But at last he did make up his mind. A year later he was in Buffalo. The West, he had already found out, was no Eden after all: a man, he wrote, had to do something other than merely to pluck and eat; he had to sow and reap and plan and accomplish. But it was vastly better here than back home, even though Ela was still of the opinion that if a person "was doing any way decently at home, he had best not migrate at all." If, however, one "had run ashore, it was a good plan to go to the West where chances to get wealth certainly are better than in the old states." In 1836 he was still working westward and had got to Plainfield, Illinois, where he found himself blessed with health, though he had, he said, been through the pestilences that walk in darkness. He had as yet found no mine of precious metal. Neither had he met with any extraordinary facilities for amassing wealth and gaining honors. Still, he was "tasting daily of Industry's growing sweetness." Note that capitalized "Industry." Here was a genuine Yankee. By their fruits one might know of their Industry.

In the spring of 1839 Ela, aged twenty-seven, was in Rochester, Wisconsin Territory, laboring in the heat of the day, making fanning mills. "I have got the frames dressed for 60 mills," he wrote, "and Basswood lumber on the ground to finish them; have got a shop raised. . . . My path is slow and by no means sure and it is full of rugged toil." But his path *was* sure, no matter what he wrote or thought, and it led him into a most successful business in the manufacture of wagons and all sorts of farming equipment. By 1846 he was serving in the legislature, and had already composed and was circulating a petition to drive RUM out of Wisconsin.

The banishment of rum was natural to Ela, but only incidental. To many a Yankee the banishment of rum was the one and the sole reason for emigrating. The antirum exodus started as early as 1830, when Lucius Manlius Sargent left Boston to lecture thoughout the United States on the evil. After him came John Newton Stearns of New Ipswich, New Hampshire, to travel at the West and denounce the taking of drams. On the heels of Stearns went forth a whole army, the Cold Water Army, many of them Amazons, to fight the hellish distillate where it was running full-flood in the Mississippi valley. In this army, and outstanding, were Judith Ellen Horton Foster of Lowell, Massachusetts, and Mary Hannah Hanchett of Canaan, Connecticut, and Mary Greenleaf Clement Leavitt of Hopkinton, New Hampshire. They are forgotten today, but in their time they were as well known as the much later Carry Nation, though more ladylike of method; and they were as much a part of the Exodus as were the migrating lumberjacks, who were toting, besides their axes and saws, as great and as enduring a thirst as could be imagined.

Thus did the Yankees leave New England, one after another, from western Connecticut to farthest east in Maine, for every reason under the sun, and for no reason at all—by the thousand, by the hundreds of thousands, man and boy, woman and maid, pimp and pastor, missionary and "madam," Mormon and Perfectionist, to search out the nearest as well as the most remote counties in all of the states and territories at the West, and there to drive their stakes, to found a town, to establish their schools and bethels, to start a business or to follow a trade or profession.

The Lord, of course, called a great many of them forth to do His work. Hard times, just as surely, drove even more of them out, probably a hundred to one. For what was there left for a Yankee to do, other than work in the factories of the rising industrial centers? Illinois and Wisconsin were shipping in wheat. Michigan's lumber was making the Penobscot and the Kennebec and the Androscoggin regions a back number. Nails, once the biggest home industry in all New England, were now being made by machines in New Jersey. The old handmade product could not compete. As for maple sugar, God save us, it was being made in York State, in Ohio, in Michigan and Wisconsin, from which no little of it was finding its way to markets in New York City and Boston. This seemed, in Vermont, in New Hampshire, and in rural Massachusetts and Connecticut, to be the last straw.

A Yankee, true enough, might invent something, or improve upon something already invented, and peddle it to other Yankees—in the ancient tradition of the Yankee peddlers who had been going to the West and South these many years, selling clocks and calf weaners and lucifer matches and combs and mirrors and other small trumpery called Yankee Notions. A large number of Yankees did become part-time inventors, in their desperate need; but, though a few of them had great successes, a majority of them failed.*

Now and again there came some idea that seemed to hold the salvation of the decaying towns, the communities which the railroads had passed or had failed to build into cities, and the surrounding countryside. One such idea which became a mania was the raising of silkworms and the manufacture of silk. Down in Connecticut, at South Manchester, Ward Cheney and his brothers had been experimenting with the tree called *Morus multicaulis,* a variety of mulberry. In 1834 the Cheneys' nursery seemed to indicate that this tree could be successfully raised in New England. Editors of newspapers and writers on agricultural subjects took the idea and quickly made it into a sensation, stressing the fortunes which unquestionably could be derived from mulberry cultivation and the subsequent production of native silk. It was a gorgeous thing to consider, and the idea spread with almost the speed of sound. Here at last was evidence that the Lord pointed the way for His own people in these times of their greatest woe. Did not God make the mulberry bush, and the worm, and even Man? Combined, they should make fine silk in the sight of the Lord.

"During the years 1835 and 1836," wrote the town historian of Candia, New Hampshire, a man filled with understatements, "a considerable number of the people of Candia Four Corners and other towns in the vicinity became much interested in the subject of producing silk." The virus was at work. Dr. Isaiah Lane and Captain Abraham Fitts, prominent worthies of Candia, together with a group of fellow citizens, purchased a stock of mul-

* See Chapter XXI.

berry shoots and a colony of cocoons, and planted the trees with the greatest assurance. This planting cost a deal of money, but almost everybody wanted a hand and a few dollars in it. Even "a young and popular school mistress invested all she had earned." In due time, related the Candia historian, "enough leaves were produced to feed the few silk worms that were hatched from the cocoons." Possibly by this time a small worm of doubt had also entered the business; but the citizens of Candia Four Corners went on. "The next thing to be done was to reel off the extremely fine thread of silk covering the cocoons. Hannah Lane and two or three other women managed to reel silk enough to make a few small skeins for sewing."

By the autumn of 1836 the enterprise had produced more doubt, and heartaches, than silk. "It was found that the climate was rather cold," wrote Candia's historian (and to anyone who has lived in New Hampshire his use of the modifying "rather" shows his blind local patriotism). It was found rather cold, he wrote, for the health of the silkworms. And, too, "a considerable capital would be required to make the business a success." He closed the subject by remarking that "the failure of the enterprise caused much disappointment to the parties concerned."

The mulberry-bush mania swept New England much in the manner of the Bridegroom and Second Advent, and died almost as suddenly.

Before the mulberry disaster there had been a mania for collecting ginseng root and shipping it to China; and after the mulberries came another exotic affair, that of growing poppies and making opium, right on the farm. This did not grow into a mania, probably only because memories were long and still retained impressions of the shoddy work of the silkworms of a generation before. But the opium delusion removed the spare cash of those farmers who listened to the slickers who came with poppy seeds, which were cheap enough, and the opium-making machinery, which came high indeed. The seeds grew well enough, even in central Vermont, but the end product, raw opium, turned out to have no market. It was not, it appeared, in a "pure enough state for manufacture," and thus could not be used to make the drug which, so the salesmen had piously observed, would be used only for the alleviation of pain—surely a Christian thing—and would not, of course, find its way into the dark channels supplying smokers with the product.*

Many desperate villagers in all six states made attempts to found industries in their hamlets. Guilford in Vermont tried manufacturing, one after another, such things as bedsteads, boots, bricks, brooms, buttons, carriages, combs,

---

* The information regarding opium-making in Vermont came to me from an old native of the Waterbury region, who had seen, when a youth in the eighties, various rusting parts of machinery stowed away in Waterbury barns, and had heard the story of the fiasco from his elders. I have been unable to document the story by printed material.

harmonicas, harness-trim, hats, inkstands, linseed oil, malt, ox-yokes, plows, and even whisky. None lasted longer than four or five years.

The town of Waltham, Massachusetts, later to become world-famous for its watches, was before that the Kerosene Capital of New England. The industry got under way in 1855, when Luther and William Atwood succeeded in producing fine burning oil from what was called petroleum pitch, imported from Canada. The product was so obviously superior to anything the Yankees knew that the business grew rapidly; but it was later moved to Portland, Maine and continued as the United States Chemical Company.

Few of the industries of the hamlets brought in much cash, or lasted long. It might be bright dawn, or high noon, for the few important textile and manufacturing cities, but, by Godfrey, it was evening in the hills and the valleys back from the railroads. The old men of the crossroads talked endlessly as the farms continued to revert to sheep pasture, and at last to forest. The sheep, which had at first seemed the road to salvation, had been the idea of William Jarvis, native of Boston, long-time consul at Lisbon in Portugal, who put New England into the sheep business in 1810. In that year he bought a farm in Weathersfield, Vermont, and stocked it with the Merino breed of Spain and Portugal. Their fine wool brought as high as $1.50 a pound. The craze ran its course. For years afterward the echo of Merino bells remained to wake people in the night. It seemed an omen of evil.

It *was* something of a knell, too; but it was only a sort of obsequies for the New England that the old men had known, that their fathers and grandfathers had known. The old order was passing before their eyes. The new order was arriving even as they looked and wondered, for few, then or now, have been able to comprehend the changing world of the current moment. It is much simpler to prophesy the distant future than it is to assess what goes on today. So, the bemused Yankees, or many of them, could only look and wonder as the old landmarks disappeared.

Emigration, immigration, the railroads, the new manufacturing cities, these and the Exodus were removing the old order, the order of flint and steel, of cocked hats.

The Exodus to the West continued. Yet New England's population did not decrease, but climbed steadily. It had continued to rise even during the tremendous going-out between 1830 and 1860. In 1830 fewer than two million people lived in the Yankee domain. By 1860 the number had passed three million. At or near the turn of the century, 1900, there were six million people in Yankeeland—though they were not all, or nearly all, of Yankee birth and parentage.

Nor did what statisticians, with their fondness of labels, call Wealth, with a capital letter, show a decline. Far from it: Wealth in Yankeeland continued to rise steadily and to reach, by the end of the century, the incomprehensible sum of seven billions of dollars.*

Both population and Wealth continued to mount after 1900. But the population after about 1850—or perhaps 1845—was decreasingly of old Yankee stock; and the Wealth was far less of farm than of city. The old New England, for better or worse, was dissipated and blown away in the smoke of the manufacturing cities, in the smoke of the westbound steamcars; and its blood, for better or worse, was getting large infusions from Canada, from Ireland, from Scandinavia, from Italy, from Poland, from every nation in Europe. In the schoolrooms of Hartford, of Brockton, of Pawtucket, Biddeford, Manchester, and Barre, the kids still sang of Sweet Liberty and raised their little voices in praise of the Pilgrims' Pride. Yet, the blood of the Pilgrims was thinning by the year, almost by the month. It was thinner here at home, perhaps, than in any number of new towns at the West, places like Marietta, Oberlin, Beloit, or even Portland in Oregon.

Thus the Jeremiahs of the crossroads and the pulpits had been right after all. It *was* night, and midnight, for New England—that is, the New England they had known and were still talking about. But in all truth it was scarcely noon for the New England that had come into being.

* *New England Trends*, published by the First National Bank of Boston, 1939 issue.

CHAPTER XIX

LESSER MIGRATIONS

THE SOUTHWEST was never a goal for any great number of New Englanders. The settlement of Utah by the Mormons was of course planned and carried out by the notable Vermonter, Brigham Young, and many of his chief lieutenants were Yankees. Otherwise, however, and except in the case of Texas, New England played an extremely small part in forming and populating what are today the southwestern states.

But it was different with Texas. The first American settlement in all Texas was planned by a native of Durham, Connecticut, named Moses Austin and was carried out most successfully by his son Stephen, one of the great colonizers of all time. The last president of the Texas Republic was born in Great Barrington, Massachusetts. And the peer of all Texas businessmen of the nineteenth century was a native of Springfield on the Connecticut River. Let no proud citizen of the largest state forget these Yankees among its pioneers and founders.

Connecticut-born Moses Austin and an older brother migrated to Richmond, Virginia, about 1784, and began operating a lead-mining business, working slaves. Moses was something of an explorer, and a couple of years later he went west in search of further mining possibilities. He found them in southwestern Missouri. He got a grant of land and founded the town of Potosi, setting up a furnace, a shot tower, and other things necessary for the commercial manufacture of lead; and later added a sawmill, gristmill, and store. For the next twenty years he prospered, and he became a noted man in the region. His mistake was in helping to organize the Bank of St. Louis. This institution crashed in 1819.

Moses Austin was then approaching sixty, but he turned away to a still newer frontier, the Spanish province called Texas. In 1821 he went to San Antonio and came away with a permit from the commandant-general of the Eastern Interior Provinces to establish a colony of three hundred American families on Texas soil. He died soon after, but not before his son had promised to carry out the colony plan.

Stephen Fuller Austin had never been enthusiastic about his father's colonization scheme; but now at twenty-seven, with Moses dead, he turned with singular devotion to the idea. He proceeded with the greatest dispatch to select, in person, a fertile and well watered piece of land on the Gulf. A year later, in 1822, he led some three hundred families to the site and planted the first legal settlement of Anglo-Americans in all Texas. Meanwhile, Mexico had established its independence of Spain. He hurried to Mexico City, just then a most turbulent place, and returned to his new settlement with the grant fully confirmed by the Mexican administration.

For the next decade Stephen Austin was the first man in Texas—executive, lawmaker, supreme judge, military commander. He learned to speak Spanish. He genuinely liked the Mexicans. He said, and honestly, that he was determined to "fulfill rigidly all the duties and obligations of a Mexican citizen." He brought in more than seven hundred additional families from the United States and settled them on the land. In time he came to favor the independence of Texas, rather than its annexation to the United States, and in 1836 he became secretary of state of the Lone Star Republic.

Stephen Austin was a grave and gentle man, and a lonely one, for though he was surely one of the outstandingly successful colonizers on a frontier celebrated for its turmoil, he seems never to have had any close friendships. He never married. He died in office of the Texas Republic in 1836, aged forty-three.

The last chief executive of independent Texas was Anson Jones of Great Barrington, Massachusetts. He had long been an adventurer in far places. He had also studied medicine, and in 1827 was pronounced a doctor by Jefferson College, at Canonsburg, Pennsylvania. In 1833 he arrived in the new Brazoria, Texas, and established himself in practice. He appears to have been a fast worker. He served as physician in the Texas army, was elected to the Texas congress, and in 1844 was elected president. Two years later he surrendered his authority to the newly elected governor of the new state of Texas, and retired to his ranch on the Brazos, which he called Barrington. Later he was defeated in the United States senatorial contest, and presently committed suicide in Houston. Jones was probably little more than an opportunist. Stephen Austin and no other "opened the door to Texas and by leadership of high order held it open."

Through this open door entered William Marsh Rice, a native of Springfield, Massachusetts in 1838. He promoted and operated stage lines, and got into many another business. He induced a brother, Fred, to come to Houston, where the latter made good in banking. At the outbreak of the Civil War,

Rice, an avowed Unionist, picked up and moved across the border into Mexico, where he continued to thrive until war's end; then he returned to his Texas home and became one of the organizers of a railroad. One may judge that he did very well. When he died in 1900, his estate was estimated at $11,000,000, a goodly portion of which was used to found Rice Institute, which opened in 1912 and continues as a liberal arts college of the first rank.

Although Arizona never has attracted many Yankees, its first territorial governor, appointed in 1863, was John Noble Goodwin, born in South Berwick, Maine and graduated from Dartmouth College. When he arrived in the territory fewer than six hundred Americans were living there. Most of these were southern in birth or sympathy. Goodwin met the situation with great tact by appointing many of them to office and, through concentrating interest on the good of the territory rather than on the outcome of the war, accomplished much that otherwise could not have been done. He established the capital at Prescott, which was named for the historian; and in 1865 was sent to Washington as territorial representative.

At least one other Yankee had a stake in Arizona. Dwight Bancroft Heard, born in Boston, had migrated first to Chicago where he dealt in wholesale hardware to considerable profit. His health failed, and in 1895 he settled in Phoenix, which became the state capital, as a rancher, farmer, and investor. He headed a large cattle company. He cultivated 7,000 acres, turned it into small farms, and gave a good deal of his time to reclamation laws and projects. He stoutly opposed admission of Arizona and New Mexico as one state. Probably his greatest contribution was the promotion of the growing in Arizona of long-staple cotton, for which purpose he spent some time in Egypt, getting information that he applied successfully.

Tradition has it that people from every state were in the wild rush when Oklahoma Territory was opened to settlement. Doubtless there were; but the Yankees must have been few indeed, for they failed to leave any New England influence in that rambunctious region. But many years before the rush a Yankee named Samuel A. Worcester had established Park Hill Mission in what was then Indian Territory and set up the first printing press in the whole immense area. His was a gentle and an appealing story, for he was no go-getter, no founder of states or towns. He devoted his life to efforts for the improvement of the battered remnants of a great people, the Cherokee nation. When he migrated, he migrated as a Cherokee, not as a Yankee; and his memory is fresh to this day, ninety years after his death, to Americans of Cherokee ancestry.*

* So says Marion L. Starkey in her fine *The Cherokee Nation,* published in 1946.

Samuel Worcester came of a family long noted in Massachusetts and New Hampshire, a cousin of Joseph who compiled the *Universal and Critical Dictionary,* a nephew of Noah the Friend of Peace who as early as 1814 proposed a league of nations and a world court. Samuel was born in the city of Worcester, but reared in small Peacham, Vermont, where his father taught him farming and typesetting. After graduation from the University of Vermont and Andover Theological Seminary, he was ordained minister at the Park Street Congregational, or Brimstone Corner, Church in Boston. He set out at once as missionary to the Cherokees in eastern Tennessee.

The remarkable Cherokee scholar Sequoya had but recently devised an alphabet for his people's language, accomplishing in a decade what had taken the white race, with no model to work upon, centuries. But to achieve its purpose "talking leaves," as Indians termed books and letters, must be printed. The Cherokees wanted a printing press to make Cherokee talking leaves. Worcester got them one and supervised the cutting and casting of types for the eighty-six characters; then he moved to Georgia, where the Cherokees had been shifted, to teach them typesetting and to help publish *The Phoenix.*

The state of Georgia was not hospitable to foreigners who sought to improve either the knowledge or the status of people of color—any color; and in 1831 Worcester was arrested on the charge of having no state license to reside among Indians, convicted, and sent to the penitentiary, to reflect for four years. A year later the case was reversed on appeal to the United States Supreme Court; but he was held a while longer in the Georgia jailhouse.

On release Worcester transferred his work to the Cherokees living in what is now Oklahoma, and in 1835 set up Park Hill Mission, erecting the buildings with his own hands—church, school, boarding house, homes for teachers, and a printing office, where he set up the first press in Indian Territory. With Cherokees working enthusiastically with him, Worcester printed and distributed thousands of copies of the Bible and other works, including the Cherokee Almanac. He died in 1857, revered by the people he had made his own, and his Park Hill Mission flourished for many years. As late as 1920, his granddaughter, Alice Mary Robertson, who carried on as a teacher and as superintendent of Creek schools, was elected to Congress. The largest dormitory for women at the University of Oklahoma is named in her honor.

The Southeast portion of the United States apparently attracted no greater number of New England people than the Southwest; yet Florida once had a veritable Yankee in command of its Confederate troops, as gallant an officer as any Southerner-born: General Edward A. Perry, born in Richmond, Massachusetts, in 1831, who attended Yale College for a time, then left to teach school in Alabama, and at last began the practice of law in Pensacola, Florida, where he was well liked and most successful. When war came, he personally raised a regiment of soldiers, was made colonel, later brigadier general, fought bravely, and was wounded twice. In 1884 grateful Floridians made him their governor. And at least one Yankee left his name on Florida's map. This was Henry S. Sanford of Woodbury, Connecticut, son of a wealthy textile manufacturer, who entered the American diplomatic service and at one time was our minister to Belgium. In 1870 he bought a large tract of land on Florida's St. John River, set out extensive orange groves, built a sawmill and store, and founded the village of Sanford. It was at first regarded by natives as a nest of Yankee vipers, for he brought in much Negro help and treated his help well. Later he established a colony of Swedes at New Upsala. He was also one of the projectors and builders of the South Florida Railroad.

Montana received a more typical town builder than Sanford when Paris Gibson arrived. He was a native of Brownfield, Maine, graduated from Bowdoin College in 1851. Gibson was among the Yankee pioneers in Minneapolis, where he made and quickly lost a fortune. In 1879 he moved into Montana, bringing the first large band of sheep in that territory. He made his home at Fort Benton, and got around a good deal. He was struck and greatly taken with a likely townsite near the great falls of the Missouri. With backing from James J. Hill, just then pushing his railroad west from Dakota, he founded the town of Great Falls, marking out wide streets and a fine park system. The railroad came, too, and the village prospered. For the rest of his life Gibson was connected with Great Falls and the development of water power, coal mining, sheep raising, and the building of railroads. In 1901 he was sent to the United States Senate; but his great work was done in the state itself. He liked to be called "the Friend of Reclamation," and he did work much to that end. He had the greatest respect for education, says a biographer, and took an active part in establishing the University of Montana, and worked for its betterment until a week or two of his death, at eighty-five, in 1920.

The first frame house in Gibson's Great Falls was put up by H. P. Rolfe, from Vermont, who had been for a while superintendent of schools in Helena, and for a time editor of the Butte *Miner*. The mayor of Great Falls elected in 1889 was the Hon. J. H. Fairchild, one of the many Maine Fairchilds. An early citizen of Great Falls who became prominent was A. G. Ladd, also from the Pine Tree State.

An unusual pioneer was Benjamin F. White of Massachusetts, who came to help found the town of Dillon looking, said a contemporary, "like a French general of the armies." He was an astute and pervasive man, and in '89 was appointed territorial governor. One of Montana's supreme court judges at the time was Hiram Knowles, native of Hampden, Maine, who made his home in Butte.

What is now Missoula was once called Wordensville in honor of Frank L. Worden, one of the town most effective pioneers. Worden himself asked the legislature to change the name. He was born in Marlboro, Vermont, in 1830, and got to Montana by way of California and Oregon. In 1856 he was fighting Indians as a member of the Oregon Volunteers. Two years later he opened a store at Walla Walla and was appointed first postmaster of that village. Two years more, and he was on his way into Montana, with seventy-five horses loaded with goods to establish a store in the new gold-mining region. The enterprise was highly successful from the first, so much so that it attracted the attention of robbers, who made an abortive attempt to carry off the safe in Worden's one-room log building. There was then no organized law in Montana, but he was a popular man and the Vigilante Committee at near-by Alder Gulch was happy to look into the matter. Presently, four men were hanging from trees, by their necks.

Worden & Company later opened branch stores at Deer Lodge and other new settlements. They put up the finest gristmill in all Montana. They sawed logs into lumber and mine timbers. Worden was one of the founders of Missoula's First National Bank. During the lean years of the *Weekly Missoulian* he financed that paper. In 1883, when the Northern Pacific rails were approaching, he laid out the city streets and was the leading spirit in construction of a city waterworks. When he died in 1887, honored throughout the state, the press hailed him as the Father of Missoula, which, except for his exceptional modesty, would still be Wordensville.

Both Maine and Vermont contributed men who had something to do with the forming of the Dakotas. One was Bartlett Tripp, born in Harmony, Maine, who went west in 1861 to teach in Salt Lake City, then to work as a construction engineer on the Central Pacific portion of the transcontinental railroad. In 1870 he settled in Yankton, Dakota Territory, to practice law, where he encouraged and became one of the incorporators of Yankton College. He later served long and actively as a regent of the University of South Dakota. He was chosen to preside over the territorial convention, and was also appointed chief justice. In 1893, the Honorable Bartlett Tripp became American minister to Austria-Hungary.

When Tripp was presiding over the Dakota convention one of its most voluble delegates was Richard F. Pettigrew, born in Ludlow, Vermont, who had migrated to Wisconsin with his parents and got his education at Yankee Beloit. He moved to Dakota in 1870 and became a leader in the development of Sioux Falls. Although he was a nonconformist in religion and politics, and opposed to all private ownership of land, he was elected one of the first two senators from South Dakota. He wrote books on economic subjects. In his public utterances he was so bitter that his nickname, which pleased rather than irked him, was Old Pale Malice. In 1917 he so bitterly opposed American entry into the war that he was indicted, though never tried, as an obstructionist. He had the indictment handsomely framed and considered it as his most valued possession. To his death, he was a Single Taxer, and in this and in many other ways was a perfect example of the Green Mountain type that for many years made Vermont notorious for its ferments. A more conventional Vermonter, Charles H. Sheldon, born in Johnson, was South Dakota's governor during 1892–1896.

In 1890 citizens of the new state of Wyoming elected a Yankee to the governor's chair, Francis E. Warren, native of Hinsdale, Massachusetts, who had already been chief executive of the territory and mayor of booming Cheyenne; later he was sent to the United States Senate, where he worked for woman suffrage and fought valiantly against the Eighteenth Amendment.

Warren was a rugged type, fit to get along anywhere. As a youth he had worked on his father's farm in Massachusetts, then enlisted for the Civil War, during which he won a Congressional Medal of Honor. In 1868 he migrated to Cheyenne and went into sheep raising, in which he became the patriarch. The Warren Livestock Company was one of the great ranch outfits in Wyoming. Senator Warren died in 1929, in office, the last Union veteran in Congress. (Incidentally, his daughter became the wife of Captain John J. Pershing.) Wyoming elected another Yankee governor in 1898, in De Forest Richards, born in Charlestown, New Hampshire, who had come as a banker to Wyoming in the eighties.

In 1900 the Twelfth Census could not discover sufficient New England natives in Wyoming to warrant a listing. Yankees were there, of course, and Yankees continued to move in—mostly, one would judge, as individuals or as a family here, another family there. They generally did not arrive direct from New England, but came from some western state or other; and the only way one can know of them is through one of their number such as Foster A. Hovey and his wife, citizens of Greybull, on Wyoming's Bighorn River.

I have never met the Hoveys, though they and I used to live a few miles apart in Vermont; but through correspondence Mr. Hovey, who is obviously of a keen and a reflective mind, has given me a much better idea of Yankee immigration into Wyoming than I have been able to get from books.

"You are quite correct," Mr. Hovey wrote in 1948, "in your assumption that I myself hardly know why I came West. It was probably but certainly not wholly an economic urge. In 1918 I was working on the St. Johnsbury & Lake Champlain Railroad [a local line in northern Vermont] and stationed at Morrisville. It did not appear that either myself or the railroad had a very brilliant future. I was discontented; felt somehow shut in. I wanted to burst out and go to far places and get rich, just a slightly older version of the small-boy complex to go out West to shoot buffaloes and scalp Indians.

"I recall, on the day before I was to leave, swaggering into a Morrisville barber shop. You will understand, of course, that a barber shop is second only to the smoking compartment of a Pullman car as a place that inspires men to lie and brag about themselves. Well, I got into the chair for a haircut and told the barber, as well as the usual audience, that I was going Out West, but that I would return one day before long and buy the entire town of Morrisville. They are still waiting, thirty years after, and so am I.

"Now, as to Yankees in the West, one can find one in almost any town in almost any state. I have ranged a good deal and have never failed to find a stray Vermonter wherever I stopped long enough to get my breath. My first work in the West was for the Santa Fe railroad, at Oakland, California, where there were many natives of Vermont. Later, I was moved to Flagstaff, Arizona, and had been there but a few days when a man stuck his head in the window and said he had heard that Vermont had gone Democratic. I asked him what he knew about Vermont. He replied that he had been born in Essex Junction. Before leaving Flagstaff, we found a woman who was born in my wife's home town of St. Johnsbury.

"When I first landed in Wyoming at Worland, I was immediately introduced to the Babbitt brothers, from Rutland. When I moved to Basin, I found there a lawyer from Bellows Falls. It was the same here in Greybull, where we discovered a man from Richmond and a woman from North Danville. And many years later, we met a woman living on a sheep ranch thirty miles out of town who was born in St. Johnsbury.

"None of these Vermonters in Wyoming had come directly, but sort of filtered in, after living in one or two other western states.

"As to the reasons for Yankee emigration, there is no easy explanation. I believe there is something in the theory that we all naturally look toward the West. You will remember that Thoreau said that whenever he went walking without a fixed goal, he found himself subconsciously trending westward. Old bee keepers have a tradition that a swarm of bees always moves westward.

"I remember reading that Calvin Coolidge was proud of the fact that none of his ancestors ever went West. Why he was proud of it, I don't know; but it is a curious fact, as I well remember in my native town of Albany, Vermont, that a person who emigrated West was looked upon much in the light of a deserter to the flag. I recall hearing my elders speak in a most contemptuous tone of a former resident: 'Oh, he went out West, somewheres.' That properly disposed of *him,* and the conversation might then turn to something of importance, such as the scandalously low price being paid for maple sugar."

A native of the old Bay State was prominently identified with both Wyoming and Nebraska. John Milton Thayer, born in Bellingham, Massachusetts, served a term as governor of Wyoming Territory, two terms as governor of Nebraska, which also elected him to the United States Senate. Thayer was an early settler, moving with his family to Omaha when it was hardly a hamlet. He later commanded volunteer troops against the Pawnees. He was a graduate of Brown, and so too was the Reverend C. B. Thomas of Duxbury, Massachusetts, a Unitarian pastor who came to Omaha in 1868 to assume editorial control of the *Daily Tribune,* a power in early Nebraska.

Omaha also attracted "the most remarkable man of this, or any other, age," who was none other than George Francis Train, native of Boston, perhaps as brilliant and surely as eccentric a person as nineteenth century America produced. That is saying a good deal, but Train certainly had few if any peers in an age when individualism flourished. Author, merchant, promoter in various parts of the world, he called himself the Champion Crank and devoted most of his life to living up to the title.

Although best remembered as the man who actually made a trip around the world in eighty days, Train had genuine ability; his influence on American shipping was great and so, too, on the successful promotion of the street railroad in England, which in an age dominated by Tories must have indeed been a task. He had made and spent much of two fortunes when in 1865 he directed his attention to Omaha, headquarters for the men engaged in building the Union Pacific Railroad which he helped to promote. He bought land in Omaha and its sister-town, Council Bluffs, Iowa, to a total of 6,000 city lots; and 7,000 more lots in Columbus—west of Omaha—which he declared should be made the national capital just as soon as he was elected President of the United States and could get around to having the records and such moved from Washington.* He also built many houses for sale in Omaha and Columbus, and in the former erected the splendid Cozzens Hotel.

* The population of Columbus, Nebr., in 1940 was 7,632.

Another Yankee, who came to be rated in early Nebraska as "a financial Khan whose duplicate cannot be found," was James M. Pattee, of Enfield, New Hampshire, surely one of the few Americans who could honestly claim to be the descendant of Shakers. Pattee's grandfather had joined the thriving Shaker colony on Mascoma Lake, in Enfield township, and had there fallen in love with a Shaker girl. Because the Shakers forbade all cohabitation, married or otherwise, Pattee and the girl, who "returned his regard," fled the colony and were married. Their grandson James taught school in New Hampshire, married, and in 1854 with his wife made a tour of the West. He invested in lands in Iowa and Nebraska so well and so shrewdly that by 1871 he received the Khan rating from an Omaha writer on eminent Nebraskans.

It is only proper that at least one native of Corinna, Maine, appeared in the migration to Nebraska, for, as pointed out again and again, this small town seems to have been the source of a continuous movement into all of the West. In 1870, after pioneering in Illinois (1844), in Wisconsin (1860), and in Boone County, Iowa (1864), where he founded a paper, the *Advocate,* Benjamin F. Hilton and wife Priscilla, both natives of Corinna, moved again, this time to Lincoln, Nebraska, where they opened a hotel.

Nebraska seems somehow to have been the final harbor for many a Yankee argonaut. Consider James N. Noteware, born in Sheffield, Massachusetts, in 1817, who went to Illinois in 1844, joined the gold rush to California in 1850, recrossed the plains in 1857 to settle in Kansas, moved to Colorado in 1860, and seven years later settled down in Omaha to engage in real estate activities. The fact that Mr. Noteware became state supervisor of immigration probably did not damage his private occupation, it being a custom in the best tradition for early settlers to mix politics and business to some purpose.

Yes, Nebraska was often the last port. There was Asa C. Briggs, a Vermonter, who moved first to Kalamazoo, Michigan, then to Iowa for five years, and in 1861 to Nebraska's Dodge County, where he went to farming and into the state legislature. Even old sea captains who had been all over and back again liked Nebraska. Thomas F. Hall, a native of East Dennis on Cape Cod, had been under sail as cabin boy and in almost every other capacity including master; yet in 1866 he gave it up and moved to Omaha, where he established the first foundry and machine shop in the territory.

The town of Beatrice, Nebraska, was laid out and organized and settled by a mixed group from Illinois, a leading member of which was Obadiah B. Hewett, from Hope, Maine. One of the earliest settlers in Pawnee County was a Maine man with a perfect Maine name—Eben Jordan of Lewiston. One of his neighbors was William H. Curtis, a leading storekeeper, who had come from Portland. The true Yankee religion was not wholly neglected in early Nebraska, for in 1856 the Reverend L. B. Fifield, native of Eastport, Maine, who had studied at Amherst and had later "gathered a Congregational church in Cedar Falls, Iowa," moved to Lincoln, where he acted as chaplain at the constitutional convention and preached in the Lincoln Congregational church.

The majority of early Nebraska settlers appear to have come, about equally, from Illinois and Missouri. But there were many from New England. In 1900 Yankees living there totaled almost 12,000, of whom the greatest number were from Massachusetts, followed in order by Vermont, Maine, Connecticut, New Hampshire, and Rhode Island. The Yankee total compares with that of Colorado for the same year. The Yankees in Colorado made considerable stir, and the record of their influence on the state is clear. But, for some reason or other, the local historians in Nebraska commonly failed to note the native states of its pioneers. In a majority of cases, the Nebraska pioneer simply appears on the scene as though he had grown straight up out of the Nebraska soil.*

New England influence in early Idaho is hard to find, yet one character there in pioneer times made considerable stir. This was Edward C. Holbrook, born of Yankee parents at Elyria on Connecticut's Western Reserve. Although he was exposed for a while to the influences of Oberlin College, he liked neither these influences nor the Yankees themselves. He turned up in wild Idaho about 1863 after spending some time in California, and in 1864, while still in his early twenties, was elected the first territorial delegate to Washington. He was a rabid Democrat, and often said he regretted he had not been born in South Carolina. Delegate Holbrook was reported by H. H. Bancroft "to have drank freely of whiskey, and had much pluck and assurance, although his attainments were mediocre." Holbrook later was shot in the back and killed in front of his law office in Boise.

There is buried in Bozeman, Montana, the source of the great, the incomparable example of Yankee "influence" in the Far West, where the

---

* Still, it is possible to discover several Vermonters among the pioneers: Lawson Sheldon from Ludlow, who in spite of being a Freethinker was rated a first-class citizen of Cass County, together with his wife, who had been Julia Pollard; Waldo Lyon of Orleans, and wife Lydia Hall, from Claremont, N.H., who located in Burt County; David J. Quimby, from Grand Island, who settled in the district of L'Eau Qui Court; James A. Kenaston, from Cabot, who homesteaded in Cass County; James Clark, from Johnson, who built the first flouring mill in Dakota County; and Elipha Clark, from Johnson, who settled in Seward County. Many of the photographs of Nebraska pioneers were taken by Vermonter Edric Eaton, who opened a shop in Omaha. Although the personal habits of these Vermonters are not now known, one is glad to find that Charles G. Smith, from Worcester, Mass., who settled in Falls City, Nebr., had "unyielding habits of temperance, using neither tobacco nor alcoholic liquors of any kind."

name "Comstock" is known as perhaps is none other; for Comstock still retains the aura of precious metal and the effulgence of Nevada's great era, when the Comstock Lode bloomed wealth upon which was erected a sudden and hectic civilization. Henry Tompkins Paige Comstock, born in 1820 of the oldest Connecticut stock, was at best a dubious character; yet, of all the migrating Yankees, his name is the best known, the one surest to conjure up a time and a place.

Henry Comstock was the son of parents who migrated from Connecticut to York State, then to Canada, then to Ohio, and at last to Blissfield, Michigan, where Comstock Senior engaged in logging. Young Henry left home at an early age, to trap for the American Fur Company. He got into the Black Hawk War, then into our war with Mexico, and in 1850 was in the California gold rush, where he became something of a character and was known as Old Pancake, because of his favorite, or at least his usual, food. In the mid-fifties he meandered over the mountains to arrive, as ragged, dirty, and shiftless as could be imagined, in what is now Nevada. Prospectors had been working in this region for several years, but to no effect. Old Pancake roamed around, and at last happened on Peter O'Riley and Patrick McLaughlin who had just discovered what looked like pretty good diggings in placer gold. Comstock, as greedy as he was dirty and noisy, immediately began to bluster. He had, he said, long since staked this ground for his claim, and what was more, he was not going to stand idle and see it jumped by any come-lately. He and his alleged partner, one Manny Penrod, would take the matter to the United State Supreme Court if need be, to see that justice was done. Old Pancake was so boisterous and apparently so determined that the two Irishers gave in. Comstock had talked himself into a four-way partnership.

For the next couple of months the four men washed out several hundred dollars in gold every day. They sent a sample for assay to San Francisco, the news got out—and quiet times in the Washoe country were over. Footloose California started moving into the district, first scores, then hundreds. The boom was on. And soon, in the best tradition of mine strikes time out of mind, the proprietors of what was about to go into history as the Comstock Lode, were given their come-uppance. Here it should be borne in mind that the Lode paid out at least four hundred millions of dollars in gold and silver. Of the four men in the original partnership claim, McLaughlin sold first. He got $3,500. Penrod held out a few days and received $8,000. Old Pancake howled and blustered awhile longer and realized $11,000 for a property, as has been remarked, that had "cost him half an hour of arguments and threats." Pat O'Riley was the really tough one to buy out. He held for $40,000 and got it.

Old Pancake promptly invested his $11,000 in a store in Carson City and just as promptly went broke. He left Nevada to wander over into Oregon, then Idaho, and at last to Montana, where he looked in vain for other Comstock Lodes. He made his base of operations at Bozeman, and near that town he died in 1870, under mysterious circumstances, a victim either of murder or suicide.* Thus lived and died the Yankee who contributed nothing to the West except his name; and his name survives, one is prepared to believe, just because he talked more and louder than any one, or any two, or any three of his partners in the Washoe claim.

The loudest talkers in the West were often the promoters of towns and cities. Every new region, as it was opened to settlement, was fairly acrawl with imaginative men. A few of these heralds of Metropolis were doubtless honest souls, if badly mistaken—poets at heart, wholly carried away with their visions of tremendous centers of business and commerce rising almost overnight out of the prairie, or emerging like wood and brick mushrooms out of the clearings in the forest. Ignatius Donnelly, he of *Atlantis* and *The Great Cryptogram* and Populism, was one of these few, an honest man who founded Nininger, Minnesota, not for the purpose of getting rich, but in an attempt to attract the very best class of people who would make Nininger the Athens of the West. Nininger boomed in 1856; in 1857, the gophers and the owls were returning to their old haunts from which Donnelly and his few settlers had driven them.

Then, there were the synthetic cities dreamed up for the express purpose of selling lots to gulls. Their number was almost without end. It rose and fell with the times but was never small. So long as gulls remained, energetic men were prepared to sell them land on the Broadways and the Tremont Streets of a continuous series of new Manhattans and Bostons that studded the landscape between the Genesee River and the Pacific Ocean, from the Yazoo River to the Canadian border.

More often than not, the very land of these city lots was not owned by the people who sold them, but was merely held on option by the promoters. Thus, the promoters' investment in land was very small, and such capital as they had could be expanded where it would do the most good—which was to say in printing and lithographing. No synthetic city could survive a month without a printing press. Indeed, it could hardly come into being without one. And almost always there was a most talented artist.

It was just such a combination of imaginative text and art, and not any idealistic urge to make the prairie Free Soil that fetched John J. Ingalls to

---

* What became of Manny Penrod, a shadowy character, isn't known. He simply disappeared. The other partners did no better than Comstock with their money. O'Riley lost his $40,000 in speculation, went insane, and died a pauper, as did McLaughlin, who never rose above the status of a $40-a-month cook.

Kansas. It was in 1858. Young Ingalls was reading law in a Boston office. He had never felt the urge to go west, to Kansas or elsewhere, when there fell into his hands a lithographed poster and description of the wondrous place which Promoter John P. Wheeler said was hustling, growing, throbbing, metropolitan Sumner, Kansas, surely the mightiest city west of Manhattan Island. Young John Ingalls took a long, dazed look at the lithograph. He read the accompanying text. He quit his job. On October 4 that same year he arrived in Sumner, Kansas, and got a shock from which he never fully recovered. Said Senator Ingalls in his later, mellow days:

"That chromatic triumph of lithographed mendacity, supplemented by the loquacious embellishments of a lively adventurer who had been laying out townsites for some years past in Tophet, exhibited a scene in which the attractions of art, nature, science, commerce, and religion were artistically blended. Innumerable drays were transporting from a fleet of gorgeous steamboats vast cargoes of foreign and domestic merchandise over Russ pavements to colossal warehouses of brick and stone. Dense, wide streets of elegant residences rose with gentle accent from the shores of the tranquil stream. Numerous parks, decorated with rare trees, shrubbery, and fountains were surrounded by mansions of the great and the temples of their devotion. The adjacent eminences were crowned with costly piles which wealth, directed by intelligence and controlled by taste, had erected for the education of the rising generation of Sumnerites.

"The only shadow upon this enchanting landscape," continued Senator Ingalls, "the only shadow fell from the clouds of smoke that poured from towering shafts of her acres of manufactories, while the whole circumference of the undulating prairie was white with endless, sinuous trains of wagons, slowly moving toward the mysterious region of Farther West."

What the young Ingalls *saw* with his own eyes on that desolating October 4, 1858, was a board shack or two, and a trail of mud, resumably a road, that led off from a jerry-built boat landing into nowhere. Ingalls did not trouble to get off the boat at Sumner, but went on another three miles to the settlement called Atchison.

At the same period, Sol Miller arrived in White Cloud, Kansas, to found a weekly paper, the *Kansas Chief,* and in his first number took occasion to let go a blast against a synthetic city of the neighborhood. "A company of capitalists from Buncombe County, North Carolina," he wrote, "have recently arrived in the Territory, and purchased a gopher hole, in a high bluff on the river, where they have laid out a new town, appropriately named Gopher City. The place already contains a first-class whiskey shop (kept by a church member in good standing), a gas mill, one dry goods store, one ox-team, three speculators' offices, and one private residence. . . . The town must necessarily become the most important point on the Missouri River above New Orleans."

Editor Miller went on to say that the town plat of Gopher City was to be seen displayed in all country stores throughout the United States, and, rising to fine sarcasm, vowed that Gopher City had a permanent landing at all seasons, for the bluff on which it was built was, during high water, quite near the river. He was sure, he said, the town would be the terminus of the Wind Line & Gasport Railroad, and that the whole country, as far as the Pacific Ocean, would be dependent on Gopher City for supplies of grog and tobacco. One had better buy lots *now,* he added, because every time a stranger inquired the price of a share in the townsite, it was advanced 50 per cent.

Seriously, said Miller, there was hardly a store or tavern in the eastern United States that did not display town plats and other advertising matter of "some large city in Kansas or Nebraska, a majority of which did not contain a single house."

Fifty-odd years later, I myself watched the erection, on paper, of a stupendous metropolis along the Grand Trunk Pacific, now the Canadian National Railway, in the remote wilds of the province of Alberta. This mighty mart of commerce was called Wainwright. The time was the spring of 1911. I had just arrived in Winnipeg, Manitoba, fresh from high school in New England, and within a few days had taken a job in the office of the promoter of Wainwright.

All western Canada was then in a frenzied boom that continued for another two or three years. Winnipeg was an exciting place. Thirty or more hotel hacks, horse-drawn, met all the trains, and the cries of the drivers extolling the merits of the Queen's, the Clarendon, the Wellington, and other places created a terrific din to greet the traveler. Main Street from City Hall north to the shacks of Little Russia and Little Poland was lined with little hotels, all with large bars, that alternated with real estate offices, penny arcades, and movie and variety theaters. Portage Avenue had a higher tone, though it too was largely infested with land sharks whose places of business exhibited immense, brilliant, and imaginative paintings of the scores of new settlements destined for great things. Apparently, almost every acre of land in all that vast region between Winnipeg and Vancouver was for sale; and on many of these acres was to arise this or that city beside which Toronto—or even London in England—would presently be as a quaint hamlet. Even their names were fascinating, at least to an Easterner—Medicine Hat, Willow Bunch, Moosomin, Athabaska Landing, Swift Current, Plum Coulee, Wetaskiwin, and incomparable Moose Jaw.

Winnipeg and all western Canada were the goal of hundreds of thousands of immigrants who had come from the British Isles and from every country in Europe, with Russia and Poland leading; and of perhaps another hundred thousand Americans, who sold their farms in the Dakotas and other western states, and moved into the prairie provinces. Western Canada was the story of western United States all over again, half a century later.

The promoter of what he called Central Park in Wainwright, Alberta, was a small dynamic Englishman who, so the courts later established, had been an adventurer in many lands and had already made and lost a couple of fortunes before he turned his talents to the metropolis of Wainwright. For thirty days, or until I became aware of what really went on, I was in his main office on Winnipeg's main street. In spite of my tender years, I was no office boy, either. I was a counter man, and over the counter I accepted the cash for lots in Central Park. I did not have to *sell them*. Money was pressed upon us by the gulls who came in and demanded to purchase these astonishing bargains.

Our literature did not have too much to say concerning the condition of Wainwright of the present moment. Doubtless the promoter had learned just how far he could go with pure imagination. He did not discuss Wainwright's population, nor its homes and business edifices, though the huge oil painting of Central Park in our window certainly indicated a population of around 100,000 people. We in the office were told to discuss the future of Wainwright, and to ignore its present. That is, except for one thing: The one overpowering reason for buying lots in Central Park, which incidentally was between the four- and five-mile circles from a non-existent city hall, was that the Dominion (federal) government had already stationed there a herd of the romantic and disappearing bison called buffalo. Somehow, this fact, which our literature and salesmen drove home, as though it were an oil field, or a gold mine, or a source of water power and irrigation—this fact of the presence of a herd of bison was considered reason enough for buying a lot now, while the price remained a mere $150 for a fifty-foot-front lot. Nor were we of Central Park avaricious; there was no extra charge for a corner lot. Yet, there was in all truth, a qualification, for we specified, "Purchaser must buy four lots to secure a corner lot."

And how they bought! A continuous stream of maniacs came into the office all day long, and into the evening. I recall accepting money from one deaf and dumb man; and at least one Yankee from Maine pressed money upon us. A majority of the suckers, however, were Englishmen, fresh from the Old Country, wearing the tight trousers, the caps, and the low-cut linen collars that marked them in the eyes of Canadians and Americans. One and all, they purchased a lot in the fast-growing city where an ever wise government had established a refuge for the conservation of several hundred head of the plains buffalo. Nor did any of the suckers quibble, nor ask embarassing questions concerning the state of activity or progress in Wainwright or in Wainwright's magnificent Central Park. They looked at the great gorgeous painting in the window, they gazed at the plat itself, they chose a lot, they paid, and they went away.

So did I, at the end of a month. From that day to this I have occasionally wondered how things went with Central Park, Wainwright, Alberta, though I never developed sufficient curiosity to find out. The place did not, I'm sure, outstrip London, or even Toronto. Its population, in the latest census, was 980; and this, I suppose, included even the denizens of Central Park. For all I know, that beautiful suburb is still in the primeval state that obtained in 1911, when all western Canada was filled with poets or dreamers. As for the boom, it went the way of all other booms; but not before farms, and even city lots, had been sold in every quarter of the tremendous region separating Winnipeg and Vancouver, and as far north as the shores of the Great Slave Lake.

Anyone who witnessed the insanity in western Canada, in 1910–1913 will have been forced to the belief that the urge to gamble on a city lot in some far-off place where the loon still cries and the foxes bark, must be almost as basic in human nature as the urge for something to eat. In those four years the frontier of western Canada was exterminated, at least technically; somebody had to survey and stake out those city lots in Central Park, Wainwright, and those others lots and farms that reached almost to the Arctic Circle.

As for the technical frontier in western United States, the superintendent of the census remarked, as long ago as 1890, that it had come to an end. True, there was still a number of territories to be made into states during the next two decades; and settlers in states as old as Minnesota and Wisconsin, to say nothing of Oregon and Washington, were still grubbing stumps, still living far from railroads, and some of them still and rightly enough lived in fear of Indian attacks. These people would not have agreed with the census man's statement about the disappearance of the frontier. Technically, however, he was right. "Up to and including 1880," he wrote in 1890, "the country had a frontier of settlement, but at present the unsettled area has been so broken by isolated bodies of settlement that there can hardly be said to be a frontier line." And then he put matters in their proper place. "In the discussion of its extent, its western movement, etc.," he wrote bluntly, "the frontier cannot, therefore, any longer have a place in the census reports."

Where were the displaced Yankees when the frontier came to an end? Twenty years after, or in 1910, the state nearest to New England, or New

York, contained 93,000 Yankees who had been "born in New England of native white parents living in the United States in 1850." This was the largest state-group of theoretically pure Yankees living outside New England. Next was California, whose Yankees of the same status numbered 46,800. Third in line was Illinois, with 25,200. New Jersey, with 21,300, was fourth. Pennsylvania and Washington were almost tied, the former with 16,600, the latter with 16,300; and Minnesota contained 16,200. Of the remaining states only Michigan, Ohio, Wisconsin, and Iowa could muster more than 10,000 each, although Colorado almost reached that figure.

Oregon and Kansas were almost in a tie: the former having 7,400 Yankees; the latter, 7,300. Indiana, not surprisingly, could muster only 3,900; and of all of the states shown in the survey, Utah had the fewest, or 1,200 Yankees.*

Neither this survey nor any other shows or could show the occupations of the hordes of Yankees living outside New England. It is safe to say, however, that in 1910 a goodly number of them were schoolteachers of one sort or another. The same would have been true of Yankee emigrants in 1880, or in 1840, and also perhaps as early as 1800. In a majority of the original settlements, all the way from Ohio to California, and often in long established communities in the border states and in the Deep South, as well as in New York City, the Yankee schoolmaster, and later the Yankee school-marm, was something of an institution, often much more.

* See Rufus Stickney Tucker, in the *New England Historical and Genealogical Register,* Vol. LXXVI (1922).

CHAPTER XX

THE EDUCATORS GO FORTH

THE DEVIL was a most real character in New England. He did not employ messengers, as did the Lord with His angels, but took care of all his earthly communication needs in person, sometimes, to be sure, as a disembodied voice, merely whispering his hideous suggestions, but often in the flesh, man to man—yea, even man to maid. The Devil's labors were vast, but his industry was equal to the work in hand, and thus he got around a great deal, earning the reputation of being the most diligent preacher of all.

Happily, if ironically, the Devil did the Yankees more service than either he or they imagined; for when the Yankees became convinced, as they did quite early, that among the Devil's most cherished projects was to keep them from learning to read, lest they thus be able to decipher God's word in the Book, why, it then obviously became the duty of Yankees to see that none of their fellows remained in the darkness of illiteracy. Because learning, like rum, created an appetite which could feed only on more of itself, the Yankee grammar schools multiplied and spread, academies and institutes were founded, many of them to grow into colleges; and there came in a little to be schools for women, for the blind, for the deaf, the backward, and even schools for the teaching of teachers.

The profession of arms never stood in high favor in New England after the end of the Revolution; and the region has perhaps produced less than its share of eminent statesmen, including presidents. But in the realm of education the Yankees early took the lead. They have held it to the present day.*

Originally, Yankees considered education only as an adjunct of religion. This idea resulted in the parson-teacher, who instructed his young charges during the week, and on the Sabbath delivered the word of God to old and

* Yankees stand high in many fields. A table showing the number of natives listed in *Who's Who in America* to each 100,000 population has Vermont at the very top with 85.3; New Hampshire second with 68.9; Maine third with 64.4; Massachusetts fourth with 51.2; Connecticut sixth with 40.0; and Rhode Island eighth with 37.7.

young alike. For two hundred years and more a majority of Yankee schoolmasters were also preachers. And ever since emigration from New England
began, schoolmasters, and in time schoolmarms, have been an integral part
of the exodus.

That educators are seldom rated by the American public as heroes, and
seldom granted the monetary reward bestowed on practitioners of medicine,
or the law, is a commonplace. Yankee lawyers and doctors moved west in
astonishing numbers, and many of them achieved comparative wealth. So
did Yankee businessmen of all sorts, from fur traders to industrialists and
merchants. Yet, it can scarcely be a matter of doubt that the lawyers, the
doctors, the businessmen, taken all together, had less influence of a lasting
kind in far places of the Republic than the uncounted thousands of Yankee
educators. Here was New England's great and incomparable export. There
is no state, and scarcely a portion of any state, that has not felt at some time
or other the impact of the Yankee schoolteacher. From the metropolis of
New York to the far reaches of Montana and Texas, to the back counties
of Arkansas and Georgia, to say nothing of Alaska and Hawaii, or even
of Asia and Africa, the figure of the Yankee schoolteacher has found his
or her way, and left an impression, no matter how small or confined.

The exodus of more or less learned Yankees started long before the
Revolution. At Elizabeth Town, New Jersey, in September of 1709, the
pulpit of the Congregational church was taken over by the young and
Reverend Jonathan Dickinson, a graduate of Yale who had been born in Hatfield, Massachusetts. With great tact and considerable shrewdness he herded
his flock into the Presbyterian fold, and held them safely, cutting down on
sight any tendencies to wander; and meanwhile he laid plans for an institution of higher learning, one that should not only produce Presbyterian ministers, but also "serve in a broad sense the whole community." His first
attempt for a charter was turned down by the Anglican governor of New
Jersey, but was granted by a successor, also an Anglican. In May of 1747
the college was formally opened in Elizabeth Town, with President Jonathan
Dickinson in charge. A little later it was moved to Princeton, where it took
and retained the name of that town.

At about this time a Yankee who had migrated to Philadelphia wrote
and issued a pamphlet urging more and better education in Pennsylvania.
This was the work of Benjamin Franklin from Boston, who went on to
found a nonsectarian school which became the University of Pennsylvania.
And it was Franklin, too, who is usually credited with founding, in 1765,
the first school of medicine in the colonies.

New Yorkers have long since forgotten that when their Anglican forebears got around to establishing King's College, in 1754, they reached up to small Stratford, in Connecticut, for a man to head the institution. He was Samuel Johnson, born in Guilford, a Yale graduate who had left the Congregational clergy to open the first building in Connecticut dedicated to Church of England services. Good Mr. Johnson wanted to remain in Stratford, to combat the established Congregational or State church; but when the Anglicans of New York City told him their plans for an Episcopalian college would fail without him, he gave up his pulpit and took upon himself the first presidency of King's. Thirty-odd years later his own son, William Samuel Johnson, was called to become the first president of what had been King's but was then and since Columbia.

The tradition of Yankee presidents for Columbia did not cease, for in 1811 the trustees installed in that office William Harris, a Harvard man who had taught school in an academy at Marblehead. In 1864 they elected one of the great educators of the nineteenth century, Frederick Barnard, native of Sheffield, Massachusetts, who was to head Columbia for a quarter of a century and build it into the great university of the present era.

Frederick Augustus Porter Barnard, born in 1809, had performed wonders elsewhere before he came to Columbia. After graduation from Yale he taught in the public schools of Hartford and in a so-called deaf and dumb school there. In 1837 he went to the University of Alabama to teach natural history and mathematics. In 1854 he began teaching the same subjects at the University of Mississippi where, in spite of his nativity and accent, he was made president. In 1864 he came to head Columbia, and remained until his death in 1889. His name is perpetuated in the women's division of the present university.

There was still time, after the founding of Princeton and Columbia, for the establishment of at least one more eighteenth century college in the United States. This was Hamilton, at Clinton, New York, a labor of Samuel Kirkland's love for the Oneida Indians. Kirkland, incidentally the father of a president of Harvard, was a native of Norwich, Connecticut. He studied under the great Eleazar Wheelock, founder of Dartmouth College and teacher to the Indians, and was inspired by Wheelock's work to go forth and do likewise, in New York State. A kindly, wise, and courageous man, Kirkland lived as and with the Oneidas for many years. In 1793, with the approval of President Washington and the promise of support from Alexander Hamilton, he established Hamilton Oneida Academy, using his own lands and funds for the purpose. A little later the school received a charter as Hamilton College, and to head it came another Yankee from Norwich, Connecticut, named Azel Backus. With the help of several other Yankee presidents and an endless procession of Yankee professors, Hamilton went on to great success that continues more than a century and a half after its founding.*

One of the most precocious schoolmasters in the early days of the Yankee exodus was a Massachusetts man, Jonathan Maxcy, of Attleboro. At the age of twenty-three he became president of Rhode Island College, later Brown University, which "flourished under his administration, and his fame was extended over every other section of the Union." At the age of thirty-four, he resigned to take over the presidency of new Union College at Schenectady, New York, where ill health caused him to leave two years later. Thereupon he moved to the South and was invited to become the first president of the University of South Carolina. He accepted and for the next fifteen years labored hard to make the school something more than the mere academy of its plans. In 1820 Maxcy died, aged fifty-two, a past president of three colleges.

When Maxcy left Union College there followed him in the presidency a Yankee schoolmaster from Ashford, Connecticut, who had founded an academy at Cherry Valley, New York, and held pulpits in Congregational and Presbyterian churches. This was Eliphalet Nott, who came to head Union in 1804 and remained for sixty-two years, probably an unprecedented period in the annals of higher education. Nott found the college in hard straits financially. Lotteries, if for "good" purposes, were not then considered sinful, at least by President Nott, who proceeded by herculean effort to establish and manage a number of "drawings" which put the college on a firm foundation. Nott also moved Union College into the ranks of the Abolitionists as early as 1811. He had a hobby, too, which was research in the properties of heat; and, Yankee that he was, he invented and patented the first base-burning stove for the use of anthracite coal, which had no little influence in promoting that type of fuel, until then generally considered worthless. All in all, President Nott of Union College probably possessed more of the several so-called Yankee characteristics than are commonly given, even to a Yankee schoolmaster.

To succeed the aged Nott, Union chose another New Englander, Laurens Perseus Hickok, of Bethel, Connecticut, a huge man with a massive head, robust health, and boundless energy who once upon a time, as a young preacher in Connecticut, had been charged by his flock with unministerial conduct, such as "whistling, vaulting fences, running on the streets, and driving a fast horse." Any one of these monstrous indictments had been sufficient, on occasion, to remove a pastor in Connecticut, but Hickok sur-

* Hamilton's third president was Sereno Edwards Dwight, of Greenfield Hill, Conn.; its fifth, Simeon North, of Berlin, Conn.; its seventh, Samuel G. Brown of North Yarmouth, Me. Among Hamilton's most celebrated alumni in 1949 is Samuel Hopkins Adams, class of '91.

vived them and went west to teach at Western Reserve, where surely there
was little of whistling and even less of fast horses; and then to Union, where
in 1866 he became president.

*A wise man will hear, and will increase learning. . . . The fear of the
Lord is the beginning of knowledge; but fools despise wisdom and instruction.*

It seemed to matter little which denomination was founding a new college;
all of them commonly looked toward New England for a head. When the
Methodists of western New York got around to establishing Genesee College,
later Syracuse University, they invited the Reverend Joseph Cummings,
native of Falmouth, Maine, to be its president. When the Baptists of Rochester, New York, decided to have a university, they brought in Martin B.
Anderson, native of Brunswick, Maine, to get things under way. The first
president of Episcopal-founded Geneva, later Hobart, College, in York
State, was Jasper Adams, born in East Medway, Massachusetts, who already
had served as president of Charleston College in South Carolina.

Let the Devil raise his head where he would, there came an imported
Yankee schoolmaster-divine to hammer it back into the dark and to cause
light to beat upon the spot. There was the truly remarkable Joseph Estabrook,
born in Lebanon, New Hampshire, (Dartmouth, 1815), who came to Knox-
ville to be the first president of what developed into the University of
Tennessee. Despite his birth and background, Estabrook was not wholly in
the Yankee canon. He was something of a dandy, given to elegant clothes,
a prodigious use of snuff, and, worse, shooting on the Sabbath. But he had
taught at Amherst, both academy and college, and had married Nancy, one
of the Dickinson sisters. In 1824 he and wife moved to Staunton, Virginia,
where he conducted a polite school for young ladies who were doubtless
known as the fairest flowers of the Old Dominion. Then, in 1834, he took
the helm of East Tennessee College, which he held with a stout hand for
sixteen years, performing miracles with the aid of the crew of Yankee professors he imported from Hanover, New Hampshire. The college prospered
and flourished, going on to become the state university. But at the height
of his success President Estabrook resigned, to spend the remainder of his
life, and such money as he had accumulated, in a futile effort to produce
salt by a new process.

Was there need in Missouri to scotch the Adversary? It seemed so, and
in 1873 there came to Springfield, to organize and head Drury College,
the Congregational Reverend Nathan J. Morrison, born in Sanbornton,
New Hampshire, who had earned degrees at both Dartmouth and Oberlin,
then served as president of Olivet College in Michigan. After fifteen years

at Drury, he taught awhile at Marietta in Ohio, then moved to Kansas where, at the age of sixty-seven, he took hold of small, and poor, and discouraged Fairmount Institute at Wichita, and in a dozen years of vast labors raised it to college rank. It is now the Municipal University of Wichita.

Was the Devil in Georgia? Down from Middlebury College in Vermont went Alonzo Church, his "piercing black eyes, graceful and dignified carriage and quick temper marking him as a positive character," to take over the presidency of Georgia University at Athens and to rule both faculty and students with great assurance. Church died in Athens, in 1862, while his sons and sons-in-law were fighting on the side of the South.

It did not matter whether education was to be public or private, nor in what state of the Union—a Yankee was certain to be in the middle of it. The father of the public-school system in St. Louis was William G. Eliot of New Bedford, Massachusetts. In 1835 he organized the first Congregational society in the Missouri metropolis. A few years later he was elected head of the city school board, which in theory, and only in theory, provided for public instruction. The board had no funds, and virtually no schools. Eliot, a man of small and frail physique, was a bundle of energy. In a year's time he had conceived and secured enactment of a law providing for a tax specifically for educational purposes; and on this he erected the city's school system, excellent for the time. In 1853 Eliot Seminary (later Washington University) was granted a state charter and opened its doors. Yankee though he was, Eliot remained during the war years and labored to keep Missouri in the Union. In later years he came to display certain characteristics typical of the Yankee schoolmaster—or, for that matter, of almost any Yankee— and came out for temperance, for woman suffrage, and against legalized prostitution.

More than one Yankee schoolmaster was forced to leave the border and Southern states as Rebel oratory moved toward Secession and war. Yankee John Almanza Rowley Rogers was escorted out of Berea, Kentucky, by a large and mean armed mob. He was a native of Cromwell, Connecticut, but a product of Oberlin College. In 1858, with support of the American Missionary Association, he and his wife went to Berea where a native, John Gregg Fee, had established a nonsectarian but Abolitionist church and a one-room school. Mr. and Mrs. Rogers started teaching fifteen pupils in a shack made of loose clapboards. He was a handy sort. He made desks, maps, charts; and introduced startling innovations such as music, pictures, lectures. As the second year opened, enrollment had so increased that two additional teachers were needed. Then, in 1859, Rogers was one of the little group that drew up a constitution for Berea College, stipulating that it was opposed to "sectarianism and slaveholding." Shortly afterward an armed mob ordered Rogers and ten associates to leave Kentucky. An appeal to the governor brought reply that the state could do nothing to protect them. Rogers and friends thereupon left, and he went to Decatur, Ohio, taking the Presbyterian pastorate there with the understanding that he might leave at a moment's notice to return to Kentucky. This he did, in 1865, reopening the little school which presently secured its charter as Berea College.*

In another Berea, this one a township of northern Ohio, grew up still another successful school of Yankee parentage, now known as Baldwin-Wallace College. This Berea was the place selected in 1837 by Josiah Holbrook of Derby, Connecticut, for the founding of what he called Lyceum Village. It was to be world headquarters for Holbrook's American Lyceum, an "association of adults for mutual education." The association flowered, too. It ran a successful course and was immensely influential in many states, where its discussions resulted in the founding or the improvement of public schools. It left, as a sort of stepchild, a pattern for the Chautauqua movement. But Lyceum Village did not survive. A major portion of the capital for the village's establishment was supplied to Holbrook by another fanatic, John Baldwin, Ohio pioneer from North Branford, Connecticut, whose great ambition was to have a hand in founding a school for higher education that should admit women. His own mother, John Baldwin often told, had been refused admission to Yale College, and he thought it a shame and a disgrace.

When Josiah Holbrook gave up his idea of Lyceum Village, he left Baldwin sunk in mortgages, though not for long. Baldwin took to incessant prayer, during which, as he related it, he "covenanted with God not to spend a quarter of a dollar in any useless way, but to give all except a bare support toward any cause God might direct, if He would only show me the way out of my troubles." It was a sound Yankee bargain, and, as so often happened with New Englanders in similar cases, the Lord took him up, directing him to a place on his farm where he uncovered one of the greatest ledges of grindstone rock imaginable. In this event was the founding of the great Berea grindstone industry. Baldwin made a fortune from it. Nor did he forget his part of the bargain. He nor his family spent a penny beyond actual needs of subsistence, but put his wealth into the founding of Baldwin University, into the founding of Baker University, Baldwin, Kansas, into schools for white and colored children in Louisiana, and into high schools for boys and girls in Bangalore, India.

___

* In 1948 Berea College had 486 men students and 606 women. Every student has to work part time under the school's labor plan, and "their earnings average 50 per cent of total college expenses."

The idea of a school to teach teachers, with no reference to Holy Writ, was conceived and put into effect by Samuel Read Hall, born in Croydon, New Hampshire, in 1795, who taught school in Rumford, Maine, where he used what was probably the first blackboard in the United States. Hall was early convinced that the school system of the entire country needed immediate and drastic reform. In 1823, to this end, he opened an academy in Concord, Vermont, for the specific purpose of training men and women as teachers. This was the first normal school in the United States, and it was successful. He was presently called to Andover, Massachusetts, where he started a similar training course. In 1839, with the aid of Horace Mann and the provision of public funds, he helped to found the first state normal school in the country, at Lexington. He wrote a great deal on the subject, and his *Lectures on School-Keeping,* published in 1829, was doubtless the first book on education printed in English in the United States. Hall's training-school idea spread rapidly. New York adopted it in 1832, and several other states soon after.

Was there a village or even a crossroads hamlet in any of the six Yankee states that did not have a son or a daughter somewhere at the West, teaching school, defeating the Devil? Probably not. Many a small village sent a dozen or more. In Chester, New Hampshire, for instance, all seven children of Dr. and Mrs. John Bell became teachers. Alice, Annie, and Lucy taught in the public schools of Colorado. Bessie became professor of languages at Colorado Agricultural College. Maude was a teacher at Potsdam, New York, brother John in Idaho, brother Samuel in Colorado. Nor were the Bell girls the only Chester schoolmarms at the West. Clara Learnard was on the faculty of Almira College at Greenville, Illinois, one of the founders of which was Stephen Morse, a Chester native. Martha Learnard went to New York City, to teach in Miss Ely's fashionable school for girls. The Reverend Daniel Tenney of Chester was one of the founders of Western Female Academy, Oxford, Ohio, where Rebecca Tenney was a teacher; it later was known as Oxford College for Women. Anna Hazelton of Chester became an early schoolmarm in Pueblo, Colorado. Chester's Chester J. Wilcomb went to the faculty of Polytechnic High School, Riverside, California.

Such was the exodus of teaching talent only, from one small Yankee town in New Hampshire. Another village of the Granite State, Thornton, sent a native son named Jeremiah Rankin to head Howard University, for Negroes, for thirteen years. You could never tell what a Yankee school-master might do, for like the general run of Yankees they numbered too many individualists to remain in any groove, educational or otherwise. From the crossroads hamlet of Windham, New Hampshire, Carroll Cutler went forth to become, in 1871, the president of Western Reserve College; and to resign seventeen years later in order to spend the rest of his life as a teacher in two Negro schools, Biddle University at Charlotte, North Carolina, and Talladega College in Alabama.

The little villages across the Connecticut River in Vermont were much the same as those in New Hampshire. Charles White of Randolph, which may have been able to muster a total population of nine hundred persons, went away to head Wabash College in Indiana. The first president of Vassar College was Milo P. Jewett, who was born in St. Johnsbury. George A. Gates of Topsham, scarcely a hamlet, was in turn the president of Iowa College, of Pomona College in California, and of Fiske College for Negroes. One of De Pauw's able heads was Lucien Berry, born in Alburg on Lake Champlain. In 1857 the president of Bucknell University in Pennsylvania was Justin Loomis, born in Bennington. Little and handsome Newfane, with a population of around two hundred, sent Webster Merrifield to head the University of South Dakota. Susan Lincoln Tolman Mills, born in Enosburg, had something to do with the founding of Mills College, Oakland, California, and was its president for many years.

It would seem odd, if not incredible, to partisans of Arnold J. Toynbee's *A Study of History,* where one may learn that the state of Maine is inhabited by "watermen and lumbermen" and little else—it would seem to them incredible that the Pine Tree State was the native home of William H. Allen, born in Manchester, who became one of the great presidents of Girard College, and became also a great president of Pennsylvania's Agricultural college; and the native home of Joseph A. Sewall, born in Scarboro, president of the University of Colorado; and the native home of another Colorado president, James H. Baker, born in Harmony. Rufus Bailey, born in North Yarmouth, wrote spelling and grammar textbooks that were the most popular of any in the South from the 1830's to the Civil War. Bailey went on to head Austin College in Sherman, Texas.

One could never tell what might come forth from a Yankee crossroads. The crossroads of Derby Center, Vermont, has never known a railroad, nor is it much larger now than it was when first settled right after the Revolution; yet one of Derby's farm boys, Charles Kendall Adams, went away to be president of Cornell University, where he notably improved the teaching staff; and then president of the University of Wisconsin, where he was no less known as a teacher than as a builder.

The first president of the University of California was Henry Durant of tiny Acton, Massachusetts, who started the far western college with nine students and a faculty of two. After his death, this university was headed by

Daniel Coit Gilman of Norwich, Connecticut, generally rated as one of the country's greatest educators. Gilman was called east from California to be the founding president of the Johns Hopkins University, at Baltimore, where he remained for a quarter of a century; and under him the school went far toward achieving the tremendous reputation which it still retains.

Though farming meant less and less to New England as the nineteenth century rolled on, and as more and more Yankee farmers rolled away from the home acres, yet the region produced and sent forth a number of brilliant teachers in agriculture. One of these was Adonijah S. Welch, born in East Hampton, Connecticut, who in 1868 became the first president of the Iowa State College of Agriculture at Ames. Here was the man for the job. He himself laid out the grounds, drives, barns, other buildings, and experimental plots. He planned and directed the curriculum. More important than all else, perhaps, was the idea of the farmers' institutes which he is credited with originating, and which later became a part of the system of agricultural education in most if not all states. His wife played a part in developing the home economics department, using her own kitchen for the purpose. She made the course a huge success, copied elsewhere in many of its details.

Horace E. Stockbridge of Hadley, Massachusetts, who had performed great work for agriculture in his native state, in Indiana, and in Japan as chief chemist to the government, went to North Dakota when that farming state wanted to start an agricultural college. He selected the location, planned the buildings, named the faculty, then went off to another job.

The school at Crete, Nebraska, named Doane College, was the idea of Thomas Doane, born in Orleans, Massachusetts, who was a civil engineer and finally chief of the engineers laying the route of the Burlington & Missouri River Railroad in Nebraska. With his own funds, and with the help of interested friends, he established the small Congregational college on the plains and lived to see it thrive.

One of the most potent of all Yankee schoolmarms was Catharine Esther, daughter of Dr. Lyman Beecher. After teaching awhile in Cincinnati, she returned to Boston and there organized the Ladies' Society for Promoting Education in the West, which resulted in the establishment of schools for females in Quincy, Illinois, in Burlington, Iowa, and in Milwaukee, Wisconsin. Miss Beecher herself was an excellent teacher. She put domestic science into her schools; but she also belabored her charges with their need for higher education, even though she was against votes for women. One of her faculty, Frances Strong, was inspired in 1831 to organize Huntsville Female Seminary, in Alabama.

THIS "LITHOGRAPHED MENDACITY" OF A NON-EXISTENT CITY
BROUGHT PEOPLE TO KANSAS

READ THE INDUCEMENTS.

FIRST.—It is a NEW COUNTRY, recently opened for settlement by the building of the Atchison, Topeka and Santa Fe Railroad, and offering the best opportunity of securing a home in the West.

SECOND.—For its CHOICE CLIMATE—in latitude 38 north, the latitude of Central Kentucky and Virginia, the favorite latitude of America—RICH SOIL, and abundance of PURE WATER.

THIRD.—The large proportion of VALLEY LAND. The grant follows the beautiful and rich valleys of the Cottonwood and Arkansas Rivers its entire length, from Emporia west.

FOURTH.—HEALTH. Its altitude, 1,000 to 3,000 feet above the level of the sea, a porous subsoil and well-drained surface, no stagnant water, or overflowed lands, secure a remarkably HEALTHY CLIMATE, free from Fever and Ague.

FIFTH.—Its rapid settlement, unprecedented in the history of the West, with the cream of Eastern immigration, has given it prosperous towns, churches, schools, mills, and the conveniences of a well-settled community.

SIXTH.—We are now running trains daily from KANSAS CITY and ATCHISON, through to PUEBLO, COLORADO, there connecting with the Rocky Mountain system of railroads, and, as Kansas is the nearest agricultural State, her products will find a ready and profitable market in the extensive mineral regions developed by the extension of this road.

SEVENTH.—With all other advantages we offer our lands at the LOWEST PRICES, and on the MOST FAVORABLE TERMS of any land grant in the West.

EIGHTH.—The Cottonwood and Arkansas Valleys are destined to become densely settled—the homes of rich and prosperous communities.

PLENTY OF RICH GOVERNMENT LANDS

—FOR—

HOMESTEADS

STOCK-RAISING.

The abundance of excellent water in SPRINGS AND RUNNING STREAMS, combined with CHEAP LAND of superior quality, covered with nutritious grasses, and the finest climate in the world, make it the finest stock country in the West.

Products Will Pay for Land and Improvements.

In selecting a new HOME, cast your fortunes with a GREAT ENTERPRISE like the

Atchison, Topeka & Santa Fe Railroad,

Which is destined to be the

FAVORITE THOROUGHFARE across the Continent.

Every one seeking a New Home should, by all means, visit our lands before locating.

If you visit the Centennial Exhibition, don't fail to see the

Splendid Display of the Products OF THE

ARKANSAS VALLEY,

Exhibited by the Atchison, Topeka & Santa Fe R. R. Co., in the Kansas Building.

TERMS OF SALE.

TERMS NO. 1—Is on eleven years' time, with seven per cent. interest. One-tenth of the purchase money paid down at time of purchase, and one year's interest on the remainder. The next two years, only interest payments. Afterwards, one-tenth of the principal and interest on the remainder annually until the contract is paid out.

TERMS NO. 2—Is on eleven years' time, with only the interest, at seven per cent., for the first four years. After that time, one-eighth of the principal and interest on the remainder annually until the expiration of the contract. Terms of sale No. 2 is applicable only to lands lying west of the west line of Reno county, on the south side of the Arkansas river, and west of range 18, west, on the north side of the Arkansas river.

TERMS NO. 3—Are our Short Credit terms, where, in consideration of the purchaser paying one-third of the principal, and ten per cent. interest on the remainder, and the balance in one and two years, we make a discount of TWENTY per cent. from the price.

TERMS NO. 4—Is a cash sale, where we make a discount of TWENTY per cent. from the appraised value.

For full particulars, and any special information desired, address,

A. S. JOHNSON,
Acting Land Commissioner for the
A. T. & S. F. R. Co.,
TOPEKA, KANSAS.

HO! FOR THE NEW KANSAS

We invite the attention of all who are contemplating a change of location, or who want

A FARM OR HOME

IN THE WEST

TO THE SPECIAL ADVANTAGES OF THE

LANDS

OF THE

ATCHISON, TOPEKA & SANTA FE R. R.

SITUATED ALONG THE BEAUTIFUL

Cottonwood and Arkansas

VALLEYS

IN

SOUTHWESTERN KANSAS.

"THE BEST THING IN THE WEST."

THE RICH VALLEY

LANDS

OF THE

Atchison, Topeka and Santa Fe

RAILROAD COMPANY,

SITUATED ON THE BEAUTIFUL

Cottonwood and Arkansas Rivers,

IN

SOUTHWESTERN KANSAS.

2,500,000 ACRES

FOR SALE ON ELEVEN YEARS' CREDIT.

Send for a circular, giving full information about PRICES OF LAND, TERMS OF SALE, Exploring Tickets, and Rebate of Fares to Land Buyers, and containing the best Map of Kansas ever published.

Address,

ARTHUR GORHAM,
Assistant Land Commissioner.

A. S. JOHNSON,
Acting Land Commissioner,
TOPEKA, KANSAS.

GEO. W. MARTIN, KANSAS PUBLISHING HOUSE, TOPEKA, KANSAS.

COME, YOU YANKEE SETTLERS,
AND SEE WHAT
THE SANTA FE RAILROAD
HAS WAITING FOR YOU

THIS RAILROAD BOOKLET FAIRLY TEEMED WITH
"SPLENDID OPPORTUNITIES" FOR SETTLERS

Left: STEPHEN F. AUSTIN CARRIED OUT THE TEXAS COLONIZATION PLANS OF HIS YANKEE FATHER. Right: ELIPHALET NOTT, ONE OF THE UNNUMBERED EDUCATORS WHO HAD GREAT INFLUENCE OUTSIDE NEW ENGLAND

A RECORD SHIPMENT OF CONCORD COACHES
LEAVING THE NEW HAMPSHIRE CITY FOR THE WEST AND WELLS, FARGO

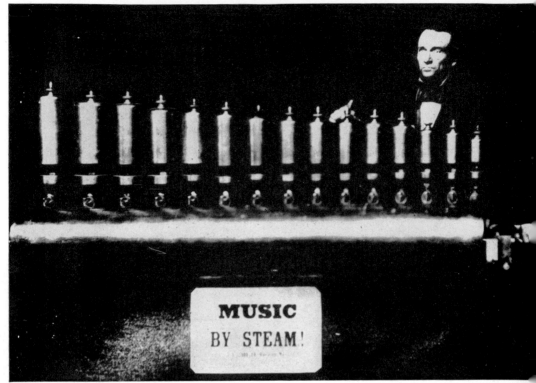

YANKEE INVENTOR STODDARD AND HIS PRIMEVAL CALLIOPE

YANKEE INVENTOR
GLIDDEN, THE
BARBED-WIRE KING

Charles H. Pinkham

MRS. PINKHAM,
WHOSE VEGETABLE COMPOUND FOLLOWED THE FRONTIER

VERMONTER SILE DOTY

BAY STATER ENOCH PRATT

When the true spirit struck a Yankee hard, there seemed to be no end and no boundaries to his efforts. David S. Richardson, born in Cornish, New Hampshire, in 1821, and educated at Kimball Union and Dartmouth, was credited with the founding of six academies in North Carolina. He also founded and edited the *North Carolina Journal of Education*. Still filled with urgency, he next moved to Alabama, where he established a military academy. In 1884 he moved again, this time to Oakland, California, where he taught school until his eighty-second year.

Not all Yankee schoolmasters were liked in the South. Alva Woods of Shoreham, Vermont, and Harvard served a brief spell as president of Transylvania College, Lexington, Kentucky, then moved to take the helm at the University of Alabama. But his outspoken dislike of slavery resulted in many "incidents," then, in 1837, in wild riots of students. Woods resigned, to take his Abolitionist teachings elsewhere. Nor were Yankees welcome in the South as late as 1887, when Edward C. Mitchell of East Bridgewater, Massachusetts, went to New Orleans to take the presidency of Leland University, for Negroes. He endured insults and even boycotts; but this graduate of Colby, who had taught in London and Paris, possessed sufficient charm to make many friends for the struggling college, in good time. For thirteen years he continued to exert a large influence in the state.

A fine example of the wide influence of a teacher-missionary of the first rank was that of George H. Atkinson, native of Newburyport, Massachusetts, and a product of Dartmouth. With his bride, young Atkinson set out for the Oregon country in 1847, going by way of the Horn and the Sandwich Islands, a voyage of more than a year. He conducted his religious work with great tact, organizing Congregational churches in Oregon City and elsewhere, and he also conducted a continuous agitation for public schools.* Moreover, he had a large hand in the founding of what are now Pacific University, and Whitman College, bringing west to head the former a remarkable Vermonter named Sidney Harper Marsh. Atkinson was no less interested in material progress, and his writings and many addresses on agriculture were considered to be of the greatest influence all over the Oregon country. He was also responsible for starting a brisk migration of Yankee schoolmasters to the northwest coast, including three of the first presidents of Pacific University. Working closely with Atkinson were the Reverend Elkanah Walker of North Yarmouth, Maine, and the Reverend Cushing Eells of Blandford, Massachusetts, whose great ambition and satisfaction was the founding of Whitman

* In 1950 almost one-tenth of Portland's public-school teachers from outside the Pacific Northwest come from New England, as follows: Massachusetts, 31; Maine, 11; Vermont, 5; New Hampshire and Connecticut, 4 each; Rhode Island, 2.

College at Walla Walla, the first chartered institution in Washington Territory.*

It was of course proper that Ohio's first institution of higher learning,
at Hudson—now Western Reserve University, at Cleveland—was known
as the Yale of the West. The town itself was founded by David Hudson
of Connecticut. The college was largely founded by Yale graduates, and its
first president was George E. Pierce, Yale 1816. Its original buildings were
constructed—handsomely, too—by Simeon Porter, a son of Connecticut
emigrants to Ohio. The remove of the college to Cleveland was brought
about chiefly by a half-million-dollar gift from Amasa Stone, from Massachusetts, whose son Adelbert was drowned while a student at Yale.

The school at Yellow Springs, Ohio, called Antioch College, was the
last work of perhaps the greatest Yankee educator of them all: Horace
Mann, born in Franklin, Massachusetts, in 1796. Though he had begun a
career in the law, he was far from content. In him was the urge, strong
though vague, which stirred so many Yankees; and in 1837, when for the
first time the state of Massachusetts provided for a secretary of education,
at a salary of $1,000 a year, Mann gave up his lucrative practice to take it.
He remained in office twelve years. When he came to office, male teachers
in the elementary schools were paid an annual wage of $185; women teachers,
$65. One-sixth of the children of the Bay State were being educated in
private academies; one-third had no educational chances at all.

Mann changed all that. In 1839 the state passed an act providing for
a minimum school year of six months. More than two million dollars was
expended for better schoolhouses. Salaries of male and female teachers were
raised 62 and 54 per cent respectively. And the proportion of private-school
to public-school expenditure decreased from 75 to 36 per cent. Mann had
put the state of Massachusetts into the business of education; and this miracle
inspired other states, at least in the North and West, to do likewise.

In 1852 Mann was persuaded to become the first president of the new
Ohio college at Yellow Springs. He also taught, taking the subjects of
political economy, intellectual philosophy, and natural theology. The school
had every reason to be successful, but it wasn't: lack of funds, plus bad
management, wrecked it, and it was sold for debt. (Later it was reorganized,
and it has long been a most successful institution, using the work-and-study
plan.) Mann's health collapsed along with Antioch, and within a few weeks

* In both Oregon and Washington the various sects were quick to set up their schools.
Methodists, Catholics, Quakers, Congregationalists, and others, one and all, established what
Dr. Ralph Fenton has termed watertight compartments of sectarianism.

he was dead. But his great work in his native state lasted and spread; and he is always credited with the ensuing period that was so marked by educational reform and progress as to be known as the Common-School Revival in the United States.

It was perhaps not incidental that Mann's sister-in-law, Miss Elizabeth Peabody, was influential in founding the first free kindergarten in the United States, in Boston, in 1860. For several years Miss Peabody edited and published the *Kindergarten Magazine,* and lectured effectively on the subject.*

It was of course teaching in common or public schools that occupied a majority of the Yankees who left home to educate young people in the West and South. No one has ever been so rash as to estimate their number. It must be huge, for they started leaving early and are still leaving more than a century and a half later. Almost every town history of New England lists men and women natives who went forth to teach in foreign parts. A large number of them seem not to have returned home, at least not to remain; and so their obituaries appeared in newspapers of forty-two states.

One wonders what they taught, these Yankee marms and masters who swarmed all over the West and South. Their talents were as varied as their personalities. The best of them surely believed in free inquiry which, in spite of all that has been said of the "liberalizing influences of the frontier," was often dangerous on the frontier. Frontier society, West or South, was basically against any free inquiry in matters of the intellect. (The Populist revolt and other radical doings of the Midwest in later years had their sources in left-wing Puritanism.) The frontier was quick to adopt things like the Colt revolver, the barbed-wire fence, and the mowing machine, and it also wanted free education; but many a Yankee schoolmaster in Ohio, Illinois, and other parts was dismayed to discover hostility, not only to Latin and Greek and poetry, but to such assorted Yankee notions as prison reform, spelling reform, school-text Temperance, and college-text doubts as to the moral and economic values of Slavery. The bright light that was Oberlin, indeed, was often dimmed and more than once all but extinguished because of its welcome to dangerous ideas—which, however, did not include any doubts in regard to the Congregational, or at times Presbyterian, Jehovah.

In all the emigrating Yankee teachers there was probably the Yankee instinct of resistance. The world was filled with evil forces that were to be

* In later life, the good-hearted Miss Peabody was taken in by an alleged Indian educator, who called herself Sarah Winnemucca and said she was operating a place of learning for Piutes. Miss Peabody responded generously, and even canvassed friends to contribute to a fund that apparently sank into the sands faster than it could be replenished.

resisted, and if possible demolished. It might be Slavery, it might be Rum, it might be tobacco or meat, or even the use of condiments like pepper. The evil could be Methodism, or Catholicism. It surely could be "desecration" of the Sabbath. It might also be banks, or railroads, or the Masonic order. But worse than any of them, worse than all combined, was the evil of illiteracy. On this one idea all the Yankees were agreed: if illiteracy were resisted and abolished, then all men would see and understand God's ways, and the United States would be the home not only of the brave and the free, but of God's own chosen people.

Most Yankee schoolteachers agreed, publicly at least, that there was a God, even though he appeared to have singularly conflicting ideas. They agreed that the correct, the only pronunciation of "half" was something like "harf." They agreed that Industry called for a capital letter; and as one they cried aloud against illiteracy—which was glory enough. As for the rest, Yankee schoolteachers could not be fitted into any intellectual mold.

Probably a majority of the migrated teachers sought to *drill* into their charges the hard facts of reading, writing, and arithmetic, using great energy, some patience, and the perseverance of a manufactory. On the higher levels they doubtless used the same methods with Latin, Greek, and the more or less rigid rules of what was called Moral Philosophy.

Not until late in the nineteenth century were Yankee education, and Yankee pedagogues, thoroughly divorced from theology. But earlier than that Yankee theology had been somewhat modified; it was no longer deemed necessary, for instance, to explain that David really had not "danced before the Lord with all his might," as the Book had it, but had merely jumped up and down in a wholly innocent manner.

All natural teachers must possess something of the missionary spirit; and Yankees were properly indoctrinated with it at such special missionary factories at the theological seminaries at Bangor and Andover, and also of course at all the Yankee colleges. At its best, this spirit was as hot to disseminate the beliefs of Charles Robert Darwin as it had been earlier to spread the verities of Jonathan Edwards.

At their worst, or perhaps even at their average, the teachers from New England appeared smug in the West—not loudly opinionated, but emanating a cold, clear belief, as silent as it was positive, that almost anything out of Massachusetts, or Connecticut, or any other Yankee state, whether education or religion, whether speech or deportment, or merely a certain brand of salt codfish, was by that fact superior to all else.

As already related, many a new college at the West somehow or other began life with a New England man as its first president. Many another

Yankee president followed the first.* As for Yankee professors, they have been almost as numerous as the common schoolmasters and schoolmarms. By all odds a most unusual such professor, whose influence went far beyond the classroom, was Charles F. Dowd, born in Madison, Connecticut, in 1825.

The Temple Grove Seminary for Young Ladies at Saratoga Springs, New York, was surely as improbable a place as any other for the emergence of the first great American reformer in regard to Time; but that is where good Professor Dowd was teaching—in fact was the principal—when in 1869 he came forth with a suggestion that the people of the United States adopt what he called Time Belts, several in number, and forthwith regulate their clocks in accordance with these time standards.

In stagecoach days and earlier, time had not been an important matter. But in 1869 railroads were long since a part of life in the United States. Their trains had to run on a schedule; but the many towns and cities they served could not agree on time. The matter of time, in 1869, was pretty much chaos in a nation of the extent of the United States. Consider Buffalo, New York. On its ornate railroad depot were three clocks, each operating on the different time favored by one of the three railroads using the station. In Pittsburgh, there were six different times in use. There were at least twenty-seven local times in Michigan, thirty-eight in Wisconsin, twenty-seven in Illinois, a mere twenty-three in Indiana. A careful traveler, going from Eastport, Maine, to San Francisco, California, changed his stem-winder twenty times on the trip.

Into this confusion came Yankee Professor Dowd, a man of ideas. Probably because his was a sound and workable plan, the public showed either hostility or complete disinterest. Professor Dowd was exactly, as things turned out, fourteen years ahead of his time. But he did not merely suggest the matter and let it drop. Instead of troubling the general public any more, he directed his proposals to executives of the railroads. He wrote hundreds of letters. At his own expense he published pamphlets outlining the simplicity and worth of his time standards. The railroads were becoming interested when the Panic of 1873 gave them so many troubles that the matter of Professor Dowd and his Time was dropped. He kept up his barrage of propaganda, and in 1876, with the immense help of William F. Allen of the *Railway Guide,* a first General Time Convention was called. Allen was

* It could interest few to cite them all, or to relate their successes; but a few examples will indicate the patent desire in foreign parts for New Englanders to head what are known as institutions of higher learning: Purdue University, James H. Smart of Center Harbor, N.H.; Colgate University, George E. Merrill, Charlestown, Mass.; Denison University, E. B. Andrews, Hinsdale, N.H.; Pennsylvania State College, George W. Atherton, Boxford, Mass.; University of Michigan, James B. Angell, Scituate, R.I., and Harry B. Hutchins, Lisbon, N.H.; University of Minnesota, Cyrus Northrop, Ridgefield, Conn.; University of Montana, Charles H. Clapp, Boston; University of California, Benjamin Ide Wheeler, Randolph, Mass.

just the man to modify Professor Dowd's original plan and at last get the major railroads to agree on adopting it.

The modified plan called for five time zones—Intercolonial, Eastern, Central, Mountain, and Pacific. The last four, all in the United States, were based on the 75th, 90th, 105th, and 120th meridians west of Greenwich, and were approximately in the longitudes of Philadelphia, Memphis, Denver, and Fresno. The plan was adopted on October 11, 1883, by the General Time Convention, and noon of October 18 was selected as the moment the railroads should put the reform into effect.

If today one should think that the Dowd-Allen reform was accepted whole-heartedly by the general public, or even by the United States government, then one would indeed be mistaken. Announcement of the impending event met with much opposition. In Bangor, Maine, the mayor vetoed a city ordinance that provided the town should adopt Eastern Standard time. Columbus and Fort Wayne delayed action because of the allegedly bad effects Central Standard time would have on the honest workingmen of those regions —a group ever favored by all opponents of change. In Tennessee a Reverend Mr. Watson defied the Louisville & Nashville Railroad to hamper God's sun and pounded his Waterbury watch into pulp with a claw-hammer, right in the pulpit; because, so he cried, the coming time standards had made all watches worthless. In Iowa, another man of the Gospel shouted that the hosts of Hell were attempting to take over the universe, and damned the Time Convention for the pride that goeth before a fall.

The United States government ignored the whole matter and did not for another thirty-five years even so much as acknowledge it. Then, on March 19, 1918, Congress passed the Standard Time Act, thus giving sanction to something that had been in effect for a generation.

Incidentally, the Dowd-Allen reform was put into effect with none of the horrible wrecks and hideous collisions that had been freely prophesied. The only casualties were the fairly large number of persons who did not read the newspapers, or did not understand what they had read. They missed their trains.

Such was the extracurricular influence of Yankee Professor Dowd, and one is happy he lived to see his reform fit into American life so well that a new generation came to think of time standards as something which had come into being simultaneously with the Republic itself. There was bitter irony in the fact that one day in 1904 good Professor Dowd was killed at Saratoga Springs by one of the very railroad trains whose departures and arrivals he had done so much to regulate. But his had been a great and lasting influence, not only on the young ladies of Temple Grove Seminary, but on every last person in the United States.

CHAPTER XXI

THE INVENTIVE YANKEES

IT WAS PROBABLY inevitable that Patent No. 1, issued by the United States Patent Office on that morning in 1790, when it first opened for business, was granted to Samuel Hopkins, of Burlington, Vermont, who had devised what he described as "an improved method of making pot and pearl ashes." There is no evidence that Mr. Hopkin's process brought about any revolutionary change in what was then a leading industry; but the fact that a Yankee was there at the Patent Office, waiting for the doors to open, was indicative of the New England bent for invention. For a century afterward Yankees were to stand in the very front rank of American inventors, both in number and in the wide influence of their work.

The Yankee schoolmaster stemmed from the peculiar Yankee religion, plus a desire for some occupation more satisfying than the slavery needed to make a living on a Yankee farm. It is probable that the Yankee's inventiveness had the same sources. His God blessed the hardy individualist, the self-reliant, while the thin soil still drove him to supplement his miserable agricultural income; hence, he made gadgets to sell, or to lighten his own labor. But these may have been little more than contributing forces. The inventor of the first submarine, David Bushnell of Connecticut, surely was inspired by a patriotic wish to sweep the feared British navy from New York harbor and Long Island Sound; while Eli Whitney of Massachusetts, who was both schoolmaster *and* inventor, devised the epochal cotton gin in a matter of eight days out of a sense of gratitude to the kindly widow of General Nathanael Greene, who had befriended him.

Thus the reasons behind New England's dominating position in American invention, from the time of the Revolutionary War down and into the twentieth century, are too complicated to be assessed by a layman, and must be left to the licensed and patented professors of psychology, who are a positive crew and have doubtless long since pronounced, if they have got around to the Yankees yet, that they were wonderfully inventive because of sexual repression.

Whatever the inventive urge was, it drove them sore hard indeed, and in their inventive success lay the survival of a New England that had been defeated in agriculture, was being defeated in shipping, and no less defeated in politics. New England's inventors put her into the business of manufacture. More than that, New England's inventors, including those who never left her borders, exerted a huge and lasting influence on the rest of the United States, and occasionally upon the world.

New England's inventors are commonly thought of, by those who know nothing at all of the matter, to have been improvers of kitchen clocks, and makers of Yankee Notions. They did put good clocks into American homes, and that fact is scarcely a footnote to their accomplishments. Consider the range, not the relative importance, of four Yankee inventions. John Locke of Lempster, New Hampshire, perfected, during 1844–1848, the electro-magnetic chronograph, which the United States Coast Survey said "completely changed the art of determining longitudes," and which Congress officially declared to be a "wonderful invention," thereupon awarding $10,000 to Locke. In 1866, Thaddeus Sobieski Coulincourt Lowe of Jefferson Mills, New Hampshire, produced the first artificial ice in the world. In 1872 Luther C. Crowell of West Dennis, Massachusetts, invented the square-bottomed paper bag, now in universal use, plus a machine to make bags. In 1881, Frederick Grinnell of New Bedford, Massachusetts, patented the automatic sprinkler that bears his name.

There was no such thing as a "typical" Yankee invention, though a number of Yankee inventors appear to have possessed in common certain characteristics, including an aptitude, or fault, for sudden and violent changes of direction and, more often than not, winding up with a success other than the object which they had set out to accomplish. Take Rufus Porter. He was born in 1792 in Boxford, Massachusetts, and got a total of six months' schooling at Fryeburg Academy in Maine. He did not like shoemaking, to which he had been apprenticed, and went away to Portland to fiddle at dances. During the War of 1812 he painted gunboats, then began to wander, teaching school in several Maine villages; putting up wind-driven gristmills; painting houses in Boston, New York, and Baltimore.

In Virginia, about 1820, he devised a camera, got a handcart, and went on the road making portraits. Somewhere he stopped long enough to invent a revolving almanac, which failed to find a market. He soon turned up in Hartford, Connecticut, with plans for a twin boat to be propelled by horse power. Hartford promoters would have nothing of it; so, he went back to the road with his camera, and now added the art of painting murals. These could hardly have been better than primitive paintings, but he seems to have done very well with his brushes and made some money. He lost it in 1825 while trying to promote a cord-making machine, which he had invented, in Billerica, Massachusetts.

Porter wandered on for another fifteen years or so, inventing a clock, a steam carriage, a corn sheller, a fire alarm, and a washing machine. He never troubled to patent anything, but sold his models for small sums. While in New York he was offered an interest in a newspaper and immediately decided to spend the rest of his life as an editor. He moved the paper to Boston, named it the *American Mechanic,* and started publishing the first scientific newspaper in the United States. It prospered, too, but now Porter was obsessed with other ideas. He sold the paper. He invented a revolving rifle which he sold to Samuel Colt for $100. He joined the Millerites. He learned electroplating. All these things seemed somehow to inspire him to bring out a new periodical—on August 28, 1845, named the *Scientific American*—which, more than a century afterward continues healthy, and is run along the very editorial lines he set down in his prospectus. But Porter, typically, sold it after six months, in order to write an urgent book entitled *Aerial Navigation; or, New York & California in Three Days.* Nothing apparently came of the scheme implicit in the book's title. He wandered off again, but eventually settled down in Bristol, Connecticut, where he devised gadgets up to and including much of his ninety-third year.

Porter was the perfect inventor-type, whose pride lay only in inventing something, anything. Samuel Colt was different. He combined good business ability with inventive genius. He was a native of Massachusetts, and got the idea for his revolving pistol while a lad at sea, by musing on the revolving steering-gear. As everyone knows, he built his revolver, one of the most deadly and hence most useful gadgets any inventor ever gave the American West, into big business. But Colt was no one-track mind in invention. He devised notably successful land mines and under-water torpedoes. And when the Connecticut River flooded his plant in Hartford, he fortified his dike with willow trees, which held the river to its banks, but which presently grew out of hand. Instead of trimming them and burning the debris, Yankee Colt imported a whole village of basket weavers from Germany, set them up near the Colt factory, and they began turning out the willow furniture that had a great vogue along the Atlantic coast.

Colt's gun was a fine piece of workmanship, but it never had a monopoly in the West. Out there, if a man did not carry a Colt's, he probably carried one of the weapons made by two other Yankees—Horace Smith, a native of Cheshire, Vermont, and Daniel B. Wesson, born in Worcester, Massachusetts

—or, if a rifle, then one of the fine guns made either in New Haven by Oliver Fisher Winchester, or in Ilion, New York, by Eliphalet Remington, a native of Suffield, Connecticut. Their very names identify the weapons.

Did the western frontier have greater effect on the Yankees than Yankee inventions had on the frontier?

Incidentally, one of the earliest examples of the machine-tool industry in New England was that founded in Windsor, Vermont, by Richard S. Lawrence and partners, who made all the machinery for the famous Enfield Armory in old England, where Sharp's rifles and other weapons were turned out for the Crimean and other wars which Britain required to make her Great. Another successful machine-tool factory was founded by still another Vermonter, he being Francis A. Pratt, born in Woodstock, of the firm of Pratt & Whitney; and there was Joseph R. Brown of Warren, Rhode Island. who founded Brown & Sharpe.

Second only, perhaps, to Mr. Colt's revolvers as an influence in the West, was the Concord coach, built in the New Hampshire town from which the celebrated vehicle took its name. Both the gun and the coach so permeated the old West that no romance of the time and place, either on paper or in celluloid, is complete without them. The Hollywood canon of horse opera, in truth, is centered on the gun-coach combination. They are instantly recognizable to millions of Americans and foreigners who know nothing about them save that the one was used to hold up and rob the other.

The perfectionists who devised America's most romantic piece of rolling stock were Lewis Downing and J. Stephen Abbot. The former, who was born in Lexington, Massachusetts, went to Concord, New Hampshire, in 1813, to open a wheelwright's shop. For several years he repaired the sleds and plows of the village, made a few chaises, a few Concord buggies. In 1826 he felt it was time to build a passenger-and-mail coach for the stage business, just then come into full flower; and, needing expert advice, sent to Salem, Massachusetts, for help. This appeared in the person of young J. Stephen Abbot, who turned out to be much better than good. The coach was built and promptly sold.

Downing had found in Abbot an artisan after his own honest heart. The two formed a partnership, and for the next twenty years made stagecoaches that seemed to grow better with every rig. They did not of course invent the stagecoach, which came from England; yet they devised many an improvement. They strengthened it even as they made it lighter, and so modified the whole as to have a just claim for inventing the American stagecoach. Competitors found it increasingly difficult to match "the lightness, durability, and elegance" of the Concord brand.

In 1847 the partnership was temporarily dissolved. Abbot retained the old shops, while Downing, with sons Lewis and Alonzo, erected a new manufactory. Both families continued to make vehicles that probably had no peers anywhere. Then, in 1865, the two firms merged, to remain so, and to keep more than four hundred employees busy for another thirty years. With Abbot-Downing, the making of coaches approached being a dynamic religion. Old Downing himself constantly ranged the shop, seeing everything, saying little; but when he noted a piece of faulty work he would pick up a hammer and smash or otherwise ruin it so that it must be done over. The care began in the forest, where either an Abbot or a Downing selected the best trees of white ash or oak. The elm for the hubs got the same treatment. The panels were of prime basswood and were curved by the slow process of clamping their edges around a form, then placing them in front of an open fire, where they were intermittently moistened, until properly shaped. When an axle was ready for the thread, four stout men took hold of four levers of a die and walked in a circle until the thread was made. Abbot-Downing held to a firm belief that, though Time might be, as some said, Money, it was of infinitely less value than quality. . . .

The Concord coach became stronger as it became lighter. It also grew more decorative. From England, Abbott-Downing imported John Burgum, whose talents with bright paints were so apparent that he was made "chief orna-menter"; and for the next several decades he and his stable of artists made every Concord coach a thing of beauty, or at least something that could not very well be ignored.

The rush of '49 to California carried two Concord coaches to San Francisco, the first of many with which Adams & Company, Wells-Fargo, and minor express outfits took the mails and the passengers to the diggings and toted gold back from Hangtown, Bottle Springs, Angels Camp, and such places, a shotgun guard on the seat beside the driver. It was to be Abbot-Downing all over again in the Pikes Peak rush a decade later, into Colorado. Moreover, until long after the completion of the first two transcontinental railroads, Concord coaches continued to travel the west. What appears to have been the last stick-up of one took place as recently as 1893.

In addition to business from the booming West, Abbot-Downing made coaches for the new White Mountain resort hotels, and for big-city hotels all over the country, including rigs for the Astor, Brevoort, and Fifth Avenue in New York. Most hotel men were explicit about the door decorations. For a decade or more a likeness of Stephen A. Douglas was specified for many southern hotels. In the North and West, Webster, Pierce, J. Q. Adams, and Frémont were favored, though there were partisans of pretty females, such as the actresses Mary Anderson and Fanny Davenport. Potter Palmer of

Chicago, a man who usually knew just what he wanted, was certain about the Concord coaches for his new hotel; he asked Abbot-Downing to paint both the bodies and the running parts canary yellow, and put on each door an elaborate picture of the Palmer House itself. In the Far West, the favored body colors were red and green, with yellow for the running parts and plenty of scrollwork in gold leaf, and bright landscapes on the door panels.

The Concord's beauty was obvious at a glance. Its marvelous lasting qualities could be appreciated only by experience. On one occasion the Downieville stage of Adams & Company, operating on the Mother Lode, went off a narrow cliff and rolled a good hundred feet among the boulders. Nothing broke, though the vivid landscapes on the panels were scratched up. One of Wells, Fargo's rigs got even rougher treatment; it went off a steep pitch in California's Nevada County, the horses with it, to roll over and over a distance of three hundred feet down into roaring-full Greenhorn Creek. The front wheels became detached, the door paintings partly obliterated. Otherwise, everything, including passengers, horses, even the harnesses, survived intact. Concords simply could not be broken, or smashed.

As often as not an order for harnesses came to Concord with an order for a coach; and these, by "an understanding," were turned over to another Concord firm, that of James R. Hill & Company, makers of "the most splendid harnesses manufactured in the United States." Hill & Company were just as careful, just as thorough, and just as honest as Abbot-Downing; and it was both a common practice and most convenient for Adams and Overland and Wells, Fargo and other large purchasers of stagecoaches to order their leather goods along with their rolling stock.

Probably the peak for both Abbot-Downing and Hill came long ago— to be exact, on the 15th of April, 1868, when a whole trainload of their master work went out of Concord: a long, glittering procession of flashing vermilions and yellows, consigned, one is pleased to know, to Wells, Fargo & Company, at Omaha and Salt Lake City. There were Hill harnesses in that stupendous shipment, too, and with the harnesses went Mr. Samuel Parker, a lone passenger, to ride to the end-of-steel and there assume responsibility— to see that the harnesses were put properly on the horses and the animals properly hitched to the superb coaches which, under the banner of Wells, Fargo, were "to ply between the Eastern and Western divisions of the Pacific Railroad."

Most fortunately, some local photographer was alert on the great day, his big awkward camera set up in an open field along the Concord Railroad tracks; and there he caught the locomotive *Pembroke* hauling the train of "fifteen long platform cars," on each of which rested two of Abbot-Downing's special western jobs; and four box cars in which were sixty four-horse sets of Hill's harnesses, and proud but lonely Mr. Samuel Parker, agent-extraordinary for the combined firms of Concord's coach and harness makers. John Burgum, master decorator for the coach firm, was stirred mightily by the special train; and later, with the photograph in front of him, he took paints in hand and embalmed, in true and vivid colors and in one tremendous long painting, this climax to his career as artist-in-residence at Abbot-Downing.*

Even on its great day in 1868, the railroads were already encroaching seriously on Abbot-Downing's business; and after the railroads was to come the internal combustion engine. Together they served to bank the fires in the Abbot-Downing forges, one after another. The stout old firm attempted to enter the new age by building fire engines and assorted motor trucks, virtually by hand and with the same care they had devoted to their coaches. But their hearts obviously were not in it. They had made in their time some three thousand Concord coaches, all by hand. The motorcar business in America had no place for such artisans; although there seems never to have been a formal closing of the works the last Abbot-Downing employee got his gold-headed cane in 1928, and the long since shadowy plant was closed.

It was a New Hampshire man, too, who perfected the one and only indispensable invention that permitted settlement on the great plains. This was barbed wire, without which a large portion of the United States would probably be uninhabited to this day. The inventor was Joseph Farwell Glidden, born in Charlestown. Glidden was not one of those casual Yankee inventors; he knew he had a rattling good thing in his barbed wire, and he devoted all his one-track energies to making it successful.

He was born in 1813. He migrated with his parents to York State, then returned for some schooling at Middlebury Academy in Vermont. For several years he taught school and worked on his father's farm. In 1843 he bought two secondhand threshing machines, hitched on a couple of rugged teams, and started threshing his way west, stopping here and there to thresh for farmers in Ohio and Indiana, then in Michigan, and at last, after two years, in Illinois, where he purchased a claim near De Kalb.

Glidden liked to keep up with things. He never missed a county fair, and at one of these events in 1873 he saw an exhibit of barbed wire. It had been a failure; it wouldn't "work." He saw what was wrong; the barbs would not stay in place. He began forthwith to experiment at home, using two strands instead of one. It was typical of his kind—a man who migrated west *in* a threshing machine—it was typical that he rigged up an old coffee mill

* Mr. Burgum's quaint and striking painting of Concord's great day is to be seen, its colors as bright as the dawn, in the New Hampshire Historical Society's building at Concord.

so that by turning the crank, the wire was twisted to produce and hold the barb firmly in place. He thought he had something pretty good. He got a patent, though later he had to fight infringement suits and also to stage several of his own.

With his converted coffee mill Glidden turned out enough of the product to fence his home acres, and to start manufacture for sale in a small way. He was soon broke and in debt. He tried vainly to sell a half-interest in his patent for $100; a year later a neighbor took a chance with $265. In 1876 success arrived: Glidden sold his patent rights to Washburn & Moen of Worcester, Massachusetts, for $60,000, plus a royalty during the life of the invention. The Washburn concern now engaged H. W. Putnam of Bennington, Vermont, to devise an automatic machine for making the wire. This he did to perfection. And barbed wire was far and away the most sensational invention introduced on the great plains.* In 1875 a mere 600,000 pounds of it was made and sold. A year later the amount was almost 3,000,000 pounds; in 1877 the figure was 12,000,000, and in 1880 almost 90,000,000 pounds were manufactured. The top year seems to have been 1901, when the total ran to almost 300,000,000 pounds.

This astonishing increase was made in the face of bitter attempts to discourage its use. Cattlemen had for many years run their herds where and as they would. There was no reason why they shouldn't; for, even though the railroads on the plains had unloaded a large amount of their land by selling it to naïve farmers, it could not be successfully farmed unless and until it could be fenced. There was no timber for rails on much of the plains. There were no millions of stones, as there had been in New England. Desperate farmers had tried the Osage orange and other hedge fences. They proved too expensive and none too efficient. Not until barbed wire was perfected could the lands of the plains be made into farms.

Fence of any sort was a natural enemy of the cattlemen. So, when Glidden's product began to appear, fence wars broke out in Wyoming, Nebraska, New Mexico, and Texas. These were extremely cruel, and were carried on with wire-cutters plus the gadgets invented by Yankees Colt, Winchester, Remington, and Smith & Wesson. State legislatures hurriedly passed laws about fences; several made fence cutting a felony. The pro-fence men won. "When I saw a barbed-wire machine at work, making the stuff," said a cowboy, an anti-fence man, "I went home and told the boys they might just as well put away their wire-cutters." And though Joe Glidden and Washburn & Moen had to wage another war, this one with other makers of barbed wire, they at last won out, and all made their fortunes. So did a truly inspired salesman, John Warne Gates, the son of New England parents, who worked

* So declares Walter Prescott Webb in *The Great Plains* (1931).

so effectively as to become known as the Barbed Wire King, and later as Bet-a-Million Gates.

Barbed wire made the 160-acre homestead both possible and profitable, except in the dry regions. In those arid wastes, settlement awaited a proper fence no more than it did a supply of water. This was presently assured by the invention of a new type of windmill, and it, too, was the work of a Yankee, Daniel Halladay, a young mechanic of Ellington, Connecticut. Windmills of course date from beyond knowing. What young Halladay did was to devise "a windmill which governed itself by centrifugal force, being held to the wind by a governing weight and so arranged that when it revolved too fast this weight would slowly rise and thereby reduce the area of sail presented to the wind." Out of this invention grew the Halladay Windmill Company of South Coventry, Connecticut, which in turn became, in 1857, the United States Wind Engine & Pump Company of Batavia, Illinois. Halladay continued to improve the device. The Union Pacific gave it a fine boost when it ordered seventy windmills to supply water to its locomotives while laying rails across the dry plains. During the seventies and eighties the manufacture and sale of windmills increased in about the same proportion as that of barbed wire. The two final things needed for homesteading the Great American Desert had arrived.

Thus did inventive Yankees meet the needs of the West; namely, a six-shooting gun, barbed wire, windmills and, in many places, the rugged Concord coach. Mr. Colt, Mr. Glidden, Mr. Halladay, and the Messrs. Abbot and Downing had worked well.*

Long before barbed wire crossed the plains, the magic strands of the telegraph had reached the Pacific Coast. Every child knows that the telegraph was perfected by Samuel Finley Breese Morse, who happened also to be a very good painter in oils. Morse was a Yankee, born in the parsonage of the First Congregational Church at Charlestown, Massachusetts. A number of Yankees contributed supplementary inventions to the telegraph; one of the most important was the telegraphic printing machine, the work of Royal Earl House of Rockland, Vermont, which is still in use, in its modernized form, wherever the keys click and stutter.

The first means of distributing Yankee inventions were the Yankee peddlers, mostly from Connecticut, who went forth into the land of the

* Charles Jasper Glidden, born in Lowell, Mass., a cousin of the barbed-wire man, was something of an innovator, too. In Lowell he installed the first telephone exchange anywhere, then pioneered and made a fortune promoting long-distance telephone systems. He is remembered for the Glidden Trophy (automobile touring) which he established in 1905.

heathen with packs, or in wagons, loaded with trumpery and a few excellent things.

Folklore to the contrary, wooden nutmegs were not their leading item of merchandise. This hardy myth, long since believed as a verity, was given wide circulation in 1836 by David Crockett, politician and professional funny man of Tennessee, who wrote of one Job Snelling, a Yankee peddler on the southern circuit, that Job's father had invented the wooden nutmeg; that Job's mother had invented the first white oak pumpkin seeds; that his Aunt Prudence had thought up a method of steeping corn husks in tobacco water to make handsome if unbearable wrappers for cigars; and that Job himself had developed the art of producing cayenne pepper from mahogany sawdust. This, said Job, was a profitable and safe business, "for the people have been so long accustomed to having dust thrown in their eyes that there isn't much danger of being found out."

Yankee peddlers sold many things; but their leader was clocks, good clocks, first made on a mass production basis by Eli Terry, born in Windsor, Connecticut, and his partners Silas Hoadley and Seth Thomas. So well did these men and their peddlers labor that by the 1840's Connecticut-made clocks were standard furniture in the homes of rich and poor in all of the organized states and territories, and were in the covered wagons crossing the plains to the Oregon country.*

Among the most celebrated Yankee peddlers was Jim Fisk of Vermont, who drove all over northern New England with a handsome team of horses, his great wagon ajingle with the gaudiest tinware to be had. He did very well at it, then migrated to New York City where, in good time, he came to be a buyer and seller, and wrecker, of railroads. One of the worst failures as a peddler was Amos Bronson Alcott, of Connecticut, who toured the South trying to sell Yankee notions and would have starved had he not thrown away his pack and begun teaching school. Alcott married and could never support his family; but one of his daughters, Louisa May, was equal to the task, by writing what she herself described as "moral pap for the young."

Yankee watches began to appear long after Yankee clocks had crossed the continent, or after Aaron F. Lufkin, native of Freeport, Maine, had designed the first factory-made watch in the world and organized a firm out of which grew the Waltham Watch Company of Massachusetts. Still later came the first watch to sell at one dollar, made in Waterbury, Connecticut, which was the highly successful idea of Robert H. Ingersoll, born in Delta, Michigan, of

---

* The modern counterpart of the old Yankee peddler stems from the one-man brush factory, opened in Somerville, Mass., in 1906 by Alfred C. Fuller, whose excellent product and well trained salesmen scarcely need an introduction.

parents who had migrated from Connecticut. Waterbury was a hive, both of invention and of manufacture. A Waterbury man, Daniel Marks, with his brother Amasa, devised artificial limbs of so improved a pattern that the Marks company was awarded a contract to supply the disabled Union veterans of the Civil War.

Environment probably had something of a guiding influence on certain inventors, on Winslow Lewis, for instance, who was born at Wellfleet on Cape Cod, and reared at sea. In 1810 he was given a patent for a startlingly powerful lighthouse lamp. It was tried out at Boston Light and was so much better than anything seen before that the government had it installed in all federal lighthouses. Another environmental influence surely was that of Boston on Joseph Francis, born there in 1801. He spent many years perfecting a good lifeboat, which at last he accomplished with corrugated metal. One of these, placed at a life-saving station on the New Jersey coast, got a genuine workout in January of 1850, when the British ship *Ayrshire,* with two hundred passengers, was wrecked off Squan Beach. The single Francis lifeboat rescued all but one of the passengers. Francis went on to invent a watertight wagon for the army, the grandfather of modern "amphibians," as well as patent floating docks, and harbor buoys. But it was his "perfect lifeboat" that went all over the world and brought him honors from crowned heads, and a diamond-studded gold snuffbox from Napoleon III.

It was a single event, not environment, that inspired Silas Clark Herring to the manufacture of the first fireproof safes. Born in Salisbury, Vermont, Herring worked in stores, sold lottery tickets, and by 1834 had arrived in New York and established a wholesale grocery business. His business was wiped out in the great fire of 1835, including the contents of his safe. A little later he met one Enos Wilder, who held patent rights on a plaster of Paris lining for metallic safes, but could get nobody to promote it. Reflecting that the contents of no safe had survived the fire of 1835, Herring went to work on Wilder's idea, experimented a bit, improved the mixture, tested it well, then started to manufacture the Salamander safe. New York and all other cities of the time were prone to fires; nobody had as yet come out with a safe that could protect its contents from anything but theft and water. Herring used the press to sing the marvels of the Salamander; and whenever one of his safes went through a fire, as many did, and the contents were found to be in perfect condition, he took immense amount of space in the papers to publicize the fact. In 1845, a Salamander survived a fire that destroyed the *Tribune* building. It was the only one to do so. By mid-century, Herring's Salamanders "covered the country," and they were also notable for the artistic scenes painted on their doors.

Nor was it environment that led the Reverend Ebenezer Brown of Chesterfield, Massachusetts, to become the world's first manufacturer of detachable collars, but good luck, plus a clear understanding of values. Mr. Brown had held Methodist pulpits in Stowe, Vermont, and elsewhere, and was once sent to New Orleans to convert the Catholics. They were not interested, so he returned north in 1821, to preach some more, and to retire because of ill health. He opened a small dry-goods store in Troy, New York, just to pass the time, and met Mrs. Orlando Montague, wife of a blacksmith. Her husband's collars had a way of getting soiled every day, and she reflected upon this matter. She soon got the idea of cutting the collars from the shirts and washing them separately. In this manner, one shirt might well do for two or three days, with a clean collar every day. Much laundry work was thus saved.

Well, the Reverend Ebenezer Brown, now in dry goods, thought well of the idea. He bargained with a number of women in the neighborhood to make, wash, and iron these detachable collars, paying them in goods from his store. He packed the collars in paper boxes, by sizes, and put them on the market. Women were ready; they bought them as fast as they could be made—and both the detachable collar and the modern laundry came simultaneously into being. This event of vast significance took place in 1829, and Brown discovered right off that his few women could not take care of the market. So, with one George Jones, from Poultney, Vermont—of whom more later—he founded the firm of Brown & Company and moved to New York City, where scores of women labored at the new neckwear, which men were to suffer for another hundred years and more, Herbert Hoover being the most eminent example of the last die-hards of the Troy Collar Era. The Troy name survived the collar, as a favorite title for laundries all over the United States.

Thus did Yankee Ebenezer Brown and Hannah Lord Montague labor to lasting effect.

A Yankee woman played an important part in another Yankee invention, that of paper patterns. She was Ellen, the wife of Ebenezer Butterick, a native of Sterling, Massachusetts, who was a tailor and among other things made shirts for men. One day in 1858 she suggested that shirts might be made with little trouble from graded patterns of thin paper. This was inspiration, whether or not her husband knew it. He was at least no man to block progress, and he cut out a batch. They worked finely. In 1863 he and Ellen started making them for the market, and they were very popular. The Buttericks moved into Fitchburg, rented an abandoned academy building, hired help, and started mass production. Ellen now suggested that mothers all over the land would welcome patterns by which they could make their children's clothes, at home, on one of Mr. Howe's new sewing machines. She was right again. The demand for these patterns was little short of sensational. The quarters in the decaying academy building were not equal to it. In 1867 the Buttericks moved to Brooklyn, where they put up a big factory. They hired agents who penetrated to the least hamlet and frontier town. They founded a magazine to tout their patterns. A decade later they were selling six million Butterick patterns annually, and their market was increasing. They opened branches in London, Berlin, even in Paris.

Although Yankee inventors were more given to machinery than to clothing, at least one other Yankee contributed something in this line. He was Charles Goodyear, born in New Haven in 1800, just the fanatic needed to prepare a future for an oddity known as India rubber. Goodyear got his first patent for treating this material in 1837, but troubles beset and followed him. His family all but starved, and would have starved except for the generosity of friends, while he experimented, and organized tin-pot companies, all of which failed to promote his genuinely important invention. Goodyear was the perfect character of the Inventor. "If you meet a man," wrote a contemporary, "a man who has an India rubber cap, stock, coat, vest, and shoes, with an India rubber money purse without a cent of money in it, that is he." But in 1844, after troubles to madden a saint, Goodyear received celebrated Patent No. 3633, for the vulcanization of rubber. He did not make a fortune, or anything like it, but few other Yankee inventions have had greater influence.

If the hamlet of Brimfield, Massachusetts, cared to mark the town as the native home of men of importance, it might well honor Samuel Guthrie, born there in 1782, a doctor of medicine who liked to experiment with chemicals, and whose puttering resulted in 1831 in what he called "chloric ether," but what turned out to be chloroform, antedating independent discoveries of the same compound in France and Germany. And Brimfield could well honor Thaddeus Fairbanks, too, whose tinkering resulted, also in 1831, in the platform scales, which were the first great revolution in the measuring of weight since Roman times.

Young Fairbanks moved from Brimfield with his parents in 1815 into the wilds of northern Vermont, where they settled at St. Johnsbury and started an iron foundry. Thaddeus was forever making something. In 1826 he patented a plow with a cast-iron moldboard; and later a cookstove. At odd times he worked in the local hemp mill, where he was struck by the awkward method of weighing hemp—by hoisting a load of the material, cart and all, on a huge pair of steelyards. How much better, he thought, to drive the cart and load onto a platform! Thereupon the young man devised a weighing machine with just such a platform—the first of its kind anywhere;

and in 1831 he was granted a patent. Together with brothers Erastus and Joseph, Thaddeus Fairbanks organized a company to make the Fairbanks scales, which in good time went into the great stock yards of Chicago and Omaha, into the cotton and tobacco fields of the South, into every last store in America, and at last were to be found in every country of the world. As early as 1846, the scale was being used in China by a mandarin of progressive tastes who—said an up-and-coming Fairbanks advertisement—found it handy for "weighing his precious jade."

Somewhat later came another Yankee, Francis M. Strong of Pittsford, Vermont, to invent and patent a ball-bearing platform scale which was made in quantity by the Howe Scale Company of Rutland. That company, together with the Fairbanks concern, now makes two-thirds of the nation's scales.

The modern passenger and freight elevators stem from the invention of a Vermonter named Elisha Graves Otis, born in 1811 in Halifax, who migrated to York State as a building contractor. To speed his work he devised a fast hoist with an automatic safety appliance that would prevent the car from falling should the rope break. He was something of a showman, too, and created no little stir at the American Institute fair, held in New York in 1854, when he stood on a full-size model suspended high in the air, while the rope was deliberately cut. The safety device held the car in place, and the crowd marveled. In 1858 Otis patented the first steampowered elevator and founded the business that thrives, under his name, almost a century later.

The astonishing success of a few of the earliest New England inventions was probably the cause of the invention mania that occupied the spare time of thousands of Yankees for many years, and much of their time which, possibly, was not spare. The decade of the fifties was perhaps the most prolific of patents. In New Haven, during the period 1849–1882, George Beckwith published an almanac which, among other things, paid considerable attention to the granting of patents to Connecticut inventors.* From his columns one gets a pretty good idea of the extent of the inventive urge of the time, and with it a wonderment that the men of Connecticut found time to do else than devise gadgets and patent them. They seem, moreover, to have thought of almost everything. On March 3, 1857, the following inventors were probably made happy by the receipt of patents: Henry Bushnell,

* Mr. Beckwith's picture appeared on his almanac's cover for many years; but, unlike virtually all other advertisers, before or since, who use their likenesses thus, he was a realist; his portrait aged gradually with the passing years. In 1850 it showed a young, beardless man. By 1859, there is a beard, plus a slight aging. By 1880 the almanac maker is a true patriarch, fearfully aged, yet genial-looking.

New Haven, for a ship's hammer; Elizur E. Clark, New Haven, machine for cutting pasteboard for boxes; Purchase Miles, Hartford, curtain rollers; Samuel Colt (*the* revolver man), "an improvement in the mode of lubricating fire-arms"; and Rufus Sibley, Bristol, an improved bomb-lance. This gadget, a whaling weapon, was apparently a favorite with inventors, for there were several other patents issued in regard to its improvement, one in 1859 going to Isaac Goodspeed of Norwich.

What a whittling, what a pounding and stewing, and what a testing must have been going on in barns, sheds, shops, and houses all over New England! Yes, and what a figuring of future profits! On July 12, 1859, patents arrived for C. B. Bristol, Norfolk, for something described as a combination flesh-fork and skimmer; for David Cook's improved fruit basket, for Robbins Shaler of Madison and his improved confectionery safe. Two weeks later Charles Goodyear, tired but game and still trying, received a patent for "improvement in the manufacture of india rubber fabric"; and within a few days appears another name soon to be famous, that of Alva Goodrich, who had been cooking rubber mixtures and now received a patent for "improved vulcanized gums." In September patents came to J. N. Treadwell, for a machine that scoured and hulled buckwheat; to G. Munger, New Haven, who had devised some sort of writing tablet. In October the Connecticut inventors included Mortimer C. Camp, New Haven, who had built a surf boat and wanted the design protected; and William H. Lewis, Glastonbury, who had merely designed a handle "for fork or spoon."

After the Civil War began, Mr. Beckwith's almanac listed fewer patents, but right down to April of 1861, when the shooting started, his columns continued to list scores of patents. On a single day in March of 1860, patents were received for the following things: sausage machine; a skeleton for hoop skirt; composition for silvering metals; a knitting machine, an elastic belting, a cultivator, a drop-letter box, a coffee pot, washing machine, lock, and a pump.

Inventions may have dropped off in the war years, but in 1867 the Beckwith almanac was advertising "Hall of Patents, 102 Orange Street, New Haven. . . . Inventors Invited to Call." But after the war one notes a trend away from invention in the Beckwith columns; the editor is now more interested in all kinds of insurance, and the doings of the officials of the fast-growing life and fire insurance concerns at Hartford. Some Christians might and did look upon insurance as a gross impiety, a doubting of the proper goodness of Deity; but the true God of the Yankees actually favored insurance, against either fire or death, for wasn't insurance merely a lottery for the *public good?* From the earliest times, Yankees had conducted lotteries for the building of academies and colleges, aye, and for the erection of churches. Further, the death of a breadwinner, or the destruction of a home or barn by fire, might well put a whole family "on the town." The towns of Hartford in Connecticut and Montpelier in Vermont waxed prosperous by insuring men against the possibility that their families would become public charges. So, too, did a foreign town, that of Newark, New Jersey, which a Yankee named John Fairfield Dryden, born near Farmington, Maine, put into the industrial insurance business on a huge scale, with his Prudential Company. "Insurance is Thrift," said Yankee Dryden who, having been born and reared in Maine, knew the meaning of thrift.

Two of the great patent wars of mid-nineteenth century were connected with the reaper and the sewing machine. The reaper did not concern New England much, though Cyrus McCormick was obliged to make war on certain Yankee inventors transplanted in the West; but the sewing machine was first and last a Yankee invention, and the man who had more to do with its perfection than anyone else was Elias Howe, born in 1819 in Spencer, Massachusetts. Howe received his first patent in 1846, and for the next decade had a running fight on his hands. By 1856 his machine had triumphed, however, and within a few years was being made in mass production at Bridgeport, Connecticut. Invention ran in the Howe family. Elias's uncle William Howe, also of Spencer, devised and patented the Howe truss bridge, much used in the Midwest. A relative, John I. Howe, of Ridgefield, Connecticut, invented a machine that made solid-head pins, in one piece, and also a machine to stick the Howe pins in papers. This machine was credited with putting common pins, theretofore an expensive and none too reliable luxury, within the reach of everybody. And it was still another, Samuel Gridley Howe, though no close relation, who in Boston thought up the process for making raised letters, by which the blind might read with their fingers. For many years what we call Braille was known as "Howe Type."

Here and there a Yankee was working in chemistry, and as early as 1813 David Melville of Newport, Rhode Island, obtained the first American patent for making coal gas. The process worked, too, but though Melville managed to place a few of his lamps in several factories, the gas-lighting industry had to wait for further improvements in lamps. Seth Boyden of Foxboro, Massachusetts, however, had quick success with a number of inventions, including patent leather, on which was founded a big industry.

A few Yankees applied chemistry with great success to the field of ready-made therapeutics. The justly revered Painkiller, both the name and the elixir, were the inspiration of Perry Davis. Born in 1791 in Dartmouth, Massachusetts, he learned the shoemaker's trade and set up shop in Taunton, where, "in order to get relief from pain, he discovered a compound which he named Painkiller." This seemed to be a pretty good article, and Davis, a pretty good businessman, established a factory in Providence, Rhode Island, for the manufacture of his remedy on a large scale. He prospered from the start. He was devout, too, and gave generously of his money to the Baptists, and for such godly works as Temperance. Upon his death, son Edward Davis carried on the business, which grew greater by the year until "the fame of the compound had gone all over the world. . . . Christian missionaries carrying it to heathen sufferers were admitted to sacred places where outsiders had never entered."*

Though it was never claimed that a sovereign tonic called Ayer's Sarsaparilla admitted Christian missionaries into the sanctums of the heathen, this remedy nevertheless achieved a great vogue in the continental United States. It was merely one of the several medicines concocted by James Cook Ayer, M.D., University of Pennsylvania, a Yankee born in 1818 in Ledyard, Connecticut. He bought an apothecary's shop in Lowell, Massachusetts, and entered the new field of patent medicines with a brew of his own labeled Ayer's Cherry Pectoral. In 1855 he added Ayer's Sarsaparilla, and though this tonic may never have cured anybody of anything, it surely made all who used it feel a great deal better; and Dr. Ayer invited these improved men and women to say so, in letters which he printed in newspaper advertisements throughout the country. He took a brother, Frederick, into the business, and the firm expanded. From time to time the Ayers added new remedies: an ague cure that achieved great popularity in the frontier settlements of the West where ague seemed to be an occupational hazard of plowing virgin soil and of cutting virgin timber; and a "hair Vigor." Dr. Ayer was a most versatile man. He bought heavily in Lowell textile mill stock, reorganized the companies, devised new machinery; bought timber lands in Florida and put up sawmills there which he operated from his base in Lowell; was awarded patents for an ore reducing process. And, because of a famous feud with the Boston & Lowell Railroad, he built a parallel line, the Lowell & Andover. In 1871 the village of Groton Junction, Massachusetts, was renamed Ayer in his honor, and he presented the town with a fine hall.

Efficient and able though he was, Dr. Ayer never became a part of the American legend. That niche in the realm of patent medicine was reserved

* I can vouch for the fact that Painkiller got around. On arrival at a remote logging camp far up the British Columbia coast, many years ago, I discovered that one of the favorite items in the company store was Perry Davis's Painkiller, each bottle of which carried a likeness of good Mr. Davis, a benign-looking man who peered forth from the quaint steel engraving with a serene if somewhat austere countenance. The remedy was much used externally and internally by the loggers, who considered it to have great thaumaturgic properties. I can state from direct knowledge that Painkiller was also well known and revered in the logging camps of Minnesota, Oregon, and California.

for Lydia Estes Pinkham, born in Lynn, Massachusetts, in 1819, who lived but sixty-four years yet achieved a fame that is more lustrous, nigh seven decades after her death, than it was in her lifetime.

The young Lydia Estes was a child of her era. She taught school in her native town, became a devout Grahamite, and attended all rallies for Abolition and Woman's Rights. In 1843 she married Isaac Pinkham, a widower. Mr. Pinkham is reputed to have been a kindly and an affable man, but "of no great vigor." He tried farming, "trading," and the manufacture of kerosene oil. Vigor or no, children began appearing in the Pinkham household; but supporting them was too great a task for Isaac. Yet, by a pleasant irony, it was one of Isaac's many follies that led directly to the Pinkham fortune.

Never able to refuse a friend, Isaac had "gone on a note" for one George Todd, a Lynn machinist. He had to make good the note, to the extent of twenty-five dollars, and the best Todd could do as reimbursement was a formula, which he described vaguely as "a cure for the weaknesses of females." This Isaac turned over to Lydia, who had an active animus against doctors and was always brewing some sort of home remedy for herself and family. Now she tried out the Todd formula and concluded that it produced one of the finest remedies of her experience. She gave away bottles of it to her friends, who felt better at once; but she had no thought, at first, of making it a commercial product. Not until 1873.

In that hard year Isaac, who had been dabbling in a Lynn real estate subdivision, lost his shirt in the panic.* The Pinkhams were left virtually penniless. Lydia now began to brew and sell a few bottles of the Todd formula, for which she still had no name. Two years later, however, she prepared a batch for the open market and called it Lydia E. Pinkham's Vegetable Compound. The name was magic, and the preparation was to become an American classic.

In the seventies, "vegetable" was a word to conjure with. It had all the connotations of something safe, simple, and reliable. It was close to the earth, hence had the virtue of Nature; and hadn't Mr. Emerson and others said that Nature was God? Mrs. Pinkham also had other reasons. For thirty years Moffat's Vegetable Life Medicines had been on the market, along with Brendreth's Vegetable Pills, and they had been credited with the cure of almost everything from baldness to the plague.

Even so, Mrs. Pinkham's Vegetable Compound had hard going until she decided to patronize the press. But when she started to advertise, the remedy picked up quickly and began selling at a great rate, as well it should. Con-

---

* But not his socks. He never wore them. This fact was made known by Robert C. Washburn, biographer of Mrs. Pinkham, who remarks that the going without socks was one of the few subjects on which Mr. Pinkham held a positive opinion.

sider: "A FEARFUL TRAGEDY, a Clergyman of Stratford, Connecticut, KILLED BY HIS OWN WIFE, Insanity Brought On by 16 Years of Suffering with FEMALE COMPLAINTS THE CAUSE. Lydia E. Pinkham's Vegetable Compound, The Sure Cure for These Complaints, Would Have Prevented the Direful Deed."

With such things going on, what clergyman, or, for that matter, what layman, would oppose his wife's need for something that would prevent her from committing a capital crime?* Moreover, Mrs. Pinkham, who was a wise and kindly woman, had no little insight of what today is called psychology. For many years she replied, without interposition of secretary or even typewriting machine, but in her own hand, to the thousands of letters that came from women all over the United States, asking her advice. Her biographer believes that most of Mrs. Pinkham's advice was sensible, perhaps much the same that would be given today by a psychiatrist. In any case, the Compound went on to glory such as seldom has been granted to a medicine, patent or otherwise; and Mrs. Pinkham went fair into the American legend.†

Mr. Davis's Painkiller, and Mr. Ayer's Sarsaparilla, and Mrs. Pinkham's Compound were to be found in every false-front store in all the false-fronts settlements of the West, and in the imposing brick pharmacies of the new western cities. Bottles of them sat on the shelves of sod-hut and log-cabin homes in all the states and territories. One has not the least doubt that these remedies performed almost miraculous cures, or that they made all the customers feel much better, and look with better cheer upon the often dismal and melancholy acres they were engaged in bringing to the plow.

An astonishingly large number of the pioneers managed not only to survive the harsh early period, but to prosper. As their homes grew larger and better, they gradually acquired things that had scarcely been possible in the previous era—for instance, an Estey Parlor Organ. This was made in Brattleboro, Vermont, after 1850, by Jacob Estey, and was a notice of culture

* Another thing: Mrs. Pinkham's checks for advertisements were notably prompt. Grant Angle, founder and editor of the *Mason County Journal,* Shelton, Wash., told me that in the difficult early days of his paper, in the eighties, the small but certain checks from Mrs. Pinkham were often his only cash income for a week or more. Mr. Angle was of the belief that many a country newspaper would never have survived except for the steady, sure income from the Vegetable Compound. This subject might well make a rewarding thesis for one of the Nieman Fellows at Harvard.

† In the wild and rugged Sultan Basin of Snohomish County, in western Washington, there is a hole in a mountain that is still known as the Lydia E. Pinkham Gold Mine. It is, or was, the property of Mrs. Pinkham's heirs, who used occasionally to visit it, coming all the way from Massachusetts, taking home with them small samples of ore. I once visited this worthless mine, and reflected again on the curious fact that comparatively few Yankees, including the notorious old Pancake Comstock, ever did well with mines. Yankee Russell Conwell knew this when he composed his famous lecture "Acres of Diamonds."

and of comparative wealth. For many years Estey himself took to the turnpikes, his great wagon filled with his small organs; but then his business grew too large, and he remained at the factory, where he added to his instruments that noble tremolo stop called the Vox humana, which lived up to its name, giving forth a golden sound like that of Jenny Lind, or perhaps, as the more pious had it, like the throbbing alto of Abby, of the Singing Hutchinsons. Estey sent out a swarm of agents. He used the newspapers. You could buy an Estey organ on the easy payment plan; and most purchasers must have kept up their payments, for by the eighties the Estey Organ Company was making eighteen hundred instruments a month.

Estey organs went everywhere in the West that a wagon could go, and often went on from there strapped to the back of a mule. Almost every little bethel in the backwoods had an Estey, and so had almost every brothel, little or big. Miners and lumberjacks, and all other men away from home, wept to the sound of Estey's Vox humana, whether it was a Stephen Foster number, or "The Old Rugged Cross." . . . "I struck one chord of music," wrote Miss Adelaide A. Procter, "like the sound of a great Amen."

Or, when culture came to the point of requiring a really fine piano, like as not it would be one of those made in Boston by Jonas Chickering, a New Hampshire native whom William Steinway called the father of American piano making. Chickering, like Abbot-Downing of the Concord coach, might be found every day in his immense factory, in mechanic's apron, making certain that the instruments were as perfect as man could make them.

A revolution in furniture took place after old Benjamin Gilbert, tanner of Georgetown, Connecticut, who disliked to see anything go to waste, invented a machine for weaving the waste horsehair around his tannery into a furniture covering that is too well known to need description. Generations suffered as they sat on it. After about 1826, and until the late eighties, the more prosperous western pioneers could buy the beautiful glass made on Cape Cod by the Boston & Sandwich Glass Company, organized and run by a Yankee family headed by Deming Jarves.

Steamboats, railroads, motorcars, one and all, have been cited, and properly so, for their influence on migrations. To them should be added another machine, the invention of a Yankee who never migrated farther from his native home in Vermont than Worcester in Massachusetts, yet may have had no little effect, of a subjective nature, in prompting Yankee lads, and boys elsewhere, to leave their homes. This inventor was Joshua Stoddard, born in 1814 in small Pawlet among the Green Mountains, and his influence on migration was the steam calliope, that great, sweet, lusty voice of the outdoors which, surely more than clowns, or bands, or spangles, removed young men from the farms and put them on the road, to wander to the far ends of the United States and all the way between. No sound, perhaps, unless it be the magic voice of the locomotive, has had more effect on the movement of individuals than the urgent, promising, and musical notes of what its creator called the American Steam Piano.

Joshua Stoddard was primarily a bee keeper, and a good one. Raised on his father's farm in Pawlet, he tended many hives of bees and came to love the insects as other people loved dogs or cats or horses. He got a little schooling at Pawlet Academy. In young manhood he married and moved to Worcester, and there continued to keep bees and devote his spare time, in typical Yankee style, to tinkering. He wanted to "improve" the common horse-drawn hayrake.

He was something of a poet and mystic, and it was unquestionably these qualities that took his mind off the starkly utilitarian hayrake, for a time, and set him to work on the useless, by all good Yankee standards, calliope. Stoddard read a good deal, and lived rather joyfully in constant expectation of the end of the world, the date of which he liked to calculate in the manner of Adventist William Miller and other "timist" theologians. Yet he took the finest care of his many bees, and their production of honey gave a decent living to the Stoddard family, and also permitted him some opportunity to work, first, on his hayrake tinkering, and second, on the immortal instrument whose sweet voice should stem from captive steam and should carry like that of Stentor.

When Stoddard began working on this idea, in the forties, the locomotive whistle was a new sound. For his new machine he made fifteen whistles of graduated sizes. These he attached in a row to the top of a steam chest. There was no keyboard to his first model. Instead, he adapted the basic idea of the music box, by providing a long cylinder with pins driven into it and so placed that, when revolved, the pins pressed the valve stems and thus blew the whistles to play a tune. It wasn't quite so simple as that, for the ingenious part of the business was the use of pins of different shapes, whereby notes of varying length, right down to eighth-notes, could be played.

Stoddard had no difficulty getting a patent, which was granted on October 9, 1855. On the previous Fourth of July, he gave a demonstration, with the instrument set up on Worcester Common and his daughter, Jennie, turning the cylinder. The Steam Piano was a great success, even though it had to compete with a battery of artillery firing salutes to Liberty and Independence. Later that year the instrument again appeared in public, this time on board a flatcar of a railroad excursion from Worcester to Fitchburg and return. The great voice gave forth with music the like of which had never been heard before, and created a sensation for a mile or two on each side of the tracks.*

Late in 1855 Stoddard and others organized the American Steam Music Company and started manufacture of the instruments, for "use on steamboats and locomotives." Next year the company staged an exhibition in the waters around New York City by setting up an instrument on a tugboat. Oddly enough, in view of its subsequent history, the steam piano's first success was on steamboats running from New York to Albany, though John Van Ambergh, the impresario who later teamed with Barnum, bought one for use with his tent show. Who gave the Stoddard invention the name of Calliope seems not to be of record; pronunciation of it has never been a thing of agreement in the United States. Both cally-ope and cal-eye-o-pee are used, the latter being rated the more elegant.†

In 1858 the American Steam Piano Company built a special job to go on the Hudson River boat *Armenia*. This was a thirty-four-whistle affair, complete with piano keyboard, which was a tremendous success and was used continuously until 1870. Other keyboard instruments were made for use on Ohio and Mississippi River boats, and one, possibly two, were put into the circus business. But by then it did not matter to Stoddard. Typically, for an inventor, he was pushed out of the American Steam Piano Company, with nothing for his pains.

The calliope, of course, went on to classic success. Which of the big circuses took it up first is of no moment, for one and all, big and little, the outdoor shows of the United States soon possessed each a steam calliope. Its position in the street parade was at the very end of the line, and to most Americans it was, and perhaps still is, the very symbol of the circus.

As for Joshua Stoddard, he fooled no longer with musical instruments, but resumed labors on his improved hayrake, receiving patents in 1870 and 1871. The rake was manufactured under his name and was much used for many years, both in New England and at points west. This success probably encouraged him, for he went on to invent a fire escape, in 1884, though nothing came of it, nor from a fruit-paring machine which he patented in 1901, in his eighty-seventh year. But his beloved bees were faithful to the end, which came in 1902, in April, just the time when a score or so of

---

* In later years the ungrateful city of Worcester passed an ordinance prohibiting the playing of Mr. Stoddard's invention within the limits of the municipality.

† In *Reedy's Mirror,* years ago, some bard made use of both pronunciations in verses beginning:

> Proud folk stare after me,
> Call me Calliope;
> Tooting joy, tooting hope,
> I am the Calliope.

circuses were taking to the road all over America; and in every parade, you may be sure, was one of Stoddard's patent steam pianos, sizzling, smoking, rocking, vibrating, blowing the living daylights out of "Over the Waves," telling the villages and their hinterlands that the big show was about to begin, charming alike the city folk and the rustics as Calliope of old, mother of Orpheus and chief of the Muses, had charmed in her time—calling from the farms the plowboys, the milkers, the pitchers of hay as the Sirens had called mariners—sometimes, to be sure, to their doom, but always to their instruction. There never has been any other sound quite like it. Then or now, no circus was a circus that did not have the stout, bewitching voice of the old bee keeper of Pawlet and Worcester.

CHAPTER XXII

OF CERTAIN EMIGRANTS

IN THE CONTINUOUS EXODUS from New England over many years were no few emigrants who for one reason or another seem to be worthy of consideration outside the general run of pioneers and settlers in the new western regions. The influence of several of these men was not on one but on several states, occasionally upon the entire country. Others became of great influence in places where Yankees were extremely rare and were usually loathed, hated, boycotted. Still others contributed to the founding of what have long since been American institutions and are generally accepted as being indigenous to American soil, or at least stem somehow from the Declaration of Independence or the Constitution. For instance, the modern American hotel.

The American hotel was the great work of Isaiah Rogers, who was born in 1800 in Marshfield, Massachusetts. Until he designed the Tremont House, opened in Boston in 1829, the public house in the United States was just that and no more—a structure with a place to eat and a place to sleep, built with little thought of utility and even less of comfort. The Tremont was the first revolutionary change in hotels and hotel keeping since the first "ordinary" was opened in Massachusetts Bay Colony early in the seventeenth century. From it stems the American hotel of today.

Rogers was the son of a shipbuilder who wanted him to be a farmer. Instead, he apprenticed himself to a Boston carpenter, and later entered the office of Solomon Willard, prominent as a master mason, who also practiced architecture and did a little sculpting. After a few fruitful years with Willard, about 1826, young Rogers established his own office in Boston; and in 1828 he got his first big commission—to design a public house for a group of well-to-do citizens who wanted their city to have an outstanding hotel, the finest in the United States.

The completed Tremont House was little less than a national sensation. It was most luxurious for the time. Its lobby and dining room and meeting rooms were considered lavish. The bedrooms could be used singly or in suites —which was a striking departure. There were water closets, toilets, bathrooms. All rooms were connected with the lobby desk by bell signals. The kitchens were elaborately equipped. And the exterior, fashioned in the Greek Revival style, was as severe as it was beautiful.

Hotel keepers came from afar to see the new wonder, and Rogers was besieged with commissions. First, he designed and took charge of construction of the Bangor House (still, in 1949, one of the better hotels in Maine). He then moved to New York City to design and superintend building of the Astor House, much larger and even more elegant than the Tremont, which was to set the style and pace for Manhattan hotels for many years. He next went on into the South, where he planned and built several of the most famous hotels of that region, including the Exchange in Richmond, Virginia, the Battle in Mobile, the Charleston in South Carolina, the truly magnificent second St. Charles in New Orleans, the Galt in Louisville, the enormous Maxwell House in Nashville, and, in the West, the celebrated Burnet House in Cincinnati. Rogers also designed many other public buildings. He always championed the Greek Revival, and managed to keep his severe classicism alive even in his later life—he died in 1869—when rococo and gingerbread horrors were spreading across the United States, in response to the birth of the Gilded Age. But Rogers had worked well and most effectively to take his place as the father of the American hotel.

If it seems odd that the first modern hotel in New York City should have been designed by a country youth from Marshfield, Massachusetts, it is perhaps odder that a majority of New York City's modern newspapers should have been founded by wandering printers and journalists, native Yankees to a man. The earliest, the *Evening Post,* was established in 1801 by William Coleman of Boston, with the financial backing of Alexander Hamilton, and rose to great influence after 1828, when William Cullen Bryant, born in Cummington, Massachusetts, took over as editor. More revolutionary was the *Sun,* the first penny paper, which made its appearance in 1833 with Benjamin Day, of West Springfield, Massachusetts, as editor and publisher. The *Sun* almost, but never quite, failed in its early period; and in 1838 it was bought by Moses Yale Beach, a native of Wallingford, Connecticut, who with his sons made it into a highly successful newspaper. Its greatest fame, however, came after 1868 when it was purchased by Charles A. Dana, born in Hinsdale, New Hampshire, who "had few early advantages beyond the good blood of Puritan ancestors." Dana had spent five years as a member of the famously unsuccessful Brook Farm group in West Roxbury, Massachusetts. Then he became editor of the Boston *Chronotype,* a strongly Congregationalist paper, which Dana all but wrecked with his editorials of doubt concerning the patented, standard, steam-heated Hell of a majority of his readers. Dana then went to New York, to become city editor for Horace Greeley, another New Hampshire migrant. Dana soon split with Greeley, bought the *Sun,* and built in into stiff competition to the *Tribune* and the *Times.*

Greeley, a native of Amherst, had founded the *Tribune* in 1841, a paper that soon became of the widest influence, in New York and all over the North and the new West. No paper was ever more a "Bible" to its readers than the New York *Tribune* under Horace Greeley.

Greeley's paper survives as one-half of the New York *Herald Tribune,* and its great modern rival is the New York *Times.* This also was a Yankee venture, being founded by the George Jones of Poultney, Vermont, who had made a little money as the "company" of Ebenezer Brown & Company, originators of detachable collars for men.* Jones teamed with Henry J. Raymond, son of Connecticut parents and a graduate of the University of Vermont, to found the *Times* in 1851. For the next forty years Jones was editor and publisher of the *Times,* which won a justified reputation for its effective attacks on the Tweed Ring. But he was as shy and retiring as Horace Greeley was bold. There was less written about Jones during his lifetime, and since, than was the case with any other prominent newspaperman of the period.

The *Post,* the *Sun,* the *Tribune,* the *Times*—all have weathered the jungle of New York City journalism, and flourish a century after their foundings by emigrating Yankees.†

One could well ponder the newspaper talent that came from the farms of New Hampshire alone. Dana and Greeley have been mentioned. Quite as remarkable was Stilson Hutchins, born in Whitefield, who went to Iowa in 1855 and there founded the Dubuque *Herald.* In 1866 he founded the St. Louis *Times.* In 1877 he established the Washington *Post.* From Greeley's home town of Amherst came also George W. Kendall, who worked briefly with him in New York, then went South and in 1837 founded the New Orleans *Picayune.* David Atwood, born in Bedford, went west to Madison and established the *Wisconsin State Journal.* And there was Horace White of Colebrook, a great editor of the Chicago *Tribune* before he went to the New York *Evening Post.*

A New Hampshire farm boy, Benjamin Franklin Keith, had a great deal to do with a large portion and a whole era of the American theater that is remembered, fondly enough, as vaudeville. If any Yankee left his mark

* See Chapter XXI.
† The *Sun* has disappeared since the above was written.

on Manhattan, and some four hundred other cities, it was Keith. Nothing in his formative years indicated the career ahead of him. He was born in 1846 at Hillsboro Bridge, New Hampshire, and spent his first seventeen years working on farms as a hired hand. Then he saw his first circus, which had set up its tents in some country town of western Massachusetts. One can hope that it was Joshua Stoddard's Steam Piano, or calliope, that removed young Keith from the plow; in any case, he was completely dazzled by the circus. He left the farm and went promptly to work for Phineas Taylor Barnum, of whom all that need be said here is that he was a native and the great ornament of Bethel, Connecticut.

Benjamin Keith's first job with the circus was as a "grifter," selling a gimmick prepared especially for the yokel trade and called a blood tester. . . . "A slow, even flow of the secret chemical which is hermetically sealed in this crystal glass bulb, denotes a perfect blood condition, my friends . . . no feverish symptoms." He did very well, but he wanted a show of his own. In 1883 he opened a combined museum and theater in Boston, and here he met Edward Franklin Albee, a native of East Machias, Maine, who had also traveled with a circus. Keith and Albee joined forces in what, by the turn of the century, was perhaps the best known partnership in American show business. They invented vaudeville, a continuous and remarkably cleaned-up version of what had been going on for years under the name of variety, in saloons, museums, and honky-tonks, and made it into the favorite "family show" of the United States. They did this by supplying complete bills of variegated entertainment, changed weekly or oftener, to some four hundred theaters. A majority of these houses took the name of "Keith's," which for more than three decades, or until the cheaper movies came, was a guarantee of quality in the variety type of entertainment.

The city of New York's greatest booster of all time was a Yankee, Horatio Alger, Jr., native of Revere, Massachusetts, who graduated from Harvard, entered the pulpit, then went away to New York with a manuscript in his pocket. The manuscript was entitled *Ragged Dick* and related the rise to riches of a street urchin of New York. It was easily the publishing sensation of 1866, and Alger was started on his long career as a writer for boys. He simple rewrote *Ragged Dick* one hundred and twelve times, under as many titles and with the names of the characters—but nothing else—changed. These books sold a total that has been estimated at two hundred million copies. They were, naturally, trash. Yet, his formula was so compelling that farm and village lads all over the United States were prompted to pack their carpetbags and take off for New York City, there to make their fortunes. A number of them did just that, too.

But it was neither the Alger books nor yet the steam calliope that removed George Presbury Rowell from his father's farm in wild and remote Concord, Vermont, where he was born in 1838. Rowell left home for a most conventional Yankee reason—to teach school. Three years of pedagogy sufficed, and in 1858 he went to work in the advertising department of the Boston *Post.* In 1865 he launched an agency to handle advertising, the first of its kind, in that he bought columns of space in country weeklies for a one-year period, which he retailed to advertisers at a saving to them and a handsome profit for himself. The idea caught on. In 1867 he moved his agency to New York, and it quickly became, and for years remained, the most original and successful venture in the growing business of advertising. Then, in 1888, Rowell brought out the first issue of *Printers' Ink,* which sixty-odd years later continues to be something of an authority in the advertising world. He died in 1908, and properly enough at Poland Spring, Maine, the mineral water of which he had successfully promoted.*

No site in Concord is marked as the birthplace of great huckster Rowell; but not far off, in Wallingford, Vermont, a small brick house bears a legend: *Boyhood Home of Paul P. Harris, Founder of Rotary International.* Not only that, but the organization which Harris created, the father of all so-called service clubs, has bought this neat home, which belonged to his grandfather, and made it a shrine, complete with portrait of the Founder. Paul Harris was a Yankee who just happened to be born in Racine, Wisconsin, of Vermont parents. From babyhood to graduation from the University of Vermont his home was Wallingford. In 1896 he opened a law office in Chicago—and Wallingford began to exert its undoubted charm.

In Chicago, in spite of his modest success at the bar, he was a lonely man. He longed for the scenes of Wallingford: its wide main street, wholly arched in summer by majestic elms and maples; the starkly beautiful colonial houses; the quiet and the cleanness of what was then and is now one of Vermont's most attractive villages. He longed for such scenes. He longed for the good familar people of Wallingford. Chicago was in too much of a bustle to be friendly. Business and professional people had no way of meeting socially. In 1905 lonesome Paul Harris founded Rotary, a social or get-together organization for business and professional men, which has grown to have chapters all over the world. It was Rotary, too, that started the typical America phenomena of service clubs.

Much older than Rotary is the Masonic order, and the nearest to a Masonic saint in the United States was a Yankee, born Albert Pike in Boston in 1809.

---

* I found it difficult when I was recently in Concord, Vt. (pop., 353) to look on this somnolent, pleasant hamlet in the narrow valley of the Moose River and realize that from it came the chief mogul and early brains of the highest-pressured business in the United States. It somehow seemed against nature that it should be so.

Pike was one of the oddest emigrants that ever left New England. He had gone to school in Framingham and Newburyport, then taught school in a number of villages in Massachusetts. In 1831, "the restraints of New England life becoming irksome," he started west. At Independence, Missouri, he joined a party of traders heading into the Southwest. By 1833 he was again teaching school, this time in Arkansas. He got into politics, married, and became editor of the *Arkansas Gazette,* in which, despite the place of his birth, he advocated admission of Arkansas as a slave state.

Pike commanded a cavalry outfit in the Mexican War. He fought at least one duel. He was admitted to the bar. During the Civil War he rose to the command of a brigade; but he seems always to have been in controversy with superior officers, including President Jefferson Davis. At war's end, his property confiscated, he became a wanderer, stopping awhile in Memphis to edit the *Appeal,* and at last settled in Washington, where he remained to his death, in 1891. Here in Washington he performed the labors that were to make him revered in the Masonic lodges of the United States, at least fifteen of which honor his name in their titles; and his labors were published, during 1872–1905, as *Morals and Dogma of the Ancient and Accepted Scottish Rite of Freemasonry.* He had previously done much to "revise and improve" Masonic ritual in all degrees of the order.

Albert Pike was a colorful character, of huge build, with a Jovian countenance and hair rolling down over his shoulders, and wore a vast beard. He was many-sided, for he not only wrote learnedly on Roman law but had poetry published in *Blackwood's,* the famous British magazine, and other periodicals. Moreover, he wrote what are considered as the best lyrics to the immortal "Dixie." All in all, Albert Pike was probably unique among Yankee emigrants.

Possibly Silas Doty, born in St. Albans, Vermont, was also unique in the New England exodus. In his age Doty claimed to have robbed more houses, to have stolen more property, and to have broken out of more jails and prisons than anyone else alive in his time, which was the seventy-six years following 1800. His boast seems pretty large, yet there is evidence that he lived up to most if not all of it.

Sile Doty, as he was known, was born into a large and apparently decent farm family, which migrated to York State in 1809. Here young Sile was apprenticed to a blacksmith. He liked to experiment with locks, too, and was shortly something of an expert. He also liked brisk business, so he worked both sides of the street, by supplying burglars with keys to fit the locks he had installed on the homes and places of business of honest people.

Sile Doty was an artist at crime but not too successful a practitioner of it. In his penniless old age he wrote that "not even the certainty of being hanged

would have prevented me for one moment from taking something I wanted."
He took, first and last, a great deal; including, on one famous occasion, the
watches and other valuables of *all* the members of the Michigan legislature,
as they slept soundly from their arduous duties in a Lansing hotel. His main
profession was burglary, though he had spells of working as a coiner, a
highwayman, a stealer of slaves, and on two or three occasions, a river pirate.
After some two decades of more or less petty crime, and numerous jail breaks,
he arrived at Adrian, Michigan, in 1836 with a wife and children. Here he
set up a blacksmith shop as a blind for his planned activities. His idea was
to build a modest empire for counterfeiters and a few gangs of thieves, the
operations of which he would direct. He established agents in Chicago,
Detroit, and Cincinnati to dispose of stolen goods, and to distribute his brand
of queer money.

The Doty gangsters appear to have been moderately successful; but things
at last warmed up, and he moved to Indiana, where he settled near Angola.
Here he committed a murder for which he was sent to the state prison at
Jefferson for life. He had served most of a year before the verdict of the
lower court was reversed and he was remanded to the La Grange County
jail, to await a new trial. A year in the pen had given him a great urge to be
outside. He sawed a hole in the jail wall and fled to Logansport, where he
was recaptured, handcuffed, and confined aboard a canalboat for transportation to Fort Wayne. The craft moved along the quiet waters behind four
horses, the weather was fine, and the officers drowsy. Doty sat up and removed his shackles. He jumped into the canal, reached shore, and untied the
horses, one of which he mounted and rode away. But they took him again,
and this time the constables vowed they would hold him. They put him in
the Angola jail and attached leg irons weighing twenty pounds, which were
riveted to his ankles and linked with heavy chain. When things had calmed
down a bit Doty took a thin-bladed knife he had sewn inside his belt, just
in case, and cut a hole through the jail wall. Getting out of there proved to
be a task; but get out he did, the heavy irons still on his legs, and made his
slow way to the nearest barn. Here he stole a horse which he rode side-saddle
to a near-by house where he kept a set of his professional tools. With these
it was simple for the master to free himself. Angola did not see him again
for a long time. Within a few weeks he was a civilian employee—so he later
said—of General Zachary Taylor's army in Mexico.

At the end of the Mexican War, Sile Doty showed up again in his old
haunts, with a sack of Mexican gold, a serape and a long knife, and some
dandy Spanish profanity. Nothing, apparently, was said about the old murder
charge, so he picked up where he had left off, by stealing horses, robbing
freight wagons, and committing other crimes of no great imagination. Michi-

gan laid hands on him and sent him to the pen in Jackson, where he spent fifteen years—much of it, surprisingly, as a trusty. On release, in 1865, he resumed his practice. Three more prison terms were still ahead of him, each shorter than the previous one, causing the now white-haired old reprobate to observe that if his sentences continued to diminish, he would at last be permitted to steal without danger of punishment.

When he was seventy-five, Doty was discharged for the last time from the Michigan penitentiary. He made himself a new set of tools, and with these moved upon the suburbs of Toledo, Ohio, plundering stores and homes of a four-horse wagonload of stuff, which he turned over to a confederate to sell. Instead, that dishonest man boxed the stuff and shipped it away, cheating Doty of his share. A few days later, old Doty, now reduced to traveling on foot, reached the home of a son in Reading, Michigan, after walking ten miles; and there he died, March 2, 1876, the sole Yankee outlaw, its seems probable, to have achieved any notable notoriety outside New England. The St. Albans *Messenger,* in his native town, does not seem to have marked his passing, but the Angola *Herald* in Indiana did right by the Vermont emigrant. On March 15 it ran a banner line across its front page: THE LAST OF SILE 'DOTY!—Death of a Wonderful Man—What an Eventful Life!

More in keeping with New England emigration was the export of missionaries; and of the thousands of these none turned out to be more effective, from the national viewpoint, than the group which gradually infiltrated the Sandwich Islands. These islands, which later became Hawaii, were an object of Yankee missionary effort as early as 1819, when Hiram Bingham of Bennington, Vermont, and Asa Thurston of Fitchburg, Massachusetts, voyaged there with the idea of converting the natives to Christianity. Ten years later reenforcements began arriving from New England, which continued until approximately a hundred Yankees were at work on the heathen.* Among these was the Reverend Daniel Dole, born in Skowhegan, Maine, and his wife, who was Emily Ballard, and who in 1844 gave birth to a boy, Sanford Ballard Dole, marked for great things. Other Doles left Maine during the years and went to the Islands—among them James, who proceeded to build up a business in sugar and pineapples that became an empire of itself, and Edmund P., who rose to prominence as a statesman. As for Sanford Dole, his was perhaps the greatest single influence in changing the Sandwich Islands, which was a monarchy, into the republic of Hawaii, then into a territory of the United States. He served six years as president of the

* Prominent in the hundred was Titus Coan, of Killingworth, Conn., who, on a single Sunday baptized 1,705 Sandwich Islanders. Others in the hundred were Ephraim Clark, Haverhill, N.H.; Dwight Baldwin, Durham, Conn.; and William Richards, Plainfield, Mass.

republic, then became the first governor of the American territory of Hawaii. Annexation had been strongly favored by the Honolulu *Bulletin,* under the guidance of Wallace R. Farrington, a native of Orono, Maine, who later became governor of Hawaii Territory.

The occupation and eventual annexation of Hawaii were for many years a subject of hot contention in the United States. Many writers denounced it as a steal, as imperialism of the worst sort. Others said it was an enslavement of a whole people to big business in the forms of sugar and fruit. The editor of the *Congregationalist* of Boston, however, looked at the matter quite differently. "The stupendous change," wrote Howard A. Bridgman, in 1920, "from a race of filthy and degraded human beings to a self-governing and Christian nation was brought about in less than a century by the self-sacrificing labors of a hundred New Englanders and the expenditure of about one million dollars." Both the critics and the friends of annexation spoke truthfully. The great fact, of course, was merely that annexation of Hawaii by one of the stronger powers was wholly inevitable. It was too late in history for any island rich in economic possibilities to retain its primitive condition.

A missionary to other Pacific islands who was interested only in business and not in conversion of the natives, was Edward Henry Green, born in Rockingham, Vermont. He made a quick and considerable fortune in Manila, dealing in tea and silk, and might be better remembered today had he not married a remarkable woman named Henrietta Howard Robinson, a native of New Bedford, Massachusetts. In 1867 she already possessed a fortune by inheritance from her father and an aunt; and on their wedding day she and Edward made an agreement that each should remain wholly independent of the other in all financial matters. Good businessman though he was, Edward Green lived ever after in the shadow of his wife's uncanny way with money. Hetty Green, as she was to be known, moved upon the New York Stock Exchange, theretofore considered a place for males only; but she soon demonstrated what a fatuous notion *that* was. She liked railroad stocks, and engineered several astounding coups that must have left officials of the Louisville & Nashville, the Reading, and the Georgia Central wondering what manner of magic had bulled the stocks of their lines to ridiculous heights. She also bought and sold other stocks, and traded in real estate.* She usually appeared wearing what had once been a black dress, but had taken on the mixed brown and green shades of old age; and she carried an umbrella and handbag of approximately the same era as her dress. In the handbag, she carried Graham crackers on which she munched from time to

* Said her brief sketch in *Who's Who in America:* " . . . and probably the greatest woman financier in the world; interested in nearly every large corpn. and enterprise of magnitude all over the world; personally manages her large property in stocks, bonds and real estate . . . "

time and remarked she was thus saved from paying the "prohibitive prices" of New York restaurants.

The newspapers, naturally, began to notice Hetty as a character. They played up her shrewdness less than her grasping and penurious disposition. She seemed not to mind in the least, calculating doubtless that the stressing of her stinginess would have some effect in keeping her from the importunities of strangers who wanted gifts. She gained added protection by adopting an ostentatiously obscure and Spartan mode of life. And she always carried a loaded revolver, reported by one newspaper writer to be one of Smith & Wesson's small-calibered weapons, which she vowed was "mostly to protect myself against lawyers. . . . I'm not much afraid of burglars or highwaymen." Thus she lived and died (1916) to the great joy of Sunday supplement readers, and she left an estate of more than one hundred million dollars, which made her unquestionably the richest Yankee woman in all of the Exodus.

But, if a fellow Yankee had had his way, Hetty Green would have left no money at all. Josiah Warren did not believe in metal money or in paper currency; the only medium of exchange he planned for his anarchistic Utopia was time-money certificates showing the "hours of useful work" performed by the bearers. Warren, now as forgotten as he was frighteningly notorious in his day, was born in 1798 in Boston. He was given a good musical education, then at the age of twenty-two emigrated to Ohio. He settled in booming Cincinnati. For a time he taught music, and also established a factory to make a lard-burning lamp he had invented. He later invented and patented a self-feeding cylinder printing press.

For all his inventiveness in practical things, and his successful lamp manufacturing business, Warren was a man of soaring ambitions to improve man's lot. These took him well into the abstract, where he dreamed up a new kind of heaven on earth. At about this time the Owens of Scotland had arrived to found a colony in Indiana based on various ideas of cooperative effort and named New Harmony. Naturally enough, it attracted Warren. He soon discovered that New Harmony was populated by a number of highly talented and original people, and by a much larger number of uncommonly lazy parasites; and though he was one of the most energetic and enthusiastic colonists he gradually saw that the drones were too many. When the colony arrived at its foreordained collapse, he left, bitterly certain that no progress could be made with any sort of cooperation between men. There and then he became the first American anarchist.

Anarchist Warren was no man to sit around a cracker barrel and mouth the philosophy of anarchism. He was a man of action. In Cincinnati he opened a Time Store to demonstrate one of the first steps necessary before the

United States could be turned into an orderly, rational, and happy state of anarchy. Time Stores, which were to be opened in all parts of the country, would accept in exchange for goods only the Labor Notes issued by some sort of minimum central office. The specimen Labor Note he used for demonstration bore the legend: "Due to Bearer, Eight Hours Labor in Shoemaking, or One Hundred Pounds of Corn."

Warren was no man for violence. Not from him came the almost universal belief that an anarchist was a maker and user of bombs. He established a periodical, the *Peaceful Revolutionist,* for printing which he himself made press, type molds, type, and stereotype plates. About 1851 he came to believe that success for his anarchist state could be hastened if he moved to an area of great population. On Long Island at what is now Brentwood, New York, he founded the town of Modern Times, a nucleus around which was to be established the first unit of an anarchistic United States. His show piece here was the Equity Store, an elaboration or perhaps a refinement of his Cincinnati Time Store. By 1859 Modern Times had achieved great notoriety among conventional Americans as a gathering place for all of the eccentrics and disgruntled in the United States. There was even a Queen of Modern Times, an actual woman—a "most beautiful woman," said Moncure D. Conway, who saw her in the summer of 1860; but what her place was in the colony is not now clear.

Among Warren's sponsors and closest friends was a Yankee from Templeton, Massachusetts, Stephen Pearl Andrews, who much earlier had been driven out of Texas and Louisiana for his outspokenness on abolition, favored Warren's ideas, but thought they were only half-measures. What he wanted was a Panarchy, the whole world in one universal nation; and to this end he devised a universal language called Alwato, and set forth his plans for society in a huge volume entitled *The Basic Outline of Universology.*

Modern Times, of course, went out of business, and neither Warren's nor Andrews's notions made any measurable progress—unless the current idea of a United Nations has some of its roots in Andrews's Panarchy. But Josiah Warren and Stephen Andrews are good evidence that New England exported revolutionary ideas, along with occasionally revolutionary inventions.

Gideon Putnam's notion of a colony was anything but revolutionary. For almost one hundred and fifty years, since 1802, it has been known as Saratoga Springs. He was born in Sutton, Massachusetts, a nephew of General Rufus Putnam, already mentioned in connection with the founding of Marietta, Ohio. Although he did not join his uncle's colony he was himself something of a pioneer and colonizer. Shortly after marriage he and his wife moved into Vermont, where they cleared land on the site of present

Middlebury College. They moved again, to Rutland for a brief period, then to Bemis Heights, New York, on the old battlefield of Saratoga. In 1789 they built their home on land that is now in the center of Saratoga Springs, and Gideon started making staves and shingles by hand. These he rafted down the Hudson for sale in New York City. Later he erected a sawmill. He bought three hundred acres of land on which were the medicinal springs, known to the Indians and used by them since time out of mind.

The springs on Putnam's land were still in their primeval state. A few abortive attempts had been made to capitalize them, but no one before him seems to have considered them as the foundation for a permanent resort. In 1802 he started construction on the first wing, seventy feet long, of a gigantic hotel which he named Union Hall. This became the famous Grand Union Hotel. He platted a village. He laid wooden pipes to carry the waters of the various springs to another building on which he began construction, which was to be Congress Hall. Meanwhile, he used the press to announce the curative properties of "Congress Water," and to describe the comforts of his hotel. He died in 1812, before he had completed even half of the improvements he had projected; but even this early his Saratoga Springs was well started on its long career as a fashionable watering place.

Whether Gideon Putnam would have approved the Saratoga Springs resort known later to generations of Americans isn't to be known. The place became famous less for its medicinal waters than for what more than one Yankee preacher described as its gambling hells, its horse racing, and its elegant barrooms. Still untold numbers of people did go to Saratoga Springs for the express purpose of drinking Gideon Putnam's Congress Water, and probably they went away refreshed in body and in spirit. The water was bottled, too, and shipped to all parts of the country, where it was drunk, among others, by the the numerous disciples of Yankee Sylvester Graham, the great food reformer, who pronounced Congress Water to be the one and sovereign medicine needed by mankind.

There was another effective Putnam in the Yankee emigration—George Palmer, born in Brunswick, Maine, who went to New York City and founded the publishing house later to be known as G. P. Putnam's Sons. This was most honorable in a day when the piracy of foreign books was common, in that George Palmer Putnam would not publish a contemporary book "except by arrangement with the author." Although it was said of him that he suffered at times because of a tendency to estimate public taste too highly, his house thrives in mid-twentieth century, along with at least two other notable Yankee-founded publishing firms, that established in 1838 by Daniel and William Appleton, from Haverhill, Massachusetts, and, much later, that established by John Farrar, an emigrant from Burlington, Vermont.

What Henry Louis Mencken always designates as the Free-State of Maryland was never in the main stream, nor even a small branch, of Yankee migration; yet the great city of Baltimore was most fortunate in receiving at least two emigrants from New England. One was Arunah Shepherdson Abell, born in East Providence, Rhode Island, who established a newspaper in 1837 which he named the *Sun* and in the next half-century made it into one of the outstanding daily journals of the country. Enoch Pratt, a native of North Middleboro, Massachusetts, was the other.

When he was fifteen years old, Enoch Pratt left school for a clerkship in Boston, remarking to his parents, "I suspect I am old enough to do considerable business." It wasn't an idle boast. Seven years later he arrived in Baltimore with $150; and in the next sixty years he had almost unparalleled success in iron, transportation, banking, and fire insurance. He took, says a biographer, the New England qualities of "shrewdness, honesty, quick wits and public-spiritedness to the predominatingly Southern city," and made a fortune, which he devoted to the promotion of education and health.

Pratt was a man of small stature. He had piercing blue eyes, the thin straight lips not uncommon in Puritan stock, and a square jaw. He dressed as quietly as a country parson, and he was in his private life as careful of money as any hill farmer in Vermont. He was also as bold as they came. In Baltimore he not only openly opposed slavery, but was a generous donor to the American Colonization Society, which sought to organize a Negro republic in Africa; and during the Civil War he was Baltimore's leading supporter of the Union cause. Long before his death, he had given large sums to hospitals and schools; and endowed the noble library that bears his name with exactly $833,333.33 which, he provided, should be permitted to accumulate until it had reached one million dollars, the city to pay 5 per cent interest in the meantime. Typically, Pratt prided himself on this arrangement, for the city had been paying but 4 per cent on its bonds; 5 per cent for the library, he said, was "good business." Enoch Pratt puzzled Baltimore. He was probably good for Baltimore, too, and Baltimore was surely kind to him.

At some future time, when Americans have at last achieved an interest in the past of their country, a comprehensive account of their many migrations may be feasible. In any such all-inclusive accounting, the early and late movement of emigrating Yankees must have the first consideration, not because of their number, great though it has been, but because of their influence. And no listing of New England emigrants is complete that does not mention Galusha Aaron Grow, a native of Windham County, Connecticut, who probably did more than any other to destroy the very frontier to which a vast majority of Yankees had been migrating. His career was crowned, though not ended, in 1861, when he witnessed passage in the House of Representatives of the Homestead Act, for which he had been fanatically working for more than a decade.

Yankee Grow was born in 1822, and was but four years old when his father died. Mother Grow, however, was a fearless and an enterprising woman. Taking her children, Widow Grow set out in 1834 to pioneer in the Tunkhannock valley of Pennsylvania. Near what became Glenwood she purchased four hundred acres, and opened a store. Twelve-year-old Galusha and a brother went to work clearing timber, making field, and helping in the store. Their activities soon centered on lumber and hemlock bark. Galusha became a prodigious bark spudder, for he grew to six feet two inches, and was as stout as an ox. He must also have been wise beyond his years, for Widow Grow permitted him, when he was fourteen, to take a boatload of bark and lumber down the Susquehanna for sale at Port Deposit.

The business of the Grows prospered, and in 1840 Galusha went away to college, at Amherst in Massachusetts, and was graduated four years later, returning to Pennsylvania to study law in the office of F. B. Streeter, at Montrose. After admission to the bar in 1847 he formed a partnership with David Wilmot, at Towanda. Partner Wilmot's name was to become historic in connection with the Wilmot Proviso.

Galusha Grow was sent to Congress in 1850, and was its youngest member. His first speech was significantly on the subject of man's rights to the soil. His ideas had been formed by observing the activities of land speculators, a large number of whom he considered to be the most rapacious and unconscionable men at large; and by noting the sufferings, even the disasters of settlers that were largely brought about by the land sharks. Such things had made him in fact if not in name something of a Single Taxer, for he believed, and often declared to Congress, that the only valid claim to the ownership of land was its occupation and use by its owner. In his second term he introduced in the House a bill providing that every applicant be given a quarter-section, or one hundred sixty acres, of government land, with the understanding that he himself should settle on the land.

Grow's bill did not pass, even though it received stout aid from a freshman representative from Vermont, Justin Smith Morrill.* But Grow did not give up. He continued to rewrite his bill and to introduce it, and to work

* Who later as Senator Morrill contributed much in the way of legislation by introducing and fostering the Land Grant College Act. This was inspired by Morrill's feeling that the educated Americans, surer than others to educate their sons, were perpetuating a monopoly of education "inconsistent with the welfare and complete prosperity of American institutions." More than fifty agricultural and technical colleges, including the agricultural branch of Cornell University and the Massachusetts Institute of Technology as well as the so-called cow colleges in the West, were firmly established under the two Morrill Acts, of 1862 and 1890.

for any other bill that would grant land to individual settlers. The approach of secession, however, kept Congress in an uproar. In the forensic battles that were tearing the Congress apart, Grow stood in the first rank. He not only was an imposing figure on the floor, but was a dyspeptic and shunned all drink at a period when members of Congress drank too much for their own or their country's good; and he was thus always dependable, ready to take the floor at a moment's notice. He proved particularly able in goading the fire-eating southern members to desperation, which he enjoyed as thoroughly as the Yankees Charles Sumner and Benjamin Wade.

Try as he would, Grow could not get any sort of homestead bill passed so long as southerners sat in the House and Senate. So he bided his time, meanwhile devoting his efforts to defeating every one of the many land speculators' schemes put forth by the catchpoll creatures of lobbyists. It was said of Grow that he could scent a land-steal bill quicker than anyone else in House or Senate; and because of his first-hand knowledge of the methods of land sharks, he was bitterly competent in talking them down once they got to the floor.

When secession at last cleared the Congress of its southern members, Grow knew that his chance had come. In 1861 he was elected speaker of the House, and presently had the superb joy of watching passage of the Homestead Act, which was later signed by President Lincoln. The act was not Grow's original bill, nor was he wholly responsible for it, or even for its passage. But his influence surely was greater than any other single influence in this connection. The act, more than any other law, hastened the end of the frontier.

The Homestead Act was abused times without number, abused by the very people whom it sought to protect; yet it was a vast improvement over the chaotic conditions of squatter preemption. Under its provisions two hundred and forty-eight million acres of frontier have been "homesteaded"—a verb which the heirs of Noah Webster long ago admitted to the pages of the American lexicon.

The barbed-wire fence of Yankee Glidden and the plains windmill of Yankee Halladay were the contributory factors that made Yankee Grow's homestead idea workable on the ultimate frontier, that land which the maps used to designate as Great American Desert, and which became America's great empire of grain. Aye, the waste land had budded and bloomed like the rod of Aaron of old. It is somehow heart-warming, too, to know that the dyspepsia of Galusha Aaron Grow, as well as his effective activities in Congress, may well have been caused by his ferocious and consuming hatred for land speculators.

CHAPTER XXIII

THERE SHE STANDS . . .

THERE SHE STANDS, New England in mid-twentieth century, the ancient and native home of the race called Yankees.

She has been buried and buried again, buried deep, these past hundred years and more. Other Americans, not Yankees, buried her, singing the obsequies of her political power, of her agriculture, her shipping, her industries, and her intellect.

There she stands, mid-century; and that she stands at all is a matter of some wonderment, for the outlanders publish her obituary every little while.

What can she show for her long and honorable past save a few historical shrines, and graveyards without number? True, the shrines are well kept and the slabs in the cemeteries have quaint and amusing inscriptions in their slate and granite. But, God help you, *what* sort of nourishment can they derive from the Green at Lexington, handsome though it be, or from the iron-fenced Old Granary in Boston? They taste not of manna, but of the bitterness of ashes. Their flowers are no longer living garlands, but wreaths of the valley of the Shadow. . . .

In forty-two states, and in the territories of Alaska and Hawaii as well, one hears it said, as though it were a documented and patented verity, that the once great country of the Yankee is Necropolis.

Call them Ishmael no longer. Their great strength, as well as their weakness, was that they were at odds with almost everybody, including themselves, and thus they performed marvels to prove that they were right. It was a wonderful thing to be *certain;* to possess neolithic assurance. This came from history. Yankees read history, all history, in the light of piety; and they discovered, in the temporal unfolding of the divine and Congregational plan, that the entire past, up to the year of their Lord 1620, had been merely a prologue to the founding of the New England commonwealths. They spent their strength fashioning their land of Canaan to their liking, then went

[351

forth in the attempt to do the same for the less fortunate parts of what became the United States.

But call them Ishmael no longer. Their harpoons of iron have rusted away. Their bomb-lances of ideas either have long since been accepted as foundations of the Republic, or have been stowed away as curiosities. Leviathan may still make a path to shine after him, yet there are none to follow the wake. The Lord may still call upon them to go forth—for all the Yankees know—but they can no longer understand His word. The confusing babel around them is too much. . . .

Where, pray, are their great voices that once echoed to the far reaches of the nation?

It was, sir, a small college—Mr. Webster had said—yet there were those who loved it. Even their hermits could be eloquent, for Thoreau had observed, of old Brown of Ossawatomie, that he was the sort to leave a Greek accent slanting the wrong way, in order to right up a falling man. Yankee women, too, spoke up in meeting, and it turned out that Dorothea, granddaughter of Dr. Elijah Dix, had something to say. I proceed, gentlemen—she told the General Court—to call your attention to the present state of insane persons within this Commonwealth. And lo, the walls of ignorance built around the sick of mind came tumbling down, even as those of Jericho. . . . Another Yankee female, who had seen the glory of the coming of her Lord, sent her brothers, and cousins unto the fourth generation, and many another, away to trample the grapes of wrath, even to die, to the thunderous hymn she wrote between midnight and dawn, in an army tent near Washington. . . .

But where are their voices *now?* Where are their whalers, their peddlers, their traders? Where are their divines, their inventors, their reformers of this and that, where are their schoolmasters, their makers of states?

As long ago as the Fourth of July, in 1876, the Reverend Frank E. Howe thought he knew. On that glorious day of the Centennial he stood in the hot sun on Grafton Common, in Massachusetts, and spoke not only for himself and the audience before him, but for all the Yankees resident in New England. "Who cares," he cried, "for the growth of New England? Who cares, so long as she can continue to give principles and institutions and men to the Nation?" He paused a moment, then replied to his question. No Yankee, he said, cared whether or not New England grew apace, so long as the whole nation became New Englandized. He was not contradicted.

The eloquent Mr. Howe was of course rhetorical. There may, too, have been something of whistling in the dark. Certainly there was an assurance equal to smugness. Yet above all he spoke truthfully. He said in words what a majority of Yankees believed on that Fourth of July in 1876, and what they believe three-quarters of a century later—that, no matter the status of

New England, her people had gone forth in continuous waves to spread Yankee notions and institutions in all parts of the country.

It is what people believe about themselves that counts. They act or they fail to act according to their beliefs.

A few years after Mr. Howe, another Yankee looked at his brethren. He was Francis Parkman of Boston, a writer who had seen a good deal of the American West. Now he looked at his rural New England. He thought that it had largely disappeared. He spoke of its narrowness, its prejudices, its oddities, and its unconquerable strength, all of which, he said, were among the things of the past; or, where they did linger, it was in some remote corner that the whistle of the locomotive never reached. New England, Mr. Parkman went on, had spread itself in swarming millions over half a continent, changing with changing conditions; and even that part of it which still clung to the ancestral hive had transformed and continued to transform itself.

The Yankees had indeed spread over half a continent. Their character had doubtless changed somewhat. But look you to what changes *they* had wrought upon half a continent. . . .

In the meantime, what was left in New England? What of the ancestral hive? It was still something of a hive, praise be, though the swarm was of species mixed beyond knowing. As for the law that was given unto them by old Bradford at Plymouth Plantation, that those who labored not should have no corn—it might be weaker than of old, but it was still in the statutes. The word Industry might now be written *without* a capital letter, yet it was still held in some respect, even if many a granite Yankee complained bitterly that the word itself had no more meaning in these latter times of weakness than the making of potash, or the reduction of a sperm whale for illuminating oil.

Times of weakness? Yea, and times of impiety. It was not so in 1849, when on a Friday in July, off the town of Chatham on the Cape, a huge whale was sighted, then promptly taken by the inhabitants. On the following day another whale was taken in the same spot. Then, on Sunday, as if to try the faith of these people, still another great monster appeared. "Not a boat was sent in pursuit," reported the *American Messenger,* a weekly paper of Boston.

"The inhabitants of New England," said an observer of a hundred years ago, "are of a character equal in strength to the austerity of their beliefs."

So, doubtless, are they to this day, though the austerity of their beliefs has been softened. (Weakened, say the surviving men of granite.) It was softened by the hordes from the Old World who swarmed into New England while Yankees were swarming into Ohio, Kansas, and Oregon. And it was softened again by Yankee philosophers who, as Yankees came to fear less the unreasonable forces of nature, saw that their God was a more genial God than they had at first supposed. He was also a God more remote than of yore. He was surely easier to live with. Yea, God's controversy with New England had come to an end. The Sabbath now belonged not only to God but to His chosen people.

The swarming immigrants brought a complexity in their religions, and even though the Yankees themselves had invented a number of religions of their own they still, one and all, spoke directly to the Lord without intermediary. With each of their homemade religions, it seemed, there was even less of divine authority than before. Now, with the immigrants, came a church armed with the same sort of absolute authority that had caused the Pilgrims and Puritans to leave old England. So, it was little wonder that the Yankees, who relied chiefly upon their individual consciences for guidance, feared it, found it alien, and were ready to believe the worst that any scoundrel could concoct about its clergy.

Meanwhile, however, the spindles turned in Lowell, in Woonsocket, in Manchester, watched by pretty girls from Ireland, while gadgets of metal flowed in continuous streams from the hands of Poles and Letts in the factories of Bridgeport and Meriden; and mountains of pulpwood, felled by *canadiens* and Finns, were digested into paper at Millinocket and Berlin Falls. Thousands of men from Scotland and Italy took their chisels in hand and wrote *Here Lies* in slabs from valleys of granite and marble at Barre and Rutland. In Montpelier and Hartford, insurance clerks born in Cork or Montreal filled in papers that gambled on the lives of locomotive engineers in Texas and the houses and barns of settlers in North Dakota. English and Scandinavians in Hartford and New Haven made weapons with which to protect the honest if illegal stills in the Carolinas, or to rob Dexter Horton's fine new bank on Puget Sound.

Nor was all the industry and busyness in field and factory. From forty-two states, as well as from much of the rest of the world, there came—and come— thousands upon thousands of outlanders to drink at the very font of learning in North America, which bubbles forth at places named Hanover and Bowdoin, Boston and Cambridge, Providence and Middlebury, Amherst and Williamstown, Worcester and New Haven. Yes, and Wellesley and Northampton. Many come as students, hungry for learning and technology; others come as snobs, for, even though the outlanders have buried New England over and over, there surrounds the hoary Yankee universities some aura of infinitely greater effulgence than is to be found in the West or South.

The several *d*'s in "Harvard Yard" can be heard as properly pronounced in
Des Moines and Tacoma as in the First Parish Church (Unitarian) in
Cambridge. . . . Graying males of Oakland and Kansas City smile nostalgic-
ally when the radio brings them the song about Morey's, a drinking saloon in
New Haven, Connecticut.

> Mr. Speaker, it is not generally known, but is yet a fact, that the
> colleges of New England harbor one-fifth of all the books in all the
> colleges in the United States. . . . And may I extend my remarks, sir,
> to point out that the endowment funds of New England colleges amount
> to more than a quarter of all such funds in the entire country.

Yet, what of yonder buildings, vast and silent, lining the banks of so
many Yankee streams? Their brick walls remind of colleges, for here and
there some wan ivy clings and climbs, and there are great bells in their towers.
Those bells, stranger, have not rung in years. Once upon a time they were
pealed nigh at dawn, a tocsin to start five hundred thousand spindles to turning, to set amove the flying shuttles, all to the end that the wives of farmers
along the Kaw and the Minnesota should have proper cotton drawers and
the bemused natives of Oahu should cover their nakedness. . . . Those
spindles, outlander, and those shuttles still spin and whir, but in the county
named for a Mr. Gaston, in North Carolina, where the hide of a Yankee was
once prized even above that of a fine raccoon. . . . The Yankees freed the
slaves, O Lord, then moved their New England mills near to the fields of
cotton, to enthrall the natives of the South with a music new to them, and
to leave Fall River with another topic than that of Miss Lisbeth Borden, and
to bequeath Manchester an empty brick shed, full two miles long, drowsing
by the falls of the Amoskeag.

> But, Mr. Speaker, may I remark here that in the matter of *woolen*
> manufacture New England retains her ancient preeminence. The great
> looms of Lawrence, of Nashua, and other of our cities produce three-
> fifths of all such goods made in the nation. As to other textiles, sir, we
> must admit that they are now made in larger amount elsewhere, a condi-
> tion due in no small part to the flighty American woman—the slave of
> fashion, sir, if I may coin a phrase—who without reason, and most
> suddenly at that, ceased to buy our fine calico and gingham, which had
> been the favorites of her mother, her grandmother, and her great-grand-
> mother, and demanded clothing made of a synthetic and damnable
> material called rayon. A passing fancy, sir, but most grievous.

It was typical of John Whittier, whose mother was a Greenleaf, that he
ignored the clatter of the many shoe factories in Haverhill and Amesbury,

to write of barefoot boys. The swarthy man with the brooding eyes loathed the rising Yankee industries. He saw them making a new kind of slave, just when Yankees were going forth to free the chattels of the South. So, he ignored the cordwainers, who had once grandly called themselves the Knights of St. Crispin but were now automatons chained to machines, to apply venom to the South, a place of woman's shriek beneath the lash, of manhood's wild despair; and to idealize an older, a simpler, a better time, when Maud Muller raked the sweet meadow, and when snow drifted gently down through loose shingles on a farmhouse roof. Old Whittier would doubtless have been pleased, had he lived to see the Yankee cordwainers departing for Tennessee, for Wisconsin, for Missouri and California, taking their wretched machines with them.

> Yesterday the chairman of the committee on industries reported that, though many factories in Maine, Massachusetts, and New Hampshire had been closed, New England continued to make better than one-third of all the leather boots and shoes in the United States. He said also that, no matter where shoes were manufactured in America, nearly all of them were manufactured on machinery made and owned in New England and rented out on a royalty basis. The chairman added that more than one-half of all of the textile machinery in the country was made in New England.

This is all very well, and it is quite smart of the Yankees to retain such a basic interest in manufacture, no matter where it is carried on. It has permitted the daughters and widows of State Street in Boston to don their lavendar taffeta once a quarter, to adjust their whalebone collars, and to visit the board rooms and safety deposits, there to see that the coupons are cut precisely along the dotted lines, and to wonder, possibly, why anyone should prefer to manufacture something in St. Louis, or Gastonia, or Milwaukee—and thus be obliged to live in such barbarous places.

Yankees of old were wont to risk their capital anywhere, no matter how distant from New England, no matter the size of the risk. (God, you comprehend, was at that time obliged to create providential opportunities for Yankee advancement.) But the children and grandchildren of the men who financed Calumet & Hecla, and Rumford Baking Powder, and the Atchison, Topeka & Santa Fe Railway, and such crazy enterprises, are content with less risk and a sure 5 per cent. A considerable army of genteel men wearing hard collars and high lace shoes advise the old ladies who, though in God they may still trust, like also to know what Messrs. Kidder and Peabody and Hornblower and Weeks and Lee Higginson think of these newer concerns, these late-comers who are manufacturing recent inventions such as electric lights and horseless carriages. Rich or poor, however, the Yankees know where to put a portion of their cash.

> The First National's survey, made public this week, shows that New England has about one-third of all mutual savings-bank deposits in the country, and more than 18 per cent of all savings deposits. Savings deposits of all banking institutions in New England are $504 per capita, as compared with $160 for the remainder of the country.

Savers of pennies, savers of string, eaters of shoebox lunches on trains, wearers of shiny clothes, of hideous vintage hats, tippers of nickles and dimes. . . . Hold, sir—hold. You hardly do us justice. Any old porter on the cars between Boston and the District of Columbia will tell you that Mr. Coolidge, who was surely a Yankee, *always* presented a tip of fifteen cents. What would you make of us, anyway? Would you have us of New England be like you of the outlands—improvident, lavish merely for the sake of show? Do you not recall the rebuke given you westerners who had complained about the economy of Yankee tourists and had induged in stale witticisms regarding their penuriousness? Why, San Francisco's *Daily Bulletin* took you severely to task, saying that these Yankees whom you had maligned were the very people who devoted more of their incomes to educational and charitable purposes than any other people on earth. And remarked further that the people of California—few of whom, said the *Bulletin,* had a hundred dollars to their names—had better emulate the Yankee and cease to talk windily of millions, while wondering where next week's rent was coming from.

Industry is fortune's right hand; frugality, her left. Would you rather not be laughed at for your economies than be hounded for your extravagances when the rent is due? Frugality itself is a handsome income. He is rich who owes nothing. A man in debt, said Mr. Emerson, is so far a slave.

But libel the Yankee if you will. He is today the most set-upon, the most abused, the most caricatured American of all. He is, in fact, almost the only American who pays no heed to libels about him. Who is the favorite villain of the stage, of the movies, of novels? He is a *Yankee* banker, name of Peabody or something similar, and not Cohen and Guggenheim. The favorite spiritual mountebank of the stage and movies and novels is not good Father O'Houlihan, but the Reverend Dr. Sears, or something similar, patently a Congregational minister. The simple clown is not Rufus Rastus Johnson Brown, but a clod from Pumpkin Center, Maine. The desire that results in dreadful adulteries is compounded under New England elms. The mourning that so becomes Electra stems from murder and incest, committed on a pretty New England farm.

Uncle Tom's Cabin is not to be shown on the screen because it reminds that Negroes once were slaves—and not because of its cruel Simon Legree, born a Yankee. *Oliver Twist* is banned because of Fagin, a Jew; and the clever magicians of Hollywood have at last produced *The Three Musketeers* without the unfrocking of a Cardinal Richelieu.

The time rapidly approaches when the only safe target of libel in the United States will be the Yankee of the old stock; nor is he likely to give a tinker's dam for't. He is content in his smug belief that Yankees are above and beyond libel, as secure as are Yankee legends, such as the Horseman of Boston named Revere, as Colonel Allen at Ticonderoga, Nathan Hale at the gibbet, and the flowering of New England's bards and philosophers. Almost the only canard he will rise to refute is that his forebears were burners of witches. They were *not* burners of witches; they hanged them by the neck. . . .

Libels of the living Yankees are as of the wind. But, sir, commit no improprieties with History. Do you not know what a foreigner, a brilliant Frenchman named De Tocqueville, as sharp an observer as ever was, said of the United States a hundred years ago? He declared that the social theories of the entire United States came direct from New England. He remarked that the principles of the Yankees had not only spread to neighboring states; they had "interpenetrated the whole confederation." He marveled in two fat books about these Yankees. He found that their civilization had been as a beacon lit upon a hill which, after it had diffused its warmth immediately around it, then tinged even the distant horizon with its glow.

> Mr. Moderator, is there yet time, and if so is there still sufficient freedom to permit a member of a minority called Yankees to express an opinion, and to cite a few facts? If so, Mr. Moderator, may I rise to remark that the notions of the old Yankees have indeed interpenetrated the whole confederation of states. Narrow, sir, as that Yankee culture may have seemed, say, to the Episcopalians, and narrow and harsh to the Quakers, yet it was the only valid culture to withstand the rigors and disintegrating effects of the wilderness frontier. Consider, too, its magnificent vitality. It splintered, true enough, yet in every splinter remained something of the basic vitality—as witness those who call themselves Mormons or Adventists or Unitarians or Christian Scientists. And who, pray, was and is the shining light of the Baptists, if not Roger Williams, late of Providence Plantations? . . .

Yes, indeed, the Presbyterians were dynamic, too. They had a much stronger organization than the Puritans. They also were superb tamers of the frontier. One doubts that America ever saw more efficient pioneers. Yet I bid you read your history right. A full century before those stout people came, the Yankee Puritans called Congregationalists had founded schools and colleges, had founded a new form of civil government. For a hundred years they had already cherished learning, and their beacon lit upon a hill had surely tinged the farthest horizon with its glow. If there is still, three hundred years later, a widespread respect for learning in America, then its sources are in the rock-bound New Canaan of the Yankees—and not elsewhere.

Three hundred and thirty years after establishment of the first New England settlement near the Rock that was called neither Peter nor yet Paul, but Plymouth, the surviving Yankees have adjusted themselves to living in a world that is no longer, except in very small part, their own. They come close to being, if they are not already, a minority in their own region. The old Yankee blood grows thinner, though slowly, by intermarriage with other stocks. In another two centuries or so the Yankee may well be extinct. What his descendant will be like must be left to prophets in the field of anthropology. All that it is safe for a nonprophet to say is that the New Englander of the future will in all likelihood retain a few of the deep-seated characteristics of his forebears.

Those forebears were at one and the same time the hottest of sectarians, and the peers of all daring innovators.

They believed that religion never more surely established its empire than when it reigned in the hearts of men unsupported by aught beside its native strength.

They sought to deal directly, individually, with their Lord; their pastors were merely referees in their discourses with Deity. This was their strength. They bottled up God's prerogative in a covenant, a bargain. They reduced Him to the role of an economic schoolmaster. He rewarded his good pupils. He punished the bad ones for neglect of their lessons. The good pupils understood they were to *feare God & walke in hys wayes*. They were to labor with all their might to extend His provinces, to defend those provinces against Satan, apparently the only personage feared by God.

> It hath pleased the great God to enter into a treaty with us his poor creatures, the articles of which agreement are here comprised. God, for his part, undertakes to convey all that concerns our happiness. . . .

Even "happiness" was carefully described by this careful people. It comprised "health, maintenance, credit, prosperous successe in our callings & lawfull dealings, deliverance out of troubles, and such like." Here were success and mortality, linked together as they were nowhere else in the world. Elsewhere, prosperity might be considered as the result of luck and Industry. Not so in New Canaan. In the Yankee economy, luck was wholly eliminated.

Nor was diligence alone enough to warrant prosperity, which was the result of diligence plus the very *right* to well-being, the latter being one of God's promises in the Covenant.

Nor are you to think that riches brought depravity. This could not happen where riches were an award for piety. So long as the Yankees kept their hearts right for the Lord, all was well. That is why the old Yankees sought, with almost equal diligence, both material wealth and moral satisfaction—which was to say, well-being in this world, a heaven in the world yonder.

    Truly, Mr. Moderator, was not theirs a tremendous daring, to thus inveigle Him into partnership with the Yankees, that He should advance them materially in exact proportion to their piety? Sir, it was a most audacious thing to conceive, and to carry out. And mark you, were they not also trying to prove that well-being on this earth was no longer an arbitrary award of despotism and ignorance? that well-being came from justice and reason?

But now, three centuries after the Covenant, is the summer of the Yankees done? Do all things stand upon them with a weather-beaten face? Has the wheat rotted in the shock? Is y₎ whole cuntrie—as old Bradford complained—filled with woods & thicketts yᵗ hideth wilde men of savage heiw & strang oppinions? No. It is merely that the summer of the Yankees' dynamic expansion and exodus is largely done. Nor does it matter overmuch; for the Yankees left the barns and the storehouses of the nation well filled— filled with assorted abilities and notions, many of which, whether or not recognized as such, are a part of "the whole confederation."

Well-being in this world? Heaven in the next? If these are goals of any number of us today, then we owe something to the curious people who established New Canaan in America, then attempted to expand it into each of forty-two other subdivisions of the Republic.

You visitors, you tourists, you summer people and travelers from far and near who have come to see the Yankee Necropolis—look you well by all means at our uncounted gravestones, smile at the naïve and the preposterous legends in their slate and granite. Look you, too, at our historic sites where Liberty began to be born. Go gape at our halls of learning, at our dry, spare churches, whence so many went forth to carry Yankee light into far swamps.

Look well at every last hamlet you pass, too, and know that at some time or other this molding village was aburst with energy, that here was born at least one man, and perhaps one woman, who contributed something more to his native land than a vote or a length of homespun.

Look well at all these; but do not, outlander, in your tourist hurry, fail to contemplate those fences of granite that wind the long way through Connecticut, into Rhode Island and Massachusetts, that mark the fields in Vermont, and encompasses whole pastures in New Hampshire, and even penetrate far into Maine. View them closely, look at them hard and long, and reflect if these granite bones of New England do not possess a permanence singularly adapted for a fence. We Yankees are not, as a people, much given to symbolism; yet we have poets among us, even as in the olden time, and our poets like to say that the granite bones of New England men possess a permanence particularly adapted for the underpinning of a nation.

You say that our poets are wrong? that the New England character is neolithic and is thus unsuited to a more plastic age? Very well, then. What would you consider as a base for the underpinning of the nation? Surely, you do not mean that the state, the government, should be the source of energy, of enterprise, of intellect? That is not the way in which the small republic became a great nation. Much of the energy and even more of the intellect which have characterized America stemmed from New England sources. And those sources were *men and women,* individuals, whose character, despite popular myth and libel of recent years, was not solid granite. Call it a granite base, if you will, but remember that it was dynamic, too—dynamic enough to form the core of American thought and American action these three centuries.

Aye, the Puritan, the Yankee, the New Englander has indeed been the butt of much sport and ridicule. He has been attacked and demolished for his narrowness, for his calm assurance that he alone was right. But, sir, you must either admit that somehow or other he accomplished prodigies; or you must cite some other group of people who accomplished more, or even as much, in the New World. Such a people does not come readily to mind.

It was inevitable that the race of the Yankees should be swallowed by later immigrations and dissipated by the scattering of the Yankees themselves. There is, however, a residue of New England character in all parts of the United States. It has been influenced, changed, probably softened, perhaps weakened, by millions of non-Yankee Americans; yet it has been strong enough to impress itself in some measure upon non-Yankees who, in their second generations, are less like the Irish, the Germans, the Scandinavians, and the Italians than they are like the people who once upon a time lived at Plymouth and around the shores of Massachusetts Bay.

But what are the tidings? How goes the nation? In the middle of the twentieth century there seems to be no solid, no granitelike assurance. Many Americans say that we are without a positive philosophy, that we are confused, that we search here and there and in vain for some anchor rock that is more than a treacherous reef. No such doubts contaminated the thinking of the old Yankees. Perhaps that is why their notions interpenetrated the whole confederation. At the head of those notions was Industry, along with a rigid moral code for which there was not, nor is, another name. And somewhere in their baggage of notions was Economy, which one of their number, who was Noah Webster, declared to be "management without loss or waste." The foundation of all their notions was, of course, their belief, so clear and so unshakable as to mystify those who did not have it—their belief in a Power from which they could draw, as water from a well, the strength needed for their prodigious works of both mind and body. You must comprehend that when a Yankee went out to pick rock and build a fence, he picked rock and built fence to the glory of his God. When he went out to break path through snowdrifts, it was to the glory of God. If he went to capture Louisburg, he captured Louisburg to the glory of God. When he decided to defy George the Third, it was for the glory of God that he defied him, because he understood that he, a Yankee, was at work with God. Yea, because he knew that he had an ally in the Almighty, this man succeeded. . . .

Simple and austere notions they were. They survive, here and there, but they are not held in any esteem by the mass of Americans today, who dismiss them as old-fashioned, as backward, as narrow, as antiquated. Perhaps they are. But they were notions formulated by an amazingly durable and most effective people who thought that their legs were made to stand upon. For three hundred years, more or less, that belief and those notions served them and America well. I could wish, sir, that we in mid-twentieth century were better acquainted with old Bradford of Plymouth Plantation, he, the governor of the Pilgrim colony, who was certain that *all greate & honorable actions are accompanied with greate difficulties, and must be both enterprised and overcome with answerable courages.*

The Rock at Plymouth may have been overdone as a sentimental symbol. But the spirit revealed by old Bradford, and the generations following him, might well point the way, might even fill the void of which an uneasy "whole confederation" has become increasingly conscious.

ACKNOWLEDGMENTS AND BIBLIOGRAPHY

To THE MANY GROUPS and institutions which made possible the assembling of material for this book, I tender my heart-felt thanks, which I offer also to the individuals who with insight and often with enthusiasm were of immense help. One and all, they contributed toward making the work easier than otherwise would have been the case. I owe much to:

The historical societies of the six New England states and their wonderful libraries at Portland, Boston, Concord, Montpelier, Providence, and Hartford; the public libraries of East Machias and Portland, Maine; the Athenaeum and the Public Library of Boston; the American Antiquarian Society, Worcester; the New York Public Library; Oberlin College library; Chicago Public Library; Iowa State Historical Society; State Historical Society of Wisconsin; the Church Library of the Latter-Day Saints, Salt Lake City; Historical Society of Montana; Historical Society of the State of Idaho; Oregon Historical Society; Reed College library, Portland; Washington State Historical Society; California Historical Society; Historical Society of Southern California. Newspapers: Worcester *Gazette;* Beloit *Daily News;* Northfield (Minn.) *News;* Portland *Oregonian.*

Among the many individuals to whom I also owe much are Katherine Anderson, May Blanchard, Theodore C. Blegen, William D. Bowell, Clarence Brigham, Mrs. Fred W. Brown, Mary E. Brown, R. C. Brummer, Frank W. Buxton, Howard S. Cady, Charlotte D. Connover, Wilson S. Dakin, George N. Dale, Timothy Dale, Walter Davis, Norman Dodge, Milton T. Dunten, George W. Ebey, Robert T. Edwards, Laura Eldridge, E. Marie Estes, Constance Ewing, Dr. Ralph Fenton, Lincoln S. Ferris, Clara E. Follette, Chapin Foster, Arthur H. French, Edmund Fuller, Ida Mann Gammons, Charles G. Gilson, Russell Gordon, Gertrude E. Hall, Mary Lee Hall, Alma Hallenborg, Paul Hauser, H. H. Hewitt, John Edward Hicks, Mrs. Preston Holt, Janet Rogers Howe, Elmer Hunt, Dorothy Johansen, Carl W. Jones, Frances Kemp, Priscilla Knuth, Evelyn Sibley Lampman, Sinclair Lewis,

Milton E. Lord, W. William Lund, Gertrude McDevitt, Robert Mahaffay, Florence F. Mainie, Eugene Melder, Earle Newton, Philip H. Parrish, William J. Peterson, Lancaster Pollard, Louise Prichard, Elizabeth Ring, Ethel Robinson, Herman Roe, Marian B. Rowe, E. L. Sanderson, Bill Schilling, Nondes Schmehl, Dorothea E. Spear, Eleanor S. Stephens, James F. Stevens, P. M. Stone, W. F. Trundy, Nell Unger, Esther Watson, Alta West, Elaine White, Walter M. Whitehill, Ruth Williamson, George Willison, and Elsie Wolfe.

Once again, too, I must cite the incomparable aid given me by the Library Association of Portland, Oregon, and the Pacific Northwest Bibliographic Center at the University of Washington, to which I am everlastingly in debt. Following is a list of the works which proved especially helpful.

Adams, Charles Francis, *Three Episodes of Massachusetts History*. Boston, 1896 (2 vols.).

Adams, Herbert L., "Gen. John M. Thayer," in *Nebraska History Magazine*, Lincoln, July–Sept., 1922.

Allen, Walter C., ed., *The Society of California Pioneers*. N.p. 1948.

Appleton's Railroad and Steamboat Companion. New York, 1848.

American Messenger (monthly). Boston, 1848–1853.

Atwater, Francis, comp., *History of the Town of Plymouth, Conn., . . . Also a Sketch of Plymouth, Ohio*. Meriden, Conn., 1895.

Bagley, Clarence B., *History of Seattle*. 3 vols., Chicago, 1916.

———, "The Mercer Immigration: Two Cargoes of Maidens for the Sound Country," in *Oregon Historical Quarterly*, Vol. V, No. 1 (Mar., 1904).

Bailey, Robert G., *River of No Return: The Great Salmon River of Idaho*. Lewiston, Ida., 1935.

Baldwin, Frederick W., *Biography of the Bar of Orleans County, Vermont*. Montpelier, 1886.

Bancroft, Hubert Howe, *Works*. San Francisco, 1875–1890.

Barber, A. D., "Vermont as a Leader in Educational Progress," in Vermont Historical Society *Collections*, Vol. V. Montpelier, 1943.

Barber, Edward W., "The Vermontville Colony: Its Genesis and History, with Personal Sketches of the Colonists," in Michigan Pioneer and Historical Society *Collections*, Vol. XXVII. Lansing, 1900.

Barrows, John Stuart, *Fryeburg, Maine*. Fryeburg, 1938.

Barry, Louise, "The Emigrant Aid Parties of 1854," in *Kansas Historical Quarterly*, Vol. XII (May, 1943).

———, "The New England Emigrant Aid Company Parties of 1855," in *Kansas Historical Quarterly*, Vol. XII (Aug., 1943).

Beckwith, George, phonographer, *Beckwith's Almanac*. New Haven, 1849–1882.

Bell, Charles H., *History of the Town of Exeter, N.H.* Exeter, 1888.

Beloit, The Book of. Beloit *Daily News*, 1936.

Bierce, Gen. L. V., *Historical Reminiscences of Summit County*. Akron, Ohio, 1854.

Blegen, Theodore C., "The Pond Brothers," in *Minnesota History*, Sept. 1934.

Bond, Beverley W., Jr., *The Civilization of the Old Northwest*. New York, 1934.

Bookwalter, J. (land commissioner, St. Paul & Manitoba Railway), *Minnesota as It Is*. St. Paul, *c*. 1888.

Bourne, Edward E., *The History of Wells and Kennebunk, Maine*. Portland, 1875.

Boyd, Julian Parks, *The Susquehannah Company*. New Haven, 1935.

Boynton, C. B., and T. B. Mason, *A Journey Through Kansas*. Cincinnati, 1855.

Bradford, William, *Of Plimouth Plantation*. Boston, 1898.

Brayer, Herbert O., "Boom-Town Banker, Central City 1880," in *Bulletin of the Business Historical Society* (Boston), June, 1945.

Bridgman, Howard A., *New England in the Life of the World*. Boston, 1930.

Browne, George Waldo, *The History of Hillsborough, N.H.* Manchester, 1921.

Bruce, William George, "Memoirs," in *Wis. Mag. of History*, June, 1933.

Brunson, Ella C., "Alfred Brunson, Pioneer of Wisconsin Methodism," in *Wis. Mag. of History*, Dec., 1918.

Burdette, Robert J., ed., *American Biography and Genealogy*, California ed., 2 vols., Chicago, n.d.

Butler, Nicholas Murray, ed., *Education in the United States*. New York, 1910.

Caldwell, Martha B., "The Eldridge House," in *Kansas Historical Quarterly*, Nov., 1940.

————, "The Stubbs," in *Kansas Historical Quarterly*, May, 1937.

————, "When Horace Greeley Visited Kansas," in *Kansas Historical Quarterly*, Vol. IX (May, 1940).

Carter, Rev. Nathan F., *History of Pembroke, N.H., 1730–1895*. 2 Vols., Concord, 1895.

Caughey, John Walton, *California*. New York, 1940.

Chase, John Carroll, *History of Chester, N.H.* Derry, 1926.

Child, Wm. H., *History of the Town of Cornish, N.H.* 2 vols., Concord, *c*. 1911.

Christensen, Thomas P., "Denmark: A Stronghold of Congregationalism," in *Iowa Journal of History*, Jan., 1926.

Christianson, Theodore, "Backgrounds of Minnesota," in *Minnesota History*, Mar., 1938.

Cleland, Robert Glass, *A History of California: The American Period*. New York, 1922.

Clugston, W. G., *Rascals in Democracy*. New York, 1940.

Coburn, Louise Helen, *Skowhegan on the Kennebec*. 2 vols., Skowhegan, 1941.

Cole, Cyrenus, *Iowa: Through the Years*. Iowa City, 1940.

Colt, Mrs. Miriam Davis, *Went to Kansas, Being a Thrilling Account of an Ill-Fated Expedition to That Fairy Land, and Its Sad Results*. Watertown, N.Y., 1862.

Cowley, Matthias F., *Wilford Woodruff: History of His Life and Labors*. Salt Lake City, 1909.

Craigie Papers, 1788–1796, relating to sale of lands in the Ohio Country. In American Antiquarian Society.

Crocker, Prof. Henry E., *A History of New England*. Boston, 1879. Especially Vol. II, Appendix, "New England in Chicago."

Davis-Stewart Letters, 1855–1889. Unpublished, in possession of Janet Rogers Howe, Sudbury, Mass.

Dore, Benjamin, "Journal," in *Calif. Hist. Soc. Quarterly,* Vol. II, No. 2 (July, 1923).

Douglas, Truman O., *The Pilgrims of Iowa.* Boston, 1911.

Edmunds, A. C., *Pen Sketches of Nebraskans.* Omaha, 1871.

Ela, Richard Emerson, Letters 1830–1854, in *Wis. Mag. of History,* Vols. XIX–XX (1936).

Engle, Flora A. P., "The Story of The Mercer Expeditions," in *Washington Hist. Quarterly,* Vol. VI, No. 4 (Oct., 1915).

Fairchild, James H., *Oberlin: The Colony and the College 1833–1883.* Oberlin, 1883.

Fisher, Lucius G., "Pioneer Recollections of Beloit and Southern Wisconsin," in *Wis. Mag. of History,* Mar., 1918.

Folwell, William Watts, *A History of Minnesota,* 4 vols., St. Paul, 1922.

Galveston, Harrisburg & San Antonio Railway Co., *Immigrants' Guide to Western Texas.* Boston, 1876.

Gammons, Ida Mann, ed., Wright Papers (1818–1867), in N.H. Historical Society, Concord.

Gaston, Joseph, *Portland, Oregon: Its History and Its Builders.* 3 vols., Chicago, 1911.

Gilbert, Douglas, *American Vaudeville.* New York, 1940.

Gilbert, Frank T., *Historic Sketches of Walla Walla, Columbia, and Garfield Counties, Washington Territory.* Portland, 1882.

Goodykoontz, Colin B., "The People of Colorado," in *Colorado Mazagine,* Sept., 1946.

Gregory, John G., "Early Wisconsin Editors," in *Wis. Mag. of History,* June, 1924.

Griffin, Simon Goodell, *A History of the Town of Keene, N.H.* Keene, 1904.

Hafen, Le Roy F., "Colorado Cities," in *Colorado Magazine,* Sept., 1932.

Hale, Edward Everett, "Christian Duty of Emigrants: A Sermon Delivered at the Old South Church in Boston, May 9, 1852," in *The Journal for the Prevention of Pauperism.*

———, *A New England Boyhood and Other Bits of Autobiography.* Boston, 1900.

Hale, Jesse D., "The First Successful Smelter in Colorado," in *Colorado Magazine,* Sept., 1936.

Hatch, Louis Clinton, *Maine: A History,* Vol. III. New York, 1919.

Havighurst, Walter, *Land of Promise.* New York, 1946.

Hayes, Lyman S., *The Connecticut River Valley.* Rutland, Vt., 1929.

Herriott, F. I., *Did Emigrants from New England First Settle Iowa?* Des Moines, 1906.

Hibben, Paxton, *Henry Ward Beecher.* New York, 1927.

Hickman, Russell K., "Speculative Activities of the Emigrant Aid Company," in *Kansas Hist. Quarterly,* Aug., 1935.

Hill, Mabel, "Paul Hill: Railroad Builder," in *Nebraska Hist. Mag.,* Jan.–Mar., 1937.

Hoskins, E. B., *History of Lyman, New Hampshire.* 1902.

———, *Historical Sketches of Lyman, New Hampshire.* Lisbon, 1903.

Hubbart, Henry Clyde, *The Older Middle West, 1840–1880.* New York, 1936.

Hunt, Elmer Munson, "Abbot-Downing and the Concord Coach," in *Historical New Hampshire,* Nov., 1945.

Hurd, Harry Elmore, *Yankee Boundaries.* New York, 1949.

Hyde, Orson, *Sketch of Travels and Ministry.* Salt Lake City, 1869.

Jackson, James R., *History of Littleton, N.H.* Cambridge, Mass., 1905.

Johnson, Samuel A., "The Emigrant Aid Company in Kansas," in *Kansas Hist. Quarterly,* Vol. I (Nov., 1932).

———, "The Emigrant Aid Company in the Kansas Conflict," *Kansas Hist. Quarterly,* Feb., 1937.

Johnson, Thomas S., "Moses Ordway, Pioneer Presbyterian Missionary," in *Wis. Mag. of History,* March, 1919.

Kansas State Historical Society, *Collections,* Vols. IV and V. Topeka, 1896.

Kellogg, Amherst Willoughby, "Recollections of Life in Early Wisconsin," in *Wis. Mag. of History,* June, 1924.

Kellogg, Louise Phelps, "The Mission of Jonathan Carver," in *Wis. Mag. of History,* Dec., 1928.

Kent, Dorman B. E., *Vermonters.* Montpelier, 1937.

Keyes, Willard, Diary, 1817–1819, in Archives Wis. Hist. Society, Madison.

Kimball, President Heber C., *Journal.* Salt Lake City, 1882.

King, C. Wendell, "Social Cleavage in a New England Community," in *Social Forces,* Mar., 1946.

Lang, H. O., ed., *History of the Williamette Valley.* Portland, Ore., 1885.

Langsdorf, Edgar, "S. C. Pomeroy and the New England Emigrant Aid Company," in *Kansas Hist. Quarterly,* Aug. and Nov., 1938.

Lapham, William Berry, *Centennial History of Norway, Maine.* Portland, 1886.

———, *History of Bethel, Maine.* Augusta, 1892.

Larned, Ellen D., *History of Windham County, Conn.* Worcester, Mass., 1880.

Lazenby, Marie, "Down-Easters Out West," in *Reed College Bulletin,* Vol. XXV, No. 3 (1947).

Leonard, Delavan L., *The Story of Oberlin.* Boston, 1898.

Lewis, Franklin F., "The Career of Edward F. Lewis," in *Wis. Mag. of Hist.,* June, 1920.

Lewis, Oscar, *The Big Four.* New York, 1938.

———, *Sea Routes to the Gold Fields.* New York, 1949.

Little, William, *The History of the Town of Weare, N.H., 1735–1888.* Lowell, Mass., 1888.

Lovejoy, Clarence E., *Complete Guide to American Colleges and Universities.* New York, 1948.

Lovejoy, Julia Louisa, "Letters 1856–1864," in *Kansas Hist. Quarterly,* May, 1947.

———, "Letters from Kansas," in *Kansas Hist. Quarterly,* Feb., 1942.

Lower, A. R. M., *Colony to Nation: A History of Canada.* Toronto, 1946.

Ludlum, David M., *Social Ferment in Vermont, 1791–1850.* New York, 1939.

Lyford, James Otis, *History of the Town of Canterbury, N.H., 1727–1912.* Concord, 1912.

Lyman, Prof. W. D., *An Illustrated History of Walla Walla County, State of Washington.* N.p., 1901.

Marberry, M. M., *The Golden Voice: A Biography of Isaac Kalloch.* New York, 1947.

Marquis, Albert Nelson, ed., *The Book of Minnesotans*. Chicago, 1907.

Massachusetts General Court Reports: Senate No. 156, Mar. 29, 1865.

Mathews, Lois Kimball, *The Expansion of New England*. Boston, 1909.

Meader, J. W., *The Merrimack River, Its Source and Its Tributaries*. Boston, 1869.

Meigs, Col. R. J., *Biographical and Historical Memoirs of the Early Pioneer Settlers of Ohio*. Cincinnati, 1852.

Michigan, *Guide to the Lands of the Jackson, Lansing & Saginaw Railroad Company*, Mason, 1875.

Michigan Historical Commission, *Michigan Biographies*. 2 vols., Lansing, 1924.

Middlesex Gazette, Middletown, Conn., 1818–1825.

Miller, Perry, *The New England Mind*. New York, 1939.

Mills, Minnie Tibbets, "Luther Calvin Tibbets," in *Quarterly of the Hist. Soc. of Southern Calif.*, Dec., 1943.

Minnesota and Its People. 4 vols., Chicago, 1924.

Minnesota in Three Centuries (by various authors). 4 vols., St. Paul, 1908.

Minnesota: Its Advantages to Settlers. 6th ed., St. Paul, 1867 (pub. by the state).

Minnesota: Its Agricultural and Mineral Wealth. St. Paul, 1888.

Missouri Pacific Railway Co., *Indian Territory, Oklahoma and the Cherokee Strip*. St. Louis, 1894.

Monroe, Ira Thompson, *History of the Town of Livermore, Maine*. Lewiston, 1928.

Moore, Jacob Bailey, *History of the Town of Candia, N.H.* Manchester, 1893.

Morton, Zylpha S., "Harriet Bishop," in *Minnesota History*, June, 1947.

National Bureau of Information, *The Richest Region of the Rockies: A Guide to Colorado*. Denver, 1884.

New-England Emigrant Aid Company, History of the. Boston, 1862.

New Hampshire Historical Society, *Collections*, Vol. I, (1824).

New Hampshire Intelligencer, and Grafton & Coos Advertiser, Jan. 17, 1821, to June 16, 1827. Haverhill.

New Hampshire Patriot & State Gazette, 1821–1826. Concord.

New Hampshire Pensioners of Revolutionary War, list, in Archives of New Hampshire Hist. Soc.

Newson, T. M., *Pen Pictures of St. Paul, Minnesota, and Biographical Sketches of Old Settlers*. St. Paul, 1886.

Niles, Elisha, Diary, copied by Clara Louise Weed, 1933, New Haven, Conn.

North, James W., *The History of Augusta, Maine*, Augusta, 1870.

Northern Pacific Railway, *A Description of the Soils and Climates of the Regions Traversed by It*. New York, 1884.

The Northfield Raid: A Story of the Heroism of Pioneer Citizens of Northfield, Minnesota, Who Frustrated an Attempt by the James-Younger Gang to Rob the First National Bank on Sept. 7, 1876, Northfield, Minn., 1933.

Noyes, Harriette Eliza, *A Memorial of the Town of Hampstead, N.H.* Boston, 1899.

Noyes, John Humphrey, *History of American Socialisms*. London, 1870.

————, *Male Continence*. Oneida, N.Y., 1873.

Noyes, Pierrepont, B., *My Father's House*. New York, 1937.

Oneida Community, *Handbook*. New York, 1871.

Oregon Land Company, *Information Concerning the Willamette Valley . . . of Oregon*. Salem, 1889.

Parker, Benjamin F., *History of Wolfeborough, N.H.* Cambridge, Mass., 1901.

Parker, Robert Allerton, *A Yankee Saint*. New York, 1935.

Partoll, Albert J., "Frank L. Worden, Pioneer Merchant," in *Pacific Northwest Quarterly*, July, 1949.

Paxson, Frederic L., *History of the American Frontier*. Boston, 1924.

Payne, Charles E., *Josiah Bushnell Grinnell*. Iowa City, 1938.

Peck, Henry H., *Connecticut Almanac*, 1882–1889, New Haven.

Peterson, Harold F., "Early Minnesota Railroads and the Quest for Settlers," in *Minnesota History*, Mar., 1932.

Plummer, George F., *History of Wentworth, N.H.* Concord, 1930.

Porter, Florence Collins, and Helen Brown Trask, eds., *Maine Men and Women in Southern California*. Los Angeles, 1913.

Portrait and Biographical Record of Portland and Vicinity, Oregon. Chicago, 1903.

Portsmouth, N.H., *Journal of Literature & Politics*, Mar. 6, 1824, to Jan. 7, 1826.

Quaife, M. M., "Wisconsin's First Literary Magazine," in *Wis. Mag. of History*, Sept., 1921.

Quarles, Joseph V., "Letters 1837–1843," in *Wis. Mag. of History*, Mar., 1933.

Randall, Oran E., *History of Chesterfield, N.H.* Brattleboro, Vt., 1882.

Raney, William Francis, *Wisconsin: A Story of Progress*. New York, 1940.

Richman, Irving B., *Ioway to Iowa: The Genesis of a Corn and Bible Commonwealth*. Iowa City, 1931.

Ridlon, G. T., *Saco Valley Settlements and Families*. Portland, Me., 1895.

Ring, Elizabeth, ed., *A Reference List of Manuscripts Relating to the History of Maine*, Pt. 1. Orono, 1938.

Roberts, Brigham H., *A Comprehensive History of the Church of Jesus Christ of Latter Day Saints*. Salt Lake City, 1930.

Robinson, Orrin W., *Early Days of the Lake Superior Copper Country*. Houghton, Mich., 1938.

Rosenberry, Lois K. M., *Migrations from Connecticut After 1800*. New Haven, 1936.

Runnels, M. T., *History of Sanbornton, N.H.* 2 vols., Boston, 1882.

Saunderson, Henry H., *History of Charlestown, N.H.* Claremont, 1876.

Sawyer, Rev. Roland D., *The History of Kensington, N.H., 1663–1945*. Farmington, Me., 1946.

Schafer, Joseph, "Hiram Moore, Michigan-Wisconsin Inventor," in *Wis. Mag. of History*, Dec., 1931.

———, "The Wisconsin Phalanx," in *Wis. Mag. of History*, Vol. XIX (June, 1936).

———, "The Yankee and the Teuton in Wisconsin," *Wis. Mag. of History*, June, 1923.

Shankle, George Earlie, *State Names . . . Seals and Other Symbols*. New York, 1938.

Showerman, Grant, "Charles Durwin Parker," in *Wis. Mag. of History*, July, 1926.

Shuck, Oscar T., *Representative and Leading Men of the Pacific*. San Francisco, 1870.

Sibley, John Langdon, *A History of the Town of Union, Maine.* Boston, 1851.

Smith, Albert, *History of the Town of Peterborough, N.H.* Boston, 1876.

Smith, Joseph, Jr., *Book of Mormon.* Salt Lake City, 1871.

Snowden, Clinton A., *History of Washington,* Vols. V, VI. New York, 1911.

Soule, Frank, *et al., The Annals of San Francisco.* New York, 1854.

Starkey, Marion L., *The Cherokee Nation.* New York, 1946.

Stevens, Dr. J. V., "The Pioneer Wisconsin Family Physician," in *Wis. Mag. of History,* June, 1934.

Stillwell, Lewis D., "Migration from Vermont (1776–1860)," in Vt. Hist. Society *Proceedings,* Montpelier, 1937.

Stone, Wilbur Fiske, *History of Colorado.* Chicago, 1918.

Suckow, Ruth, "Iowa," in *American Mercury,* Vol. IX, No. 33 (Sept., 1926).

Sumner, William Graham, *Folkways.* Boston, 1940.

Swisher, Jacob A., *Iowa, Land of Many Mills.* Iowa City, 1940.

Thompson, Charles Miner, *Independent Vermont.* Boston, 1942.

Thompson, Robert Luther, *Wiring a Continent.* Princeton, 1947.

Thwaites, Reuben Gold, *The Story of Wisconsin.* Boston, 1891.

Thwing, Charles F., *A History of Higher Education in America.* New York, 1906.

Trumbull, H(enry), *Western Emigration Journal of Doctor Jeremiah Smipleton's* [sic] *Tour of Ohio.* Boston, 1819.

Tucker, Rufus Stickney, "The Expansion of New England," in *New England Hist. and Geneal. Register,* Vol. LXVVI (1922).

Turner, Frederick J., *The Frontier in American History.* New York, 1920.

United States Biographical Dictionary and Portrait Gallery of Eminent and Self-Made Men: Iowa volume. Chicago, 1878.

Upham, Warren, "Minnesota Geographic Names," in *Minnesota Historical Society Collections,* Vol. XVII. St. Paul, 1920.

———— comp., "Minnesota Biographies, 1655–1912," in *Minnesota Historical Collections,* Vol. XIV. St. Paul, 1912.

Usher, Ellis B., *Puritan Influence in Wisconsin.* Madison, 1899.

Vermont, *Heads of Families at the Second Census of the United States Taken in the Year 1800.* Montpelier, 1938.

Waldorf, Dolores, "Gentleman from Vermont, Royal H. Waller," in *Calif. Hist. Soc. Quarterly,* Vol. XXII, No. 2 (June, 1943).

Wallace, William Allen, *The History of Canaan, N.H.* Concord, 1910.

Wayne, History of the Town of. Augusta, Me., 1898.

Webb, Walter Prescott, *The Great Plains.* Boston, 1931.

Wheeler, Edmund, *The History of the Town of Newport, N.H., 1766–1878.* Concord, 1879.

Wheeler, George Augustus and Henry Warren, *History of Brunswick, Topsham, and Harpswell, Maine.* Boston, 1878.

Whitcomb, Mary R., "Abner Kneeland: His Relations to Early Iowa History," in *Annals of Iowa,* Apr., 1904.

White, William Allen, Address as President of the Kansas State Historical Society, in *Kansas Hist. Quarterly,* Topeka, Feb. 1939.

Whittemore, Rev. Edwin Carey, *The Centennial History of Waterville, Maine.* Waterville, 1902.

Whitwell, Gertrude Howard, "William Davis Merry Howard," in *Calif. Hist. Soc. Quarterly,* Vol. XXVII, No. 2 (June, 1948).

Wiley, Edgar J., comp., *Catalogue of the Officers and Students of Middlebury College, 1800–1927.* Middlebury, Vt., 1928.

Willard, James F., "The Union Colony at Greeley, Colo.," in Univ. of Colo. *Historical Collections,* Vol. I. Boulder, 1918.

Willison, George F., *Here They Dug the Gold.* New York, 1946.

Wilson, Carol Green, "A Business Pioneer in Southern California," in *Quarterly of Hist. Soc. of Southern Calif.,* Dec., 1944, to Sept., 1945.

Wilson, Forrest, *Crusader in Crinoline.* Philadelphia, 1941.

Winsor, Justin, ed., *Memorial History of Boston, 1830–1880.* 4 vols., Boston, 1881.

Wisconsin Doomsday Book, Town Studies, Vol. I. Madison, 1924.

Wisconsin, State Hist. Society *Proceedings.* Madison, 1884, 1893, 1902.

Whitcher, William F., *History of the Town of Haverhill, N.H.* N.p., 1919.

Worcester, Samuel T., *History of the Town of Hollis, N.H.* Nashua, 1879.

Wright, Doris Marion, "The Native-Born Population of California," in *Calif. Hist. Society Quarterly,* Vol. XIX (1940), p. 339.

Youmans, Theodora W., "A Pioneer Church at Prospect," in *Wis. Mag. of History,* Vol. IX, No. 3 (1926).

INDEX

Abbeyville, Ohio, 43
Abbot, Downing & Co., 316–319
Abbot, J. Stephen, 316 ff.
Abbott, Collamer M., author, 121
Abbott, Isaac, 84
Abbott, Joshua K., 93
Abel, Elijah, 33
Abell, Arunah S., editor, 348
Abington, Mass., 230
Ackley, Iowa, 137
Acton, Mass., 305
Ada, Mich., 82
Adams, Alvin, expressman, 159
Adams, Alvin, Judge, 141
Adams, Annie May, 244
Adams, Charles Francis, 240
Adams, Charles K., heads college, 305
Adams, David, 16
Adams, Elmer E., 181
Adams, George J., 55
Adams, Isaac, 92
Adams, Jasper, heads college, 301
Adams, John Q., settler, 92
Adams, Samuel Hopkins, 300
Adams, Stephen, 16
Adrian, Mich., 87, 342
Agawam, Mass., 232
Alabama, University of, 299, 307
Albany, N.Y., 17
Albany, Vt., 287
Albee, Franklin, 253, 339
Albion, Me., 66
Alcott, Amos Bronson, 322
Alden, Hiram, 84
Alden, Thomas, 178
Alden, Timothy, 19
Aldrich, Hazen, 52
Aldrich, Solomon, 16
Alexander, N.Y., 112
Alford, Mass., 93
Alger, Horatio, Jr., 339
Algona, Iowa, 164

Alleghany College, 19
Allen, Electra, 96
Allen, Ethan, 2, 13–14, 255
Allen, George W., 91
Allen, Henry, 102
Allen, Jesse, 32
Allen, Josiah, 168
Allen, Lovatus C., 92
Allen, Nathaniel, 32
Allen, Phineas, 16
Allen, William F., 119
Allen, William H., 305
Alling, Ethan, 32
Allis, Mich., 89
Almira College, 66, 304
Almy, John, 91
Alpena, Mich., 86
Alton, Ill., 197
Ames, Edwin G., 237
Ames, Jesse, Captain, 179
Amherst, N.H., 84, 179, 338
Amherst College, 8, 41, 166, 301, 349, 354
Amity, Ore., 232
Anamosa, Iowa, 141
Anderson, Martin B., 300
Anderson, Samuel F., 92
Andover, Mass., 57, 92, 235, 304
Andover, Ohio, 29
Andover, Vt., 51, 159
Andover Theological Seminary, 133, 150, 202, 282
Andrews, Christopher C., 178
Andrews, Constant A., 111
Andrews, E. B., heads college, 311
Andrews, John A., Governor, 246
Andrews, Rebecca, 56
Andrews, Stephen Pearl, 346
Andrus, Joseph, 17
Angell, James B., 311
Angle, Grant, editor, 331
Angola, Ind., 342
Ann Arbor, Mich., 112, 169

[373

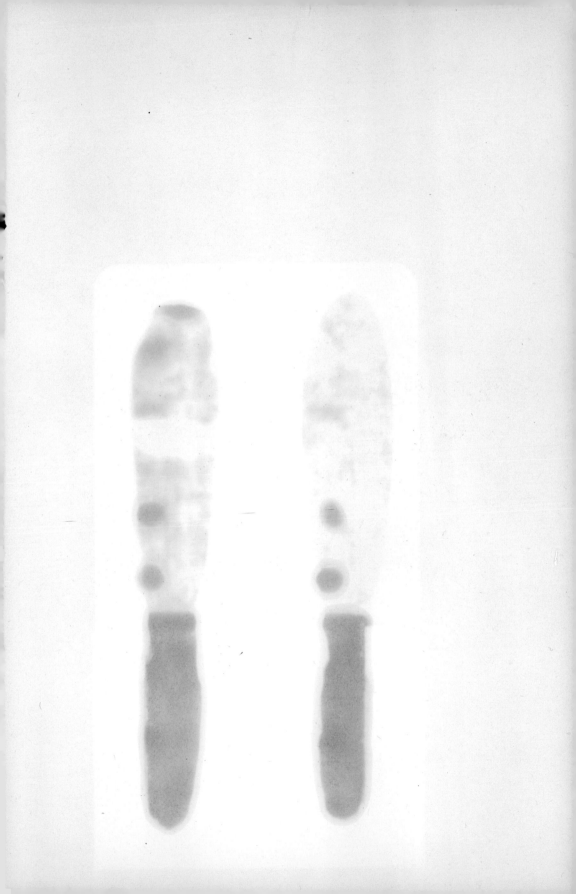

DATE DUE	
DEC 1 1 2004	
GAYLORD	PRINTED IN U.S.A.

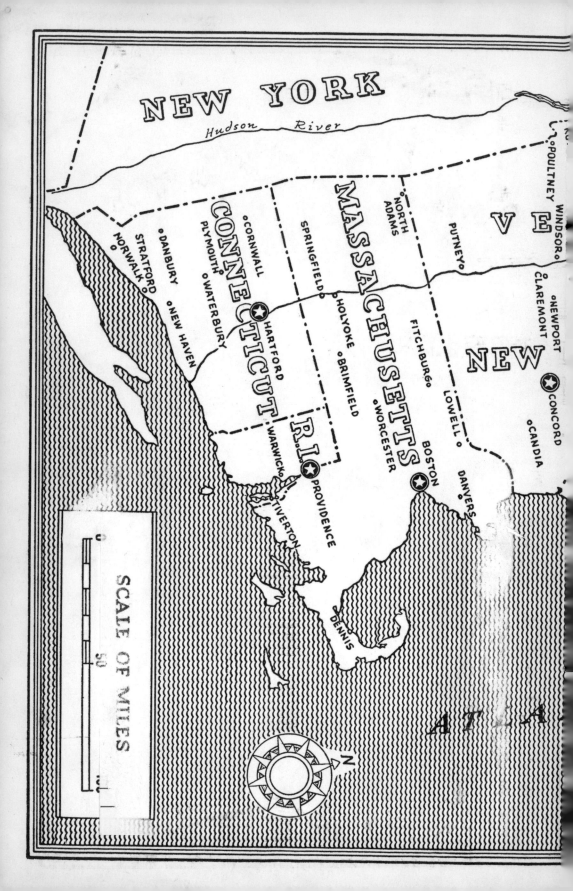